Black Identity

Black

Identity

Rhetoric, Ideology,
and Nineteenth-Century
Black Nationalism

Dexter B. Gordon

Southern Illinois University Press
Carbondale and Edwardsville

Library of Congress Cataloging-in-Publication Data
    Gordon, Dexter B., 1955–
    Black identity : rhetoric, ideology, and nineteenth-century Black nationalism / Dexter
B. Gordon.
    p. cm.
    Includes bibliographical references (p.) and index.
    1. Black nationalism—United States—History—19th century. 2. African Americans—
Race identity—History—19th century. 3. African Americans—Communication.
4. Rhetoric—Political aspects—United States—History—19th century. I. Title.
    E185.625 .G625 2003
    320.54'089'96073—dc21   2002003897
    ISBN 0-8093-2485-7 (cloth : alk. paper)
    ISBN-13: 978-0-8093-2735-5 (pbk. : alk. paper)
    ISBN-10: 0-8093-2735-X (pbk. : alk. paper)

Printed on recycled paper. ♻

The paper used in this publication meets the minimum requirements of American National
Standard for Information Sciences—Permanence of Paper for Printed Library Materials,
ANSI Z39.48-1992. ⊚

To the memory of Mur and Mamma

Murell Gordon (1925–89)
Eutedra Perkins Gordon (1927–70)

my beloved parents, both of whom labored manually from their teen years with love, faith, and the expressed commitment that their sixteen children would have the option of laboring mentally should they so choose. And to their children, my siblings

Leonard (Reds)
Norma (Storma)
Keith (Busta)
Owen (Rev. Bredda Pal)
Jennifer (Peg)
Beverly (Vanigee)
Yasmin (Del)
Donovan (Danny)
Geneita (Little)
Rohan (Presley)
Andrew (Nev)
Patrick (Mike)
Claudia (Cuddy)
and
King
and
Stanley
(who came later)

all of whom provided me, their middle sibling, with my first sense of community and of the importance of doing my best as part of that community.

Contents

Acknowledgments   ix

Introduction   xi

1. The Making of a Constitutive Rhetoric of Black Ideology   1
2. The Narrative of Oppression: Preserving Slavery   40
3. Early Roots of Black Nationalism: The Birth of the Black Subject   69
4. Contesting Blackness: The Rhetorical Empowerment of the Black Subject   101
5. Black Nationalism Matures: The Black Subject as Public Citizen   124
6. The Ideology of Black Nationalism and American Culture   161

Notes   207
Works Cited   217
Index   245

Acknowledgments

This book is the product of many years of academic toil and many thoughts from astute minds. I am indebted to both individuals and institutions for my intellectual development, throughout which I have received constant and crucial emotional support from my family and friends. Fellow students through the years and now my own students have contributed in various ways to my development as a scholar.

My formal education began in Jamaica and took several detours before it ended at Indiana University. I wish to express my gratitude to a number of outstanding teachers and scholars who guided me along the way. I am especially grateful to Phyllis Jennings for laying the foundation at the Old Harbour Bay Primary School; to Jean Blake of St. Jago High School for infecting me with her love of literature; to Billy Hall of Jamaica Theological Seminary for insisting that students garner from the library and bring to the classroom the fruits of their labor; and to Mark Fackler for making graduate school at Wheaton College stimulating and interesting.

I discharge only some of my debt by citation in the pages that follow to the works of scholarship that helped give form to my thought.

Thanks to the Department of Communication Studies at the University of Alabama and to the University of Puget Sound for resource support and, in the case of Puget Sound, a small grant. I thank the faculty of the Department of Communication and Culture at Indiana University for the intellectually challenging but supportive environment that framed the latter stages of my scholarly development. Thanks to James Andrews who as chair of the department provided my first appointment as an associate instructor, thus affording me tuition coverage and access to the classroom.

Bob Ivie, Carolyn Calloway-Thomas, and Richard Blackett generously provided time and scholarly insight. Special thanks to John Lucaites, whose careful reading and rereading of the various drafts and whose insightful criticisms and guidance influenced the formulation of this study and whose thoroughgoing approach and intellectual rigor served as a guide to my own concept of an effective strategy for this arduous process of academic writing.

Finally, one does not get to this point without the help of "a crowd of witnesses," people whose encouragement and support function as buoys during turbulent times. This crowd includes family and friends. Special mention must go to some who helped in significant ways and at crucial points in the process: Althea Bailey, Georgia and Orville Beckford, Sandra and Lance Brown, Flo and Clinton Chisholm, Manuela Douschand, Sharon Downer, Stafford Gaynor, Francis Gordon, Tajuana Gordon, Ray James, Grace Livingston, Roy Locke Jr., Huntley Manhertz, Leonie Moore, Janet Morgan, Darryl Neher, and Gloria Smith.

A project like this invariably costs a family in various ways, often unrecognized. Special thanks, therefore, to my children Donja, Janelle, LeVar, and Amara. Finally, I thank my wife, Sharon, who has been my main source of encouragement. Together, we have worked with much creativity and innovation to survive and thrive as we negotiated the various challenges of getting through this project.

Introduction

This book sprung from a desire to understand the ways in which the movement led by Marcus Mosiah Garvey, Garveyism, functioned to fulfill its gargantuan task of effecting a movement of "a people," not just leaders or select groups but the entire African diaspora. That broad desire became a more manageable first step: understanding the early rhetorical formation and functioning of the ideology of black nationalism in the United States. In this regard, then, the book is a beginning and not an end. Much more rhetorical analysis of the various facets of black nationalism throughout the African diaspora has yet to be completed. I hope this book serves as an invitation to more voices to join the talk.

Anglo-America's rhetorical construction of blacks as "slaves" or "free blacks" was part of an effort to divide and alienate African Americans while naturalizing the white supremacist structure of antebellum America. In response, black advocates sought to bring about their own liberation by rhetorically constructing an ideology with a new collective identity for themselves that addressed black ideological alienation even as it challenged the prevailing Anglo-American ideology. Central to that rhetoric was an ideology of black nationalism.

For abolitionists such as Henry Highland Garnet, the voluntary submission of black people to their abject condition in slavery was "SINFUL IN THE EXTREME" (Garnet 3: 407). This participation in and lack of resistance to slavery were acts that alienated them from their ancestors, their heroes, the fruits of their labor, and most significant, themselves. Slaveholders, as abolitionists saw them, were diabolical and had neither the intention nor the ability to be active subjects for black liberation. In sum, black abolitionists sought to place the responsibility for the abolition of slavery in the hands of blacks as the only means of eliminating their alienation. I establish this thesis through a comparison of representative examples of American black abolitionist discourse.

Rhetoric, race, and alienation are central to this study; thus, the first chapter engages various theories about these concepts and the problems they spawn. For example, rhetorical critics in the United States have only relatively recently engaged in significant and sustained analyses of race as a problematic of rhetoric that as a social force shapes liberal democracy. Of course, the issue of multiculturalism as part of American public culture is itself a recent phenomenon, yet it presents us with momentous challenges of unity and diversity, survival and suffocation, creativity and barrenness, and inclusion or death, all of which must be worked out as part of our public negotiation of power and in our public talk. To move ahead, we constantly reach back for cues. An understanding of the struggles of the past will help us as we become frighteningly aware that they are not past.

Through a rhetorical analysis of the discourse of black abolitionists, I examine the ways in which these displaced Africans used their own sense of alienation to confront their oppression, premised as it was on race. Rhetoric was their primary tool, functioning as they were in the margins of American society. Black abolitionists like Maria Stewart, David Walker, and Henry Garnet used rhetoric as an effective tool to defend themselves and their people against the devastation of slavery's multiple weapons of torture and against the dominant white supremacist network that supported it. Fundamental to the life of slavery and oppression in America was proslavery rhetoric: the discourse that sought through every available means to convince all people, especially blacks and whites, that blacks were natural slaves and whites their natural masters and mistresses. It is as blacks respond to these rhetorical efforts to define them and delimit their lives that we see an open rhetorical contestation of histories and futures, of epistemologies and ontologies. Perhaps more significant, we see how rhetoric functions materially to shape identities.

The use of representative examples or anecdotes of black abolitionist discourse allows me to highlight specific speeches and articles as emblems of a black social and political consciousness. It also facilitates a focus on individual speakers and writers as representatives of public consciousness and social and political activism (Benson 48–49). In the consideration of identity formation and social activism, this approach lends itself to reflections on the role of the broader community, as well as the forms and functions of sociopolitical discourse. Contemplation of this broader context is further enhanced by a comparative approach in which related examples of abolitionist discourse are studied together in an effort to tease out points of connection and disconnection that advance our understanding of the constitution of a black collective identity. The notion that any single selection or set of selections is representative invites an array of problematic implications. In this study, a ready problem is the dominance of masculinist discourse. This problem endures because it is emblematic of black nationalism.

Chapter 2 provides an analysis of Robert Walsh's *An Appeal from the Judgements of Great Britain Respecting the United States of America.* I use this text as a representative anecdote about the discursive narrative of oppression in antebellum America to show its materially rhetorical emergence within the context of American slavery and point to its rootedness in the discourse of the church and proslavery America. In this process, I analyze such standard proslavery documents as Thomas Roderick Dew's *Review of the Debate in the Virginia Legislature of 1831 and 1832*, Thornton Stringfellow's "The Bible Argument: Or, Slavery in the Light of Divine Revelation," James Henry Hammond's "Letter to an English Abolitionist," and William Harper's "Memoir on Slavery." This effort to show how Anglo-Americans sought through various rhetorical means to defend slavery in the shadow of liberty is a prerequisite to the exploration of the narrative of black nationalism, as it represents the immediate adversarial rhetorical culture within which black nationalism emerges and, as such, provides the context for its development.

Chapters 3 through 5 examine representative examples of black discourse that point to the development of black nationalism and its inherent new black identity. I focus on the ways in which this ideology unified and mobilized blacks while it challenged Anglo-American conceptions of black identity and authenticated its own. I group related aspects of this discourse into three comparative case studies that highlight some of the tensions manifest in black abolitionism after the emergence of the separatist ideology of black nationalism, as well as the dialectic tensions of the black nationalist ideology itself. Here I must choose from thousands of black abolitionist documents.

Any selection of rhetorical artifacts for such a study invariably confronts the challenge of its justification in the face of the exclusion of others. I could have started with the earliest petitions for freedom by blacks from 1661–1784 or followed the exemplary work of Essien Udosen Essien-Udom in *Black Nationalism* and begun with the remarkable Paul Cuffe. The writings of Cuffe, Prince Hall, or William Hamilton or any selection from the post-Revolutionary generation of black activists make for important study. As early as the seventeenth century, blacks in America expressed strains of what we have come to call "nationalist sentiments," recorded, for example, in Herbert Aptheker, *A Documentary History* (1: 1–79) and discussed by Sterling Stuckey (*Ideological Origins* 1–29). However, there is no gainsaying that black abolitionist arguments in nineteenth-century, antebellum America mark the best organized and most significant public declaration of black nationalist sentiments against slavery; thus, my focus on this period and the signal rhetorical artifacts within it. I begin with two representative black abolitionist publications from the 1820s that allow for exploration of the development and function of black nationalism.

Chapter 3 examines what are arguably the foundation documents of black nationalism: Robert Alexander Young's *The Ethiopian Manifesto, Issued in Defense of the Black Man's Rights, in the Scale of Universal Freedom* and David Walker's *Appeal to the Colored Citizens of the World, But in Particular, and Very Expressly, to Those of the United States of America*. Here I take a cue from Stuckey's *The Ideological*

Origins of Black Nationalism, which describes these two documents as embodying the origins of black nationalism, and examine the birth of the black subject within the context of blacks having previously been defined as less than human.

Chapter 4 looks at an intramural debate related to the genesis of an exclusive focus on black efforts within the convention movement to bring about black liberation, the Whipper-Sidney debate of 1840–41. Significantly, this debate is a contestation over blackness. The exchange includes William Whipper's three letters of 3, 12, and 17 January 1841, first published in the *Colored American,* 30 January and 6 and 20 February 1841, and Sidney's (Garnet's pseudonym) "Four Letters, in response to William Whipper," also first published in the *Colored American,* 13 and 20 February and 6 and 13 March 1841. In this comparative analysis, I point to the development of the black nationalist ideology as these protagonists seek to interpellate, or call out and position, their black subject as a social activist in preference to the previously-taken-for-granted white social activist.

Chapter 5 scrutinizes and compares Garnet's "Address to the Slaves of the United States of America" (delivered before the National Convention of Colored Citizens, Buffalo, New York, 16 August 1843) and Martin Robison Delany's "The Political Destiny of the Colored Race on the American Continent" (a report to the delegates at the first National Emigration Conference in Cleveland, August 1854). Frederick Douglass's *Oration, Delivered in Corinthian Hall, Rochester* ["What to the Slave Is the Fourth of July?"], an address delivered in Rochester, New York, to the Rochester ladies antislavery society on 5 July 1852 will serve as a foil to my reading of Garnet and Delany. These speeches, by the leading spokesmen for black abolitionism of their day, represent significant milestones in the efforts of black abolitionists toward self-definition and self-determination. Garnet's is the premier effort to bring to the platform of the National Black Convention movement the principles of black nationalism. "The Political Destiny" is, in Stuckey's words, "Delany's most trenchant statement on black nationalism and must be considered one of the seminal political documents in American history" (*Ideological* 22). "What to the Slave Is the Fourth of July?" reflects Douglass's expansive view of the black struggle and thus represents the broader and more moderate perspective in black abolitionism, allowing me to tease out some of the tensions and rhetorical problems created as part of the separatist-integrationist dialectic within abolitionism. Also, it allows me to examine the ideology of black nationalism in its most mature state in antebellum America as blacks contended with what it meant to be national and international social actors on their own behalf in the face of recalcitrant material and symbolic alienation.

Chapter 6 discusses the findings of this study and their implications for rhetorical theory and for our understanding of black nationalism. Here I explore a number of problematic features of black nationalism, among them the seeming absence of the voice of black women in the development of the ideology of black nationalism. While the significance of black women in abolitionism is established, not so their role in the development of black nationalism. There is also the issue of the role of black nationalism in the broader program of black abolitionism.

More important, I follow Michael Calvin McGee in advancing a materialist conception of rhetoric of abolitionism by demonstrating such a rhetoric at work in nineteenth-century black abolitionism ("Materialist's Conception"). In this rhetorical approach, I am concerned with both the description of the historic role of discourse in the black struggle for freedom and justice and the critical rhetorical reconstruction of the past to establish points of intersection with the present. As J. Robert Cox notes, "we must view history ideologically and argument as a form of 'presentist' reasoning. [We understand the past then], only in terms of our present need" ("Memory" 1). Somewhat similar to Celeste Michelle Condit and John Louis Lucaites, I point to possible options for understanding and engaging the effort toward justice within our shared communities. These options include a consideration of the role of collective memory and more inclusive approaches to theories of rhetoric, alienation, and other contemporary social phenomena.

Rather than accept race as a fixed and changeless phenomenon, critical rhetoricians can provide a useful service to our fragmented communities by theorizing race and alienation and exposing the ways in which race is still used systematically for ideological and material benefit. This service becomes even more significant as race prejudice becomes more sophisticated. An understanding of the rhetoric of black abolitionism is an asset to this effort, as well as to multicultural America's broader effort to confront race as we negotiate a new century. If the people who make up the multiplicity of cultures, ethnicities, and "races" in the United Sates, including blacks and whites, are amicably to share common communities, we need some understanding of each other's social and political culture. Otherwise, we will return repeatedly to our racialized stock responses, as many have done in their response to the September 11 destruction of the World Trade Center Towers in New York. In so doing, we only escalate our racialized rhetorical warfare, exacerbating what *Newsweek's* Howard Fineman calls the "uncivil war consuming America" (31). My contribution is an understanding of African American political culture through a reconception of the development and functioning of black nationalism.

Black Identity

1

The Making of a Constitutive Rhetoric of Black Ideology

The Million Man March of 16 October 1995 pushed the debate about "race" to the forefront of American public discourse.[1] As such debates engross the nation, some troubling questions are asked, particularly those about the identity, place, and role of "black people" in America. The answers that prevail will greatly affect the nation's effort to negotiate the tenuous issue of race in the twenty-first century. Indeed, according to the then newly appointed president and chief executive officer of the NAACP, former Democratic congressman Kweisi Mfume, "race relations are at their most pivotal point since the 1960s" (Mfume).

Not only has the Million Man March pushed race to the forefront, but even more significant, it has demonstrated the potential power of a black nationalist ideology to unify and mobilize blacks in the face of material and symbolic alienation in the United States. Along with the established nationalist ideology of the leader of the march and the Nation of Islam, Louis Farrakhan, the repeated claim that the marchers were coming to Washington to answer the question "What is to be done?" rather than to ask the government for something served to highlight what Vincent Harding has called "the core ideology of the march" (Address).[2] In Farrakhan's words, "we didn't come to Washington to petition the government for a way out of her, but to find a way out of our affliction" (Farrakhan 20). If, as Louis Althusser contends, "there is no practice except by and in an ideology," then for Farrakhan, black action would be generated within a black ideology (170). The ideology of black nationalism emphasizes black self-definition and self-determination in contrast to the continuing efforts of white Anglo-America to define blacks and determine their role in the debate about race.

I use the term "race" throughout this study with an awareness that race as a classification of humans into immutable biological categories with qualitative differences among them is a discredited enterprise. Yet "race" and its attendant and chromatically inaccurate color descriptors, especially "black" and "white," enjoy almost universal usage today, though often without the pernicious assumptions of the innate physical, mental, and moral superiority of one group over another. Race, then, is a social category. Still, it functions problematically to homogenize large groups of people and to facilitate the continuation of racism, with its systematic advantage to one group over another. In this study, largely about the negotiation of life framed by race and racism, I use the terms with a clear sense of their entailments. Other related terms, such as "racialism" and "race prejudice," do not enjoy wide currency in the United States; thus, they are not of major concern here.

The problem of race in the United States is an old one. In *The Souls of Black Folk,* first published in 1903, W. E. B. Du Bois lamented the experience of blacks in the United States and expressed his outrage at the Southern practice of implying that blacks were a problem in the society. When whites approached him, he noted, they seldom asked him a direct question that indicated such a problem; however, veiled in their comments was the question, "How does it feel to be a problem?" (3). More recently, in *Race Matters,* Cornel West wrote, "nearly a century later, we confine discussions about race in America to the 'problems' black people pose for whites" (2). And still later, in *Race Rules,* Michael Eric Dyson marshalled compelling evidence to establish his claim that, in the United States, race still rules. So, for example, a common issue in America's water cooler talk is the striking phenomenon of blacks and crime. In 1995, the Sentencing Project, a Washington, D.C., think tank, indicated that "almost one in three (32.2 percent) young black men in the age group 20–29 is under criminal justice supervision on any given day—in prison or jail, on probation or parole," up from the 23 percent reported in 1990. Subsequent reports have painted an even gloomier picture while raising disturbing questions about race and American democracy. For example, of an estimated 3.9 million Americans, or one in fifty adults, who have currently or permanently lost their voting rights as a result of a felony conviction, 1.4 million are African Americans. This number includes 13 percent of all black men, who are disenfranchised at a rate seven times that of Americans as a whole (Mauer and Huling 1). As blacks continue to pursue their struggle for freedom and justice, the constitution of their identity remains an issue in the incessantly acrimonious debate about race in America.

For the most part, the statistics are used by whites to construct a picture of the violent and dangerous criminal element in the United States. Such a criminal element is presented to and accepted by Americans as a menace that threatens the very fabric of American society. The general consensus seems to be that American society (read Anglo-American society) needs to protect itself against this foreboding element by putting the members of this group in prison. The popular support for this notion is indicated in the political and popular trends reported in 1999 by the Sentencing Project. It notes that "the past decade can be viewed as an 'experiment' in the 'get tough' approach to crime." Further, it claims that the proposal to lock up offenders, rather than deal with the larger societal problems such as drug treatment and unemployment, has been a basic campaign issue for more than twenty years. The implication is that this platform has met with public approval (Mauer 5). The problem for blacks is that this violent element is constantly projected by American media and by white public officials as black, young, and male (Sentencing Project; Mauer and Young). There is no denying that disproportionate numbers of young black men are identified as the victims and perpetrators of violent crimes in the United States, as is explored in William Oliver's *The Violent Social World of Black Men,* for example. The issue here, however, is how these numbers are accounted for, interpreted, and used in the majority white society as part of the construction of black America and, by implication, white America. Ellis Cose demonstrates this problem when he points to the arguments of white public officials like Daniel Patrick Moynihan, then senior U.S. senator from New York, and Ed Koch, former New York mayor, who contend that crime in America is a black problem (*Rage,* especially chapter 5). The young black male has thus become the most feared element of American society.[3]

Black males do not, however, commit more or different crimes in comparison with other groups but, as is the case with the disparity in sentencing for possession of crack cocaine versus powdered cocaine, black males are often treated more harshly by the criminal justice system.[4] The step from this picture of the violent, young, black male to the designation of violence and criminal behavior as a black pathology is short. In a fallacious leap, blackness is then readily and deleteriously conflated with violence (McGee, "Technical Terms"). The black subject in this scenario and in the mind of white America becomes one that should be watched, controlled, and dominated for the good of the larger society. So, for example, in 1995, *Time* darkened the face of O. J. Simpson to make him fit the image of the murderer, an image already established in the American mind as black (Cover, *Time*). Following a general outcry from African Americans against this racist act, *Time* offered an explanation suggesting that this was an artistic and not a racist product ("To Our Readers"). Sometime later, *Time* printed six letters reacting to the June 27 photograph, five of which accused the magazine of being racist and unfair in this act (Letters).

While contemporary white perspectives continue to focus on "black people" as a "problem people," the Million Man March painted a different picture (West, Race Matters 2). The statistics about the number of young black men in prison or otherwise entangled in the legal system served as a rallying cry for the Million Man marchers. There were expressions of disgust at the implications of injustice by the predominantly white justice system, as well as anger at the self-destruction of young black men. Several speakers described African Americans in contradistinction to the image presented by whites in the mainstream media. These black leaders said the white-dominated media presented African American men as dangerous, drug-pushing gangsters who refused to work and African American women as welfare dependents who continue to bear too many fatherless children. In this media presentation, both men and women were portrayed as refusing to carry their share of responsibilities as American citizens. As Haki R. Madhubuti notes in reflecting on the march, "black men had been painted and brushed by those in power as somehow deficient, irresponsible, lacking in moral and ethical character, unable to speak truth to power or themselves" (2). In challenging the mainstream media to reflect accurately on the march, Farrakhan noted, "All of these black men that the world sees as savage, maniacal, and bestial. Look at them. A sea of peace. A sea of tranquility. A sea of men ready to come back to God. Settle their differences and go back home to turn our communities into decent and safe places to live" (17).

Labeling blacks as a problem is part of a rhetoric that constructs blacks as "Other" and involves "the creation of an 'us against them' frame that alienates and disenfranchises citizens of color" (McPhail, "The Politics of Complicity" 345). Against the background of alienation and disenfranchisement, the Million Man March brought black men together in a powerful demonstration of solidarity and popular support. For people such as Farrakhan, the image of African Americans as a problem is not only inaccurate but racist. The march's background themes of atonement and restoration, then, framed Farrakhan's call for black men to return to the (black) family and take their rightful place in American society. To make this return, Farrakhan argued, blacks must assert their true identity, an identity based on their ancestral achievements. Accordingly, in Farrakhan's terms, blacks need a knowledge of their own history, and not from a white perspective (Farrakhan). "By the end of the march, everyone was saying Farrakhan's name" (G. Curry, "After" 37); this phenomenon, along with a postmarch increase in African American involvement in community organizations, indicates that Farrakhan had struck a responsive chord among those gathered in his immediate audience and beyond.[5] In a later assessment, the march was dubbed "a black nationalist triumph of unparalleled scope"; the "golden event" of American black nationalism (M. West 81, 82). But the question remains: How does the ideology of black nationalism function in the broader context of African American political culture?

The answer to this question demands an understanding of the context of black nationalism and that of African American political culture. In our efforts to make sense of the present, we search the past for material, social, and political warrants that make the present what it is. In so doing, we re-collect and re-member pieces from what Edwin Black calls the "garbage heap of facts" that serve our particular purposes ("Second Persona" 109). In this way, our memory functions ideologically, and because of this ideological function, efforts to theorize social reality "must concern [themselves] in an unprecedented way with the past" (Cox, "Memory" 5). As Ernest Bormann observes, "whenever a movement deals with race relations in the United States, the historical rhetoric continues to intrude into the contemporary campaign" (241).

As a critical theorist, I am concerned with the past as a useful tool. The contextualization of African American political culture, then, requires a remembering, a re-constructing of the "historical forces and potentialities that condition [the] present social relations" that make up African American political culture (Cox, "Memory" 2). Michael O. West's "Like a River: The Million Man March and the Black Nationalist Tradition in the United States" provides an important genealogical tracing to connect Farrakhan and the march to antecedent black nationalist developments but with a focus on people and programs. Mine is a focus on antecedent rhetoric. From this perspective, the key forces and potentialities in question are to be found in the rhetorical and historical roots of the ideology of the Million Man March. From one perspective, at least, these roots are grounded in the efforts of the black abolitionists to develop a rhetoric through which they could constitute blacks as a nation. Therefore, an explanation of the ideological functioning of black nationalism in contemporary African American political culture requires an examination of the public rhetorical efforts of black abolitionists.

To constitute a black nation, language and its public enactment in speeches, pamphlets, letters, petitions, broadsides, et cetera must embody speakers and audiences in collective social relations that enable or disable action. One might reasonably expect at this point a definition of black nationalism. However, I intentionally omit such a definition to draw attention to my treatment of black nationalism as a rhetoric. While I intend to focus on the broadly accepted notion that black nationalism entails a call for black autonomy in culture, economics, and politics, more important is my emphasis on black nationalism as a rhetoric—an ideological discourse in process, constantly responsive to the exigencies of the contingent situations in which it operates—as against the more popular notion of black nationalism as a philosophical ideal. Charles McKelvey, for example, in a chapter titled "The Philosophy of Black Nationalism," treats black nationalism as a philosophy and discusses the works of several scholars who address the philosophy of black nationalism, including Harold Cruse, Nathan Hare, Du Bois, Franz Fanon, and Kwame Nkrumah (152–81). In other words, I examine the way that blacks pragmatically create and recreate themselves as they negotiate their American experience in situ. This examination shows that the black identity construction in question is not so much the result of a commitment to a philosophical ideal as it is a contingent, socially constructed reality carved out of the harsh realities of slavery. It is a rhetoric, a discourse in action, that remains fluid in response to the vicissitudes of American life. As we explore the rhetorical undertakings of blacks, we see the emergence of their self-defense, self-definition, and self-determination. With this rhetorical focus, I emphasize key connections among words, ideas, and political action.

In this study, I commence investigating the public rhetorical efforts of select black abolitionists, who happen to be male, to show how blacks such as the Million Man marchers, faced with alienation and disenfranchisement as a part of their daily experience, developed collective practices of empowerment that cohere as a constitutive rhetoric of black ideology. An important first step in this process is a statement of the problem of alienation. To this end, I demonstrate that treatments of black abolitionism provide little accounting of how the ideology of black nationalism developed and that those accounts that do exist either ignore or undertheorize the role that rhetoric plays in the process. Next, I show that our theories of ideological alienation accentuate the problem by their failure to take "race" into account. Finally, I advance a rhetorical conception of ideological alienation as a means of reconceiving black nationalism. To examine the ways in which the ideology of black nationalism emerges in nineteenth-century America, I use the lenses of Maurice Charland's conception of a constitutive rhetoric ("Constitutive Rhetoric"). To explore the central concepts of race and rhetoric, I employ Molefi Asante's Afrocentrism, Mark Lawrence McPhail's "coherence," and Aaron David Gresson III's "recovery," all of which are contemporary theoretical explorations of the rapprochement between race and rhetoric (Asante, *Afrocentric;* McPhail, *Rhetoric;* Gresson).

The Ideology of Black Nationalism

According to C. Peter Ripley et al., the editors of *The Black Abolitionist Papers,* "black abolitionism transformed antebellum black Americans and left its mark on Afro-American identity, life and institutions" (3: 67). However, for all the considerations of black abolitionism as social and intellectual history, there is little accounting for how the ideology of black nationalism developed as a public discourse. The accounts that exist either ignore or undertheorize the role that rhetoric plays in the process.

The lack of accounting for the way in which the ideology of black nationalism developed as a public discourse is accented by the failure of theories of ideological alienation to take race into account. Strikingly, much of black nationalism's public manifestation is in its rhetoric. The need to address this problem becomes more pressing in the face of the significant increase in the chronicling of the efforts of blacks to overcome the challenges of both material and symbolic racism and oppression during the period of legalized slavery and since its demise. This increase is part of the new wave of black studies research since the 1960s.[6] Though not comprehensive, *The Black Abolitionist Papers* is a signal event in this regard, as it successfully fulfills its mission of publishing "the documentary record of African Americans involved in the movement to end slavery in the United States" (Ripley et al., *Witness* xvii). This documentation is an important starting point and, as such, is a part of our ongoing effort to come to grips with the ideology of black nationalism and to theorize about its function in contemporary political culture. These *Papers* represent a necessary but not sufficient cause to nullify John Blassingame Sr. and Henry Louis Gates Jr.'s 1985 lament that "African and African American materials continue to be either inadequate as research tools or, more often, simply unavailable at all" (Kinney xi).

Jane H. Pease and William H. Pease's *They Who Would Be Free: Blacks' Search for Freedom, 1830–1861* and Benjamin Quarles's *Black Abolitionists,* called "the two most perceptive interpretations" of black abolitionism, have settled some fundamental questions about blacks and their role in the struggle for freedom in antebellum America (Ripley et al., *Witness* 281). Quarles's *Black Abolitionists* settles the issue of the presence and participation of blacks in abolitionism. Blacks were pioneers, as well as symbols of the struggle. Pease and Pease investigate "how Northern blacks saw and sought freedom" (vii). In so doing, they provide definitive evidence that while blacks were active in antislavery efforts between 1830 and the Civil War, black endeavors toward freedom went beyond antislavery organizations and programs and often beyond abolitionism per se (ix). The work of Pease and Pease, and of Quarles, which have become standard texts on black abolitionism, provide detailed surveys of the black effort but do not provide sustained investigation of specific properties and functions of the discourse emerging from such efforts, such as ideology. Still, these works do provide the backdrop against which such sustained analyses must be done.

Vincent Harding's *There Is a River* builds on the groundwork laid by Quarles, Pease and Pease, and others before them to provide "a comprehensive and organic historical survey of the black movement toward freedom [and its] search and struggle for justice, equality and self-determination," and to suggest "some of the critical themes, ideologies, and questions" (xxi–xxii). It is increasingly acknowledged that blacks were not just significant in this struggle but that theirs was the *primary* role. For example, Celeste Condit and John Lucaites in *Crafting Equality* contend that white abolitionists played a major role in the struggle for equality and that they were more visible and represented more of a national presence than blacks but that the primary role in the struggle was fulfilled by blacks (70). Central to our understanding of this fundamental role is that black radicalism predated and shaped the better known white radical abolitionism, in which the work of William Lloyd Garrison is often highlighted, a point affirmed by Condit and Lucaites. Paul Goodman's crowning work, *Of One Blood,* further illuminates this pivotal role of blacks. Goodman not only demonstrates that it was the work and witness of blacks that led to the conversion of Garrison to radical abolitionism (a point highlighted earlier by Condit and Lucaites) but also provides a detailed tracing of the conversion of a host of other white abolitionists to radical abolitionism following Garrison. Among these are Elizur Wright Jr., Beriah Green, James Birney, and Sarah Grimké and her sister Angelina Grimké Weld (36–102). *Of One Blood* expands Gilbert H. Barnes's *Antislavery Impulse* and provides further insight into the role of Protestant evangelicalism in abolitionism. By focusing on abolitionism's originating ideas and activists, Goodman draws attention to David Walker's radical brand of abolitionism as a part of the central role of blacks in the herculean struggle to defeat slavery. Important to considerations of the black discursive struggle for liberation is the specific role of black women.

The role of women, a longtime companion to the role of blacks, is also being addressed more, and with it, the role of rhetoric. *The Abolitionist Sisterhood* is a collection of essays that focuses on "the complex political culture of antislavery feminists," both black and white (Yellin and Van Horne 3). Karlyn Khors Campbell's timely reminder that women have always adequately articulated their own causes, in her two-volume work *Man Cannot Speak for Her,* should be heeded by rhetorical scholarship, which is often masculinist in its orientation. Marilyn Richardson's *Maria W. Stewart, America's First Black Woman Political Writer: Essays and Speeches* has drawn attention to the early and salient contribution of this black woman who confronted oppression, at great risk, to challenge other black women (and men) to respond to their oppression through self-definition and self-development. Shirley Wilson Logan's *We Are Coming: The Persuasive Discourse of Nineteenth-Century Black Women* and *With Pen and Voice: A Critical Anthology of Nineteenth-Century African-American Women* and Carla Peterson's *Doers of the Word: African American Speakers and Writers in the North* point to important early rhetorical work by women and to the incorporation of African cultural connections and spirituality in their rhetorical practices. Shirley J. Yee's *Black Women Abolitionists* focuses on the collective role of black women in abolitionism as a way of filling the gender gap in African American abolitionist scholarship, and Beverly Guy-Sheftall explores the challenging lives of black women between 1880 and 1920 by studying the attitudes of the rest of the society toward them.

These are important perspectives, as the inclusion of women, and black women in particular, allows for a focus on discrimination based on sex as one of the many contradictions and ironies inherent in the struggle of the abolitionists

(Yee 1). In addition, the study of women's discursive practices draws attention to the tension between masculinist and feminist discourse in the rhetorical struggle for black liberation. That this study focuses on the rhetoric of black men is neither a claim to their greater importance nor a slight of the role of black women. I am cautioned by the resonant voices of activists and scholars such as Sojourner Truth, Maria Childs, Michele Wallace, and bell hooks, all of whom, along with multiple other black feminist scholars, point to the deficiency of the synecdochical use of masculinist discourse. Said differently, to use the stories and struggles of black men as exclusively representative of the black struggle in the United States is to demean black women in the most egregious fashion. Sadly, to continue "men's depreciation of women's influence" was identified by Garrison in 1832 as one of two errors that hindered the most progressive movement of the nineteenth century. The other was "women's depreciation of their own influence" (*Colored American* 13 May 1837; Goodman 173). Patricia Hill Collins's observation that a range of people, rather than a select few, make theory and intellectual traditions is a timely caution against elitism (xiii). Rather than to claim comprehensiveness or exclusivity, this study is an acknowledged attempt to treat one important aspect of black abolitionism. The growing body of literature about the role of black women is equally significant. To provide a sustained theoretical engagement of the development or function of the black nationalist ideology, I look for connections in the literature about the struggle for the freedom and the identity of blacks.

The introductory essay in Sterling Stuckey's *The Ideological Origins of Black Nationalism,* which discusses black resistance efforts in the first half of the nineteenth century within the context of ideology, is a significant precursor to my approach to black abolitionism. I extend Stuckey's notion that those "who sang of independence and freedom and referred to themselves as Africans" (3) were espousing a black nationalist ideology by examining select nineteenth-century black nationalists whose program emphasized political and economic nationalism rather than cultural nationalism (1–29). Whereas Stuckey's focus is on establishing the origins of the ideology of black nationalism, my focus is on the development and rhetorical functioning of this ideology. My interest is in identifying how blacks constructed this ideology in their discourse and then how this discourse functioned ideologically to advance the black cause. Stuckey's *Slave Culture* also addresses aspects of black nationalist ideology important to my study and thus provides significant groundwork on which I build. *Slave Culture's* objective, however, is to show "a continuing Africanity [as part of] the governing principles of black culture in slavery *rather* than their manifestations since that time" (viii; emphasis added). The latter, of course, is my focus, and where Stuckey sees "Africanity" as a philosophy, a principle guiding behavior, I discuss it as a rhetoric, a discourse constituting a collective black identity as a means of mobilizing black collective social activism. Such a rhetorical focus allows me to explore the contingent nature of the various efforts to construct, reconstruct, and contend for black identity. A rhetorical approach also facilitates my focus on the creative and pragmatic undertakings of activists employing language as a major tool in their effort to create and control social reality and thus exercise power.

Rhetorical scholarship that addresses black abolitionists and examines their discursive efforts to dismantle slavery, confront racism, and effect black liberation has emerged as part of a mode of critical scholarship to confront traditional rhetorical studies. This critical rhetorical scholarship demands of the broader study of rhetoric a deepening of its social analysis, a more reflexive posture in its critique, and a broadening of its scope. This mode of critical scholarship was part of what Asante calls a "symbolic 'revolution' which began with the Civil Rights Movement" (Asante, *Afrocentric Idea* 179). Since the early appeals for recognition, such scholarship has made important contributions to the discipline. The early call was highlighted by Franklin Haiman's 1967 essay "The Rhetoric of the Streets," in the *Quarterly Journal of Speech*—the flagship journal of the discipline—which urged that American rhetorical criticism broaden its scope and look beyond "the Faneuil Hall rally or a Bughouse Square soapbox" to examine the "rhetoric of the streets" (99, 114). With similar concerns but seeking criticism's expansion in both scope and function, Robert Scott and Donald Smith's 1969 *Quarterly Journal of Speech* essay "The Rhetoric of Confrontation" wrote that "a rhetorical theory suitable for our age must take into account the charge that civility and decorum serve as masks for the preservation of injustice and that they condemn the dispossessed to non-being" (8). The push for a rethinking of rhetoric's substance was advanced significantly by Scott's contention that rhetoric should not be seen as secondary in the construction of truth—making truth effective—but as primary; a means of producing truth and knowledge. In his essay "On Viewing Rhetoric as Epistemic," Scott argued that rhetoric is epistemic and thereby launched a fruitful debate about the characteristics and the significance of this often praised, often maligned, but always captivating phenomenon.[7] The debates that followed these significant rhetorical productions opened the way for important considerations of rhetoric previously ignored as outside the norms of rational rhetorical culture and thus beneath (not just beyond) the scope of rhetorical criticism. In 1977, for example, Karlyn Khors Campbell endorsed Scott and Smith and demonstrated the validity of their claim with her specific focus on "The Rhetoric of Radical Black Nationalism," the title of her 1971 *Central States Speech Journal* essay. Still, from the beginnings of race and rhetoric studies in the 1960s through the 1980s, as McPhail points out in the introductory essay in his *Rhetoric of Racism*, with few exceptions, the small number of studies that moved beyond the descriptive mode failed to theorize race, racism, and the epistemological groundings of arguments contesting these social constructions. Such efforts as Robert C. Dick's *Black Protest: Issues and Tactics,* though useful, are largely descriptive of black rhetorical strategies as contrapuntal to those of whites (1–12).

More recently, however, along with studies of women's rhetoric, critical rhetorical scholarship about the broad issue of blacks and their role in the struggle for freedom in America has moved beyond fundamental issues of establishing scope and significance and beyond naturalist descriptions of rhetorical practices. Even so, in her contribution to Julia T. Wood and Richard B. Gregg's 1995 speculative anthology, *Toward the 21st Century: The Future of Speech Communication,* Campbell points to the dearth of treatments of the rhetoric of marginalized groups. Her essay "In Silence We Offend" renews Campbell's calls to the discipline for self-examination. She intones, "We have only made a small beginning in critical work analyzing discourse produced by marginalized groups" (137). These more recent and more nuanced studies theorize rhetoric and race as central elements of this African American struggle. I survey and build on these efforts to provide a more focused treatment of the ideology of black nationalism.

Asante's *Afrocentricity* and *The Afrocentric Idea,* Condit and Lucaites's *Crafting Equality,* McPhail's *Rhetoric of Racism,* and Gresson's *The Recovery of Race in America* are leading examples of this new trend in rhetorical scholarship to provide crucial understanding of the role of rhetoric in the black struggle.

Asante is in the forefront of this more recent development in rhetorical scholarship that calls into question the privileged discourse of traditional rhetorical criticism. His theory of Afrocentricity is outlined in his 1980 publication *Afrocentricity* and expanded in 1987 in *The Afrocentric Idea,* which was revised and expanded in 1998. Asante presents his Afrocentric method as a project "concerned with establishing a worldview about the writing and speaking of oppressed people" (*Afrocentric Idea* 173). Although, as Wilson Jeremiah Moses indicates, Asante was not the first to use the term "Afrocentrism," he is clearly its chief proponent and has been for the last twenty years (*Afrotopia* 1–2). Asante's *Afrocentricity* and *The Afrocentric Idea,* which Moses describes as a "creative, and in some respects brilliant, but rambling theoretical work," articulate an Afrocentric theory of rhetoric (2).

This rhetorical theory pays attention to "African ownership of values, knowledge, and culture" as a way to understand the discourse of African people and that of other oppressed groups and, even more important, as the lenses through which we can understand and achieve other ways of knowing (*Afrocentric Idea* 181). This alternative epistemology is necessary to give new scope and vision to literary theory in general and rhetorical theory in particular, both long held hostage and blinded by their "essentially European" epistemic with its binding commitment to the fundamental concepts of Western thought: rationality, objectivity, and progress (179). The symbolic revolution in rhetorical studies since the 1960s has highlighted the inadequacy of Europe-centered rhetoric to account for the discourse of the oppressed. This European rhetoric invariably sides with the dominant culture, forcing scholars to confront the need for a radical ideological break from Eurocentrism to facilitate the liberation of the oppressed. Afrocentricity provides such a break and challenges Eurocentrism, especially its effort to universalize its mode of knowledge. Eurocentric views reflect the program of colonization whereby Europe dominated not only the geopolitical world but also the information about the world, including the language in which it was communicated. Such a process intensifies the domination and, as Kenyan novelist Ngugia wa Thiong'o notes in *Decolonizing the Mind*, promotes mental death and despair for those among the colonized who seek liberation (3; *Afrocentric Idea* 183). Afrocentricity not only challenges Eurocentrism but argues for an architectonic treatment of the twin problems of European cultural forms and Western expansionism that stalk literary theory. Asante promotes a transcendent rhetoric guided by pluralistic cultural values and grounded in specific cultural experiences to reclaim philosophical ground. Such a rhetoric transcends ideological or racial divides "to perform the task of continuous reconciliation" (183). Afrocentricity is a rhetorical recovery project for Africans and, by extension, for all; as Asante contends, it is "the centerpiece of human regeneration" (1). This concept is based on Asante's "belief in the centrality of Africans in post modern history" and on the power of Afrocentricity as "the highest and most conscious ideology" to captivate by "the force of its truth" (6). Asante proposes, for universal consideration, transcendent Afrocentric discourse with its three fundamental themes: "(1) human relations; (2) human relationship to the supernatural; and (3) humans' relationships to their own being" (184).

The question, for Asante, is how to proceed so that Eurocentrism, Afrocentrism, and other contending voices contribute to the creation of a more inclusive society. In advancing his probes, Asante confronts rhetorical theory with its most debilitating blind spot—Eurocentrism—as he promotes the expansion of rhetorical theorizing to include multiple voices and multiple perspectives. Asante responds to Eurocentrism's dominance not only of rhetorical theory but of all social theory in Western scholarship, even when the object of study is African American discourse. He strikes a militant tone as he calls Africans everywhere "to the vanguard of this collective consciousness of Afrocentrism! Teach it! Practice it! And victory will surely come as we carry out the Afrocentric mission to humanize the world" (6).

Asante represents the emergence of a knowledge community that seeks public validation for its social procedures and practices. Such an emergence bumps up against what Patricia Hill Collins calls "the Eurocentric masculinist knowledge validation process"; such a bumping is also experienced in efforts to advance a black feminist epistemology (201–20). Still, though difficult, these new challenges are necessary, for as Thomas Kuhn has long established in *The Structure of Scientific Revolutions,* it is appropriate—indeed, necessary—for scholars to explicate the fundamental assumptions and credentialing processes used to validate experts and their regimes of knowledge production. Notwithstanding the shortcomings of Afrocentricity, Asante's "calling out" of Eurocentric scholarship is part of a scholarly community that advocates important considerations in social theory, including a demand for more reflexivity in the approach of critics who use Eurocentric scholarship. Afrocentricity presents itself as a complement to Eurocentric scholarship even as it contributes to the call for more thorough-going explorations of the social locations from which theorizing and critique are done. Black feminist studies and whiteness studies, for example, are contemporary critical enterprises that have chosen to take seriously the notion of grounding critique and theory in visible and specific local spaces and practices. In contrast, Eurocentrism, broadly generalized, operates behind the veil of universalism and neutrality.

Asante and Afrocentricity have faced scathing, if often, disingenuous criticism that suggests, for example, that Afrocentricity promotes myths as history, replaces white ideology with black ideology, and foments disunity in the United States. In the 1998 revised and expanded edition of *The Afrocentric Idea,* Asante answers his most strident critics both polemically, in his preface, and more substantially in the expansion of the Afrocentric idea. In this later development of his work, Asante presents the "Afrocentric idea" in more measured tones. It is "a model for intercultural agency in which pluralism exists without hierarchy and respect for cultural origins, achievements, and prospects is freely granted" (xii). Even so, this model demonstrates "the illogic in empiricist epistemologies and questions the conceptual cosmologies that give rise to the concept of the foundation of civilization in a Greek miracle" (xii). Still, the claims of exclusive insight to Afrocentric scholarship and Asante's militant tone render Afrocentricity susceptible to challenges raised by critique interested in more than polemical exchanges and more than a defense of Europe from what is seen as an academic onslaught by Afrocentric perspectives. Of these various challenges, perhaps the most significant is the contention that, politically, Afrocentricity seeks to replace the totalizing discourse of Eurocentrism with its own new totalizing system—a replacement of one epistemology with another, one ontology with another—and that, philosophically, it shares with Eurocentrism similar essentialist notions and foundationalist thinking.

Writing about the same time as Asante, literary critic Henry Louis Gates Jr. published his award-winning *The Signifying Monkey: A Theory of Afro-American Literary Criticism*. As the subtitle indicates, this work focuses on literary criticism rather than rhetorical theory. Gates presents, however, a clear theory of rhetoric centered in African American discourse. For Gates, "Afro-American culture is African culture with a difference as signified by the catalysts of English, Dutch, French, Portuguese, or Spanish languages and cultures which informed the precise cultures that each discrete New World Pan-African culture assumed" (4). Moses links Gates's *Signifying Monkey* with Stuckey's *Slave Culture* to argue that both scholars present Afrocentric theories without using the term "Afrocentric" (*Afrotopia* 13). Not only does Gates construct an Afrocentric theory without naming it as such; he also develops a rhetorical theory with a very narrow conception of rhetoric. As Patricia Bizzell and Bruce Herzberg observe, "rhetoric for Gates means tropes" but tropes that are constitutive of language (1545). Gates, like Geneva Smitherman before him, studies black English and black speech, but she focuses on language per se while he looks to rhetoric and demonstrates that blacks employ unique rhetorical tropes in their speech and language in general. Signifying is the master trope of black rhetoric, as Gates notes. It has evolved from African Americans' use of the trickster figure, the signifying monkey, derived from the African usage of the trickster god Esu Elegbara. This usage is evident in the language of Africans, African Americans, and those elsewhere in the African diaspora. Jamaicans, for example, employ in their signifying practices the cunning of the trickster figure Anansi. Theirs is a language in which the contradictions and especially the hardships in life are managed artfully, with dynamism and fluidity, to both survive and thrive in the face of overwhelming odds. Adaptability and ambiguity are the hallmarks of this rhetorical tradition, as black life in the diaspora is about repetition and revision. Gresson sees in Gates's work a covert message: "*The Signifying Monkey* is a message and a model of recovery" (185). Though, like Asante, he was engaged in an Afrocentric project, Gates articulated no express challenge to Eurocentrism, and thus the response he received, while it included both praise and blame, was not as strident as that offered to Asante.

Asante's provocative work has generated an ongoing debate that has spawned a plethora of publications. This debate is summarized by McPhail and by Moses ("From Complicity"; *Afrotopia* 1–17). An exhaustive critical analysis is beyond the scope of this project, but Gresson, for example, demonstrates elements of the much needed thoroughgoing analyses by rhetorical scholars. It is sufficient for now to point to McPhail's critique of Afrocentrism, which I discuss below, and of the debate about it, very little of which is in communication journals. Yet Afrocentricity is clear in its challenge to rhetorical scholarship. To be relevant and useful, such scholarship must critically address discourse from the margins and those hailed by its appeal, with means available not only in European guise. Race and rhetoric, for example, then must be addressed with creativity, skill, and a clear understanding of the multiplicity of cultures to be considered. Rhetorical critics have responded significantly but not sufficiently.

Condit and Lucaites's *Crafting Equality* takes a rhetorical focus in its study of the ways "Anglo- and African-Americans have negotiated and managed [the meanings of the word "equality"] over the past 225 years in the public and pragmatic context of crafting a national political identity" (ix). Treating the term "equality" as a contested ideograph, Condit and Lucaites posit that this contestation and negotiation of meaning point to a futuristic approach that demands that multicultural societies move away from polarizing, exclusive approaches to more inclusive and cooperative ones, which may lead to interbraided results. In this study, the authors combine a focus on rhetoric as central to our social and political relationships and an awareness that broadening the scope of discourse communities to be studied serves to enhance American rhetorical scholarship, long marked for its limited scope and function. In so doing, Condit and Lucaites demonstrate a critical rhetorical scholarship that provides illuminating insight into the ongoing efforts of individuals and groups who contest the formation of civil morality through symbolic interaction, even where such groups, or elements of such groups, are outside the norms of traditional rhetorical culture. This significant perspective is the creative embodiment of the call to the discipline treating rhetoric to broaden its scope and deepen its critical practice.

McPhail, too, challenges American rhetorical scholarship to continue its evolution toward more bridging of gaps and overcoming of barriers. In his *Rhetoric of Racism*, McPhail explores "the relationship between language and negative definition in the social construction of racism and the conceptualization of rhetoric as coherence." Beginning with his assessment of communication scholarship that discusses race, racism, and rhetoric as largely descriptive, McPhail sets out to extend the more promising efforts and to address the need for rhetorical theorizing about the "relationship between race and the underlying assumptions of Western thought concerning both language and difference" (3).

These more promising studies include that of Marsha Houston Stanback and Barnet Pearce, whose "Talking to the Man" is a study of interracial communication that points to the transactional nature of such symbolic interaction and thus to the shared responsibility of each group for the outcomes. This shared responsibility is true even in asymmetrical relationships between blacks and whites. Haig Bosmajian's *The Language of Oppression*, which discusses the power of language to name and define people with both positive and negative consequence, also provides a basic understanding of oppressive language as that which dehumanizes victims. This issue of negative consequences is key to McPhail's study. Bosmajian's work also influences several subsequent studies of language and racism, including Dianne Hope's "Communication and Human Rights," which extends Bosmajian's language of oppression to specific considerations of sexism and racism. Hope, too, indicts communication scholarship. She sees it as susceptible to being identified as irrelevant and inappropriate for its lack of attention to the important symbolic and social dimensions of sexism and racism. Three other studies addressing race and rhetoric are important to McPhail's study: Teun A. van Dijk's *Communicating Racism,* Robert Entman's "Modern Racism," and Margaret Anderson and Collins's anthology *Race, Class and Gender.* The study by van Dijk of white racism as it is passed on among whites points McPhail to the importance of exploring the social and symbolic elements of racism by examining not just intragroup communication but intergroup communication as well; the rhetorics of both "oppressor" and "oppressed" and the epistemological ground on which they stand. Entman's study of modern racism highlights the construction and communication of racism through local television news, functions in which blacks are affirmed and demeaned simultaneously. Again, this study approaches but does not explore important implications of racism as a way of knowing in which differences are constructed negatively by all parties and as such all are complicitous in the process. Anderson and Collins, in their approach to the study of race, class, and gender, demonstrate an awareness of the epistemological problem of traditional approaches, which reproduce hierarchical viewpoints that frame "oppressed" groups as "other" without adequate consideration of their views and voices as part of the process. Here, McPhail sees negative difference at work, a difference also present in the views of the "others" not acknowledged in Anderson and Collins's scenario of the undesired "social problems"–based approach to the study of race, class, and gender discrimination. As McPhail argues, the main problem with these and other approaches to the study of social questions is the assumption that race, class, and gender issues are prerhetorical and that persuasion and argument can bring much-needed resolution. McPhail rejects such approaches as complicitous and doomed to failure.

Instead, beginning with the notion that rhetoric is epistemic, McPhail examines the rhetoric of racism through an exploration of the epistemological foundations of race and the influence of such foundational assumptions on racism in black-white relationships. Racism premised on the fallacy of race is, for McPhail, a phenomenon promoted by argument, an antagonistic discourse, which "turns back upon itself to expose the consequences of an epistemic stance grounded in negative difference" (*Rhetoric* 3). McPhail contends that language used to distinguish "oppressed" peoples from their "oppressors," including the language often used by the "oppressed" themselves, is grounded in notions of persuasion and argumentation that are themselves premised on negative difference. For McPhail, such a rhetoric of persuasion and argumentation, grounded in essentialist epistemology, has proved unable to adequately address the vexing historical problem of racism. The challenge, as McPhail sees it, is to develop an epistemic stance that addresses "the consequences of negative difference." His solution is a generative rhetoric of coherence.

To develop his rhetoric of coherence, McPhail looks to the work of Kenneth Burke and Ernesto Grassi, both of whom attend to the inherent qualities and functions of language. Burke, who identifies humans as "inventors of the negative," is discussed for his observation of the negative in language, Grassi for his focus on the affirmative. In the end, McPhail sees both theorists as settling for complicity, Burke by his acceptance of the notion that "the negative is the essential ground for language" and Grassi for his "rejection of science in favor of poetry" (17). Still, McPhail explores racism and develops his notion of coherence by reconstructing both Burke and Grassi.

McPhail based his theory of coherence on the notion that balance and harmonious energy are essential for successful human communication. This kind of balanced, coherent communication, McPhail contends, is the only way to overcome the imbalance of racism. The interdependence and complementarity promoted by coherence, McPhail argues, is the way to move from complicity, with its reification of oppositional stances, to a dance toward balance and progress. He notes, "Methodologically, coherence invites a focus on the common grounds that bind seemingly contradictory positions, so that we might more effectively understand and address the social construction of difference" ("From Complicity" 126).

McPhail's theory of complicity and coherence is crucial to my study, since he sees oppositional discourses, including the discourse of black nationalism, as complicitous and, as such, lacking the necessary conditions to fulfill the goal of emancipation. Coherence has been used by McPhail to critique both the rhetoric of racism and the rhetoric of emancipation. In his essay "From Complicity to Coherence: Rereading the Rhetoric of Afrocentricity," McPhail undertakes a critical analysis of the debate about Afrocentricity and of Afrocentricity itself. He sees Afrocentricity as complicitous in its essentializing of negative difference between itself and Eurocentrism, but he also sees the theory, especially as revealed in the earlier works of Asante, as containing the *essential* elements to be viewed as an important component of a healthy multiculturalism. In this regard, McPhail articulates three elements of rapprochement between Afrocentricity and coherence theory: (1) the offering of an alternative epistemology to the foundationalism and externalism of Western thought, one that acknowledges the role of subjective conviction; (2) the affirmation of concrete personal experience or personal acceptance as the final arbiter justifying true belief; and (3) the call for the minimizing of inconsistencies as necessary to achieve an accurate connection between mind and material experience (129–30).

McPhail views Asante's response to his critics and concludes that "the rupture between theory and practice ultimately undermines the Afrocentric ideal" (131). McPhail also attends Gresson's recovery rhetoric to indicate that Gresson's insight into the scope and functioning of black conservative rhetoric is useful. He notes, however, that Gresson overlooks the complicity of the "collectivist camp" who supposedly are advancing freedom but are unable so to do, suppressed as they are by their essentialism shared with the Other whom they oppose ("Complicity of Essentializing Difference" 163). While McPhail uses coherence and complicity effectively to critique Afrocentricity and recovery, identifying each as fruitful but flawed, there are challenges facing coherence. While coherence exposes epistemological flaws in Asante's Afrocentricity and Gresson's recovery, for example, the question of praxis haunts coherence.

The practical political challenge of establishing the common ground on which to balance the generative rhetoric of coherence is not a simple one. As Ernesto Laclau and Chantal Mouffe suggest, seeking emancipation from points of marginality is likely to further polarize already antagonistic subordinated groups and those who run the system. Instead, subordinated groups, such as black nationalists, might be more effective if they seek a point of equilibrium somewhere between unity and identity. McPhail is correct in his observation that a shifting of cultural critique away from differences between races and onto differences within racialized contexts of domination and subordination will better serve the interests of racial equality. Yet, as Mary S. Strine suggests in her "Cultural Diversity and the Politics of Inquiry: Response to Mattison and McPhail," the challenge is one of locating spaces of inquiry within the politics of location. Where black nationalism functions as white racism's "mirror image," it is patently implicated in and complicitous with racism. However, where the political options are to be constructed as nonbeings, the way white racist rhetoric has characterized blacks in the past, or to become the "shadow and echo" of white racism, the way many black conservatives have, to stand in contrast will remain more attractive. These black conservatives often face the charge that they are traitors of the black cause. Put simply, the challenge of coherence is a challenge of the need for practical political action. In the murky waters or on the tenuous terrain of American political life, where race matters so much that public intellectuals and political activists, especially black ones, are often forever "fixed" by their expressions on race, to be an essentialist is to be redeemable; to be a "traitor" is not. As Gresson notes, though blacks have resisted being defined in essentialist terms, racial essentialism has long been for blacks an important political weapon (34).

Still, McPhail's highlighting of the problematic entailments of the essentialist groundings of racist rhetoric demonstrates that the rhetoric of domination and the rhetoric of freedom must be critically addressed. In Foucauldian terms, such essentialism inscribes black nationalists in the racist power games that they are trying to fix (Foucault 99). Gayatri Spivak's notion of strategic essentialism provides a possible way out of this dilemma (51). Raka Shome employs Spivak's conception in her performance of a postcolonial critique (46). In employing strategic essentialism, the critic acknowledges that any act of criticism calling into question the misrepresentation of a racial "Other," in this case the "Other" of white supremacy, is itself open to the charge of being essentialist. However, such essentialism need only be a necessary strategic act: temporary grounding for the production of a critique. For Spivak, any deconstructive move necessarily includes some act of essentializing. The way out of this quandary is through a reflexive stance—an acknowledgment of one's complicity, to use McPhail's term—but to note that this essentialist act is a strategy and one that cannot lay claim to any "fixed" or "authentic" identity. Viewing black nationalism's essentialism as a strategic political stance significantly alters the nature of its complicity as part of the rhetoric of racism. It also allows for a pragmatic approach to black nationalism and to other emancipatory practices such as Afrocentricity, shackled as they often are by what Gresson calls "the code word 'essentialist'" (55). Such an approach takes into account an important caution that we note differences in "motives, morality, and possible outcomes" (to borrow from Gresson's comparison of Asante and Julius Lester) when making observations about a rhetoric of freedom and a rhetoric of domination sharing common essentializing tendencies (55). Strategic essentialism, then, provides a way out of the bind of dismissing out of hand or even significantly weakening rhetorical moves with laudable motives, morals respecting human dignity, and emancipatory potential. To be effective, Burke contends, the Other must find a way to speak the language of the "us" (*Rhetoric* 563; qtd. in Gresson 55). With the same goal of theorizing race and rhetoric but in a way different from McPhail's more philosophical conception of coherence, Gresson takes a psychological approach and proposes a rhetoric of recovery.

Gresson's psychological approach takes as its center Joseph Campbell's contention that the problem of contemporary societies is their search for all meaning in the individual, unlike earlier ages in which meaning was found in the group or in the world (3). Gresson addresses African American rhetoric by exploring the tension between the collective and the individual. In this undertaking, Gresson's approach is also an extension of the work of Richard B. Gregg, who earlier introduced the notion of the ego-gratification function of rhetoric. In his 1971 essay "The Ego-Function of the Rhetoric of Protest," Gregg explored "protest rhetoric" and highlighted what he called its "ego-gratification" function. In this process, discursive appeals—often seen as lacking the necessary civil and rational elements of persuasion—"persuade," affirm, and empower members of a social movement by helping them to overcome feelings of privation. This provision of in-group psychological gratification is one aspect of the dual effect of such rhetoric. The other is the generation of fear in the minds of opponents. Such a rhetoric often is impolite and does not bear the mark of traditional rationality. It is effective, however, when it reconstitutes the dominance and submission that mark the social relationship in which its primary audience is the dominated group. With this insight, Gregg established the rhetorical framework on which subsequent theorists would build. Gresson built on Gregg's perspective to argue not only for a "rhetoric of creation" to be used to foster "symbolic equality" but also, later, the development of his more full-blown theory of a rhetoric of recovery.

Gresson identifies his *Recovery of Race in America* as "a rhetorical study of loss and recovery." He contends that there are "two particular losses which are central to American life: white Americans' loss of moral hegemony and black Americans' loss of the myth of racial homogeneity" (ix). Gresson then explores the rhetorical structure of the response to these losses. This important study is Gresson's exploration of the ways in which African Americans rhetorically manage an ongoing liberation struggle beyond the apogee of the Civil Rights era. Ultimately, Gresson is interested in plumbing the nature of what he calls contemporary "racial recovery discourse" to exert its influence on rhetorical theory development. Gresson's theory of recovery promises insight into the way black nationalism functions as part of the liberation struggle in America.

Recovery is, for Gresson, a human necessity: a response to loss with an effort to regain balance by taking back that which has been lost. "Recovery discourse," then, is "talk about recovery" that addresses the emancipation of self and Other with recollections of a past before the experience of loss. Recovery is a special form of discourse perhaps best described in Mikhail Bakhtin's terms as a "speech genre", a genre employed by any individual or group that has experienced loss. It is within this type of speech that we find the *topoi* or "common places" that are then used in rhetorical strategies of recovery *(Speech Genres)*. In Gresson's scheme, the rhetorics of "betrayal and consolation," "failure," and "self-healing" are all "recovery rhetorics" (4). These recovery rhetorics share a cast of components:

> (1) a motive to recover something perceived as lost through violation, failure, or betrayal; (2) the use of narrative to describe a discovery with inferred relevance for both one's own and the Other's ability to deal with duplicity and uncertainty; and (3) an implicit invitation to identify with and accept the liberative powers of that discovery. (5)

Recovery rhetorics employ a narrative structure to tell their story, a story often marked by reversals and ironic inversions. It is a signifying practice that employs metaphors and myths to "twist reality, a reality of self and Other" (24–25). For example, the notion of "reverse racism" marks the birth of modern white racial recovery rhetoric (9). Gresson's insights into the rhetoric of recovery provide an understanding of the role of rhetoric in the effort of African Americans to re-cover the concept of race.

Following the work of Gregg and Gresson, Stephen Goldzwig uses the no-tion of symbolic realignment to explain the rhetorical function of Farrakhan's discursive acts. In the process, he extends Gregg's and Gresson's notions of rhetoric used in a process of reestablishing balance for a marginalized or deprived audi-ence to argue that such rhetoric also functions to symbolically realign the rela-tionship between speakers and their audiences. This realignment creates concep-tions of leadership and group relationship that provide motives for action within the group (Goldzwig).

That the theme of recovery seems to be at the core of African American dis-course is understandable given the tragic sense of loss that marks African diasporic life. Asante, for example, appeals for an approach that acknowledges the centrality of African cultural values as the basis for understanding and healing. Similarly, McPhail's notion of coherence is an argument for the process of black emanci-pation to be viewed as possible only through a rhetorical engagement between "oppressed" and "oppressor" without the disabling shackles of negative differ-ence. Gresson sees recovery as a necessary exercise that includes but, in complex ways, goes beyond oppositional discourses to fuse disparate individual and col-lective fates and identities (Gresson 212). Accepting these themes as central to African American discourse enhances my effort to examine the ideological struggle inherent in the rhetorical process. With these more recent efforts as al-lies then, I explore the recursive interplay between and among ideological alien-ation, rhetoric, public memory, and race as a continuation of this more recent approach to the study of African American discourse and as an effort to fill the void of theorizing about the development and functioning of the ideology of black nationalism.

Ideological Alienation and the Black Experience

Theorization about the development of a black nationalist ideology excludes key rhetorical dimensions, a problem accentuated by the failure of theories of ideological alienation to take race into account. I demonstrate this failure in a critique of theo-ries of ideological alienation. I also argue that understanding the efforts of blacks as an ideology that functions as a constitutive rhetoric provides a useful frame-work for the exploration of African American rhetoric and the continuing struggle of blacks to deal with their experience of alienation in America. I show that the collective black practices that constitute the ideology of black nationalism emerged in the response of blacks to their American experience of alienation. The question is this: In what ways do blacks publicly struggle with the issue of who they are and where they belong as part of their American encounter?

The black experience in America from 1619 to the present has been one of a minority group surviving in the midst of an antagonistic white majority. Slavery, segregation, and Jim Crow laws are just some of the more visible and vulgar manifestations of this antagonism. According to Robert Fogel, these developments are based on "age-old sentiments on slavery with a new emphasis on race that justified white dominion over blacks" (202). White supremacy, bolstered by slavery, was further reinforced by black servility. Thus, as Fogel concludes, "although the sources and degree of the intensity of early racism remain a matter of debate, it is agreed that the degradation of color was increased by servility" (202).

This system meant that because of their color, blacks were forced to fill a subservient role in the society. This servility functioned further to conscript them to an underclass, which was then designated as their rightful place. Blacks confounded such designators by demonstrating their skills and abilities. However, even when blacks worked as skilled artisans, white supremacists argued that these instances were exceptions (Condit and Lucaites 169). Both during and after legalized slavery, then, blacks have for many years contended with a lack of social cohesion, whether related to the disruption of families caused by slavery, an unwillingness or inability to connect with an oppressive Anglo-American culture, or a sense of disconnection from themselves and other blacks as the result of systematic oppression.[8] This lack of social cohesion is, in Durkheimian terms, the experience of "anomie," or alienation (De Vos xiv).[9] Blacks were alienated from fellow blacks; from Africa, the homeland of their ancestors; from fellow humans (whites); and perhaps most significant, from themselves. There was a loss of control over the most prominent mode of production, which was rhetorical access to the dominant public fora, and the major product, which was black identity.

The striking evidence of crime and punishment in black communities is another scenario of alienation (Berry, xiii). All available data indicate that blacks have always been overrepresented both as victims and offenders in crimes, and the arrest and conviction rates for blacks are much higher than those of whites. Compared with the total population, blacks are "twice as likely to be victims of robbery, vehicle theft, and aggravated assault, and 6 to 7 times as likely to be victims of homicide," which has only recently been bested by AIDS-related illnesses as the leading cause of death among young black males (Jaynes and Williams 498; Centers for Disease Control and Prevention). The high rates of criminal justice control over young black men result in much more than the temporary loss of freedom for these men. As the Sentencing Project contends, "the consequences of this situation for family and community stability will be increasingly debilitating" (Mauer 4). *A Common Destiny*, identified by Walter Shapiro in *Time* as "the nation's most definitive report card on race relations in 20 years," opens by stating that, "we describe many improvements in the economic, political, and social position of black Americans. We also describe the continuance of conditions of poverty, segregation, discrimination, and social fragmentation of the most serious proportions" (Shapiro 13; Jaynes and Williams ix). Though "the world of black Americans has always been a part of American society, the black and white worlds have also always been mostly separate," and, consequently, blacks live as "a society within a society" (Jaynes and Williams 163). This separate black society is due in part to the search by blacks, in response to the experience of alienation, to articulate a way of life of their own. Black alienation is thus partly the effect of the nationalist ideology of a predominantly white society.

This white ideology defines the racial superiority that has been the hallmark of American practices since the initial encounter of blacks and whites (Kinney 225). As a consequence, the American sociopolitical landscape, with its ideal of equality, is overshadowed by the inventory of social realities embodying such racism, including the efforts of the white population to dominate and subjugate blacks. For example, in 1919, from June to the end of the year, there were twenty-six so-called race riots in the United States, as blacks from the South moved in large numbers to the North in search of a better life (Lewis 62; Woodward 113–16). These riots occurred mainly in large northern metropolitan cities where, again and again, whites attacked migrant blacks, contending that they were a threat to whites. Such racist practices were not new. The oppression visited by physical conditions, such as those of slavery, have always been complemented by the arguments of slaveholders and the narratives they constructed to support their system of subjugation.

My interest is in the way alienation functions rhetorically. Beyond the physical and symbolic conditions themselves, blacks point to their awareness and feeling of alienation; especially as slaves, they indicated that they knew "what it is to live 'far from [their] native clime/Under the white man's menace, out of time'" (Harding xii). In the case of the black experience, alienation is constituted by the language of blacks and whites. Alienation, then, is a phenomenon that includes more than just oppressive material conditions or the loss of social cohesion as a material reality. In this regard, white language functions to marginalize blacks on the basis of race, and alienation manifests itself when blacks comply by acquiescing to the descriptors imposed upon them within such language. Unfortunately, a rhetorical understanding of alienation, with race as a pivotal issue, is absent from contemporary discussions of social theory.

While I cannot review all the literature on ideological alienation here, I do consider the Marxist notion of class-based alienation in an analysis of the major proclivities toward a theory of alienation that it has spawned.[10] Because alienation is an effect of ideology, a consideration of the theories of alienation must begin with an examination of "ideology" itself. With welcome exceptions such as the [Birmingham] Centre for Contemporary Cultural Studies' *The Empire Strikes Back: Race and Racism in 70s Britain,* which seeks to theorize ideology, race, and class by following Karl Marx, conceptions of ideology focus primarily on class, to the exclusion of race. This bracketing of race accentuates the lack of theorizing about a black nationalist ideology because, notwithstanding the protestations of many whites, race is of primary importance both in the dominant white ideologies that seek to oppress blacks (some more explicit than others) and in the ideology of black abolitionists that sought black liberation. Cedric Robinson's outstanding study *Black Marxism* engages much of the problematic of blacks and Marxism to demonstrate their mutually antagonistic, if at times beneficial, relationship. The problematic of the way race is implicated in ideology is a pivotal issue.

In *The German Ideology,* Marx and Friedrich Engels invert the idealist conception of ideology espoused by Georg Wilhelm Friedrich Hegel in favor of a materialist account. Marx and Engels see people as creating their own history, not through the abstract notion of consciousness but through the experience of their material life. They thus present two concepts of ideology. The first treats ideology as an inversion of reality:

> Consciousness can never be anything else than conscious existence, and the existence of men is their actual life-process. If in all ideology men and their circumstance appear upside down as in a *camera obscura,* this phenomenon arises just as much from their historical life-process as the inversion of objects on the retina does from their physical life-process. (Marx and Engels 14)

Their second concept of ideology treats it as the expression of the ideas and interests of the ruling class. According to Marx and Engels,

> [t]he ideas of the ruling class are in every epoch the ruling ideas: i.e., the class which is the ruling material force of society, is at the same time its ruling intellectual force. The class which has the means of material production at its disposal, has control at the same time over the means of mental production, so that thereby, generally speaking, the ideas of those who lack the means of mental production are subject to it. (Marx and Engels 14)

Marx and Engels present these two conceptions of ideology as a way of critiquing ideologists within the dominant class who present this inverted view of life. In their view, history should not be presented upside down. To correct this erroneous view of life, Marx and Engels argue for an examination of the material basis of ideology, an investigation of the impact of the order of production in any given epoch upon the sense of social and political consciousness. Following Marx and Engels, I see ideology as rooted in the perceived consciousness of humans, a consciousness that emerges from their experience of material conditions. As Bakhtin contends, "consciousness takes shape in the material and being of signs created by an organized group in the process of its social intercourse"; as such, as McGee convincingly demonstrates, rhetoric is a material experience of life in society (Bizzell and Herzberg 1213; "A Materialist's Conception"). Marx's diagnosis of ideology is therefore a social analysis, with social transformation as its goal (Giddens 166–68). A survey of the Frankfurt School's extensive treatment of ideology is beyond the scope of this study. Also, while the marxissant tradition represented in the work of Walter Benjamin, the Max Horkheimer–led early Frankfurt School, with Theodore Adorno and Herbert Marcuse, and the work of Georg Lukács has expanded Marx's definition, it has maintained his perspective of ideology.[11]

With a broader perspective, Althusser presents ideology as a practical characteristic of every type of society. For him, ideology is essential for the conversion and molding of people into beings able to respond to the demands of existence within such societies. In his terms, ideology "is the 'social cement,' the indispensable source of social cohesion: through ideology, human beings live as 'conscious subjects' within the totality of social relations" (179). If Althusser is right in his conceptions that ideology is "an inherent feature of the conduct of social life," then it is an inherent feature even of theories of ideology and alienation (183). In this respect, it is important to reflect "a critical awareness of how [racial] borders have been (and continue to be) systematically policed and for whose ideological benefit and material profit" (qtd. in Awkward 15).[12] The Althusserian concept of ideology is developed further by the Birmingham School of Cultural Studies in *The Empire Strikes Back* where they seek to articulate the relationship between ideology and race. Marx's notion of sectional interests as basic to the theory of ideology is also a useful guide here. With this conceptualization, one of the chief uses of ideology is the critique of domination. Here ideology can also be affirmed as "modes of belief which mobilize political activity against the *status quo*," the existing state, which functions ideologically to establish and maintain its preeminent position (Giddens 186; McGee, "'The Ideograph'" 4). As ideologies establish particular perspectives, they also dominate other perspectives through the process of alienation.

Bertell Ollman notes that Marx defines alienation as the absence of unalienation, and argues that, "for Marx, unalienation is the life man leads in communism" (131). Ollman illustrates the concept of alienation versus unalienation by contrasting it with disease versus health: "we only know what it is to have a particular disease because we know what it is not to" (132). In Marxist terms, then, alienation is a malady, an unhealthy condition that should be remedied. Alienation is manifested as a loss of control of the decision-making process as it relates to work and the products of such work. In this state, one is separated not only from work but also from fellow humans as "competition and class hostility has [sic] rendered most forms of cooperation impossible" (133–34). People who experience this kind of cleavage exist as abstractions who have "lost touch with all human specificity" (134). These splintered beings can experience reunification only through communism. This reunification is "the positive transcendence of all estrangement—that is to say, the return of man [and woman] from religion, family, state etc., to his [and her] human, i.e., social mode of existence" (134).

The emphasis in Marx's theory is in the category of class. Class struggle results in alienation, and the elimination of class under communism is consequently the solution to the problem of alienation. Marx sees class, like human character, as determined by social conditions, which then directly affect individual power and needs. Social conditions also work to create interests, which individuals seek to satisfy. For Marx, then, any group that experiences common social conditions develops similar powers, needs, and interests and, as a result, develops into a social class. This class will be intrinsically hostile to other classes that develop under different conditions; the result is class struggle (121–22). Marx's theory proceeds on the assumption that class is materially determined, to the exclusion of considerations of its social construction. By extension, alienation is not considered to be socially constructed. In response to critics, Engels is deliberate in clarifying that "the determining element in history is *ultimately* the production and reproduction in real life" and that the economic element is not "the *only* determining one" (R. Williams 267). Still, as James Aune has observed, the role of rhetoric in this process is thus bracketed and marginalized (Aune 158). This is a significant shortcoming of the Marxist theory because, as I will argue, rhetoric functions to establish individuals as belonging to particular social units, groups, or in Marxist terms, classes (Burke, *Rhetoric* 27–28). The predominance of the Marxist concept of alienation based on class has resulted in a lack of attention to the rhetorical dimensions of the problem of alienation and to race as a distinct social grouping that often confounds the Marxist notion of class. This deficiency needs to be addressed, as alienation is important in any consideration of the marginalization of one group by another, and the discourse of marginalized groups often reflects both an awareness of alienation and a rhetorical effort to overcome it. Indeed, the success or failure of discourse from the margins is largely dependent on its ability to provide a reconfiguration of alienation and identification as they affect the relationship of the margins to the center. This dependence is acute within a context of unchanging oppressive social conditions, such as those experienced by American blacks, especially during the nineteenth century. Such rhetorical reconstruction challenges the dominant forces and provides a frame of acceptance and affirmation for the group in the margin.

Richard Schmitt avers "there is widespread agreement that alienation is not merely a feeling but consists of definite social conditions . . . but it is also agreed that if people are alienated they must feel alienated" (8). In the first statement, Schmitt points to the dominance of the Marxist conception of alienation. In the second, he begins to address the symbolic aspect of the problem of alienation as it is constructed in language. Here alienation consists not so much of "definite social conditions" but of a rhetorically constituted social construct. This is an important aspect of alienation, and such rhetorical alienation is evident in modern society.

The Cold War between the United States and the Union of Soviet Socialist Republics was one example of such alienation. This phenomenon created a cleavage in the sense of kinship that people shared with each other, regardless of where they lived. The human bond between the people of these nations was broken, and difference was established. This state of affairs was constructed primarily in the discourse between the two nations. It was rhetorically constructed alienation. According to Robert Denton, "the Red Scare was more deadly than the black [sic] plague. Our language determined what we saw, and what we thought, and what we did" (xiv). In this same vein, black alienation was an experience felt in the encounter with the language of white supremacy. This was a language that functioned in tandem with the full complex of the social conditions of white supremacist America. The language of master versus slave and superior versus subordinate was a concrete aspect of this experience of American blacks. As Walter Rodney notes, in the face of slavery and the oppressive practices of white supremacy, "even the blacks became convinced of their own inferiority" (Groundings 25). Also, the common example of the black male, of whatever social class, being referred to as "boy" by whites is a clear example of talk being used as a tool to establish difference and reinforce notions of white superiority and black inferiority, even long after slavery. These uses of language established, reinforced, and ensured that blacks felt this alienation.

For this study, the most telling critique of alienation theories, then, is that they do not account for race or, at best, they presume that race is subordinate to class. In either case, the consideration of race and the black experience requires an extension of Marx's theory of alienation. In presenting a conception of alienation without any fundamental consideration of race and the way it functions to interpellate particular groups to prescribed hierarchical roles within social formations, Marxist theories reinforce the status quo. Race calls people out; it names them, and in so doing, it places them in structured social positions. The Marxist approach to alienation, then, has itself been an alienating factor in the experience of blacks in America (Kymlicka 4–6).[13] It provides them with no sense of identity or place that resonates with their particular experience of struggle (Asante, *Afrocentricity* 33). The problem they face is precisely a problem of race, and it needs a solution that considers race a primary issue. Asante, for example, sees Marxism as an inadequate, if not inappropriate, tool. He writes, "socialism to deal with class contradictions; [black] nationalism to deal with race contradictions" ("Systematic Nationalism" 123). From a different perspective, Roy L. Brooks, in *Rethinking the American Race Problem,* argues that in contemporary America, race and class must be studied together. Still, in the 1920s and 1930s, for example, within the United Communist Party in America, "the solution to the race problem was seen as an automatic by-product of a socialist revolution and that was all" (T. Martin, *Race First* 223). Indeed, because of the emphasis on class over race, the relationship between blacks and American communists during this period was an attenuated one (221–72). As Martin's extensive discussion of the issue reveals, the result was a standoff between Garvey, the spokesman for the black "masses," and the communists. The significance of this standoff is highlighted by the fact that "[t]he bulk of Garvey's followers [and blacks in general] in the United States, as elsewhere, were workers and peasants. These were the types of people upon whom the communists would necessarily hope to build a mass movement" (222). This problem is further highlighted in Wilson Record's *The Negro and the Communist Party.*

The balkanized approach to alienation, with its focus on brute material conditions, leaves us with desideratum in our efforts to theorize contemporary social relations between blacks and whites in America. Where discussions focus on the black underclass, for example, we can point to economic inequalities. The Marxist focus is less useful, however, where we engage issues related to the black middle class, which, while it continues to succeed economically, acknowledges an experience of alienation from the rest of Anglo-American society. As Cose notes: "Although white America is keenly aware of the alienation of the black underclass, it is largely oblivious of the deep sense of racial injustice that middle-class blacks feel. And notwithstanding Shelby Steele's *The Content of Our Character,* with its 'new vision of race in America,' whether a black man 'is a judge or a janitor, race always becomes an issue'" (Cose, "The Key" 42). It is significant that a majority of the Million Man marchers was from the black middle class (Curry, "After the Million Man March"). Charles T. Banner-Haley and Sut Jhally and Justin Lewis contest the problematic but dominant Anglo-American myth of social mobility unhampered by race (blackness). Put another way, when in moments of crisis where white supremacist rhetoric dominates American popular culture or guides the ship of state, race trumps everything and frames blacks and blackness as Other. A rhetorical approach to alienation might facilitate the inclusion of race as an important consideration in social theories, thus enabling us to account for material experiences such as those of middle-class blacks.

Toward a Rhetorical Concept of Alienation

In proposing a rhetorical conception of alienation, I characterize the discourse of both blacks and whites as material rather than representational. From this perspective, as McGee points out, rhetoric is material "because of its pragmatic *presence,* [and] our inability to safely ignore it at the moment of its impact" ("A Materialist's Conception" 29). The rhetorical dimensions of alienation, then, can be seen through the basic function of rhetoric as expressed by Burke: "the use of words by human agents to form attitudes or to induce actions in other human agents." This function finds its roots "in an essential function of language itself, a function that is wholly realistic, and is continually born anew; the use of language as a symbolic means of inducing cooperation in beings that by nature respond to symbols" (*Rhetoric* 41, 43). People identify with each other when their interests are joined. Where their interests are not joined, they may identify with each other if they assume that their interests are joined or if they are persuaded that their interests are joined. Within the context of black and white relations in America, alienation occurs when blacks experience and accept the language that identifies them as joined to whites in social relations so structured to condemn them to a position of inferiority based on race. Rhetoric effects identification when it creates this kind of assumption or brings about such persuasion. In his discussion showing that rhetoric functions inherently to develop factions as it creates identification, Burke notes, "since identification implies division, we found rhetoric involving us in matters of socialization and faction" and, "we are clearly in the region of rhetoric when considering the identifications whereby a specialized activity makes one a participant in some social or economic class. 'Belonging' in this sense is rhetorical" (45, 27–28).

Establishing that the rhetorical dimension of alienation is encapsulated in the use of language to form attitudes or to induce actions in others allows us to show that while nineteenth-century black alienation was firmly grounded in material conditions, it was also constructed in the discourse of both oppressed and oppressors. This discourse went beyond the representation of mental and empirical phenomena. In the context of nineteenth-century America, this discourse was causative, with ideas, conceptions, and consciousness of stratification based on skin color as its main products. The language of master versus slave and superior versus subordinate established clear and fixed hierarchical arrangements as part of the social structure of the society. Blacks who experienced this discourse as part of its audience were circumscribed in a subservient role. This encounter virtually ensured that they would feel alienated; whites, though, experienced it as empowerment. As part of their effort to recover their sense of their own collective humanity, black abolitionists challenged this hierarchy to bring about black emancipation, and I examine selected aspects of their discourse to demonstrate how their efforts functioned collectively as a constitutive rhetoric that led to the development of a black nationalist ideology.

Ideology has long been recognized in rhetorical scholarship as central to persuasive discourse. With Ernest J. Wrage's 1947 call for an investigation of ideology in public discourse as an early marker, rhetorical scholarship has increasingly interrogated the role of ideology in discourse (451–57). A focus on ideology is evident, for example, in the work of McGee, Philip Wander, Condit and Lucaites, and Raymie E. McKerrow, all of whom employ aspects of the marxissant tradition in their rhetorical theorizing.[14] McKerrow theorizes a critical rhetoric to examine the "dimensions of domination and freedom as they are exercised in a relativized world" ("Critical Rhetoric: Theory" 91). Charland's concept of a constitutive rhetoric has emerged as part of a critical rhetorical practice that seeks to "promote a realignment in the forces of power that construct social relations" as it unmasks its own discourse of power (91). The aim is to provide an emancipatory critique by presenting an understanding of the functioning of power and knowledge in society (Foucault). As its main contribution, then, a constitutive rhetoric provides an accounting of the way subjects are constituted and employed or deployed to function ideologically in discourse. My main concern is with the issue of constitutive rhetorics and how they operate within the context of ideological contestation and identity formation. Charland explored a political struggle over language and culture; my concern includes language and culture but with the nefarious issue of "race" at its core. With racism stalking their lives, nineteenth-century black rhetors constantly undertook the double task of constituting not only their audiences but themselves as legitimate speaking beings (Smith [Asante] 7; Gregg; Terrill 70). Though often denied any legitimate role in the public domain of rhetorical interaction where American collective life was negotiated and determined, these black rhetors confronted Anglo-American notions of nationhood to contest one of the central elements of nineteenth-century public rhetorical culture, "the people." As Condit and Lucaites argue, "the people" is one of a select number of ideographs crucial to the organizing of any public rhetorical culture (xii). The centrality of the conception of the people and the rhetorical uses to which it is put is evident in America's long contestation over the Constitution's "We the people."

Because of this central issue of race, McPhail's notion of coherence and Gresson's concept of recovery, both within the stream of rhetorical practice aimed at providing emancipatory critiques, serve as important touchstones for my analyses of this rhetoric. I use both McPhail and Gresson then, alongside my expansion of Charland's formulation of a constitutive rhetoric, to explore the ways in which the ideology of black nationalism emerges within its own particular historical and rhetorical context of nineteenth-century America.

In addition to the characterization of rhetoric as material and epistemic, a constitutive rhetoric operates with the understanding that rhetoric is ontological in that it does not merely re-present and describe human ideas and empirical data but instead generates such ideas and data. In the case of nineteenth-century America, proslavery rhetoric was part of the system that created the hierarchy of white superiority and black alienation. It accomplished this by establishing what it meant to be black in relation to whites. In contrast, black abolitionist rhetoric addressed this experience of alienation. In their response, we see the emergence of ideological effects that were appellative of black alienation. These effects include the re-defining of blacks and the re-structuring of their social relations. Rhetoric creates, explains, and confronts people with realities they cannot ignore. So, to understand African American political culture and the changes that take place within it, we must acknowledge the ontological and epistemic functions of rhetoric in the historical struggle for black liberation. Of course, the past is crucial to critical theory's effort to understand the present.

Constitutive Rhetorics and Ideological Effects

A constitutive rhetoric is a critical rhetorical practice that proceeds on the notion that audiences and their identity do not transcend discourses but are fixed by the speeches, pamphlets, letters, et cetera within which they participate and by which they are persuaded to act. This rhetoric seeks to account for such audiences, especially where their identity is problematic. In so doing, a constitutive rhetoric "permits an understanding within rhetorical theory of ideological discourse, of the discourse that presents itself as always only pointing to the given, the natural, the already agreed upon" (Charland, "Constitutive Rhetoric" 133). To be more specific, a constitutive rhetoric enables us to account for the "key processes in the development of ideology: the constitution of the subject" where the subject is at once both speaker and actor in the discourse and the world (133). This ability is crucial for the development of rhetorical theory, as it uses Burkean identification to address a key deficiency in theories of rhetoric as persuasion, which cannot account for such a subject or audience that rhetoric addresses (Burke, *Rhetoric* 50; Charland, "Constitutive Rhetoric" 133). Constitutive rhetoric embraces Burke's proposal of identification as a replacement for persuasion;

it is the key issue in rhetoric that allows for its ideological effects identified by Althusser to be analyzed. In this proposal, Burke challenges the notion of an audience existing prior to and outside the scope of rhetoric, which then seeks to persuade them. He argues instead that rhetoric constitutes audiences through the process of identification. In Burke's terms, you persuade someone by *"identifying* your ways with his [*sic*]." He notes that persons may be identified in terms of something that they share and to identify one person with another is to make them consubstantial. For Burke, persuasion involves "communication by the signs of consubstantiality, the appeal of *identification*" (55, 62). Burkean identification allows for the construction of subjectivity and the ideological functions of rhetoric. In McPhail's terms, persuasion, with its foundation in argument and negative difference, precludes coherence and as such functions to reinscribe racism rather than to dismantle it. Constitutive rhetoric's accounting for the subject, therefore, advances our understanding of the power of discourse to create identity. Charland trained his critical eye on developments in Canada's political life to theorize a constitutive rhetoric.

In 1967, the year of Canada's centennial, a political organization, the Mouvement Souveraineté-Association (MSA), was launched in Quebec and was dedicated to the political sovereignty of the province. The MSA called for Quebec's independence, claimed that there was an essential unity among the social actors in the province advocating this cause, and in French, Quebec's majority language, declared, *"Nous sommes des Québécois"* ("We are *Québécois*") (Mouvement). In so doing, the MSA sought to redefine those previously identified as *Canadiens Français* (French Canadians), thus bringing into being a new political subject whose identity would be used to justify the constitution of a new state. According to Charland, the MSA's effort to call the *peuple Québécois* into being is an instance of constitutive rhetoric. The term *Québécois* gained national currency, and in 1976, MSA's successor, the *Parti Québécois* gained control of the Quebec government, asserting that those in Quebec constituted a distinct *peuple* with the rights and duties for sovereignty and the commitment to lead Quebec to independence. As part of its preparation for a referendum on Quebec's political sovereignty, the *Parti Québécois* issued the "White Paper," a formal policy statement that proposed a new political order, with Quebec as a sovereign state. In this new political order, Quebec would be culturally and politically separated from Canada while maintaining only economic ties to what the paper termed an "oppressor government." For its enactment, this proposal required a favorable vote from the citizens of Quebec on the referendum. Proponents argued that with the success of the referendum, Quebec would gain a new constitutional status and freedom from its former "oppressor," Canada. Most important for our consideration, the White Paper contended that the "new people"—the *peuple Québécois*—were non-

Canadians. To do this, it presented an historical account of the struggles of the citizens of Quebec that set them apart from "regular" Canadians. Citizens who accepted this self-description would support the effort toward separation. This effort rhetorically to construct a particular kind of subject—a people—points to the constitutive function of rhetoric. Thus, the White Paper was a striking example of a significant effort to create and employ or deploy a subject to function ideologically in a rhetoric.

In his discussion of constitutive rhetorics, Charland indicates that Quebec's claims for sovereignty were based on the "asserted existence of a particular type of subject, the '*Québécois*'" ("Constitutive Rhetoric" 134). In this undertaking, Charland makes use of three notions important to an understanding of abolitionists' discourse as a constitutive rhetoric: McGee's view of "the people" as a legitimizing force in political discourse; Althusser's concept of the "interpellation" of people as subjects; and Burke's theory of identification as the key concept of rhetoric. Having established that these concepts are active in the rhetoric of the *peuple Québécois,* Charland then uses Althusser's work on the production of ideology to identify three ideological effects of constitutive rhetoric in this discourse: the constitution of a collective subject, the positing of a transhistorical subject, and the illusion of freedom.

Constituting the Collective Subject

The constitution of a collective subject involves a rhetoric's construction of individuals into a collective subject. This collective subject is then presented as united in such a way as to allow for the transcendence of divisions such as interests, age, and class. As McGee indicates, such a collective subject does not exist in nature as a collective being but is constructed in a narrative and serves to legitimize the goals of such a narrative. In his discussion of the use of the term "the people" as a legitimizing tool in rhetoric, McGee shows that collectives are constructed by activists to serve particular ideological functions:

> 'The people,' therefore are not objectively real in the sense that they
> exist as a collective entity in nature; rather, they are a fiction dreamed
> by an advocate and infused with an artificial, rhetorical reality by
> the agreement of an audience to participate in a collective fantasy.[15]
> ("In Search of 'the People'" 240)

McGee identifies four stages in this collectivization process whereby "the people" may be rhetorically defined. First is the presence of dormant seeds of collectivization in popular reasonings within a culture that represent "the parameters of what the 'people' of that culture could possibly become." In the second stage, advocates seek to activate these dormant seeds by organizing them into political myths and presenting them to persons in an effort to create "a people." The third stage appears when masses of persons respond to the political myths presented and give them legitimacy by "publicly ratifying the transaction wherein they give up control over their individual destinies for [the] sake of a dream." The fourth stage involves a rhetoric of decay, with a decline of collective ideological commitments (240).

As part of such rhetorics, people are constituted in discourse as collective subjects with rhetorically flexible identities. The boundaries vary as to who are included or excluded from such a "people." For example, James Henry Hammond's proslavery text, a "Letter to an English Abolitionist" seeks to constitute Southern blacks as not just slaves but "our slaves" (Faust 178). Such a collective subject is predisposed to contentment in slavery and extreme dependence upon and loyalty to white slaveholders. With a distinct difference, blacks in the North are constituted as poor and ignorant, natural lackeys agitated by ungodly white abolitionists with their misguided notions of equality and of the immorality of slavery (175–79). It is not surprising that these claims were contested by black and white opponents of slavery; such contestations, however, point to the extent to which people are constituted as subjects in discourse and that their identities as such are rhetorically negotiable.

Advocates of slavery like Hammond claimed that Southern slavery was Edenic, the perfect social institution. Such a characterization is based on the existence of an ideological black subject who is naturally pliable, is in essence servile, and whose character fits perfectly the role of the compliant subject: "our slaves." From the other perspective, black activism toward emancipation becomes possible through the articulation of a collective black subject naturally aware of freedoms and rights denied them through slavery and having the characteristics of a freedom-loving people thus predisposed to reclaim such rights and freedoms: "black people." Of course, both proslavery and antislavery advocates ignore the fact that the black subjects they claim exist become real only through rhetoric, that is, that they are fictive. They also gloss over the tensions between individual identity and collective identity. However, these fictions have consequences as people live them out, making them historically material. In living out these fictions, people are transformed into what Black labels the "second persona" of a discourse ("The Second Persona" 109). Such rhetorics, then, function ideologically in that they constitute identities even as they contend that these identities are natural and pregiven. The ontological status of these people both as individuals before the process of identification and as the persona of discourse thereafter remains in question.

To account for the ontological status of audiences before their identification with a second persona, Charland uses Burke's discussion of the symbolic to challenge any notions of the givenness of audiences, persons, or subjects. He argues instead that social beings are textual in that they are constituted in rhetoric as "a structured articulation of signs" (Charland, "Constitutive Rhetoric" 142). To exist ontologically, then, is to be a subject, and audiences are, in Althusser's terms, "always already" subjects. These subject positions are not, however, fixed or seamless. New subject positions may develop along with new constitutive rhetorics. The many texts that make up our social worlds often result in what Stuart Hall calls contradictory subject positions simultaneously existing within a culture ("Signification" 107–13). Such contradictions put a strain on particular subject positions, thus necessitating the rearticulation of the subject. Constitutive rhetorics undertake this task of rearticulation by providing the subject with new interests and motives, thus resolving or containing the contradictions.

A ready example is the identity of "African American," which is constructed as the rearticulation of the "African," one belonging to the continent of Africa, and the "American," one belonging to the United States. This became necessary because the subject position of "African," while it affirmed a black heritage, made it difficult for blacks to claim a place in the United States. On the other hand, while "American" pointed to a subject belonging to the United States, its strong Anglo connotations implied a negation of the black heritage. Of course, within a constitutive rhetoric, terms such as "African American" and "American" are not just descriptive but also constitutive of subjects with particular histories and futures (Charland, "Constitutive Rhetoric" 140). This new subject position at least contains the contradiction between the subject belonging to Africa and making claims on America. This rearticulation includes the positing of new constitutive rhetorics that reconfigure old discourses. Such rearticulation is part of the effort toward black equality. It points us again to the important role of the historical narrative in our contemporary contestations over identities. In sum, this highlighting of the textuality of the subject points us to the recursive interplay between biological beings and their functioning in rhetoric that constructs and hails them as textual subjects for political ends. The critique of humanist ontology and the claim that subjects are textual helps make visible the second ideological effect of constitutive rhetorics, the positing of a transhistorical subject.

Positing the Transhistorical Subject

In positing a narrative history, a constitutive rhetoric conceives of a set of individuals as one. For example, settlers from different countries in Europe are presented as a community. Blacks from different tribes and nations in Africa are identified as "a people." In both cases, disparate individuals representing a plurality of nationalities, tribes, and cultures are identified as "one people." Such a constitution serves to mask and negate the tensions and differences among members of any given society. Not only are differences negated but such a narrative also elides and bridges distinctions between the past and the present. Time is collapsed or compressed as identification occurs in the narrative. In functioning thus, the subject constituted by such rhetorics is not just transhistorical but also transcendent. In nineteenth-century black abolitionist discourse, for example, blacks both in the North and the South are presented as one, sharing a consubstantiality with ancestors identified with a heroic black past. In this process many sociogeographical divides are elided and past struggles are featured as warranting present action. The nineteenth-century collective black subject is then called upon as "black people" to continue the work of blacks in the past, a work of heroic struggle for their cherished freedoms. As "black people," then, these nineteenth-century blacks transcend their individual differences, as well as the time differences between them as biological beings and those in the past. They are joined as one "black people" with other individuals, many long dead and, for the most part, unknown. As such, they are inscribed as real social actors with the textually construed motives of the discourse shared with historical black figures. As I show shortly, this inscription takes place when individuals experience, affirm, and choose to inhabit such a narrative. In sharing this common identity, nineteenth-century blacks everywhere felt the degradation of Southern slavery and the oppression of Northern racism while they shared a common memory of the struggles of their ancestors; in short, they were inscribed into the ideology of the discourse and therefore understood the world from its perspective.

In contending that not only do people use words but also that words use them, Burke puts it well when he claims "an 'ideology' is like a god coming down to earth, where it will inhabit a place pervaded by its presence. An 'ideology' is like a spirit taking up its abode in a body: it makes the body hop around in certain ways," and a different behavior would have come from that same body, inhabited by a different spirit (*Language* 6; Charland, "Constitutive Rhetoric" 143). It is precisely because an ideology operates like a god or a spirit who pervades a place or inhabits human bodies that it can be presented as natural, normal, and unquestioned. Subjects constituted within an ideology, then, "do what they do because of who they are." In the case of nineteenth-century blacks inhabited by this "god," this ideology, as "black people" they must struggle for their freedom, since that is what blacks faced with oppression have always done. Inhabited by the spirit of abolitionist ideology, then, these individuals are inserted into the material world of nineteenth-century America to complete the unfinished struggles of their ancestors. They undertake such action with a sense that they choose to do so freely.

The Illusion of Freedom

The battle over what Althusser calls interpellation, or the way in which people are inscribed in black abolitionist narrative versus Anglo-American, proslavery narrative, points to Charland's observation that "people are constituted in rhetoric" ("Constitutive Rhetoric" 136). Althusser identifies interpellation as a key function of ideology. It relates to ways in which people are hailed or constrained by particular circumstances and thus compelled to respond in specific ways, governed by the demands of such circumstances. He observes that

> [i]deology "acts" or "functions" in such a way that it "recruits" subjects among the individuals (it recruits them all), or "transforms" the individuals into subjects (it transforms them all) by that very precise operation which I have called *interpellation* or hailing, and which can be imagined along with the most commonplace everyday police (or other) hailing "Hey you there!" (174)

The concept of interpellation, therefore, illustrates that people are not "free" to act as they please but are obliged to respond as subjects within frameworks. This concept is further reinforced by Black's demonstration that auditors are constructed and constrained in the framework of discourse. This persona is a fiction but one that "figures importantly in rhetorical transactions" ("The Second Persona" 111). The way people are interpellated as subjects circumscribes what they can or cannot do. It not only limits their options but also points them in particular directions.

The artistic creativity, popularized by Bertolt Brecht, that affords momentary "freedom," for example, to Spike Lee's characters in *Do the Right Thing* to break out of their roles and yell racial epithets at the cameras or Woody Allen's characters in *The Purple Rose of Cairo* to walk off the screen, further illustrates that the subjects in narratives are purely textual with illusions of agency and freedom. Nelson George describes this move as a Spikeism; Lee stops the narrative and allows characters to speak to the camera (McMillan et al. 80). Within a narrative already spoken or written, protagonists are constrained to fulfill its *telos*.

However, as part of its effective ideological functioning, a constitutive rhetoric advances a narrative with protagonists who are "free" to choose their course of action. The identity of such protagonists or collective subjects is constructed so as to project inherent motives and interests as being natural. For such an identity to fulfill particular functions, subjects are constituted with a specific character, nature, or essence. A constitutive rhetoric, then, creates the kind of subject that will fulfill its political ends while projecting itself as one existing prior to and outside the discourse. It is to this "real" subject that such a rhetorical address is aimed. The subject is then presumed to be free to choose to act in accordance with or against the promptings of such a rhetoric. This presumption is in Althusser's terms "an illusion of freedom." Black nationalism claims emancipation and equality on the assumed existence of a particular type of black subject, "black people" or "Afro-Americans," while proslavery discourse claims as natural the hierarchical social order of the Old South based on a different type of black subject, the "slave." Blacks who recognize and acknowledge that they are being addressed by such discourse participate in it by accepting the self-understanding it advances—thus, individuals become part of the persona of the discourse and are inscribed into its ideology. This inscription is the process through which they are interpellated or hailed as political subjects in a process of identification and rhetorical socialization. It is after this ongoing rhetoric of identification that "persuasion" takes place. This process establishes blacks as sharing a racialized collective identity. Thus, constituted as "slaves," "black people," or "Afro-Americans," black individuals can be "persuaded" to remain in their rightful place of subjugation as slaves or agitate for their denied freedom as a people.

The ideological function of constitutive rhetoric is crucial in that it presents to the addressed the cherished and admired notion of freedom of choice. Such an illusion is further masked by the fact that unlike classical narratives, which have closure, constitutive rhetorics present unfinished histories and "leave the task of narrative closure to their constituted subjects" (Charland, "Constitutive Rhetoric" 143). In the case of nineteenth-century black nationalist narrative, the call is clear: the struggle goes on, as blacks have yet to obtain their freedom. Since slavery, the call has been in the name of equality. This call is effective in motivating individuals to associate with the textual identity, as they see themselves as respected and are thus more likely to embrace the discourse generating such respect. For constitutive rhetorics, the likely result is material action by which such individuals, as embodied subjects, affirm their subject position in the social world.

Notwithstanding Althusser's otherwise insightful perspective, however, he leaves little or no room for human experience and creativity, which are important aspects of subject formation. As Lawrence Grossberg and Jennifer Daryl Slack observe, Hall theorizes a space between "culturalism" and "structuralism" in which, he argues, the positioning of subjects as "the product of ideological practices and positionings" is overly deterministic by Althusser's structuralist approach. As Stuart Hall sees it, this approach needs to be balanced by the culturalist's emphasis on experience as a creative human social practice (Grossberg and Slack 89). Hall also argues that "the constitution of subjects and how ideologies interpellate us" is only one side of the two-sided issue: the problem of ideology discussed in Althusser's essay "Ideological State Apparatuses." The other side is the question of the "reproductions of the social relations of production." For Hall, the fracturing of the two has resulted in an unevenness in the development of the problematic of ideology, with reproduction assigned to a "(male) pole" and subject formation to a "(feminist) pole" (S. Hall 102–3).[16]

To be successful, black abolitionists had to win the battle of interpellation, that is, the battle for the way blacks would be constituted as a people, as well as the battle to restructure the social relations of production. As I demonstrate in the case studies that follow, their aim was thus the production of blacks who were human—equal to any other human being—not just the transformation of slaves into "free blacks." The objective of white supremacists, of course, has always been the opposite.

Approaching black abolitionism from the perspective of a constitutive rhetoric allows us to examine blacks' collective practices in response to their material and symbolic alienation and to delineate the emerging ideological effects. This approach is useful in that it goes beyond the notion that the audiences and subjects involved in the rhetoric of these abolitionists were always already fixed outside the speeches, pamphlets, letters, et cetera that they employed. It enables us to demonstrate how these abolitionists tried to fix what it meant to be black; to fix it in such a way that it propelled blacks to address their ideological alienation. It also enables us to see how these collective black practices functioned to re-structure the social relations between blacks and whites. The following chapters highlight the ideological functions in the rhetoric of black abolitionists, as well as in that of proslavery nineteenth-century white Anglo-America, as contesting cultures create and recreate themselves rhetorically. This approach serves as a prerequisite for an explanation of the functioning of the ideology of black nationalism in contemporary African American political culture.

2
The Narrative of Oppression: Preserving Slavery

The real world is to a large extent unconsciously built on the language habits of the group.
—Edward Sapir, *Selected Writings of Edward Sapir in Language, Culture, and Personality*

Slaveholders and their friends produced poetry, essays and novels to prove human bondage was as American as apple pie and as benign as the smile of God.
—William Loren Katz, *The Suppressed Book about Slavery*

Any study of black survival and advancement in America during the early nineteenth century must address both slavery's symbolic and material instruments: the efforts aimed at enslaving both the mind and the body. Alongside the study of the physical conditions of slavery should be an increasing study of the symbolic instruments of slavery, for, "in much the same way that literal whips were fashioned from different materials, the symbolic whips of slavery were woven from [and into] the many areas of culture" (Patterson, *Slavery* 8). My focus here is on proslavery discourse, the discourse that expressly advances a defense of Southern slavery, contending that blacks are natural subjects for enslavement.

The oppressive white supremacist culture of antebellum America, circa 1815–61, was maintained with an array of symbolic instruments that included social norms, ideas, values, and other cultural expressions such as art, media, and architecture (D. Goldberg 8). Next to slavery itself, however, racist discourse was perhaps the chief marker of prejudice supporting antebellum America's proslavery culture. This discourse shaped and expressed the white supremacist social, cultural, and moral values (Tise, *Proslavery* xv). An important feature of this discourse was a defense of slavery as a legitimate American social practice, based partly on the contention that blacks were natural subjects for enslavement. This discourse was a signal feature in the white supremacist effort to demean and dominate black lives. Alongside its affirmation of whiteness, the rhetoric sought to complement the enslavement of black bodies by enslaving black minds. However, the discourse, like slavery itself, faced challenges and changing social conditions to which it had to adapt. Nineteenth-century proslavery thought continued the themes of seventeenth-century arguments but with the remarkable development of a "more systematic and self-conscious" approach to the defense of slavery. The proslavery arguments during this era "took on the characteristics of a formal ideology" as advocates "sought methodically to enumerate all possible foundations for human bondage" (Faust 4).

The proslavery proponents of the period were conflicted about the morality of slavery and the humanity of blacks (Takaki, *Pro-Slavery;* Tise, *Proslavery*). This conflict was accentuated by the tension between Revolutionary theory and human bondage. Yet, these Anglo-Americans needed to establish a unity in their ideology. This proslavery narrative then was a part of the effort of Anglo-Americans to construct for themselves "a coherent social philosophy" (Faust 1). Their efforts are evident, for example, in the writings of proslavery advocates such as Ebenezer Newton Elliott, who sought to present the defense of slavery as a coherent, consistent body of thought (Faust 4). Still, this rhetoric tried to undergird slavery by constituting blacks and whites as naturally unequal social subjects. And though, as Tise argues, "it was not necessary to denigrate the Negro race to defend slavery," there was hardly a defense without such denigration (*Proslavery* 12).

Despite their ambivalence about the morality of slavery and their espoused commitment to notions of liberty, Anglo-Americans crafted a narrative of suppression for blacks even as they created stories for themselves to live by. The evidence is definitive that Europeans arriving in America from multiple clans and countries were united by a narrative of positive whiteness and negative blackness (West, *Race Matters* 20; Morgan 328; T. Allen 1). Theodore W. Allen, in his decisive work *The Invention of the White Race* provides definitive evidence that the "white race" is a rhetorical invention. While I do not suggest that this discourse is an "isolatable or determinative clause" of white oppressive practices, I advocate it as a significant if underexamined element (Condit and Lucaites xviii). A valid question at this point could be the often examined issue of whether slavery caused racism or vice versa. This is, in Allen's terms, the psychocultural, socioeconomic debate (1). Allen aligns himself with the "socio-economic camp" and presents credible evidence to support Eric Williams's thesis that "[s]lavery was not born of racism; rather racism was the consequence of slavery" (E. Williams 7). This is against the "psycho-culturalists" like Winthrop Jordan, who argues that they "seem to rather to have generated each other" (*White Man's Burden* 45). As Allen argues, an understanding of the connections between racism and slavery is crucial to our contemporary efforts to end racial prejudice (2–3). Even so, I endorse Peter Kolchin's prods that we examine the useful question of "how slavery and prejudice interacted to create the particular set of social relationships" in America (*American Slavery* 14). As we examine the efforts of advocates to prove *why* slavery was right, we see in their language-in-action remarkably striking features of white supremacy. "White centrality," "unity," and "superiority" versus "black otherness," "externality," "dependency," and "inferiority" emerge as symbolic tools in the construction of a cellar of black inferiority and an edifice of white superiority so important for this continued justification of slavery. These features were common to defenses of slavery whether such defenses were based on history, sociology, biology, or theology.

I undertake a genealogical inquiry of this proslavery narrative in an effort to understand how this rhetoric functioned to constitute and differently situate the collective black subject and the collective white subject.[1] The rhetorical constitution of this narrative enabled Americans to fashion and maintain the social order of antebellum America in both the North and the South but particularly in the Old South with its continuation of slavery and the oppression of blacks (Faust; Lyons; Hubbart; Perkins; Silbey; Tise, "Interregional Appeal"; Kolchin, "In Defense of Servitude"). Further, like slavery earlier, modern racism is a striking indicator that humans view the world through systems of belief and explanation that do not fully reflect the reality they are meant to describe. The need to better deal with racism and prejudice is a good enough reason to seek to fathom how proponents of slavery manufactured and maintained their systems of meaning.

In what follows, I examine the proslavery discourse that developed in the aftermath of the Revolutionary War, when the values of "property" and "liberty" took on new meaning and required a rhetorical reconfiguration. Rather than to examine all the proslavery defenses from the period, I focus on Robert Walsh's *An Appeal from the Judgements of Great Britain Respecting the United States of America* to probe the salient features of the post-Revolutionary defense of slavery.[2] This text was the signal proslavery treatise of the period. In the face of challenges from within the United States and beyond, Walsh's *Appeal* outlined the key frames that became the tenets of proslavery defenses. These frames include the establishment of blacks as marginal and whites as central to civil society; the contention that slaves were the rightful property of their owners and thus beyond the jurisdiction of outside interests, especially the federal government; and the affirmation of slavery as a legitimate, perpetual, and progressive social practice. Walsh's *Appeal* was so successful it became the blueprint for subsequent proslavery defenses, including the biblical defenses so popular in the 1830s and beyond. As we shall see, these biblical defenses, exemplified in Thornton String-fellow's "Bible Argument: or, Slavery in the Light of Divine Revelation," were often restatements of Walsh's positions argued with biblical justifications. I explore Walsh's *Appeal,* treating it as a representative anecdote.

An Appeal from the Judgements

To use Burke's terms, a representative anecdote is the form that guides the development of the vocabulary of a given system. Such a form becomes that which represents the whole of any system (in this case, the proslavery position) and (proslavery) advocates develop subsequent examples by drawing from this exemplary form. To be representative, such a form "must have scope. Yet it must also possess simplicity in that it is broadly a reduction of the subject-matter." The representative anecdote contains the "terminological structure that is evolved in conformity with it." Walsh's *Appeal* became the paradigm or prototype for the defense of slavery. All other treatises defending the institution were but "partial exemplifications" in which could be discerned the summation of Walsh's exposition (*Grammar* 60). This treatise became the representative of proslavery positions synechdochically: that part which stood for the whole. By bringing all the proslavery arguments together into a coherent whole, the *Appeal* symbolizes and is itself a summation of the systematic defense of Southern slavery in antebellum America. It was that "representative public enactment" to which all supporters of slavery variously but commonly subscribed. This treatise was the benchmark of American conservative republican nationalism and, as such, and more important for this study, provided for the proslavery community the moment of convergence, the symbolic enactment of their group identity, designed to help maintain slavery (328).

Proslavery Ideology

This work contains the "longest and most extensive defense of slavery yet published in America" (Tise, *Proslavery* 47). It is part of a genre of proslavery treatises bound together by their common agenda of maintaining the institution of slavery in America. Among these treatises are standard proslavery documents such as Stringfellow, "Bible Argument," Thomas Roderick Dew's *Review of the Debate in the Virginia Legislature of 1831 and 1832,* James Henry Hammond's *Two Letters on Slavery in the United States, Addressed to Thomas Clarkson, Esq.,* and William Harper's "Memoir on Slavery." These efforts were part of a larger proslavery narrative intertwined with the Southern sentiment and language that bolstered Southern confidence in the region's self-revered social practices.

Though not the first, Walsh's *Appeal* is acknowledged by John Adams as "the most able, the most faithful and the most ample apology for the United States."[3] James Madison declared it "a triumphant vindication of our Country." A third American "founder," Thomas Jefferson, anticipated that the *Appeal* would "furnish the first volume of every future American history" and that "the latter part will silence the libelists of the day" (Lochemes 103–4; Tise, *Proslavery* 47). This work heralded a new era in proslavery ideology as it set the tone and outlined the basic arguments to be employed in most subsequent proslavery treatises. In the wake of the Revolution, the *Appeal* was the first to show that Americans could openly defend slavery and win wide approbation from the best and the brightest in the nation. For decades following, this work was accepted as the standard history of the United States (Tise, *Proslavery* 47–50). Walsh's important rhetoric emerged as part of an interesting set of rhetorical and historical developments.

The period 1808–30 was, in Larry Tise's description, one of "intense, interconnected social reevaluation" marking the beginning of the "manifestation of a many-faceted process that transported Americans from obeisance to the heritage of their Revolution to their acceptance of far different social, economic, and political values" (*Proslavery* 41). With the closing of the foreign slave trade in 1808, slavery in America became a domestic issue. After the War of 1812, the respected *English Review* published sharp criticisms of American life. British tourists to America routinely supplied the British press with travelogues recounting their observations. In their regular discussions of these travelogues, the British press had, since 1795, provided critical assessment and often demeaning accounts of American society. Americans sometimes responded by extolling the virtues of life in the new nation. One such was Charles Jared Ingersoll who, in 1810, pseudonymously published a tract with a title and subtitle revealing its strategy, content, and purpose: *Inchiquin, the Jesuit's Letters, During a Late Residence in the United States of America: Being a Fragment of a Private Correspondence, Accidentally Discovered in Europe: Containing a Favorable View of the Manners, Literature and State of Society, of the United States, and a Refutation of Many of the Aspersions Cast upon This Country, by Former Residents and Tourists.*

Ingersoll's American encomium was written as from an unknown Irish Jesuit to a friend in Europe. He advanced an American proslavery nationalism by contending that America had created the first successful republic and that it did so with slavery. This achievement was in contrast to what Ingersoll saw as the failed French experiment in democracy. Embracing the musings of Edmund Burke, Ingersoll praised Southern slaveholders as the epitome of the spirit of liberty. He claimed that, with the use of slavery, America had effectively eradicated the vices of Europe, peasantry, mobbism, and beggary. He argued further that slavery should not be lamented, as it was "not militant with republicanism" (Ingersoll 106–7,

110, 120; qtd. in Tise, *Proslavery* 42–45). In this scheme, Ingersoll broke with traditional defenses of slavery, in use since the Declaration of Independence, which had shown deference to natural rights theory by acknowledging some conception of equality, even the white supremacist formation with its skewed notion of white equality that excluded blacks. Ingersoll's social and political values, however, had their basis not in the Revolutionary heritage but in conservative republicanism. He inverted the natural rights notion of theory as a guide to action, advocating the acceptance of social reality, with actions based on present needs. This idea was in direct contrast to Revolutionary rhetoric, which proceeded from theories of equal rights to rightful action (Tise, *Proslavery* 43, 45–50).

In 1814, the *Quarterly Review* of London excoriated Ingersoll for his ploy of using the supposedly Jesuit letters to praise American character and advocate a rapprochement between republicanism and slavery. In response, Timothy Dwight's *Remarks on the Review of Inchiquin's Letters* and James Kirke Paulding's *The United States and England: Being a Reply to the Criticism on Inchiquin's Letters*. . . . both defended Ingersoll and scoffed at Old England and its imperialism. They extended Ingersoll's proslavery republicanism, accepting his notion of the primacy of material social reality as the basis for the justification of enslavement (Lochemes 90; Tise, *Proslavery* 45–47).

The major offensive of slavery proponents in the intense, post-Revolution rhetorical war over American character, however, was the publication of Walsh's *Appeal*. In 1819, Walsh, "a renegade federalist from Maryland," joined the effort to defend American practices against the derogation of British travelers and produced a five-hundred-twelve-page, full-blown treatment of conservative American republicanism. Walsh devoted the last hundred pages of his polemic to slavery. For four decades, this text served as the standard single-volume history of the United States, eliciting American praise and British opprobrium (Tise, *Proslavery* 47; Lochemes 96–106).

Laclau and Mouffe's discussion of the unifying principle of an ideological discourse provides a point of entry into the ideological contestation of this era and the rearticulation of proslavery ideological discourse. Laclau and Mouffe identify two phases: periods of stability and periods of generalized conflict. Periods of stability occur when ideologies go largely unchallenged and

> the social formation tends to reproduce its relations following traditional channels and succeeds in neutralizing its contradictions by *displacements*. . . . [T]he dominant bloc in the formation is able to absorb most of the contradictions and its ideological discourse tends to rest more on the implicit mechanisms of its unity. (27–29)

As Laclau and Mouffe point out, the opposite occurs during "a period of generalized ideological conflict." During this period, opponents raise questions about the social formation's reproduction of its relations and the ideology's constitution of subjects, previously accepted as natural. These opponents make visible contradictions within the ideology. This conflict forces an "'identity crisis' of the social agents" and a consequent struggle between opposing forces that seek to constitute or reconstitute their own ideological unity while disarticulating the ideological discourse of opponents (27–29).

The defense of slavery preceded the American Revolution. Proponents of slavery constructed a narrative, with its roots deep in seventeenth-century religious, slaveholding America, "'to create the fiction that the enslaved people were subhuman and undeserving of human rights and sympathies'" (qtd. in Bosmajian 35). From the beginning of North American slavery, its advocates sought to convince those outside America, Anglo-Americans, and the slaves themselves of the truth of this claim. After the abolitionist crisis of 1835 and before the Civil War, the defense of slavery became predominantly a Southern phenomenon. With Walsh's systematic defense as a staple, subsequent apologists such as Stringfellow and Dew and his colleagues in the antebellum Old South directed their apologia more to equipping other Southerners with good reasons for their own defense of slavery (Faust 6–7). The proslavery position, however, was espoused by both Northerners and Southerners. It was an American phenomenon.

Proslavery and American Revolutionary Ideologies

The debate in the British and American press over the American character provided the immediate context for Walsh's discourse. A much broader problem, however, prompted the need for this particular defense of the controversial institution. Aspects of America's Revolutionary ideologies and slavery had been on a collision course since the Declaration of Independence and the ensuing war. Condit and Lucaites, in their discussion of the shortcomings of the conventional interpretation of Revolutionary ideology or ideologies and slavery, bring insight to this issue. While Anglo-Americans interpretively qualified equality, on the basis of their primary public values of liberty and property, to exclude, most notably, African Americans, American antagonists in the British press and African Americans at home actively challenged this qualification. For African Americans, this challenge was most effective in their ability to promote and use the Declaration of Independence as a means of expanding the scope of liberty while restricting the Anglo-American use of property. It is in this contestation of interpretation, then, that the conflict between Revolutionary ideologies and slavery is established, and it is the Revolution and the events surrounding it that provided the rhetorical ground for equality to be used as a basis for the challenge of slavery (Condit and Lucaites, *Crafting Equality* 40–98; Davis, *Problem of Slavery*). For the nation to claim a place of respect among European nations such as Britain and France, a resolution of this ideological conflict between American freedom and American slavery was a rhetorical necessity. This need emerged in the arguments of those who found the joint rise of slavery and freedom an embarrassment (Patterson, *Slavery* ix). Gary B. Nash shows significant evidence of several factors and arguments favorable to the abolition of slavery in the 1770s and 1780s (6–20). One of the five identified by Nash was strong sentiment against the institution based on the Revolutionary ideal of natural rights (6–7). Slavery caused no conceptual conflict when framed within Anglo-America's accepted version of the ancient scheme of the Greeks and Romans that valued liberty and property. Blacks, however, expanded liberty to include themselves, and British adversaries of slavery called attention to it as the exploitation of free human labor to create more property. In view of the challenges posed by these alternative schemes of freedom and property, American slavery became "not the peculiar institution, but the embarrassing institution" (Patterson, *Slavery* 27–34).

With the Constitution and the Northwest Ordinance of 1787 providing the legal impetus, by the 1820s, after a checkered history, slavery had been "abolished in all the states north of the Ohio [river] and firmly entrenched in those to the south" (Tise, *Proslavery* 55). This profile of slavery's ebb and flow suggests that in America's effort to be both one nation and the bastion of freedom and equality, the very soul of the new nation's experiment was wrenched and contorted by this mounting conflict. America's rhetorical response, best articulated in Walsh's *Appeal,* was an attempt to reconcile slavery and freedom in a coherent view of American civil society. The struggle to come to grips with such issues as the slaveholding practices of Jefferson, the champion of the Declaration of Independence, and George Washington, the hero of the Revolution, led to "an attribution to the Negro of characteristics by virtue of which his [or her] slavery could be explained and maybe even justified" (Patterson, *Slavery* ix; MacLeod 11). To put this development in context, a brief survey of the defense of slavery in early American history will suffice.

The Defense of Slavery in American History

American arguments in justification of slavery, from their beginnings in the middle of the seventeenth century, were largely borrowed from ancient and medieval sources including Aristotle, Augustine, and Thomas Aquinas (Jenkins 1; Patterson, *Slavery* vii–xiii; Davis, *Problem of Slavery*). The practice of human bondage and its justification were part of the European cultural heritage brought by some early migrants. Since then, the proslavery position has been a restatement of these arguments modified in response to the socioeconomic and political conditions and challenges of the period (Jenkins 2). This defense has been used in a wide variety of causes, including the definition of race.

The beginning of the eighteenth century saw the first clear public debate about the issue of slavery with the publication, in Boston, of Judge Samuel Sewell's antislavery pamphlet, countered by Judge John Saffin's proslavery response (Jenkins 3–5). During this period, proslavery arguments were often biblical and largely unchallenged, until the Quakers, led by John Woolman and Anthony Benezet, provided the first concerted antislavery effort. Before the end of the century, with the Declaration of Independence, the ensuing war, and the rise of the new nation as its catalyst, the debate took on national and international significance (MacLeod 11). The rise of slavery occurred along with the rise of liberty and equality, but as Morgan observes, the Revolution had "irreversibly altered the context in which 'all men'—and hence Negroes—had to be viewed" (Morgan 4; Jordan, *White over Black* xi).

Natural Rights and the New Nation

Slavery became a national debate in the Constitutional Conventions of 1787–88. The slaveholding delegates demanded that control over slavery be permanently reserved for the states and that there be guarantees against any congressional powers to interfere with the institution. Thus began the list of crucial compromises forged in the process of building a nation but often to the detriment of blacks (Liston 55–58). Subsequently, in the face of antislavery appeals to Congress, proslavery Congressmen limited debate on the issue by arguing that slavery was not a subject for congressional deliberation. Even so, between the Revolution and the rise of abolitionism in the 1830s, slavery was assailed by Revolutionary rhetoric based on natural rights. Proslavery writers responded with racist claims denying the equality of blacks and contending that antislavery propagandists were impractical. They countered the natural rights theory with arguments that absolute freedom and equality were impractical, as the social order of society required an essential hierarchy, with blacks, of course, at the bottom. Slavery's defenders also grounded their rebuttals in what, for them, was the manifest evidence of the institution's beneficent nature. Another significant contextual feature of Walsh's *Appeal* was African colonization.

Parallel to the rise of proslavery nationalism was the blossoming of African colonization; Anglo-Americans were increasing their advocacy for the return of blacks to Africa. Beginning with John Saffin's claim that "the Negroes [if emancipated] must all be sent out of the Country," colonization, on some scale, had consistently been a part of white America's proposed solution to slavery (G. Moore 251–56). However, the efforts gained momentum as part of the Revolutionary rhetoric. This rhetoric embraced both liberty and racism and resulted in a pro-gram seeking to end bondage while removing from "our land the alien race" (qtd. in Tise, *Proslavery* 50–51). This convolution of vice and virtue as part of the American character emerged from the notion that the nation had two main evils: slavery and Negroes. A driving force was white fear of blacks, a fear heightened by the 1789 French Revolution and especially its byproduct, the 1791 black slave revolution in Haiti led by Toussaint L'Overture (Aptheker, *To Be Free* 43–44).

It is not surprising, that for Walsh and subsequent Southern proslavery pro-ponents, the real evil of America was not slavery but the nation's "Black Jacobins" (Holland 85–86). Early-nineteenth-century Southern considerations of eman-cipation included proposals for colonization, which was thus a central issue in Walsh's treatise and in the subsequent debates about the fate of blacks.

Anglo-American Ideological Crisis and Rearticulation

British criticisms of American life highlighted the ideological crisis foisted on the nation by the performative contradiction between its espoused commitment to "equality" and the enslavement of millions within its borders. These criticisms questioned America's social formation and the reproduction of its relations. They challenged American ideology and the subjects it constituted. With contradic-tions between equality and slavery made visible, the nation needed a reconstitu-tion of its ideological unity. Walsh's *Appeal* provided just such a reconstitution. It did so with its countering of British and other antislavery criticisms and its rearticulation of an American unified vision based on conservative republican nationalism. Slavery and republicanism were woven into this new American ide-ology with its reproduction of equal whites and inferior blacks. This develop-ment was not limited to the South but was national in its scope. The South, however, would soon face its own set of ideological crises precipitated by several developments on the international scene.

The move toward abolition in the British territories brought increased oppo-sition from the outside. The Missouri crisis and the congressional debates sur-rounding it, the American Colonization Society, with its plan to establish the groundwork for general emancipation, and the bombardment of the South with more radical abolitionist propaganda disquieted Southerners. Most disturbing for whites were slave revolts, as names like Gabriel (Prosser), Denmark Vesey, and Nat Turner struck fear in the minds of slaveholding communities.

These developments created and recreated periods of ideological crisis for the Old South. Crises of confidence in the taken-for-granted productions and re-productions of Southern life exacerbated the ideological contradictions between such concepts as freedom and slavery, setting in motion the dissolution of the dominant discourse that supported the "natural" order of Southern life. This crisis was one of identity, an exigency demanding an effective rhetorical defense of the embattled institution.

In the face of challenges that Southern slavery was peculiar, inhumane, evil, and dated, the proslavery South found new rearticulations in the increasingly more strident proslavery discourse of Dew, Stringfellow, Harper, Hammond, and others (Genovese, *"Slavery Ordained"* 7). These early- to mid-nineteenth-century arguments sought to present slavery as a perpetual institution, a necessary component of liberty, and a beneficiary to all. Within this context, slavery had to be transformed. The "transient evil" that it was had to be significantly underplayed, and slavery as "a permanent good, and not only a permanent good, but the best of all social institutions" had to be highlighted much more than previously (G. Smith 3; Wish, "Slave Disloyalty" 435). Tise consistently argues that there was not an extreme swing from evil to positive good in nineteenth-century proslavery thought and that "evil and good were always juxtaposed in any thorough defense of slavery." He argues instead that with the waning of the Revolutionary heritage and the supplanting of natural rights theory by economic, social, and political ideologies, acknowledgment of the evils of slavery became unnecessary, since these evils were recognized by all. Slavery as a social good, then, could be highlighted (Tise, *Proslavery* 34–40).

Accentuating the long existent racism in American practices and extending Walsh's arguments, Southern proslavery advocates proffered slavery as a permanent good on the basis of their own physical, philosophical, and moral truths. These idiosyncratic truths included principles such as the physical inferiority of blacks and the superiority of whites, the natural subordination of blacks to whites, and the moral and biblical requirement to subject inferior, heathen blacks to the authority of superior, Christian whites. All of these notions were woven into a self-serving and self-fulfilling narrative in support of Anglo-American racism. Ironically, they supported these concepts against the backdrop of the Constitution, with its compromised depiction of slaves (all of whom happened to be black) as property and as three-fifths a person; the Bible, with its notions of chosen and cursed peoples; and white supremacist history, developed and sustained on Southern biblical interpretation. An analysis of the *Appeal,* the exemplar of this discourse, reveals the various tenets of this narrative of oppression.

An Appeal from the Judgements: Tenets of Oppression

Walsh, a magazine editor and publisher acknowledged by John Quincy Adams, then American minister to Russia, as "the first internationally recognized American author," prepared the *Appeal* as a "survey of the institutions and resources of the American republic; and of the real character and condition of the American people" (Adams, *Writings* 4: 135, qtd. in Lochemes 71; Walsh v; Lochemes 49–88). In

Walsh's view, his "series of notes and illustrations" was "wrought from authentic information" constituting the best refutation against those deriding America and its people (v–vi). To establish the nature and gravity of the charges to which Walsh was responding, I reproduce a section of his summary of British allegations culled primarily from the *Edinburgh Review* and the London *Quarterly Review:*

> The institution of slavery is the foulest blot in the national character of America; its existence in her bosom is an atrocious crime— the consummation of wickedness, and admits of no sort of apology from her situation;—the American, generally, is a scourger and murderer of slaves, and therefore beneath the least and lowest of the European nations in the scale of wisdom and virtue; and above all, he sinks, on this account, immeasurably, in the comparison with England, who, become the agent of universal emancipation. . . . America is chiefly to blame for the establishment and continuance of her negro slavery. . . . [I]t is incompatible with soundness of heart or understanding, and with the love or possession of political freedom; that no nation of Europe, not the lowest and least, presents a similar or equally revolting spectacle of servitude. (Walsh 308–9)

This was, in Walsh's view, an outright assault on American character, a "war (which is) waged without stint or intermission upon our national reputation" in the British press, its institutions of higher education, and Parliament (v–xiv). The volume is divided into nine sections, the last of which specifically treats American slavery. While an analysis of the entire text is a worthwhile undertaking, it is beyond the scope of this project. Instead, our focus here is on Walsh's discussion of slavery.

Proslavery Arguments

An Appeal from the Judgements employs arguments that later became key to specific defenses of the South. They include ascribing responsibility for the introduction of slavery to agencies other than the present slaveholders while acknowledging the rights of these slaveholders to "their property"; contending that the federal government had neither the responsibility nor the power to interfere with slavery in the states; presenting slavery as a positive good and comparing it favorably with free labor and other institutions outside slaveholding states; presenting slavery as consistent with American values such as liberty and property; establishing slavery as a perpetual institution rooted in the revered ancient republican traditions of the Greeks and Romans and the monotheistic tradition of the Jews and especially the Bible; contending that American slaveholders had made progress in improving the lot of slaves and recognizing their rights under the law; presenting blacks as naturally suited for slave labor especially in the Southern soil and climate; and most important, seeking to establish black inferiority (and white superiority) as the linchpin in the justification of the embarrassing institution. As we will see, these broad arguments functioned to establish five cardinal components of the defense of slavery.

Constituting Proslavery Subjects: Black Marginality and White Centrality

The constitution of subjects in a narrative is a key process in the production of the narrative's ideological program. As part of its effort to tell a positive Anglo-American story, the *Appeal* constitutes collective subjects hailed in specific ways and for specific functions in the narrative. The primary subjects are blacks and whites. Immigrants who had arrived on American shores "perceiving themselves to be 'Irish,' 'Sicilian,' 'Lithuanian' and so on," along with their offspring, were constituted as one people (Cornel West, *Keeping Faith* 20; Jacobson). They were whites, or Europeans, in contrast to blacks who should be seen as distinctly different on the basis of color. This rhetoric, relying on Anglo-America's accepted notions of "positively valued whiteness and negatively charged blackness," served to present Caucasians living in both the Old World and the New World as belonging to a common, superior group of human beings (20). In advancing this ideological and textual unity, Walsh's decision to identify the subjects in his treatise primarily as blacks and whites establishes a distinction between even those born and socialized in common households in America. This distinction also functions to unite disparate groups living on separate continents, such as Caucasians in Europe and in America. The textual nature of this unity is revealed by the fact that in Walsh's pamphlet the identity of the white subject remains flexible to serve the desired function of the rhetoric. Where there is the need to argue for American nationalism, for example, there are distinctions in Walsh's text between the British, Americans, and French, otherwise united as "white."

Walsh identifies blacks and whites as representing a "difference of race and colour." In presenting as natural and fixed the inferiority of one "race" and "color," and the superiority of the other, Walsh writes,

> Their color is a perpetual memento of their servile origin, and a double disgust is thus created. We will not, and ought not, [to] expose ourselves to lose our identity as it were; to be stained in our blood, and disparaged in our relation of being towards the stock of our forefathers in Europe. This may be called prejudice; but it is one which no reasoning can overcome, and which we cannot wish to see extinguished. (397)

Here Walsh seeks to establish the distinction between blacks and whites as a phenomenon fixed in nature and history. He also claims, for whites, a purity of blood, which serves as a marker for the presumed social cohesion of those with European forefathers. They are the ones not cursed with "a perpetual memento" of servility. The identities and characteristics of the black and white subject, however, were fixed neither in nature nor in the minds of all in America or in Europe. These identities were not only flexible but also highly contested in the United States and beyond.

Competing proslavery and antislavery narratives contested the true identities of these subjects and described them in strikingly different terms. This difference is evidence that the identities of these subjects undergo rhetorical revision relative to the purpose of the particular narrative and the functions to be fulfilled by its constituted subjects. The British antislavery narrative, for example, presents American slaveholders as "scourger[s] and murderer[s] of slaves." In Walsh's proslavery story, they are people of "urbanity and facility, dignity and liberality" (404). As part of Walsh's proslavery agenda, black and white subjects are positioned in contradistinction to each other, the white as standard and central and the black as peripheral and other.

The establishment of blacks as the natural, taken-for-granted inhabitants of the margins of American society is a key aspect of proslavery discourse. It establishes the structure of the society and especially the central role of whites by negation. As Robert Hariman notes, social marginality is the zone of undesirable identity: "The margin of the society contains what one is but should not be, and the disciplining of the individual to avoid the margin is the means by which one is socialized" (Hariman 44). Within slave societies, whites were disciplined to avoid the margins, the realm within which blacks were disciplined to remain. Walsh's writing represents a sustained effort to naturalize the textual marginality he constructs for blacks. The rhetorical success of this venture was an essential feature for the argued morality and cohesiveness of the proslavery textual community.

Within proslavery discourse, the institution of slavery is presented as being prior to and beyond the agency of those constituted as its primary subjects. This discourse mutes agency, limiting and, in some instances, excluding these subjects from action affecting the nature of the institution. Where such agency is granted, it is limited to the functioning of the constituted black and white subjects in the prescribed social roles of slaves and masters. Here the first tenet of oppression begins to emerge: the identification of the collective black subject as circumscribed to a servile role and subject to the surveillance of the collective white subject. Such functioning serves further to validate the relative places of blacks and whites in the society.

Walsh, who grew up in a household in Baltimore tended by slaves, opens the chapter "Of the Existence of Negro Slavery in the United States, and of the British Abolition of the Slave Trade" with the observation that "negro slavery [is] the side on which we appear most vulnerable, and against which the reviewers have directed their fiercest attacks" (Lochemes 8–12; Walsh 306). His first line of defense was to blame England for the introduction of black slavery into American society, then under British colonial rule. In Walsh's story, it was the English who were first responsible for bringing "Africa and the slave trade into view: If there is any nation upon which prudence and shame enjoined silence in regard to the negro bondage of these States, England is that nation" (306). In defending slaveholding among American colonists, Walsh argues that they "believed slavery to be strictly lawful in itself, both according to natural and revealed religion" (311). Insisting on the lack of a role for the federal government also became a patented proslavery line. Walsh writes, "as regards, then, the existence of slavery within the limits of the Union, the federal government has no responsibility" (387).

Beyond deflecting responsibility, this strategy served to establish slaveholding as the actions of citizens discharging their legal duties. Brutal and inhumane acts of authoritarianism on the part of slaveholders are then cast as the necessary routine for these slaveholders to maintain social order. Humane acts on the part of slaveholders are cast as rendering such subjects, in Walsh's words, "remarkable for their urbanity and facility" (404). This feature became more pronounced with the explosion of the biblical defense of slavery, which returned in explicit fashion in the three decades before the Civil War. With this emphasis incorporated in the proslavery story, the assigned roles of slaves and masters to be fulfilled by the collective black subject and the collective white one were further reinforced. In addition to the legal obligation, there was now an emphasis on the biblical one. Slaveholding thus fulfilled not only the legal responsibility of citizenship but the godly function of Christian duty. Even more nefarious, this story also constituted the obedient slave as Christian, while the slave who resisted remained a savage, a heathen.

With the explosion of the biblical defense after 1830, slavery as an act of God became a more explicit and common theme. For example, in 1841, "the most widely disseminated and influential" proslavery tract of the post-1830 era, Stringfellow's "Bible Argument," was published in the *Richmond Religious Herald* and then reprinted as a pamphlet (Genovese, *"Slavery Ordained"* 8). Its objective was to examine the Bible

> to make it appear that the institution of slavery has received, in the
> first place, 1st. The sanction of the Almighty in the Patriarchal age.

2d. That it was incorporated into the only National Constitution which ever emanated from God. 3d. That its legality was recognized, and its relative duties regulated, by Jesus Christ in his kingdom; and 4th. That it is full of mercy. (Elliott 462)

Stringfellow develops his argument that in the Patriarchal Age, "God *decreed slavery*—and show[ed] in that decree, tokens of good-will to the master," by beginning with Genesis 9: 25–27, which proslavery advocates embraced as the premise for launching all such arguments in favor of black enslavement (463). He argues that God decrees slavery by cursing Ham and condemning him and his posterity, Africans, to be in *abject bondage* to Shem, Japhet, and their Jewish, European, and American descendants (463). Walsh's first tenet of oppression is framed in biblical terms. Blacks as a race are under a divine curse condemning them to a role of servility, while whites are charged with the responsibility for their control. This biblical reference is depicted as an act of God that both denigrates blacks and affirms whites. By invoking God and the Bible, this proslavery narrative effectively removes from its constituted black and white subjects any sense of agency. Instead, both are constrained by the narrative to bow to the teachings of the Bible and the authority of God. In so doing, the proslavery narrative not only hailed blacks as social subjects without agency but also functioned to establish black otherness and exteriority.

Proslavery discourse consistently casts independent black action as beyond the pale of acceptable godly or civil practice and outside the bounds of the just laws of society. Blacks in the Haitian Revolution were anarchists and terrorists, and blacks in the United States agitating for their freedom, especially "free blacks," likewise were to come under more intense white scrutiny. As part of his defense of slavery and his advocacy of nationalism, Walsh contended that the success of any emancipation scheme would require colonization, since without it, America would have "a two-fold, or a motley nation; a perpetual, wasting strife, or a degeneracy from the European standard of excellence, both as to mind and body" (392). He also notes that the British, in fear after the Haitian Revolution, claimed "'the negroes [were] truly the Jacobins of the West India islands—they [were] the anarchists, the terrorists, the domestic enemy'" (238). Walsh is clear in his indictment of "free blacks" when he states

> the existence of a class of free people of colour in this country is highly injurious to the whites, the slaves, and the free people of colour themselves; consequently that all emancipation, to however small an extent, which permits the persons emancipated to remain in this country, is an evil. (Walsh 398)

For Caliban and Prospero to share a common space, they must maintain their "natural" states and only one can be master. Colonization is, therefore, the scheme of choice for Walsh, since the presence of blacks, especially as free people, represent an alarming danger of "cherishing in our bosom a distinct nation which can never become incorporated with us . . . a nation which must ever be hostile to us from feeling and interest" (398–404). True to the standard formula, South Carolina's Edwin Clifford Holland called blacks "*anarchists* and the *domestic enemy;* the *common enemy of civilized society,* and the barbarians who would, IF THEY COULD, become the DESTROYERS *of our race*" (Holland 86).

In the biblical version of the proslavery story, the black subject is aligned with the action of Ham. This action meets with condemnation and results in a curse from God. In contradistinction, the white subject is aligned with Abraham, the model whom God delights to honor. While whites are embraced in the center of the universe by God through the blessing and honoring of Abraham, blacks are cast as the troubling other who must be constrained by being made subject to white governance (Elliott 463–64).

The relative positions of the subjects in the proslavery fictive discourse follows naturally from qualities presented as their inherent characteristics: the black subject, the troubling other, governed by the surveillance of the civil white subject. It is not surprising, then, that the *Appeal* describes blacks and whites in predictably different terms.

Slaves as Property: Black Debasement and White Development

Walsh, like others before and after him, framed slaves as white property. Cast as property, the collective black subject in the proslavery narrative is always already predisposed to the control of the owner of such property, the collective white subject. This is the second tenet of oppression in Walsh's *Appeal.* Stringfellow, too, advances the notion of slaves as property but does so in biblical terms. He argues that this view of slaves was consistent with the Bible because, in honoring Abraham, God gave him slaves as property. To reinforce this point, Stringfellow points to Exodus 20: 17, "Thou shalt not covet thy neighbor's house, thou shalt not covet thy neighbor's wife, nor his man-servant, nor his maid-servant, nor his ox, nor his ass, nor anything that is thy neighbor's." He sees this as "a patriarchal catalogue of property, having God as its author, the wife among the rest" (Elliott 468). An offshoot of this patriarchal defense of slavery was the notion of the subjugation of women as a God-ordained feature of good social order. Frederick A. Ross, a pastor of the Presbyterian church of Huntsville, Alabama, put it bluntly: "God placed master and slave in the same relation as husband and wife" (F. Ross 106). As Eugene Genovese notes, "it would be difficult to find a proslavery pamphlet or book that did not explicitly root divine sanction for slavery in divine sanction for male domination of the household" (*"Slavery Or-dained"* 15). Once again, in Stringfellow's narrative, whites—more specific, white men—are not responsible for their acts of domination. They are simply compli-ant agents of the God of Israel. More interesting, this proslavery narrative justi-fies such designation, the consequential treatment, and the institution of slavery itself on the basis of the proffered nature of the property and its owner. "Slaves as property" was as much a staple of proslavery discourse as it was a point of contention in the antislavery story. The collective white proslavery subject here incorporated nonslaveholding whites as well.

As Edmund S. Morgan demonstrates, in the case of seventeenth- and eigh-teenth-century Virginia, Anglo-Americans enacted laws aimed specifically at the disenfranchisement of blacks by making whatever they might own subject to seizure and delivery to poor whites (316–37). Poor whites were also employed as overseers of black labor and, as such, were aligned with slaveholders as buffers against blacks (Zinn 172). These developments dissolved the common cause shared earlier by servants (poor whites) and slaves most notably demonstrated in Bacon's Rebellion of 1676 (Morgan 250–70, 327). More important, they al-lowed for the construction of black slavery as a positive facet of American repub-licanism. They fostered equality!

This "equality" was further reinforced by Dew's *Review of the Debate in the Virginia Legislature of 1831 and 1832,* described by William E. Dodd as "the ablest of all the works treating slavery from historical and social points of view" (149). Dew's essay was part of the proslavery effort that convinced white South-erners, including a majority of nonslaveholders, that slavery was in their best interest. The enslavement of blacks, therefore, became the argued basis for the development of what Walsh constantly refers to as a "common equality" among whites. In developing his notion of "common equality," Walsh artfully attends one of the key challenges faced by slavery proponents of the early nineteenth century. This challenge was to paint a picture of slavery that would "appeal" to America, Britain, and the rest of the world while advancing notions of Ameri-can patriotism and love for human rights.

Slavery Consistent with American Values

One way to meet this challenge was to acknowledge slavery as a necessary evil. Such acknowledgment, however, was not sufficient for Walsh. So, even before the beginning of radical abolitionism, the *Appeal* depicted slavery as a positive good. This depiction was a direct appeal to white American nationalist sentiment. Walsh ingeniously cast his white subject, the slaveholders, as patriotic and prag-matic emancipators. These white subjects embraced liberty as they defended their right to their "property" and looked for practical and safe ways to end slavery, an institution that they were not responsible for initiating. Walsh writes, "we do not deny, in America, that great abuses and evils accompany our negro slavery. The plurality of the leading men of the Southern states . . . would be glad to see it abolished, if this were feasible with benefit to the slaves" (421). However, he quickly returns to his defense of the institution: "[I]t produces here much less misery and vice, than it produces in the other countries which are cursed with it, it furnishes occasion rather for praise than blame" (421).

Here we see the third tenet of oppression, another key aspect of the rhetorical power of the proslavery narrative, its ingenious presentation of slavery as consistent with American values liberty and property. An important part of this tenet required the establishment of slavery as a perpetual institution rooted in the revered ancient traditions of republicanism and the monotheistic tradition of the Jews, especially the Bible. Walsh's notion of slaves as property functioning to establish "equality" may, within the contemporary context of property and equality, appear to be contradictory, even nonsensical. In the nineteenth-century Anglo-American mind, however, any such contradiction was repressed (Lucaites, "Irony of 'Equality'" 51). Furthermore, the conflation of liberty and property, through the early American concept that liberty was the right to own and protect one's property, made Walsh's argument persuasive to the white mind. For Walsh, freedom and slavery in America shared the same happy coexistence they shared in the ancient republics of Greece and Rome. He bemoaned the British critics who suggested that freedom was incompatible with slavery "in defiance of the lessons of history and of the true philosophy of the human mind" (404). Walsh quotes liberally from the speeches of Edmund Burke, especially in support of his arguments that in the presence of Southern slavery, "the spirit of liberty is high." He praises Southern slaveholders as those who are highly independent. In this regard, he embraces Burke's assessment that the "people of the Southern colonies are much more strongly, and with a higher and much more stubborn spirit, attached to liberty than those of the northward. Such were all the ancient commonwealths" (397, 402–3).

In firmly establishing proslavery nationalism, Walsh contends that

> all our experience in America, since the revolution, confirms the
> opinion of the orator; or, at least assures us, that the citizens of the
> slave-holding states understand quite as well, and cherish as fondly,
> the principles of republicanism, as those of the other members of
> the union. (403)

He goes further to articulate what developed into the myth of the beneficent Southern slaveholder when he writes, "the planter of our old Southern states has always been rather remarkable for his urbanity and facility as well as for the dignity and liberality of his sentiments" (404). Here noblesse oblige and Anglo-American paternalism are doing overtime narrative duty. According to the *Appeal,* the American Revolution, the discussions preceding it, and the institutions that developed as a consequence "excited a greater sensibility to human rights; a quicker sympathy with human sufferings; a more general liberality of sentiments; and a higher pride of character in the slave-holding part of our population" (408). In Walsh's scheme, slavery was a positive good. He argued that black slavery placed all whites on a level of equality engendering among white slavemasters a profound sense of justice. For Walsh, it is on the basis of their holding blacks as property that whites learn human rights and enhance their conceptions of liberty. Slavery, then, was not perfidious; it was progressive.

A part of the humanitarian effort of Walsh's white subject is the desire to put an end to slavery. As Walsh indicates, "the leading men of the Southern states . . . would be glad to see it abolished, if this were feasible with benefit to the slaves" (421). Proslavery narrative here frames its consideration of the future of slavery as dependent on that which is feasible and safe for the slaveholder and, by extension, American society and on that which is of benefit to the slave. Walsh opposed emancipation because, in his view, blacks could never be assimilated into American *white* culture and would therefore pose a constant threat of insurrection, much like he saw the poor doing in England (387–88). He claims that American slaves were in superior condition and better prepared for freedom than those in the West Indies but "they are still far from the point of being prepared to exist here out of the bonds of slavery, with advantage to themselves or safety to the whites" (388). Since, for Walsh, blacks could never attain the qualities necessary for sharing America equally with whites, in his discourse, he rejects any scheme of emancipation that is not tied to a plan of separation of blacks from whites. For him, such separation was necessary for the safety of whites and the advancement of American civil society.

Addressing the "moral and political training" necessary for freedom, Walsh argues that British policy before the Revolution precluded any such program as "incompatible with their very being as slaves" (388, 389–90). In his justification of keeping slaves in ignorance for the "safety [of slaveholders] and the ultimate happiness of his slaves," Walsh's apt summary of the dilemma of slavery and Anglo-American fears merits extensive quotation:

> You could not attempt to improve and fashion their minds upon a
> general system, so far as to make them capable of freedom in the mass
> and apart, without exposing yourself, even in the process, or in pro-
> portion as they began to understand, and value their rights, to feel
> the abjection of their position and employment, calculate their

strength, and be fit for intelligent concert—to formidable combinations among them, for extricating themselves from their groveling and severe labours at once, and for gaining, not merely an equality in the state, but an ascendancy in all respects. The difference of race and colour would render such aspirations in them, much more certain, prompt, and active, than in the case of a body of villeins of the same colour and blood with yourselves, whom you might undertake to prepare for self-government. . . . What consequences, then, might we not expect in the case of our slaves, from the sense of recent suffering and degradation, and from the feelings incident to the estrangement and insulation growing out of the indelible distinctions of nature?

I know of but one mode of correcting these feelings and preventing alienation, hostility, and civil war; of making the experiment of general instruction and emancipation with any degree of safety. (389–90)

Walsh goes on to deride Britain and the rest of Europe when he sarcastically presents the most frightful arguments ever to confront white supremacist, European thinking. He teases, "we must assure the blacks of a perfect equality in all points with ourselves; we must labour to incorporate them with us, so that we shall become of one flesh and blood, and of one political family!" (390). This is, of course, anathema. In the words of Jonathan Edwards, it would be for whites a mortifying thought (J. Edwards 36, 37). Walsh mocks, "[N]o sublime philanthropist of Europe has, however, as yet, in his reveries of the impiety of political distinctions founded upon the colour of the body, or in his lamentations over our injustice to the blacks, exacted from us openly this hopeful amalgamation" (390). Walsh argues that slavery and oppression at the hands of white supremacists had made blacks unfit for freedom and granting them such freedom would render them "idle, profligate, and miserable" (390). Caught between the Scylla of legalized slavery and the Charybdis of emancipation, then, Walsh's fellow whites, even those with the best intentions, were constrained to maintain the status quo, of course, for black benefit!

The black subject of the proslavery narrative, while in slavery, stood to benefit from white guidance and ultimately would be the recipient of white salvation. In freedom, however, this black subject became the primary focus of white surveillance. Such surveillance was to ensure that the "free" black subject did not establish common cause with those in bondage. "Free blacks," then, are a prime target for attack, as a nuisance, a problem for whites, for "you can manumit a slave, but you cannot make him a white man." The indelible mark of color would ensure that such persons would still feel connected to slaves while separated from whites. Without the restraint of white masters, they would live "in idleness, and probably in vice . . . and contribute greatly to the corruption of the slaves" (392). Such corruption, Walsh contends, would upset the otherwise harmonious relationship, "provoking the master to a severity which would not otherwise be thought necessary" (393). In the absence of any practical means of abolition, then, the humanitarian white subject is presented as laboring continuously to improve slavery for all involved.

Slavery as Progress with Black Beneficiaries

Contending that slavery has become more humane with laws respecting slaves as human, Walsh writes that "since the revolution, most of the Southern codes have been softened in regards to the slave police; and the murder of a negro is now capital except in one state" (406). He continues, "[B]efore our revolution, the negro slavery of this country was, as we have seen, acknowledged to be universally less severe than that of any other part of the world. It has undergone, since that event, a great and striking amelioration" (406). With the cessation of the importation of Africans, blacks and whites growing up together in the South, and whites exceeding blacks considerably, Walsh argues, there was less mistrust than before and "room for the kindlier dispositions of our nature to operate" (407).

The framing of slavery as a progressive and "positive program of social renovation" was in Tise's view, the "most important asset that proslavery writers derived from [American] conservative thought" (*Proslavery* 360). Here we see the fourth tenet of oppression: the presentation of slavery as a program of reform for blacks. This tenet was often called the Christianizing and civilizing of heathen savages. Walsh praises the slaveholding South for its religious instruction of slaves while Britain is indicted for having "attempted nothing towards the regeneration of the millions of heathens who have been held in bondage in her islands" (411–13). Stringfellow credits Southern slavery as having "brought within the range of gospel influence, millions of Ham's descendant's [*sic*] among ourselves, who but for this institution, would have sunk down to eternal ruin" (Elliott 491). This story of salvation for Anglo-American Christians was, to the Africans stolen from their homes, a story of death, since, as Sterling Stuckey notes, for the slave, "life in Africa at its worse was superior to domination by the white man" (*Ideological* 8).

In arguing that slavery in the South was both biblical and humane, Stringfellow, like other proslavery theologians, faced a difficult task. He had to present the Hebrews in a positive light, since theirs was the social order the South emulated, while arguing that the South in treating slaves as property had the right so to do but did better. To overcome this difficulty, proslavery arguments present the Hebrew laws as both humane and a reversal of Roman law, with its injustices to slaves (Genovese, *"Slavery Ordained"* 8–11).

In Stringfellow's view, the South did not treat slaves as property. Instead, enlightened, Christian, philanthropic Southern slaveholders went beyond the biblical requirement and protected slaves with favorable and humane laws and statutes (Priest vii). Blacks never had it so good! For this, the South expected to be lauded, and as we have seen, they were. Strategically, then, George D. Armstrong, pastor of the Presbyterian church in Norfolk, Virginia, argued that "the condition of slaves in Judea, in our Lord's Day, was no better than it is now in our Southern states, whilst in all other countries it was greatly worse" (11). Slavery was thus progressively more humane, and Southern slavery was its zenith. This line of argument became a staple in nineteenth-century proslavery discourse.

Stringfellow's effort to establish the biblical view of slaves as property and then to show that the South treated its slaves as more than property was a response to abolitionist criticism that slaves were treated as property, no better than livestock. Stringfellow contended that, in America, the service or labor of blacks, not their beings, was viewed as property. He thus argued that slaveholders respect slaves as persons and that slaves' rights "are as well defined and secured, by judicial decisions and statute laws, as the rights of husband and wife[,] parent and child." Not only theologians but also social theorists such as Henry Hughes of Mississippi and George Fitzhugh of Virginia picked up on the theme of slaves' rights. In his *Treatise on Sociology,* Hughes refers to Southern slavery as "warranteeism." For him, slaves had no rights, whereas Southern blacks had many. Fitzhugh, on the other hand, argued in *Sociology for the South* that all forms of labor were slavery, and Southern slavery should be emulated rather than abolished (Genovese, *"Slavery Ordained"* 12, 13). This argument was continued by Elliott in his introduction to the major proslavery treatise *Cotton Is King, and Proslavery Arguments.* Elliott strongly objects to the argument that slaves were chattel being used for the benefit of their masters. He argues instead that slavery was synonymous with servitude. He picks up Hughes's "warranteeism" and argues that slavery is "the duty and obligation of the slave to labor for the mutual benefit of both master and slave, under a warrant to the slave of protection, and a comfortable subsistence, under all circumstances" (vii). As Frank Tannenbaum shows, however, proslavery advocates were on tenuous grounds at best with these claims.

Tannenbaum observes, in his comparative study of slavery across the Americas, that fewer laws protecting slaves were in place in the United States than in other territories. Where such laws did exist in the United States, enforcement of them was another matter (73). Tannenbaum also notes that freedom was favored in Latin America, where slavery had become a contractual arrangement. Slaves were encouraged to purchase their own freedom, and there were multiple grounds for manumission. Within this context, social devices encouraged masters to free slaves and encouraged slaves to achieve their own freedom. Though the Latin-American practice of slavery was no less brutal, cruel, and inhumane, in that culture "the freeing of one's slaves was an honorific tradition [fulfilled] on numerous occasions" (58).

In the English-speaking Caribbean and the United States, however, slavery was seen as perpetual. Within this context was hostility toward freedom, as "the presumption was in favor of slavery." Here, manumission faced legal and various other obstacles, though it was the most likely route to freedom for the slaves (65). Supporting this view, Davis sees slavery in North America as "distinctive for its legislative and other efforts to construct barriers against manumission" (Davis, "Comparative Approach" 65). From the Southern perspective, these barriers were necessary to maintain the natural order of their society.

In defending the inhuman slave codes, Walsh argued that they were necessary for the protection of white Southerners, as blacks arriving from Africa were "barbarians" and arrived in a "savage state and unhappy mood" (405). To present slavery in a positive light, the narrative of oppression compares slavery with forms of labor elsewhere. As part of this effort, Walsh developed what Tise sees as one of the most significant features of the *Appeal,* a detailed comparison of American slave labor with European free labor (*Proslavery* 49). The idyllic life of American slaves is compared with the degeneracy of the British laboring class and British paupers whom Walsh terms a "wretched and noxious class of persons" who were "progressively increasing in number and deteriorating in character" (xlv, xlvi). As Walsh sees it, American slaves "are not worked near so hard, nor so many hours in a day, as the husbandman and day labourers in England" (307). Walsh continues, "[T]he physical condition of the American negro is, on the whole, not comparatively alone, but positively good, and he is exempt from those racking anxieties—the exacerbations of despair, to which the English manufacturer and peasant are subject in the pursuit of their pittance" (409–10). For Walsh, "the propensity to rebelliousness and violence among the lower orders" in Britain far out weighs "any evil in our situation, realized or threatened by our negro slavery" (xlv). Walsh contended, as did those who followed him, that "where slavery does not exist, there are *other institutions* generating an hundred fold more vice misery and debasement, than we have ever witnessed in the same compass in America" (405). This line of argument would be taken to its extreme in the work of Hughes and Fitzhugh. In their defense of Southern slavery, both men derogated the American poor and working classes, especially those in the North (Genovese, *"Slavery Ordained"* 12, 13; Hughes, *Treatise;* Fitzhugh, *Cannibals All; Sociology*). Walsh saw Britain as using a scheme of colonization to rid itself of its generous supply of degenerate and beggarly element, a scheme he endorsed as a necessary prerequisite for any consideration of the abolition of American slavery (xlvi).

Slavery as a Perpetual Institution and Blacks as Natural Slaves

In their effort to maintain slavery, Walsh and others presented the assailed institution as perpetual. The use of proslavery arguments to defend American nationalism and social harmony cannot be separated from the fact that those held in slavery were not just the poor or lower class. They had the distinctive features that, in the mind of white America, qualified them for bondage; they were "uncivil, unchristian, and above all unwhite" (Morgan 329). They were black! Important to the proslavery program of convincing blacks and whites of the perpetual nature of slavery was the characterization of blacks as naturally suited for slave labor, especially in the Southern soil and climate. This argument, of course, was another facet of white supremacist notions of black inferiority (and white superiority), the linchpin in the justification of the embarrassing institution. These writings provide authoritative precedent for the fifth and perhaps most widely used tenet of oppression: the labeling and defining of one group by another in such a way as to depict the other as inferior, less than human, and deserving of degradation.

Walsh's idea of black inferiority is clearly demonstrated in his observation of black skin as a perpetual memento of servility (397). These blacks were cast as naturally suited for labor in conditions that existed in the South, for according to Walsh, these conditions were "noxious to the white labourer, but favourable to the African constitution" (310). In his effort to present slavery as perpetual, with blacks as naturally filling the role of slaves, Stringfellow turns to Job 3: 11–19 to argue for *hereditary bondage* from which nothing but death brings relief. Here, Stringfellow is at one with the broader Christian proslavery discourse community, which identified blacks as the heathen and degraded descendants of Ham. This narrative theologically coded slavery as "God's punishment upon Ham's prurient disobedience [and] slaves were infidels or heathens" (Jordan, *White Man's Burden* 33).

"Black heathenism" in the Anglo-American mind was more than just a religious phenomenon. As Jordan notes of earlier English responses to "African heathenism," "they evidently did not regard it as separable from the Negro's other attributes" (*White Man's Burden* 12). These English and, I would argue, their Anglo-American progenitors treated black heathenism "not so much as a specifically religious defect but as one manifestation of a general refusal to measure up to proper standards, as a failure to be English or even civilized" (12). Of course, the eighteenth-century notion of proslavery Christianity was still applicable: "so long as the slave was a heathen or infidel, slavery was lawful" (Jenkins 18).

This phenomenon becomes understandable with the acknowledgment of the significance of race. American slaves were black, and race was the dominant subtext of Anglo-America's system of chattel slavery. In his study of race and slavery, Stanley Elkins points to what he calls "the most implacable race-consciousness yet observed in virtually any society." He goes on to observe that it developed as a simple syllogism but with precision. "All slaves are black; slaves are degraded and contemptible; therefore all blacks are degraded and contemptible and should be kept in slavery" (14). Therefore in many states, there was pressure to keep blacks in slavery "or to reduce [them] to slavery if free" (Tannenbaum 67).

Despite the plantation legend of the good master, the faithful slave, and the warm sentiments that Southerners expressed for both, the accepted notion that the slave was degraded and that blacks as a species were thus contemptible were ingrained in the institution of slavery. For Southern whites, blacks were inherently degraded and inferior, and "the very thought of such a creature existing outside of the pale of their so aptly devised system filled the most reasonable of Southerners with fear and loathing," a nightmare of Charybdis (Foner and Genovese 14).

Southern, white, proslavery advocates sought to construct their superiority and maintain their dominance in various ways. Several early nineteenth-century developments, however, such as the rise of abolitionism, the abolition of slavery in the North, the closing of the foreign slave trade, and British criticisms of American slavery challenged those notions. By the 1860s, these Southern whites were expressing both their fear and arrogance with respect to black emancipation. The stereotyping of blacks as passive and incapable had become so ingrained in the psyche of proslavery Anglo-Americans that even in the face of effective black agitation for freedom, these whites saw inevitable black failure. They argued that even with the aid of white Northern philanthropy, blacks were unable to emancipate themselves. After the arrest and execution of John Brown and his colleagues for their raid on Harper's Ferry, David Christy, a former agent of the American Colonization Society claimed "no successful organization, for their deliverance, can be effected in this country" (Elliott 24).

The black subject was so effectively constituted as docile in white, proslavery discourse that James Henry Hammond, discussing the possibility of slave revolt in the event of war, could argue that "our slaves . . . born among us, would never think of such a thing at any time, unless instigated to it by others" (Faust 178). Hammond's rhetoric is clearly grounded in the constitution of slaves and blacks in general as docile political subjects naturally suited for and contented with slavery. This subject was otherwise incompetent and inactive in any resistance or emancipatory efforts except under the influence of white instigators. Despite the relative success of this proslavery rhetoric, indeed, as part of the proslavery rhetoric, whites had to ignore black activism wherever possible, "for to do otherwise would have been to unhinge a cardinal tenet of the Southern faith—the concept of the contented slave and the impassive black" (Quarles, *Black Abolitionists* ix).

In the late eighteenth century, within the crucible of the young nation, its constitutional compromise a political necessity, American slavery was defended on the basis that it was a necessary evil. In the first half of the nineteenth century, however, with the economic success of Southern agriculture and, later, the spreading voice of abolitionism, the Southern defense of slavery evolved into a more affirmative advocacy, presenting slavery as a positive good, necessary for the continued advancement of Southern society. In the effort to present slavery as an exemplary institution, the proslavery narrative presented itself as a positive American story. The full measure of the story, however, requires that we consider the subjects it constituted as well as the program it advanced.

Proslavery rhetoric, as represented by the works of Robert Walsh, Thornton Stringfellow, James Henry Hammond, and others consistently sought to present Southern whites as a superior race in contrast to an imbecilic and inferior black race. In so doing, this rhetoric employed race to provide a semblance of social cohesion for a disparate Southern population. The designation of this group as a race of whites armed Southerners with a cohesive identity that proved capable not only of breaking barriers of time and distance but also of establishing criteria for identification and exclusion.

Placed as it was within this narrative in contradistinction to blacks, the next step in the process of establishing whites as the dominant and controlling group was the establishment of "white" as core and "black" as peripheral. With blacks occupying the zone of undesirable identity, the disciplining of whites away from this zone and the disciplining of blacks as part of it effectively socialized the community. This disciplining of the black and white collective subject established the proslavery textual community's morality and maintained its cohesiveness. These elements of "white superiority" and "black inferiority" were ably woven into Walsh's treatise and into the systematic proslavery rhetoric.

As represented by Robert Walsh's treatise, proslavery discourse constructs a narrative in which blacks are interpellated as puerile subjects with a propensity toward self-degradation. These blacks required salvific agency, which Providence assigned to whites. This narrative is what Cornel West calls the "Judeo Christian racist logic," a logic that "links racist practices to notions of disrespect for and rejection of authority, to ideas of unruly behavior and chaotic rebellion" (*Keeping Faith* 269). On the basis of these negative characteristics, presented as inherent to blacks and reinforced by positive characteristics ascribed to whites, proslavery rhetoric bolstered slavery as it buried blacks deeper in degradation.

Following Walsh, Thornton Stringfellow employs the Bible as the chief authorizing instrument in a treatise that masks Walsh's proslavery claims with Christian dogma. This biblical defense of slavery proved effective in maintaining the alienation and oppression of blacks. There were challenges to the context and relevance of Stringfellow's arguments for the biblical sanctions of slavery. Eugene Genovese is, however, more than likely correct when he claims that even though the opponents of slavery invoked the Bible in their cause, "they fail[ed] to refute the slaveholders' prime contention that the Bible did in fact sanction slavery" (*"Slavery Ordained"* 7.)

This program of black depravity is highlighted by the five tenets of oppression ensconced in the stories Anglo-America advanced to manage the ideological crisis of the early nineteenth century. This was a crisis precipitated by the challenge to American slavery by abolitionist calls from within the United States and Britain. First, the proslavery narrative constituted a collective black subject circumscribed to a servile role and subordinated to the superintendence of the collective white subject. Second, this collective black subject was identified as white property with the attendant conditions generally accepted as naturally occurring between people and their property, such as the right of the owner to dictate terms and conditions for the existence or demise of such property. The black subject was under the control of the proslavery white subject. Third, slavery in this uniquely American story was an institution that provided for the development of the important values of liberty and property, especially in the Southern mind. The enslaving of blacks was seen as leading to the flowering of equality among America's "citizens."

Fourth, in this benign story, slavery was presented as being in the best interest of blacks; it fosters their reform. The act of oppression is characterized as being in the best interest of the oppressed. Unfortunately, in contemporary times, new, subtle, and more sophisticated racism continues to be masked by the argument that in our progress we have eliminated oppression and racism, as we have advanced beyond the vulgar racism of earlier centuries. As David Theo Goldberg contends, this masking is an integral part of modernity's cloaking of racist cultures (6). Cornel West's terse rephrasing of Malcolm X sums up this issue well, "you cannot stick a knife nine inches into a man then pull it out six inches and call that progress" (C. West, Forum; Malcolm X 270).

The final and perhaps most devastating tenet of oppression pervading this proslavery narrative is the characterizing of slavery as a perpetual institution and blacks as natural slaves. This depiction reinforced the proslavery hierarchical system, premised as it was on the white supremacist conception of perpetual black inferiority. This reinforcement included the labeling and defining of blacks by whites as inferior, less than human, and deserving of degradation. Whether metaphorical or malevolent, even in the shadow of the Revolution, this white discourse effectively protected and preserved the Anglo-American value of white supremacy (Condit and Lucaites 131). Indeed, this was the rhetoric used "to justify the unjustifiable, to make palatable the unpalatable, to make reasonable the unreasonable, to make decent the indecent" (Bosmajian 9).

My genealogical inquiry has revealed the ways in which Walsh employs this logic in his effort to present blacks as naturally "other" and thus perpetuate their marginalization and exclusion from full participation in nineteenth-century American life. Notwithstanding the schizophrenia of their moral angst over the dastardly practice, the South and its defenders successfully prolonged slavery by effectively manipulating their rhetorical tools to bind the mind as their inhumane chains bound black bodies. As Charles M. Wiltse argues, "the right hand held the Bible and the left the bullwhip" (Wiltse vii).

3
Early Roots of Black Nationalism: The Birth of the Black Subject

Proclaim, that duty—imperious duty, exacts the convocation of ourselves in a body politic; that we do, for the promotion and welfare of our order, establish to ourselves a people.
—Robert Alexander Young, *The Ethiopian Manifesto*

We are a people notwithstanding many of you doubt it.
—David Walker, *David Walker's Appeal, in Four Articles*

The early years of the nineteenth century marked the end of America's first revolution and the beginning of its second. This era was, as Anne Norton saw it, "a time of tension and division, of contending cultures and conflicting loyalties" (8). It was a period of ferment among a significant, discontented group of inhabitants in the heady young nation. Blacks in America, both "slave" and "free," lived in the proud, independent nation with very little in the way of American life of which to be proud and with independence as nothing but a dim hope in a distant future. White supremacist perspectives that demeaned blackness (black intelligence, beauty, ability, and character) were pervasive American themes. Still it was within the ironic soil of the glorious Declaration of Independence and the Constitution, which promoted the idea of freedom on the one hand and American practices perpetrating black oppression on the other, that "an ideology of black nationalism would eventually take root" (Stuckey, *Ideological* 3). To secure for themselves and their communities an acknowledged place with dignified lives,

Northern "free blacks" set about creating their own revolution in an America still savoring the success of its revolutionary break with its former taskmaster.

This revolution involved the constitution of black rhetorical practices—ways of constructing and sustaining the previously private camaraderie and community—into a public voice that would "articulate in public pressing [black] survival need" (Condit and Lucaites 77). As Cornel West argues, these efforts included "selective appropriation, incorporation and rearticulation of European ideologies, cultures and institutions" (*Keeping Faith* 16). Before this black voice could effect any significant public persuasion, however, blacks had to be rhetorically constructed as human beings with the capacity to embrace the privileges of freedom, a task achieved gradually in the early discourse of black abolitionists. This achievement was revolutionary, for it marked the birth of the black public subject in a context of axiomatic general exclusion of black participation from the public sphere in American life.

The erasure and exclusion of blacks from the public sphere presented America's "colored" inhabitants with a difficult rhetorical challenge. Inscribed in both proslavery discourse and in racist America's symbols and practices as inhuman, nineteenth-century black rhetors had to construct their constitution as human and deserving of treatment as such, with limited access to the available means of public communication. Even so, conflicting sentiments about the identity of blacks existed in the South partly because of the contestation of proslavery perspectives. For example, Norton discusses sectional divergence between North and South during this period and points to John Calhoun's contention that the industrialized, urban North was structured around an aggregate of individuals; the South on the other hand, with its agricultural base, was based on communities, with the family as the first unit (153–54). Norton presents this familial model as implicitly affirming the "common humanity of slave and free" (154). Among the three sources Norton uses to establish this point is Eugene D. Genovese's reference to the 1827 declaration by the Supreme Court of Louisiana: "Slaves being men they are to be identified by their proper names." As Genovese notes, this declaration was "not without some ambiguity" (*Roll, Jordan* 444). Also, blacks present a different picture as they respond to their material experience and the daily reality of being construed as subhuman. Norton presents an insight important to the understanding of black life during the period when she observes that the "translation from a material to an ideal dimension of politics changes a quantifiable object into one which is susceptible not of proof but of interpretation . . . [and she is] interested not in what Northerners and Southerners were but in what they believed North and South to be" (8). Black activists had a different view from that of whites who supported slavery. In addition, blacks had to reclaim their voices from whites who, in the name of benevolence toward blacks, supplanted black voices with their own. In "speaking for blacks," these whites often re-presented the past, the material conditions, experiences, and desires of black people in ways that reflected white desire rather than black reality. Those who were denigrated to the point of invisibility, inaudibility, and inconsequentiality had to create a discourse through which they could be seen, heard, and respected as part of the American family (Condit and Lucaites 62; McDorman 10). Southern, white proslavery advocates sought to construct their superiority and maintain their dominance in several ways. Their physical chains contorted black bodies, and their white supremacist discourse squelched the black voice and projected black invisibility. A public black challenge would emerge.

During the period 1808–1830, with its "intense, interconnected social re-evaluation," slavery proponents were especially conflicted about the morality of the beleaguered institution (Tise, *Proslavery* 42). The abolition of slavery in the North, the closing of the foreign slave trade, British criticisms of American slavery, and the rise of abolitionism all precipitated a crisis in Anglo-America's white supremacist ideology. Since the time of the Revolution, the tension between revolutionary theory and human bondage always lurked in the shadows of American life. As part of their contestation of proslavery ideology, blacks rhetorically crafted an effective disarticulation of white supremacist discourse by articulating a discourse with a new black subject for the task of black liberation. Anglo-Americans, of course, sought through rearticulation to establish a unity in their ideology (Faust 4). Articulation and rearticulation are discursive processes used to fix meaning as part of rhetorical advocacy (D. Goldberg 8). Thus, in the crisis of the period, both the proslavery and antislavery communities sought a "system of narration" to contest for ideological dominance through their own interpellation (Donald and Hall 28).

In this contest, blacks faced the domineering apparatus of white respectability: press, pulpit, and state. Because their lives and the lives of their communities depended on their efforts, black advocates set about this task with energy, tenacity, and commitment. As Herbert Aptheker notes, the task of challenging those "who controlled the press and pulpit, who represented 'stability' and respectability and who dominated the political apparatus," required, among other things, "courage, rooted in an overwhelming conviction as to the baseness of slavery." Blacks were equal to the task, as they had experienced firsthand the indignities of slavery and had "seen their own children or their own parents sold like hogs" (*"One Continual Cry"* 21).

In the midst of this struggle was a remarkable voice, that of Maria W. Stewart. In "An Address Delivered at the African Masonic Hall" in Boston, February 1833, for example, Stewart defended the right of blacks to remain in the United States and claimed, "They would drive us to a strange land. But before I go, the bayonet shall pierce me through" (*The Liberator* [Boston], 27 Feb. 1833; Richardson, 64; qtd. in Quarles, *Black Abolitionists* 7). Maria Miller, who married James W. Stewart in Boston in 1826 and changed her name to Maria W. Stewart, is identified as the first native-born American woman to address a promiscuous (mixed) public audience and the first to deliver a public speech and leave extant texts. In doing this, Stewart confronted and broke both white and black rules of decorum that prohibited women from making of themselves "a public spectacle." She paid the price and was pressured out of the public speaking circuit and out of her hometown of Boston. Stewart moved on and became an educator in New York, then Baltimore. In 1861, she fled the war and moved to Washington, D.C., where she later became a matron of the Freedman's Hospital, following in the footsteps of Sojourner Truth (Quarles, *Black Abolitionists* 7; Bizzell and Herzberg 1031–35). With Stewart and other black women working alongside black men to elevate the race and oppose slavery, the collective public drive is reflected further in the flurry of significant events and activities that marked the early years of the new century, as blacks called for "a transformation of values and the creation of institutions designed to enable black people to move from oppression and dependency to liberation and freedom" (Stuckey, *Ideological Origins* 5). Two significant rhetorical creations at the center of this drive for liberation merit our attention: David Walker's *Appeal* and Robert Alexander Young's *The Ethiopian Manifesto*.

Walker's *Appeal* and Young's *Manifesto* served as early catalysts for nineteenth-century black activism and provided rhetorical *topoi* for the early discourse of black nationalism. Functioning ideologically, both documents helped create a collective black subject and insert it into the nineteenth-century epic struggle for emancipation. The *Appeal* and the *Manifesto* challenge the constituted subjects of the nineteenth-century proslavery narrative to fulfill their own ideological agenda: constitute a different collective white subject and, more important, a new collective black subject to contend for the basic humanity and rights of blacks as a people and as citizens. From the basis of their collective black subject, the *Appeal* and the *Manifesto* rhetorically reconstruct both the past and nineteenth-century black experience, including the use of the Bible and the Declaration of Independence, to claim a place and a future in America for its black inhabitants. In so doing, Young's and Walker's narratives help to posit the black citizen as a transhistorical subject. Both documents were catalysts for and products of a dynamic period of black activism against slavery in search of equality.

National Emergence of a Rhetoric of Black Ideology

One way to view America's story is through the eyes of radical black abolitionists. Through these lenses, we glimpse the tripartite manifestation of American racism with which antebellum blacks had to contend. First, there was slavery, which detained 90 percent of blacks in bondage; then there was the racialist structure of the society, a moral and social order that privileged whites and stereotyped blacks as either subservient or subversive; and finally, there was the resurgence of the long-held Anglo-American desire for African colonization.

In this African American story, then, the major success of the early nineteenth century was the 1808 abolition of the international slave trade (Stuckey, *Ideological Origins* 3–4). Even though proslavery forces translated this development into a boon for slavery by introducing an illicit international slave trade, expanding the internal slave trade, and increasing the price of individual slaves, this abolition was a landmark development in the struggle to topple slavery. After this success, African Americans sought to make other gains.

On 16 January 1816, at the Bethel Church in Philadelphia, blacks celebrated the establishment of the African Methodist Episcopal Church as the first independent black church in the United States. This beginning was a culmination of the work of many pioneering church leaders. They included Cyrus Bustill, former slave who became the first African American school teacher in Philadelphia and who was a member of the Free African Society, a mutual aid group founded in Philadelphia 12 April 1787 as the first African American society; John Murrant, perhaps the first ordained black minister to preach in the United States, invested by Calvinist Methodists in 1785; Prince Hall, leader of Boston's eighteenth-century black community and founder of its Masonic Order; George Liele, who, in 1799, founded the first Black Baptist churches in Georgia, before he left to do missionary work in Jamaica; Andrew Bryan, who succeeded Liele in Georgia; Absalom Jones, ordained in 1804 as the first African American priest of the Episcopal church; Richard Allen, ordained the first bishop of the African Methodist Episcopal Church in 1816 (Jones and Allen cofounded Bethel); and Peter Williams, priest of St. Phillip's African Church in New York. Since the eighteenth century, these blacks had been forced by racist practices within the white church to establish separate black churches, all of which remained under white supervision and often white ownership. The black church was pivotal in the struggle for freedom, and Bethel, a leading example, became a primary meeting place in Philadelphia for blacks to organize in opposition to the American Colonization Society (Aptheker, *Documentary* 1: 67–69).

Between 1817 and 1819, blacks from cities such as Philadelphia, Baltimore, Brooklyn, and Boston organized to reject the American Colonization Society with its scheme of transporting "free blacks" to Africa (Ripley et al., *Black Abolitionist* 3: 6). Not all blacks, however, opposed the American Colonization Society (Uya 24–40). Launched 28 December 1816, the Society enjoyed broad support of the white population, including clergy, gradualist antislavery societies, fourteen state legislatures, and many leading politicians including James Madison,

James Monroe, Henry Clay, and Daniel Webster (Ripley et al., *Black Abolitionist* 3: 5; Goodman 11–22). In contrast, "free blacks" in the North were incessant in their opposition to the scheme of African colonization because they saw it as presenting clear and imminent danger first to the "free black" community and ultimately to all blacks in the United States. In 1826, blacks founded the Massachusetts General Colored Association for black uplift and the toppling of slavery, a part of which was the effort to unite Northern blacks for continued organized opposition of the American Colonization Society (Ripley et al., *Black Abolitionist* 3: 7).

On 16 March 1827 in New York, Samuel Cornish and John B. Russwurm published the first black newspaper, *Freedom's Journal,* with its first editorial declaring, "We wish to plead our own cause. Too long have others spoken for us" ("To Our Patrons"; Aptheker, *"One Continual Cry"* 36; Stuckey, *Slave Culture* 117). On July 4 of that same year, slavery was abolished in the state. In 1829, Robert Alexander Young wrote and distributed the *Manifesto.* This publication was followed, later in the year, by David Walker's *Appeal.*[1] Walker's *Appeal* and his attack on colonization, as well as the advance of the American Colonization Society itself, initiated debates about black militancy and black responses to colonization. One significant result was the 1830 launching of the National Negro Convention, a central piece of black struggle. The initiative, in response to the 1829 expulsion of blacks from Ohio, came from Hezekiah Grice, "who Goodman identifies as 'Frederick Grice a Baltimore iceman and hog butcher'" (Aptheker, *Documentary* 1: 98–102; Goodman 32). Grice may also have been influenced by Walker's *Appeal,* which he had seen (Goodman 32). The Convention's objective was to "devise and pursue all legal means for the speedy elevation of ourselves and brethren to the scale and standing of men" (Aptheker, *Documentary* 1: 106). These events were all pivotal in the black struggle.

These developments marked the beginning of a period of organized national black response—primarily among Northern blacks—to slavery and black oppression in America, especially as it was expressed in the Old South (Condit and Lucaites 77). Created was a collective entity for the public representation of American blacks. The campaign nationalized and, as we will see, in some instances radicalized the efforts of black women and men to establish educational institutions and benevolent societies for economic and moral uplift even as they continued their protests against slavery and discrimination through their broadsides and petitions to white legislatures, an effort that dated back to at least the first recorded petitions of 1661 (Aptheker, *Documentary* 1: 1–2).

Alongside their efforts to find their own voice and oppose colonization, "free blacks" sought to convert white abolitionists from gradualism to a more radical abolitionist program, the immediate end of slavery. With the 1820s social climate favoring reform, blacks had some success with an increase in antivice activity against alcohol abuse, prostitution, and illiteracy, but the American Colonization Society, too, was thriving with the support of white abolitionists such as William Lloyd Garrison. A major development in the struggle for freedom and equality was the 1830 conversion of Garrison from support for colonization to opposition. William Watkins was a black abolitionist schoolteacher and a member of the African American community in Baltimore that strongly influenced Garrison's conversion (Goodman 42). Watkins's essays against colonization provided the themes and arguments for Garrison's 1832 publication *Thoughts on African Colonization,* which, along with Thomas Roderick Dew's *Review of the Debate in the Virginia Legislature of 1831 and 1832,* provided critiques important in the demise of the American Colonization Society (41; Tise, *Proslavery* 70). The election of Andrew Jackson in 1828 and his rejection of federal funding for the Society's program effectively killed it (Goodman 22). Another byproduct of the emerging radical abolitionist movement was the demise of organized, white public antislavery activity in the South. All this Northern activism, however, emerged against the backdrop of Southern slavery and black agitation opposing it.

Slavery insurrections, from the first recorded in New York in 1741 through Gabriel's plot of 1800, Denmark Vesey's June 1822 North Carolina revolt, and Nat Turner's rebellion of 21 August 1831, created havoc among slaveholders and their families. Most notable was Turner's rebellion in Southampton, just seventy miles from Richmond, which killed fifty-nine whites, sent shock waves through the South, and "frighten[ed] the Virginia legislature into a heated debate over emancipation in 1831–2" (Faust 21; J. F. Clarke 20).[2] Turner's uprising was just the latest in a long line of rebellions by Virginia slaves, and it evoked memories of Gabriel's frightful, if unsuccessful, plot of 1800 (Higginson, "Gabriel's Defeat"). Gabriel's conspiracy, which had been exposed by Ben Woodfolk or Woolfolk, a "faithful slave," faltered on the proposed day of action (Higginson, *Black Rebellion* 188–90; Wish, "American Slave" 311). To the alarm of slaveholders, this plot had a reported eleven hundred slaves committed to revolt and fifty thousand more expected to join after the anticipated initial success (*Black Rebellion* 192, 194; "American Slave" 311). Gabriel's conspiracy became the benchmark of slave revolts, and subsequent insurrections such as Vesey's recalled the specter of Gabriel ("Gabriel's Defeat"). *Black Rebellion* provides an account of Gabriel's, Vesey's, and Turner's uprisings.

While Turner's rebellion was the most shocking, rumored or actual slave-led rebellions from Maryland to Florida kept the South on edge (Wish, "American Slave" 313–20; Olmstead 513–14; Aptheker, *To Be Free* ch. 1). In the aftermath of the Southampton uprising, the fearful expression of "a citizen" chronicled in the many accounts of the rebellion served as an insignia of white trepidation:

"many a mother as she presses her infant darling to her bosom, will shudder at the recollection of Nat Turner and his ferocious band of miscreants" (Drewry 118). Harvey Wish contends that the many slave insurrections and slave plots of this period were concealed from the public "as effectively as if an official censorship had been established" ("Slave Disloyalty" 435). In a somewhat similar vein, James F. Clarke argues that there was always an inward sense of danger in every slave community. "There were two terrors constantly before the minds of Southern families—the dread of fire and that of poison." Clarke writes that from his experience in the South, the slaves sometimes actually used these two weapons, but that no newspaper ever mentioned them for fear they might become examples to others (*Anti-Slavery Days* 19–20). The war of 1812 had also served to heighten hushed fears about slave revolts (Wish, "American Slave" 312). During Vesey's scare, a Charleston woman wrote, "[L]ast evening twenty-five hundred of our citizens were under arms to guard our property and our lives. But it is a subject not to be mentioned; and unless you hear it elsewhere, say nothing about it" (Higginson, *Black Rebellion* 195; Wish, "American Slave" 299). Such trepidation was both widespread and long-lasting.

The mutinies by blacks aboard the slave ships *Amistad* and *Creole* in 1839 and 1841 made this predicament even more acute (Coffin 33; Catterall 565; Wish, "American Slave" 306).[3] Eaton discusses a number of developments prior to and including Walker's *Appeal* that exacerbated the fears and anxieties of whites in the South (325–26). In addition, David Brion Davis notes that the Toussaint L'Overture–led revolution that resulted in the declaration of Haiti's independence from France and the execution of Haiti's white residents raised France to "a pitch of fanaticism" and "tautened the nerves of slaveholders from Maryland to Brazil" (*Problem of Slavery in the Age of Revolution* 557). This assortment of events, along with the 1829 publication of both Young's *Manifesto* and, of course, Walker's *Appeal,* served as disquieting demonstrations of orchestrated, Northern interference in Southern life, and slave revolts were often followed by hysteria and copycat, draconian slave patrol laws ("American Slave" 312). Later, John Brown's 1859 raid on Harper's Ferry further heightened these fears.

The South saw a Northern conspiracy in the timing of Turner's rebellion, a mere eight months after the January 1831 inaugural issue of Garrison and Isaac Knapp's *Liberator* and their demand for immediate and unconditional emancipation (Oates, *Fires* 129). This suspicion was heightened by the perception of a similar militant tone in Walker's *Appeal* and the *Liberator's* editorials. In addition, the *Liberator's* publication of parts of Walker's *Appeal* led some in the South to conclude that Walker and Garrison were in collaboration with one another (Wiltse xi). Enraged by these developments, Virginia governor John Floyd and a chorus of Southern newspapers accused Garrison of inciting slave insurrection and thus propelled him to national prominence. In these specific accusations, the South was far from the truth, as Garrison and his small following of white abolitionists constantly expressed their opposition to violence. Their hope was to appeal to the conscience of slaveholders for the abolition of Southern slavery. Prior to these Southern claims, Garrison and his supporters had little recognition or support in the North for their crusade (Oates, *Fires* 129–45). These are curious accusations from the South, since as Tise observes, proslavery ideology persisted in the North in the arguments of antiabolitionists and social conservatives who sought to defend against any form of social radicalism. Tise contends that this proslavery ideology became the basis of Southern sectional arguments only after it became the ideology of the Confederacy during the Civil War (*Proslavery* 14).

Still the radical black publications, slave revolts, and other antislavery appeals added substance and credibility to the constant rumors and threats of slave revolts. As proslavery white Southerners saw it, the efforts of white and black Northern extremists to create discontent among Southern blacks endangered the very survival of the white South. Norton argues that the first two decades of the nineteenth century saw marked progress in the "efforts to integrate the black slave into the legal and social environment of the South." She then quotes Thomas Hart Benton, "who had been instrumental in securing to Missouri slaves the right to jury trial," as describing Northern antislavery agitation as "fatal outside interference" (153). In 1830, North Carolina governor John Owen expressed his belief to the legislature that "free blacks" were being used as agents in a "systematic attempt by reckless persons in the North to sow sedition among the slaves, 'distorting the peaceful doctrines of the Bible'" (Eaton 331). Wish challenges this charge and argues instead that while white men played an important role in many uprisings, abolitionist propaganda played a relatively minor role, despite Southern charges. He claims that the genealogy of revolt extends much farther back than the organized efforts of antislavery advocates (Wish, "American Slave" 310).[4]

Responding to these developments among blacks between 1830 and 1850, proslavery Anglo-America redoubled its efforts to strengthen the slave system. This response becomes understandable with the awareness that, as Norton observes, "The American Revolution had served as the model for political development in the South" (122). Against this backdrop, "[i]nformal collective violence was recognized in Southern political culture as encompassing revolution. . . . Expressions, violent or pacific, of a collective consciousness within subcultures thus merited particular attention" (122–23). This governing group of whites would have been more than a little disturbed by any expression of a black collective consciousness that challenged the rights to white governance. It is within this context that the Anglo-American effort to consolidate the slave system, including the push for the reintroduction of the slave trade during this period, is seen by Sterling Stuckey as an indication that the long held desire among blacks for autonomy "may well have crystallized into an ideology" some years before 1850 and certainly before the Civil War (*Ideological Origins* 2). Such dating contrasts with Victor Ullman's *Martin R. Delany,* which contends that Delany was America's first black nationalist. Stuckey reaffirms his position with the claim that Walker "is the father of black nationalist theory." He writes that "black nationalist theory in its truest, richest form is found, of course, in slave folklore" (*Slave Culture* 120–21, 211, 378n. 80). Kwame Anthony Appiah sees Alexander Crummell, Edward W. Blyden, Africanus Horton, and Martin Delany as individuals who could "lay claim to the title of 'Father of Pan-Africanism'" (*In My Father's House* 21). W. E. B. Du Bois attributes the increase of American involvement in the international slave trade to economic factors such as a steady increase in the price of slaves (*Suppression* 162–67). Still, this chapter embraces Stuckey's perspective on the earlier rhetorical development of nineteenth-century black nationalist ideology.

Walker's *Appeal* and Young's *Manifesto*

Early-nineteenth-century black nationalist ideology was fashioned out of the shared black experience of white oppression and, especially among activist blacks, the sense of a common need to extricate themselves from that experience. "Group—traits and preferences" shared by people of African descent were often demeaned by the larger society (Stuckey, *Ideological Origins* 6). These characteristics included skin color, arts, crafts, and general ways of being-in-the-world. Fashioned out of such a milieu, this early, black ideology advanced unity among people of African descent. Integral to this ideology was the conviction that this group was distinct, especially from their white oppressors, and as such should work together to control their own life processes and ultimately their own destiny (1–7).

Robert Alexander Young's *Manifesto* and David Walker's *Appeal* played a crucial role in the development of this ideology. David Walker was born in Wilmington, North Carolina, in 1785. His father died in slavery. His mother's status as a "free black" meant that Walker was born a free black (Wiltse vii; Stuckey, *Slave Culture* 98–99). Goodman identifies his mother as white (28). Walker acquired an education and traveled extensively throughout the country, especially in the South where he observed firsthand the cruelty of slavery. He moved to Boston because, in the words of Charles Wiltse, he could no longer endure the geographical "proximity" of degraded black life in the South (Wiltse viii). Here he sold new and used clothing. By the mid to late 1820s, Walker was identified as a leader in the black community. He led the Massachusetts General Colored Association, which was in the forefront of the effort to organize Northern blacks in opposition to the American Colonization Society. Walker became the Boston agent for and a contributor to *Freedom's Journal* and held meetings at his house to promote the paper (Wiltse viii; Goodman 28; Ripley et al., *Black Abolitionist* 3: 7). Walker also served in the Methodist church. As part of an active black community in Boston, he became the incessant black militant voice against slavery during the 1820s. He desired, however, to reach beyond those who gathered to hear his combative rhetoric in Boston or who read his polemics in *Freedom's Journal.* This desire to extend his militant message of immediate emancipation beyond Northern abolitionism to the South and particularly to the enslaved population of blacks there led Walker to pen, publish, and circulate his *Appeal* (Wiltse viii–ix; Goodman 30; Ripley et al., *Black Abolitionist* 3: 7; Stuckey, *Slave Culture* 98–137).

In contrast to the available details of Walker's life, there is not much information about Robert Alexander Young. Aptheker identifies Young simply as a free black New Yorker (*Documentary History* 1: 90). The relative high status of these men mirrored somewhat the reception of the *Appeal* and the *Manifesto.* The *Appeal* was a major influence in abolitionist circles, while there is not much specific response recorded about the *Manifesto.*

With their call for self-affirmation and self-development among blacks, in contrast to many earlier black appeals that petitioned whites, these two pamphlets advanced "the need for black people to rely primarily on themselves in vital areas of life—economic, political, religious, and intellectual—in order to effect their liberation" (Stuckey, *Ideological Origins* 1). These pamphlets are therefore arguably the foundation documents of black nationalism. Stuckey identifies the *Appeal* and the *Manifesto* as the foundation of black nationalist ideology and notes the absence of similar recognition of these two documents by other scholars. He points to three causes for this lack of recognition. First, scholars focus on Walker's call for blacks to rise up against their oppressors. Second, they tend "to interpret the past in the burning light of current concerns," one such concern being the rise of integrationist sentiment to "fever pitch" after World War II. The emphasis on integrationism resulted in a lack of focus on the nationalist concepts that permeate the *Appeal.* Third, there is a misconception that no major black nationalist ideologists existed before Martin Delany. Stuckey contends that this misconception was promoted by, perhaps more than anyone else, Harold Cruse in *The Crisis of the Negro Intellectual* (Stuckey, *Ideological Origins* 7, 9, 10). Cruse not only influenced the belief that Martin Delany was the first major ideologist of black nationalism but also implied a conflation of "back to Africa" and black nationalism. While this implication is generally a useful marker, it is also a misleading one. It suggests, incorrectly, as in the case of Walker, that a back-to-Africa call is a necessary condition of black nationalism (Cruse 5). This conflation might explain why as prominent a black nationalist scholar as Tony Martin refers to neither Robert Alexander Young nor David Walker in his list of nineteenth-century Pan-Africanists whose work influenced Garvey's. This omission might be due to the lack of reference in either the *Manifesto* or the *Appeal* to any notions of "back to Africa" or "Africa for Africans" (Martin, *Race First* 111). The production of these texts should be seen as no surprise, as Northern blacks had already established "something of an intellectual tradition" by the beginning of the nineteenth century, as Dorothy Porter writes in *Early Negro Writing* (Stuckey, *Ideological Origins* 6).

The *Appeal* is a seventy-eight-page document divided into four articles, each addressing one of Walker's four primary reasons for nineteenth-century black degradation: Article I. "Our Wretchedness in Consequence of Slavery"; Article II. "Our Wretchedness in Consequence of Ignorance"; Article III. "Our Wretchedness in Consequence of the Preachers of the Religion of Jesus Christ"; and Article IV. "Our Wretchedness in Consequence of the Colonizing Plan." The *Manifesto* is a brief, seven-page document that addresses black oppression and prophesies the liberation of Africans. Framed and influenced by religious themes, these two treatises are "enveloped in a special aura of mystery" and in places present confusing and "half articulate beliefs" (7). Both, however, exhibit "something of the primordial, the suggestion of profound beginnings, intimations of the coming sovereignty of certain ideas" and, as such, offer critical insights into the early development of this black ideology and the new black subject that provides its animus (7).

A study of these two documents as constitutive rhetorics illuminates the early development and materialization of the black nationalist ideology and its inherent new black identity. These rhetorics catalyzed black thought and action to challenge Anglo-American conceptions of black identity while authenticating their own construction of blackness. The *Appeal* and the *Manifesto* reconstituted the black subject as an agent for social change within the discourse. In contrast, they constituted the white subject as the primary agent for black debasement and against black progress. The specific responses of white America were a noteworthy marker of the challenge to Anglo-America's perspectives on black America.

As part of the general agitation for freedom among blacks in the early nineteenth century, these two documents were marked by their truculent militancy, which would elicit a vigorous response, particularly from the proslavery community. Walker's *Appeal* immediately threw white America into a quandary. Discussed across the nation, it was seen as exaggerating the sufferings and strength of blacks while underrating whites and expressing "sentiments totally subversive of all subordination in (our) slaves" (Eaton 323; Aptheker, *Documentary History* 1: 90; Litwack, *North* 253; Schor 52). Slave states were flabbergasted, and general panic resulted in a flurry of secret government meetings, witch hunts, and petitions. Georgia, Virginia, Mississippi, Louisiana, and North Carolina, for example, replenished their armories and passed new, draconian laws, including the death penalty, to further repress blacks and to punish them, as well as any sympathizers, who might have, use, promote, transport, publish, or in any way identify with Walker's *Appeal*. The mayor of Boston, Harrison G. Otis, is said to have condemned the pamphlet, declaring that his sentiment was the same as that of the mass of New England residents, including "even the free colored population of Boston" (Eaton 327, 329). White antislavery crusaders such as Benjamin Lundy and his protégé Garrison were ambivalent in their responses. Lundy described the *Appeal* as a "bold, daring, inflammatory publication." Garrison refers to Walker's pamphlet as breathing "the most impassioned and determined spirit." He later wrote it was "warranted by the creed of an independent people." Yet both Lundy and Garrison issued public condemnations in Lundy's newspaper, *The Genius of Universal Emancipation* (Aptheker, *"One Continual Cry"* 2). Of course, Garrison and Knapp published parts of the *Appeal* in the *Liberator*.

Proslavery newspapers were "thrown into paroxysms of rage." The *Richmond Enquirer*, for example, called Walker's *Appeal* a "monstrous slander" (1). Northern newspapers sympathetic to "endangered whites" joined in the condemnation. Boston's *Columbian Centinel* of 16 January 1830 indicted the *Appeal* as bereft of even a single redeeming quality and "pronounce[d] it one of the most wicked and inflammatory productions that ever issued from the press" (Eaton 328). Clement Eaton, in "A Dangerous Pamphlet," provides a good overview of the frightened response of white America, especially the Old South. This essay is especially valuable because of its sympathetic treatment of whites and the plight they faced. Walker refers to the strident response of the South to his *Appeal* in a footnote to the third edition (Aptheker, *"One Continual Cry"* 1–6, 45–53, 139–40; Aptheker, *Documentary History* 1: 90; Litwack, *North* 233–35; Schor 52). These pamphlets also had a significant impact on the black community.

The *Appeal* was a major focus point within the developing antislavery movement, and its impact is reflected in the work of the prominent black nationalist Henry Highland Garnet (Aptheker, *"One Continual Cry"* 2). The appearance of Walker's controversial document revealed, as Aptheker notes, "a jelling" of antislavery efforts, even as the work itself served as a stimulant to the forces that came to constitute the national abolitionist effort (1). Moreover, "it projects most of the arguments and questions that were used and raised in the next generation of decisive struggle against slavery" (58). As Wiltse notes, the *Appeal* marked the transition in the antislavery fight from gentle Quaker persuasion to the more militant activism championed by blacks and picked up by white abolitionists from Garrison to John Brown (Wiltse xi).

The power of Walker's *Appeal* is attributed to it being "the first sustained written assault upon slavery and racism to come from a black man in the United States" (Aptheker, *"One Continual Cry"* 54). While there is no denying the significance of this observation, the *Appeal*'s enduring relevance is due more to its affirmative stance than to what it negates. In 1848, Garnet assessed the *Appeal* in the following terms: "The work is valuable because it is among the first, and was actually the boldest and most direct appeal in behalf of freedom which was made in the early part of the Antislavery Reformation" (qtd. in "One Continual Cry" 3). Though the rebuffing of slavery and racism remains an integral part of the development of any positive black perspective, the major reason for the *Appeal*'s continued relevance is that it was one of the first documents to advance a coherent vision of black self-definition and self-determination. This vision was Walker's literary construction, and it functioned rhetorically to effect black social identity through the process of interpellation and identification. It was a key starting point in the discourse with which blacks would identify spontaneously, intuitively, and unconsciously (Burke, *Language* 310; Charland, "Constitutive Rhetoric" 133).

The *Manifesto* is also significant in this regard; it is, however, neither as sustained in its attack on slavery nor as comprehensive in its vision of black life. Aptheker is on target when he argues that the *Appeal* is of historic moment in that it powerfully "brings forward repeated strands in Negro (black) life and history" (*"One Continual Cry"* 59). Walker skillfully weaves together black life and history as he seeks to awaken in "afflicted, degraded and slumbering brethren, a spirit of inquiry and investigation respecting our miseries and wretchedness" (2). Young's objective is even more lofty; it is to raise the black race "from its degenerate sphere, and instill into it the rights of men . . . which shall lead us to the collecting together of a people" (Young 4). To achieve their objectives, both men position their reconstituted black subjects to reveal and confront both the degrading physical conditions of black life and the racist material discourse that demeans blackness. That blacks in America are "a people" or should become "a people" is the basis for their claims.

Walker confronts the proslavery discourse of white supremacy and black inferiority. He questions and undermines its passive black subject by reconstituting blacks as a people able to work for a return to their rightful place defined by their illustrious past. The claim of blacks being or becoming a people, is, in Michael McGee's terms, "a myth." It is a rhetorical construction used by advocates such as Young and Walker to advance their cause. Inherent in this claim is the notion of what John Louis Lucaites calls "an historically transcendent and homogenous, collective consciousness that constitutes, controls, and gives voice to the social and political fabric of the life of the community" (Lucaites, "Visualizing 'The People'" 270). Nineteenth-century blacks in America, individuals living disparate lives while struggling to survive blatant Anglo-American racism and prejudice in the North and brutal slavery in the South, are depicted as "a people," a unified "public." To perform the esemplastic, impractical feat of unifying blacks spread across the country, these advocates turned to rhetorical myth. Given the reality of the experiences and social conditions of the individuals in question, the rhetorical functioning of such a myth is manifest. The constitutive role of this rhetoric becomes even more evident when we consider that the very humanity of blacks was questioned by contending proslavery proclamations and practices.

Both Young and Walker confronted the challenge to black humanity posed by Anglo-America's racist depiction of the black subject. Walker avers, "all the inhabitants of the earth, (except however, the sons of Africa) are called *men,* and of course are, and ought to be free. But we, (coloured people) and our children are *brutes*" (7). Consequently, blacks, as Walker saw them, "had to prove to the Americans and the world, that we are MEN and not *brutes*" (30). He argues that whites continue to insult blacks by claiming that they are not part of the "HUMAN FAMILY" and that they descended "originally from the tribe of *Monkeys* or *Orang-Outangs*" (26, 10). Walker sees whites as continuously lying about blacks, "holding them up to the world as a tribe of talking apes void of intellect!!!!! incapable of learning" (61). To overcome the subhuman depiction of blacks, Walker advanced a black subjectivity that sought to establish the common humanity that blacks shared with whites. Thus, for example, he notes that "we are *men* notwithstanding our *improminent noses* and *woolly heads,* and believe that we feel for our fathers, mothers, wives, and children as well as the whites do for theirs" (4–5). Included is a rejection of Thomas Jefferson's thesis of black inferiority (10–15). Young affirms, "I am in myself a man . . . I claim . . . my birthright of man, so do I equally claim to the untutored black" (5).

This notion of the humanity of blacks, though unchallenged in contemporary times, was a necessary rhetorical undertaking for those consistently referred to as less than human (Condit and Lucaites 62; McDorman 10). Cornel West is somewhat accurate in his indictment of approaches like this as proceeding in an *assimilationist manner* (and in so doing elided differences between blacks and whites) and as resting upon a *homogenizing impulse* (which assumed that all black people were alike) (*Keeping Faith* 17). While Walker does not focus on them, he does acknowledge differences among blacks. He argues that Egyptians were Africans and claims that these Egyptians were "coloured people, such as we are— some of them yellow and others dark—a mixture of Ethiopians and the natives of Egypt—about the same as you see the coloured people of the United States at the present day" (8). In his indictment, West does not adequately account for the exigencies of the rhetorical situation and the constraints faced by people like Young and Walker. For these and other blacks in the nineteenth-century, establishing the humanity blacks shared in common with whites was the only rhetorical ground available for the advancement of their cause. The necessary depiction of blacks as complex human beings with a significantly different culture and history from those of whites and with significant differences among themselves, had to be the rhetorical assignment of a later generation; a legacy of the success of people like Young and Walker. From the basis of the humanity of blacks and the contention that blacks are a people, Walker and Young challenged the existing structure of American society, with whites on top and blacks, whether "free" or not, relegated to a condition of abjection and servitude (4, 7).

These two black advocates operated under the presumption that "the people" are a natural social phenomenon existing outside rhetoric and to which rhetoric makes reference. Analysis of the *Appeal* and the *Manifesto* as constitutive rhetorics, however, allows us to identify "the people" as a rhetorical construct that advances the black nationalist system of narration. The immediate cause here was the legitimation of claims that blacks should be granted the basic rights of "a people": the rights to freedom, equality with whites, and even self-determination.

That blacks were a people, then, was crucial, for only people can claim these rights. Young's and Walker's efforts signal a significant rhetorical contestation over the identity of blacks and the way they would be characterized in both proslavery and antislavery discourse. In its most benign rendition, proslavery narrative identified blacks as "slaves" and "free blacks." More representative was Robert Walsh's identification of Africans as barbarians in a savage state (Walsh 405).[5] This rhetorical contestation is crucial, since identity legitimates action. Accepting blacks as slaves effectively enhanced the claims that they were property. It also muted claims that they were human and should be treated as such. It would be unlikely, if not impractical, for slaves to have claimed the rights of a people. As shown in Young and Walker, however, those who were "free" could and did make such claims. The designator "free blacks" and the distinction made between such people and "slaves" in proslavery discourse precluded free blacks from making claims on behalf of blacks held in slavery. For white slaveholders like James Henry Hammond and Walsh, those held in slavery were "our slaves," while "free blacks" were nothing but a nuisance—lazy, idle, and a threat to American civil society—the lingering apparition of the Charybdis of chaos; the unfettered black body. In discussing the conditions in England at the beginning of the seventeenth century, when many English migrated to America, Charles, Mary, and William Beard note that "free" men and women were among the most despised. These people were serfs and laborers working in crop production who had been evicted by landlords in a widespread conversion of "a vast acreage into sheep pastures." The landlords had discovered that they could make more money by raising sheep. The evicted became "free" but ended up on the streets as beggars and paupers. Free blacks had a similar plight, and Anglo-American sentiment against them was comparable to that against the free men and women in England (31). Carshee C. L. McIntyre sees the white treatment of free blacks as "criminalizing a race." Walker's cynical depiction of this white perspective is worth repeating. He writes,

> They tell us that we the (blacks) are an inferior race of beings—incapable of self government. We would be injurious to society and ourselves, if tyrants should loose their unjust hold on us; That if we were free we would not work, but would live on plunder or theft; that we are the meanest and laziest set of beings in the world!!!!! That they are obliged to keep us in bondage to do us good; That we are satisfied to rest in slavery to them and their children; That we ought not to be set free in America, but ought to be sent away to Africa; That if we are set free in America, we would involve the country in a civil war. (66)

The division among blacks implicit in this white perspective and key to the rhetorical program of the proslavery system of narration saw its physical manifestation in the American Colonization Society's scheme to forcibly remove free blacks from the United States and "return" them to Africa. Legislation passed in 1785 by the General Assembly of North Carolina required free blacks to wear on their left shoulders "a badge of cloth . . . and to have thereon wrought in capital letters the word free" (Franklin, *Free Negro* 60; Stuckey, *Slave Culture* 98). This legislated, cloth tattoo symbolized the Anglo-American effort to distinguish between free and enslaved blacks. In contrast, by designating blacks as a people apart from their status as slave and free, Young and Walker sought both to extend the inclusive boundaries for the term "black people" and to give a new identity to the individuals who made up "the people." In so doing, the *Appeal* and the *Manifesto* began the formulation of a nationalist ideology. They also began the task of reconstructing white identity as well.

As in the case of blacks, the rhetorical contestation over the identity of whites represented a clash of political agenda. As the proslavery writer Robert Walsh knew, the claims to be made in the name of a people of remarkable "urbanity and facility," as he saw slaveholders, were different from those to be made for people characterized as "scourger[s] and murderer[s] of slaves" (308, 404). Though these claims begin as fictive characterizations in rhetoric, they develop historical and material consequences when social agents embrace and live them. Indeed, it is this historical and material consequence that prolonged black degradation, white elevation, and black alienation, and it is this to which Du Bois refers in his challenge of the "fine aristocratic life of cultured leisure" said to typify the Southern slaveholder (*Black Reconstruction* 715). Walker tries to disrupt the process of whites embodying (and blacks accepting) the proslavery rhetorical characterization of them as godly, humane benefactors of blacks while they held blacks in slavery. He presents a new construction of the white subject as he accounts for the conditions visited upon "his people" by American slavery.

Walker argues that unlike blacks, whites "have always been an unjust, jealous, unmerciful, avaricious and blood-thirsty set of beings, always seeking after power and authority" (16). For him, slaveholders were not people of "urbanity and facility"; they were tyrants (21). Those whites who wanted slaves were butchers and murderers (20). Like Walker, Young depicts slaveholders as base: for him, they are monsters and the "most deadly foe" of blacks (7, 8, 9). He declares them marked for impending judgment as part of God's plan for the liberation for blacks. He trumpets, "thou vain bloated upstart worldling of a slaveholder . . . on thee we pronounce our judgement" (7). Both documents are specific in their excoriation of white greed, as they condemn what they saw as hypocrisy in the land of liberty, an argument taken up to great effect by Frederick Douglass several years later. For Walker and Young, slavery was a manifestation of white greed, not of black degradation. This view led to a challenge of the black alienation advanced in the proslavery narrative and practices and sanctioned by black compliance.

Black Nationalism and Black Alienation

Walker not only rejects the proslavery effort to proscribe black life and naturalize black alienation but also rages against black acquiescence to their own alienation. He protests, "[M]y objections are to our *glorying* and being *happy* in such employments" (29). He bemoans, "[I]n sorrow I must say it, that my colour all over the world, have a mean, servile spirit. They yield in a moment to the whites, let them be right or wrong—the reason they are able to keep their feet on our throats" (62). For Walker, "full glory and happiness" would come only with the *"entire emancipation"* of all enslaved brethren (29). Unwilling to abdicate to whites total power over blacks, Walker presents black suffering as a divinely sanctioned, momentary punishment. He contends that the abject state of blacks in America is a temporary one, allowed by God because of black disobedience. In his view, neither the structure of the society nor a servile attitude on the part of blacks was natural, as whites tried to argue. For Young, the long, unjust oppression of blacks was about to end, for God had heard the cries of "the black, a most persecuted people" (7). Walker exhorted blacks not to submit to these conditions or to the desire of whites to rule and dominate their lives. He wrote,

> A groveling servile and abject submission to the lash of tyrants, we
> see plainly, my brethren, are not the natural elements of the blacks,
> as the Americans try to make us believe; but these are misfortunes
> which God has suffered our fathers to be enveloped in for many ages,
> no doubt in consequence of their disobedience to their Maker. (21)

The *Manifesto* is more futuristic in its vision of a militant black subject. Young
foresees the day when slaves withdraw all attachments from slaveholders and
"[d]eath shall he prefer to a continuance of his race" (8). Walker denounces the
view of whites who "are of the firm conviction that Heaven has designed us [blacks]
and our children to be slaves and *beasts of burden to them and their children*" (2).
More than a hundred and fifty years later, in his "Power at Last Forever" speech
at the Los Angeles Forum in 1985, Louis Farrakhan followed this tradition: "I
am saying from the Honourable Elijah Mohammed, that our slavery and our
suffering in America was not because God hated us. I am saying this was to fulfill a divine purpose. That is bigger than our suffering" (Goldzwig 214).

The *Appeal* refers to blacks as "coloured," "people of colour," and "Africans." The designator "Negro" is used only cynically. The *Manifesto* uses "black,"
"black Africa," "African slave," "degraded sons of Africa," or "Ethiopian." Walker
explains the origins of the term "Negro" in illuminating a parenthetical note on
"Negro Slavery" contained in a speech by slaveholder John Randolph of Roan-
oke, Virginia:

> "Niger," is a word derived from the Latin, which was used by the
> old Romans, to designate inanimate beings, which were black; such
> as soot, pot, wood, house, &c. Also, animals which they considered
> inferior to the human species, as a black horse, cow, hog, bird, dog,
> &c. The white Americans have applied this term to Africans, by way
> of reproach for our colour, to aggravate and heighten our miseries,
> because they have their feet on our throats.[6] (55)

In this explanation, Walker insightfully points to his recognition of the material
power of discourse to constitute rhetorical beings. This is a power to cause reproach as well as to repress or advance the cause of its constituted subject. The
Appeal is uncompromising in its rejection of the racist narrative of those "who
cease not to declare that our condition is not *hard,* and we are comparatively
satisfied to rest in wretchedness and misery, under them and their children" (8).
Both pamphlets set the tone for subsequent and sustained, strident rejection of
white supremacist narratives as part of the continuing struggle over the construction of the identity of blacks. This protracted struggle remains at the heart of
the black effort to obtain real equality in the United States and elsewhere.

Walker specifically points to his awareness of the significance of naming in the crucible of identity formation. (As shown in the next chapter, naming remained central to the struggle over slavery and freedom.) Not only do Anglo-Americans oppress Africans by having "their feet on our throats," but in their discourse they seek to name them and construct an identity for them that will cause reproach, as well as "aggravate and heighten our miseries" (55). It is not just the use of the term "African" in these pamphlets that is of interest here. As Stuckey points out, in the North, "almost all blacks," as late as the second decade of the nineteenth century, "referred to themselves as 'Africans' or 'free Africans'" (Stuckey, *Ideological Origins* 6). Naming here is crucial because it is an important indicator of the ingenious efforts in these works to create a black subject who has a strong African connection, as well as a place in the United States. It was an effort to constitute a subject affirming the geopolitical claims that blacks make in their individual lives. At the beginning of the twenty-first century, naming continues to be a point of contestation in the development of a black nationalist ideology and of black identity.[7] Walker's choices represent a movement in the concept of the ideological black subject, a movement from displaced African to "colored" or "blacks" with African ancestry but with a new home in America. This effort to combine the Africanness of blacks with a new but noble American identity was innovative in that there is little evidence to suggest that being identified as "American" was either attainable for blacks or desirable in the minds of either blacks or whites (Stuckey, *Ideological Origins* 7).

Whereas this American identity might be a sticking point for those who argue for a "back to Africa" call as the litmus test of black nationalism, it is in no way a repudiation of Africa, as is attested to by the prominence of references to both Africa and Ethiopia in both documents.[8] It is, however, one of the early strategic, pragmatic shifts in the fight for freedom. Many similar maneuvers would follow, as black tacticians made day-to-day choices and employed rhetorical strategies in what they saw as their fight for the very survival of the race. Genovese discusses the issue of naming within the context of Southern slavery and observes of white slaveholders and black slaves, "Both understood that names identified class and status and marked an appropriate degree of respect" (*Roll, Jordan, Roll* 445). It is perhaps in this issue of naming that the *Appeal* and the *Manifesto* most strongly reflect and promote an "African consciousness" (Stuckey, *Ideological Origins* 4). Walker further shows his awareness of the significance and power of the discourse of suppression in his reference to the use of the *African Repository* and *Colonial Journal* by Anglo-Americans to abuse blacks and present them "as the greatest nuisance to society, and throat-cutters in the world" (69). Norton speaks of nineteenth-century conceptions of violence: "Popular culture associates it with animals and primitive men" (121). In claiming black humanity and advocating black liberation, then, these two documents, especially the *Appeal,* crafted their call for black agitation artfully so as to avoid reinforcing Anglo-American notions of blacks as subhuman or primitive.

Through their call for a militant black response to oppression, both Walker and Young deftly expressed black rage. This rage served to further establish the humanity of blacks and to mobilize them to political action. Young takes aim at those holding his fellow blacks in bondage and issues his malediction: "Accursed and damned be he in mind soul and body" (6). Walker contends, "[F]or if we are men, we cannot but hate you, while you are treating us like dogs" (70). In the face of such expressions of black rage, critics have argued that nationalism is self-defeating in that it expresses hatred of whites, a pathological reverse racism. As noted above, the focus of scholars on the call for blacks to rise against their oppressors is perhaps why the *Appeal* has been overlooked as a primary black nationalist statement of the nineteenth century. What this denunciation ignores is that this rage was expressed by Walker as an opprobrium against slavery, racism, and their perpetrators, not as a general indictment of whites (Aptheker, *"One Continual Cry"* 58). Walker points to his awareness that not all whites were to be blamed in his expression of heartfelt thanks to "those among them who have volunteered their services for our redemption" (71). He notes further, "[W]e ask for nothing but the rights of man, viz. For them to set us free, and treat us like men, and there will be no danger" (70). Indeed, Walker presents an expansive, if somewhat naive, view of the future when he argues that if whites treat blacks "like men, . . . we will be your friends" (70). He continues, "[T]he past will be sunk into oblivion, and we yet under God, will become a united and happy people" (70).

The rage expressed in the *Appeal* and the *Manifesto* are but early expressions of the rage expressed by James Baldwin in *Notes of a Native Son,* theorized by Franz Fanon in *Black Skin, White Masks* and bell hooks in *Killing Rage,* popularized in the national media by Malcolm X, and maintained by younger nationalist voices such as Sistah Souljah and a slew of rap artists. It is an emotional, political response to a materially debilitating experience. As hooks argues, black rage is no more a pathology than any understandable expression of anger against injustice. It is instead an important part of black political expression in the face of bruising and oppressive white supremacist practices. hooks rejects the thesis of black rage as a pathological sign of powerlessness, advanced in Price M. Cobbs and William H. Grier's *Black Rage.* She also argues that, in *Race Matters,* Cornel West undermines the power of Malcolm X's rage by linking it with his love rather than his passion for justice. For hooks, black rage or "killing rage" is not a sickness and it is not something to be tempered: it is "a potentially healthy, potentially healing response to oppression and exploitation" (12, 13). It is not "in-rage," pathos born in blackness, but "out-rage," pathos triggered by and aimed at an external phenomenon. This expression is cathartic, even as it portends the physical violence that, for Walker, must remain a serious political option for oppressed blacks. Young is more content to await divine judgment, which for him is imminent. More important, this rage serves as a tool for the mobilization of sometimes apathetic, alienated blacks to political action. As hooks contends, rage is "a necessary aspect of resistance struggle" (16). Walker's call for action reveals his perspective that action is a sign of humanity. He pleads, "When shall we arise from this death-like apathy?—And be men!! You will notice, if ever we become men, (I mean *respectable* men, such as other people are,) we must exert ourselves to the full" (61). Rage and the threat of violence are central to the kind of retaliatory action blacks are called upon to take, for in Walker's view, whites "are afraid that we, being men, and not brutes, will retaliate, and woe will be to them" (61). Stuckey argues that Walker's "appeal to morality in the struggle against slavery was in no way diluted by his urging of his people to commit violence, if necessary" (*Slave Culture* 158). In treating violence, the *Appeal* resorts to its strong religious theme, shared with the *Manifesto*.

Religion and Black Liberation

For both Young and Walker, blacks must be ready to fight, if it is the will of God. Even so, both documents point to the coming of a Messiah who would bring about black redemption (Aptheker, *"One Continual Cry"* 58–59). For Young, God has appointed a leader to the Ethiopian people who will call "together the black people as a nation in themselves," in the right season, and prove to be their "liberator from the infernal state of bondage" (9). Young and Walker express optimism in the salvation expected with the coming of this Messiah. Walker contends that with this Messiah's coming, white "prejudices will be obliged to fall like lightning to the ground in succeeding generations" (56). Walker's optimism is grounded in a realism that acknowledges that the fall of prejudice will be neither complete nor without resistance. The *Appeal* notes that prejudice will fall; "not, however, with the will and consent of all the whites, for some will be obliged to hold on to the old adage, viz: that blacks are not men" (56). In keeping with this early, central place, religion has continued to have a prominent, if controversial, place in the rhetoric of black nationalism.

Here, religion provides for an interesting inculcation of race pride and martyrdom into black nationalist rhetoric. Walker advanced black race pride, which has become one of the primary elements of black nationalism. This pride was embraced by Martin Delany, popularized by Marcus Garvey's "race first" philosophy, and used effectively in the "black is beautiful" principle of the black power movement of the 1960s.[9] For Walker, blacks are proud of their color, and whites who think that blacks wish to be white "are dreadfully deceived" (12). In both Walker and Young, we see blackness linked to God through oppression and the coming of the Messiah. This Messiah will bring judgment upon white oppressors while bringing salvation to the black oppressed. The martyr spirit is linked to Christ, the biblical Messiah, who was killed for doing God's will and speaking the truth against the oppressive powers of his day. Similarly, black nationalist advocates like Young and Walker faced the threat of death as martyrdom, which would serve only to confirm the righteousness of their cause as it would link them eternally to the Messiah. Walker invokes the incorrigible persona of the martyr when he states, "I write without the fear of man, I am writing for my God, and I fear none but himself; they may put me to death if they choose" (54). Young similarly declaims, "Your oppressors we fear not, nor do we his power" (10). Such a rhetoric presages the efforts of Malcolm X and has become the militant stance of contemporary black nationalists like Louis Farrakhan and Sistah Souljah who constantly declare that, in the name of God and righteousness, they set their own agenda, advance their own cause, and do not fear or seek to appease whites (Souljah). Claiming the prophetic voice of the biblical and Mohammedan prophet in his "Power at Last Forever" speech, Farrakhan intoned, "Whether I lose my life is not important, because my life should be constructed on the basis of truth, and I should live for the truth, and when I cannot live any longer, I should die on behalf of the truth" (qtd. in Goldzwig 213).

Another initiative by Walker that confronts whites with the challenge to treat blacks as humans, and one that has become an important rallying cry of black nationalism, is open and official acknowledgment of the infliction upon blacks of slavery's injustices. As Walker puts it, Americans have "to make a national acknowledgment to us for the wrongs they have inflicted on us" (70). This charge has been expanded to calls for apologies and, more significant, to a call for reparations. The continuation of this theme is evident, for example, in the editor's preface to Walter Rodney's notable black power thesis, *Groundings with My Brothers.* The preface opens with an acknowledgment of the appalling conditions of black people in comparison with those of whites, declaring, "We, black people, having realized this, demand from the white people economic and political power" (5).

Within its strong religious theme, the *Appeal* advances an early version of the notion that the abolition of slavery and injustice is a necessity not only for the liberation of blacks but also for the redemption of America, for slavery is a *"curse to nations"* (3). This idea is clear from Walker's pronouncement that slavery "gnaws into the very vitals and sinews of those who are now in possession of it" and if whites continue to maintain slavery it "will ruin them and the country forever, unless something is immediately done" (68). Blacks have embraced and subsequently advanced this notion to include the claim of being what August O. Wilson calls, "the custodians of hope for America" (lecture). Here Walker not only challenges the morality of slavery but also undergirds his claim for black humanity by his positioning of blacks on the moral high ground of American life. Only human beings, and conscientious ones at that, can occupy such a role. Despite the strong appeal of religion, however, black alienation was deeply ingrained in American life. In fact, along with America's premier documents, religion played a significant role in black alienation.

An important aspect of the structuring of American society is its popular interpretation of the nation's primary documents. If Anglo-Americans took black degradation for granted, they saw white leadership and ownership of America as natural, God-ordained, and reinforced by the Bible, the Declaration of Independence, and the Constitution. Besides rhetorically contesting the identity of the black and white constituted subjects, then, the *Manifesto* and the *Appeal* also advance a view in which they engage proslavery discourse in a struggle over the interpretation of America's revered, constitutive documents.

With slavery and the Constitution as the two primary markers, the depiction of blacks as less than human was present in the distinguished documents and in the daily practices of nineteenth-century Anglo-Americans. To agitate for a place in the human and American family, however, blacks like Walker challenged these depictions as inherently proslavery. In turn, they contended that the true spirit of America was to be discovered in an understanding of the nation's founding documents as embracing all people and not just whites. In so doing, Walker was among the earliest of African Americans to advance systematic efforts to inscribe blacks in the spirit, if not the letter, of America's founding documents—an early if muted version of radical constitutionalism, which I discuss in chapter 5. Walker argued that slavery contradicted the explicit "sentiments of the Declaration of Independence," among which was the notion that alternative depictions that excluded blacks were not only aberrant but contrary to the clear spirit of the document. Anglo-American interpretations that supported slavery and oppression, then, were to be seen as expressions of white injustice. In addition to challenging Anglo-America's use of the primary document shaping America in independence, Walker also contested proslavery readings of the nation's founding guidebook, the Bible.

Young and Walker each charge that Anglo-America's oppressive practices were both unnatural and in direct contradiction to the natural law of God. Thus they challenged preachers who continued to tell "(coloured people) that slaves must be obedient to their masters—must do their duty to their masters or be whipped" (39). The *Appeal* identifies as "pretended preachers" those who present a proslavery view of Christianity (36, 48).

In contrast to the proslavery view, Walker looked to the injunctions of Jesus to his disciples in Matthew 28: 18–20 (The Great Commission) and argues, "They do not show the slightest degree of distinction. 'Go ye therefore,' (says my divine Master) 'and teach all nations,' (or in other words, all people). . . . We are a people, notwithstanding many of you doubt it" (41–42). These challenges unequivocally point to the role that rhetoric plays in the crucial contestations over the meanings and uses of documents salient to the formation and functioning of America. In their rhetorical reconstruction of these pivotal American building blocks, Walker and Young recreated and repositioned the collective black subject for the pivotal claim of America as home.

The racist perspective of blacks as less than human or at least of a lesser status than whites was undergirded by the natural rights philosophy of John Locke, which led to the prominent "belief of Anglo-American republicans that the self was 'founded in property'" (Norton 125). As Norton observes, "Locke also argued that property might include those things that men [sic] produced through labor" (125). This idea is of enormous import in the struggle over the creation of a black subject within the context of slavery, as a key element in this debate concerned the ownership of the products of black labor. This linking of property with the products of labor allows for Walker's appeal for black rights and black ownership of America on the basis of black labor, a tapping into the logic of the proslavery conservative republican scheme of social reality as the basis for civic and human rights.

Walker lays claim to at least an equal share of America for blacks as for whites. Arguing that blacks have enriched America with their blood and tears, he claims, "this country is as much ours as it is the whites" (55). Later he goes further and contends that "America is more our country, than it is the whites—we have enriched it with our *blood and tears*" (65). Walker's black nationalist argument, then, is that it was blacks, and not whites, whose blood and sweat built the United States. Set within the nineteenth-century Anglo-American republican scheme of natural rights, this argument merited white attention. Within the scheme of natural rights, "the definition of property and the determination of the boundaries of the self is made with reference to the body and the corporeal requirements and capacities of man" (Norton 125). While Young claims as a gift from God "universal freedom to every son and daughter descending from the black," Walker goes further in claiming that not only are freedom and human dignity the natural rights of blacks, as they are of all human beings, but also that blacks had added to these natural rights their sweat and blood.[10] The claim on America, then, was not only a moral claim grounded in the notion of black sacrifice—black blood—but also one based on the indisputable social reality of black labor. Walker's claim on America for blacks is different from the approach that has come to be readily associated with black nationalism's disavowal of America and the embrace of Africa as the homeland for blacks.

The denouncing of America as a racist country that had no place for blacks was one of the common themes of nineteenth-century black discourse. Though unintended, this discourse had the deleterious effect of excluding blacks from a place and a future in the United States. Even more detrimental, such rhetoric resulted in a tacit endorsement of such racist schemes as that of the American Colonization Society, which under the guise of doing what was best for blacks "given their inability to thrive alongside freedmen," served to protect slavery with its plan of forced repatriation of free blacks. Walker exposed this scheme by arguing that the Society wishes to separate free blacks from slaves because they fear that in the intercourse between the two, the free will pass "*bad habits* [on to the slaves] by teaching them that they are MEN, as well as other people, and certainly *ought and must be free*" (47). This view reflected accurately the proslavery sentiment of the American Colonization Society and its leading proponents, among them Henry Clay and Robert Walsh. Walsh argues that without white governance, blacks live "in idleness, and probably in vice . . . and contribute greatly to the corruption of the slaves" (392). Walker's *Appeal* denounced American racism and condemned all proslavery activities, including the American Colonization Society, without relinquishing black ownership of the United States. Walker posited this because, for him, "this land which we have watered with our *tears* and *our blood,* is now our *mother country*" (58).

The claim to a place in America was also used by blacks in Baltimore who identified the United States as their "only *true and appropriate home*" and those in Brooklyn who contended, "[W]e are *country-men and fellow citizens* . . . we are not strangers" (Ripley et al., *Black Abolitionist* 3: 6). By the 1830s, this approach became even more poignant and urgent after blacks had watched Cherokee forcibly moved by the federal government from the South to the West to facilitate the advance of the "Cotton Kingdom" (3: 7; Goodman 85). As Aptheker observes, Walker spoke "not as one who hates the country, but rather as one who hates the institutions which disfigure it" (Ripley et al., *Black Abolitionist* 3: 7). Walker thus prefigured other distinguished black nationalists such as Garnet and Alexander Crummell who would praise America's institutional embrace of liberty and equality, even as they subjected her racist institutions and practices to scathing assaults (Stuckey, *Ideological Origins* 21). With this approach, Walker was able to condemn oppressive practices within the United States at the same time as he rhetorically created a place in America for blacks. Bishop Richard Allen, founder of the African Methodist Episcopal Church, takes a similar approach, according to the excerpt of his letter reproduced in the *Appeal*. The letter was originally published in *Freedom's Journal* 2 Nov. 1927 (Aptheker, *"One Continual Cry"* 122–

23). While Walker is not the first to use this strategy of critically embracing America as home, his usage here is early evidence of a claim to a collective consciousness among blacks in their efforts to chart their own course and determine their own destiny.

Having rejected white supremacist perspectives of the existing conditions of blacks and of their role and place in America—in short, black alienation—Walker moved next to challenge Anglo-America's story about the black past. He advanced an early version of black nationalism's asserted, authentic recording of black history. In this undertaking, black nationalism engages in the rhetorical construction of what Warren I. Susman calls a "usable past" (7–26); that is, Walker employs the "twin rhetorics of *nostalgia* and *critical memory*." The rhetoric of nostalgia provided for a "purposive construction of the past," while the rhetoric of critical memory facilitated Walker's judgments and evaluations as it allowed for the establishment of select relationships with the past to deal with the reality of black homelessness (H. Baker 7). Here black nationalism engages in the age-old contest for the right to define the past and thereby control the future (Susman 3). In its system of narration, black nationalist rhetoric uses history not only for identification and inspiration among oppressed blacks but for legitimacy as well (J. H. Clarke vii). An important aspect of the retelling of the story of the black past is the retelling of the story of the white past.

Walker also examined the history of whites in Greece and saw "them there, cutting each other's throats—trying to subject each other to wretchedness and misery" (17). He traced their past in Rome, where "the spirit of deceit still raged higher," and finally, he observed whites in "Gaul, Spain, Britain, and all over Europe, together with what were scattered about in Asia and Africa, and [saw] them acting more like devils than accountable men" (17). For Walker, those whites who were Christians were "more cruel, avaricious and unmerciful" than those who were heathens (17). He then tracked the experience of Europeans in the New World to tell the story of "no trifling portion" of migrants to the Americas and the Caribbean. These were people who were "for stealing, murdering, &c. compelled to flee from Europe, to save their necks or banishment" (49). He invited his readers to "read the history particularly of Hayti, and see how they [blacks] were butchered by the whites" (20). This aspect of the American story is often downplayed, if not suppressed, by pro-European, conventional historiography.[11] In contrast, black nationalism highlights the story as a way of challenging white supremacy and white privileged ownership of the places these Europeans have come to dominate. Garvey, for example, would later write

> Out of cold old Europe these white men came,
> From caves, dens and holes, without any fame,

> Eating their dead's flesh and sucking their blood,
> Relics of the Mediterranean flood;
> Literature, science and art they stole,
> After Africa had measured each pole,
> Asia taught them what great learning was,
> Now they frown upon what the Coolie does.
>
> (qtd. in T. Martin, *Race First* 81, 82)

Where such white experience is revealed, black life can also be seen in a different light. Where proslavery and black nationalist systems of narration are compared, the rhetorical contest over the events of the past and their uses comes to the fore.[12]

In the construction and reconstruction of the past, both black nationalist rhetoric and white supremacist rhetoric use history—or perhaps more accurate, make history—to serve their own contemporary political ends. Aptheker's view that the oppressed use history for identification and inspiration while the oppressors use it for justification, rationalization, and legitimacy highlights the significant role of rhetoric in efforts to construct a usable past (J. H. Clarke vii). This perspective is incomplete, however, in that it frames the contestants of the rhetorical struggle so as to limit the scope of the rhetorical *topoi* available to each side. In different terms, Aptheker limits the rhetorical use of "history." If, however, we accept history as an ensemble of material from the past, then we can see the possibility of the rhetorical structuring of the past so that the subject positions "oppressor" and "oppressed" are inverted if not effaced. Without denying the constraints placed on rhetorical constructions or re-constructions of the past by the "facts" of history, we can affirm that the making of history is open to wider contestation than Aptheker acknowledges. For example, blacks did not always address their plight by reacting to the "history" of their "oppressors." Instead, as represented in the *Manifesto* and the *Appeal,* blacks did more than just respond to and reinterpret Anglo-American accounts of the past. To meet the demands of their situation, they created their own past. Indeed, from one perspective, aspects of Anglo-American popular and professional history are largely a telling of a white supremacist story often with limited accounting of the "facts." The United States is only now beginning to tell a different story from the one framed by the ideology that guided the Confederacy (Davis, "Free at Last"). James W. Loewen, in the provocative title of his popular text, identifies such history as "lies my teacher told me."

In the contest over the past, we see in the effort of the black nationalists clear evidence of what Wilson Jeremiah Moses, borrowing from St. Clair Drake, calls the "historiography of decline based on the idea that the African race has fallen from its past greatness"; early African vindicationism or, for Orlando Patterson, "contributionism" (Moses, *Afrotopia* 16). In Walker's view, for example, the ancestors of blacks in America were above servility and had achieved notable feats. Among these achievements was the defeat of whites in battle. He writes,

> When we take a retrospective view of the arts and sciences—the wise legislators—the Pyramids, and other magnificent buildings—the turning of the channel of the river Nile by the sons of Africa or of Ham, among whom learning originated, and was carried thence into Greece, where it was improved upon and refined . . . I say when I view retrospectively, the renown of that once mighty people, the children of our progenitor I am indeed cheered. Yea further, when I view that mighty son of Africa, Hannibal, one of the greatest generals of antiquity, who defeated and cut off so many thousands of the white Romans. (9–20)

These events become a part of black nationalism's combative narrative used to constitute a militant, collective black subject. In this effort, Walker provided a rhetorical revision of blacks and their past. In contrast, Thornton Stringfellow credits whites and slavery with having brought blacks to civilization and biblical salvation in his proslavery treatise "Bible Argument" (491). As Basil Davidson argues, European, white supremacist historiography "declared that Africa had no history prior to direct contact with Europe," and thus "spawned an abrasive progeny of myths" (Davidson xxii). This torturous, white supremacist historiography is strikingly summarized, aptly by an anonymous author, in an 1856 excerpt quoted by Cedric Robinson from what he calls the "fledgling but prestigious" American literary magazine *Putnam's Monthly*:

> The most minute and the most careful researches have, as yet, failed to discover a history or any knowledge of ancient times among the negro races. They have invented no writing; not even the crude picture-writing of the lowest tribes. They have no gods and no heroes; no epic poem and no legend, not even simple traditions. There never existed among them an organized government; there never ruled an hierarchy or an established church. Might alone is right. They have never known the arts; they are ignorant even of agriculture. The cities of Africa are vast accumulations of huts and hovels; clay walls or thorny hedges surround them, and pools of blood and rows of skulls adorn their best houses. The few evidences of splendor or civilization are all borrowed from Europe; where there is a religion or creed, it is that of the foreigners; all knowledge, all custom, all progress has

come to them from abroad. The negro has no history—he makes
no history. (98)

Though this specific summation comes twenty-six years after that of Walker,
the contrasting views of the black past bring into sharp relief the crucial rhetorical revisioning and the contestation between black nationalism and proslavery
white nationalism.

The effort to retrieve an imagined, glorious black past for the creation of a
better black future has become one of the most telling leitmotifs of black nationalism. This is not to challenge the veracity of these historical claims (they face
enough from ideological contestants of various stripes) but to point to their function as a part of this ideology.[13] Not only does Walker provide a rhetorical revision, if not redemption, of the black past; he also seeks to establish a continuity
between blacks in the past and the blacks of his time. In so doing, he creates a
black subject organically linked to the past and prepared for action in the present
(Donald and Hall 166). Having interpellated blacks into a collective entity by
articulating nineteenth-century blacks to the blacks in his admirably rich, militant black history, Walker contended that this collective subject should act to
bring about black liberation. In his appeal for "one continual cry" against slavery throughout the Confederacy, then, Walker was inscribing this new collective black subject in black nationalism's narrative structure as one that was active in the campaign against black degradation (38). Such a liberation was similar
to the one blacks had achieved in Haiti. In contrast to the proslavery interpretation of this event, the Haitian revolution was for Walker "the glory of blacks and
the terror of tyrants" (21). As shown in the next chapter, this argument is similar to the one made by Sidney in his "Four Letters." In these letters, Sidney extends black nationalism's system of narration as he continues the ideological
program started by Young and Walker. He focuses on the insertion of the collective black subject into the social world and contends that blacks should act
exclusively as a group to effect their own emancipation.

In the introduction to this chapter, I argue that the *Manifesto* and the *Appeal*
are constitutive rhetorics. I base this claim on the two primary ideological functions performed by these two early, black abolitionist pamphlets: (1) the constitution of a collective subject and (2) the positing of a transhistorical subject.
Young's *Manifesto* and Walker's *Appeal* both construct a collective black subject
who is the product of Africa, connected to the continent through a proud ancestral history and a celebrated past, admirable for its militant protection of freedom and dignity, but with a stake in America rooted in suffering, sacrifice, and
hard labor. Young and Walker imbue this collective subject with black pride and
dignity and then call it into action against the degradation and indignity visited

upon blacks in the United States by white supremacist oppression. In fulfilling these functions, both pamphlets become significant parts of the early development of a black nationalist ideology. Unlike the work of several subsequent black nationalist ideologists, however, neither document promoted a return to Africa as the way of liberation for blacks.

This absence of a call for a return to Africa or a claim of Africa for Africans has led to a charge of "diffuseness" in "formulation of the place of Africans in the world." Perhaps this charge is responsible for neither the *Manifesto* nor the *Appeal* having received much credit for the development of black nationalism. Yet both documents advance several elements that reveal their incontestable black nationalist bent: these are the identification of the "God of the oppressed" as "the God of the Ethiopians," the anticipation of a black messiah, and the call for blacks everywhere to become a people, like Africans (Stuckey, *Ideological Origins* 8). Beginning with Pan-Africanism, a first principle of black nationalism, the *Appeal* advocates black self-government that would be achieved through black unity as a means of transcending existing black ignorance and degradation. For Walker, this transcendence would return blacks to the true legacy of the glorious cultural and intellectual tradition of their ancestors. With these elements, the *Appeal* embraced or prefigured almost every important aspect of nineteenth- and twentieth-century black nationalism, anticipating such figures as Garnet, Lewis Woodson, Crummell, Delany, Garvey, Paul Robeson, Elijah Mohammed, Malcolm X, Sistah Souljah, and Farrakhan (Stuckey, *Ideological Origins* 8).

Of the two pamphlets, the *Appeal* is the more extensive and more developed. It is also the more advanced in its concepts of black identity and black existence in America. The *Manifesto* is the more primitive, having more of the "aura of mystery" than the *Appeal,* which may be a function of its heavier dependence on religious metaphors and ideas. Whereas the *Manifesto* points back to Africa, the *Appeal* looks to Africa but only to find groundings for the existence of its new black subject, which seeks to survive and advance in a new place. While both documents "projected much that was African into an essentially European environment," the *Appeal* laid a more direct claim to title and ownership in the New World. This claim angered the white South and the supporters of slavery.

The flailing response of the South to early-nineteenth-century developments within the black community and to Walker's *Appeal* in particular becomes more comprehensible when one considers the role of the American Revolution in the South. Anglo-Americans focused explicitly on what for them was the primary element of the *Appeal,* a call to arms. Certainly related but perhaps more disturbing for this governing group of whites was the expression of a collective consciousness that challenged the rights to white governance. The two pamphlets addressed specifically to blacks in the United States were, for all concerned and especially for whites, more than a "whisper [of] liberty in the ears of the oppressed" (Ripley et al., *Black Abolitionist* 3: 5). In these documents but more so in the *Appeal*, Anglo-Americans experienced the material embodiment of Thomas Jefferson's fearful dilemma: "We have the wolf by the ears, and can neither hold him nor let him go" (qtd. in Norton 152). For blacks, Young's *Manifesto* and Walker's *Appeal* were purposeful stepping stones in the process of creating a people. This was a people who would, one hundred years later, be hailed and called into action by Garvey in his famous dictum, "up ye mighty race, you can accomplish what you will" (T. Martin, *Race*).

The rhetorical significance of the *Appeal* and the *Manifesto* is to be found both in what they express and in what they leave unstated. Through their claim of blacks as a people, both seek to naturalize the idea of a collective consciousness among blacks that guides them to unified action. That the existence of a "black people" continues to be debated almost two hundred years after the publication of these pamphlets only reinforces the argument that such claims are problematic and have their basis in rhetoric and not in the biological world. If the claim of blacks as a special kind of people was rhetorical, more so was the extended notion that nineteenth-century blacks were a people connected with blacks before them who had achieved great feats and thus set the standard for black life. The black subject employed in both pamphlets is textual: It is a rhetorical construct born of a combination of the militancy, the creative genius, and the religious faith and optimism of both Young and Walker. This rhetorically constructed collective black subject performs the ideological function of legitimizing claims for black emancipation. That the discourse was embraced by blacks and has been accepted by some as the beginnings of black nationalist ideology points to the rhetors' appeal to elements in the black experience that had perhaps become dormant or had been pushed underground by the oppressive and debilitating white proslavery practices. As we shall see, these elements, including black pride, collectivism, creativity, heroism, and a love of independence, are still being used in the effort to reconstitute blacks, even as that use is contested.

4

Contesting Blackness: The Rhetorical Empowerment of the Black Subject

As a people, then, we entertain no chimeras concerning our *actual condition;* we feel, that though not chattels, yet we are slaves. The *necessity* of effort to extricate ourselves . . . is a common conviction. . . . In reply, we adduce the general principle as of primary import—self-exertion the great law of our being.
　　　　　　　　　　　　　　　—Sidney, *Colored American*

Time to "hang out our own shingle."
　　　　　　　　　　　—William J. Watkins, *Witness for Freedom*

We have been enslaved by *"necessity"*—we are disfranchised by *"necessity."* I hope . . . they [commence] a warfare against the complexionally distinctive feature in every institution whether formed by white or colored people. I find . . . principles and sentiments that are eternal and immutable. Principles that must and will dethrone slavery, and obliterate prejudice.
　　　　　　　　　　　　—William Whipper, *Colored American*

On 18–21 August 1840, the Albany Convention of Colored People was held in Albany, New York. This convention, the first called exclusively for black people, was as controversial as it was significant (Ripley et al., *Black Abolitionist* 3: 349). The call and, eventually, the resolutions passed by the delegates were factious and faced strong challenges from within the black convention movement, primarily because of their focus on exclusive black involvement. William Whipper, a veteran of the black convention movement, challenged this exclusivity. The result was a notable public exchange between Whipper and Sidney.[1] The strident Whipper-Sidney debate of 1840–41 was an early contestation of the boundaries of black culture and of the limits of black-white collaborative programs, in contrast to exclusively black programs, in the struggle to overthrow slavery and, with it, the racism of white supremacy. In short, this was a contestation of "blackness."

In this rhetorical contest, nineteenth-century black culture publicly paraded its heterogeneity. Such heterogeneity has reappeared in contemporary black public culture as an exigency that demands rhetorical address. It is evident in the recent emergence of a new conservative voice, represented most strikingly by Shelby Steele's 1990 publication *The Content of Our Character: A New Vision of Race in America*. This new vision of blackness challenges the old vision of the black civil rights establishment and, in so doing, presents black conservatives as a different but legitimate face of blackness. More extreme forms of the new vision contend that black conservatives represent "authentic blackness" and, as such, are *the* legitimate face of blackness. Central to this conservative vision is an individual black subject to replace the collective black identity advocated by the civil rights establishment and black radical liberation efforts. Important to an understanding of the 1840 debate is a recounting of the developments within the abolitionist movement that resulted in the exclusive Albany Convention. A brief background sketch will suffice.

Between its launching in 1830 and the Civil War, the black convention was at the center of the black struggle. As part of the broader program of abolitionism, black conventions and black newspapers, along with the black church, provided for the mental, moral, and social elevation of blacks and for the shaping of black identity. It is not surprising that the black convention was the setting in which the early shoots of black nationalist ideology were pruned and shaped.[2] Although these conventions met annually up to 1835, they lapsed thereafter, with national conventions reconvening after seven years and state conventions resuming in 1840, after five (Bell, *Minutes* i–vi; Ripley et al., *Black Abolitionist* 3: 345). At both national and state conventions, blacks and sympathetic whites gathered to reflect on and devise strategies to achieve their twofold goal of freedom and equality. These conventions invariably faced the same questions of direction, procedure, and personnel that haunted the broader program of abolitionism. Central to these concerns was the contested identity of black people.

With disagreements over a number of strategies and tactics, factions began to emerge in the Northern abolitionist movement in the 1830s. These factions

involved some personal and regional rivalries between the Massachusetts abolitionists led by William Lloyd Garrison and the New York abolitionists led by
Arthur and Lewis Tappan (Wesley 33, 34; Quarles, *Frederick Douglass* 17). At
issue were the following: (1) Should women's rights share equal prominence with
emancipation? (2) What should be the role of the church in emancipation? and
(3) Should abolitionism proceed with Garrisonian moral suasion and government
nonresistance or more direct political action? (Harding, *There Is a River* 135). This
rivalry led to a split in the Massachusetts Antislavery Society in 1839 (Ripley et
al., *Black Abolitionist* 3: 298). By the end of the decade, blacks were frustrated
with the antislavery schism, the indifference of white reformers to prejudice and
discrimination, and the recent attitude toward "free blacks," especially in the
North (3: 283, 340). These developments helped advance the cause of independent black efforts within the convention movement.

A formal break in the Northern abolitionist movement occurred 15 May 1840
at the annual American Antislavery Society meeting, when the New York abolitionists, disenchanted with Garrisonianism, formed the rival American and Foreign Antislavery Society (Schor 31). This break finally came after a pro-Garri-
sonian majority defeated the Lewis Tappan–led opposition and elected Abigail
Kelly Foster, a white Quaker activist, as the first woman to sit on the executive
board of the American Antislavery Society. For Tappan, it was understood at
the founding of the society that "[a]ll women have a right to be members but
the business [was] to be conducted by men" (Yee 7). On one side of the divide,
Garrisonians interpreted the Constitution as a proslavery document but opposed
political action and believed "moral suasion" would achieve emancipation. On
the other side were political abolitionists, who interpreted the Constitution as
an antislavery document and espoused political action. This group supported the
recently formed Liberty Party, which vigorously opposed slavery (Wesley 39).[3]
This division in the Northern abolitionist movement included a disagreement
between blacks and whites. This "was not simply a black white disagreement,"
however, as blacks sided with the different political factions (Harding, *There Is a
River* 25; Wesley 34). A vocal group of blacks that included Henry Highland
Garnet actively supported the Liberty Party and promoted the development of
separate and independent black organizations (Litwack, *North* 84–90; Pease and
Pease, *They Would Be Free* 173–205). Included was a call to relaunch the National
Negro Convention movement (Harding, *There Is a River* 120, 121; Schor 49).
This separatist call raised the troubling questions of black autonomy and the role
of friendly whites in the abolitionist movement, issues brought to the fore in the
Albany Convention of August 1840 and its offshoot, the debate between Whipper
and Sidney.

The Public Rhetorical Construction of
Black Identity: Contesting Blackness

The Whipper-Sidney debate includes Whipper's three letters of 3, 12, and 17 January 1841, first published in the *Colored American* 30 January and 6 and 20 February 1841, and Sidney's "Four Letters, in response to William Whipper," also first published in the *Colored American* 13 and 20 February and 6 and 13 March 1841. All are reprinted in Sterling Stuckey's *Ideological Origins of Black Nationalism.* This debate, which spanned the two major organs of the emerging black public sphere of the period, the black convention and black newspapers, reveals the two contending perspectives of black abolitionism. Those who promoted exclusive black involvement advanced the growing perspective of black nationalism. In contrast, those who supported a more integrationist approach argued for collaboration with interested whites. Whipper, in 1841 the chief antagonist of black separatism, concludes his trilogy by indicating to editor Charles B. Ray, "I leave you standing on the horns of a dilemma," a dilemma that has plagued the cause of black liberation ever since (Bell, *Survey* 18; Stuckey, *Slave Culture* 210; and *Colored American* 20 Feb. 1841). Stuckey suggests that Ray, as editor, solicited Garnet's letters (211).

Like that of other black abolitionists, Whipper's ambivalence about the involvement of white leadership and the peculiar interest of blacks is symptomatic of this dilemma (203–11; J. W. Johnson 12–18). While he supported integration in this debate, by the 1850s he was railing against white racism and endorsing emigration as the only option for blacks. Whipper had come to see slavery as based on color and blamed racism on white ignorance. In 1856, he endorsed emigration (Ripley et al., *Black Abolitionist* 4: 242–44, 335–36). The labels "integrationist" and "nationalist," then, are useful only in the context of a particular stance on specific issues and not as fixed descriptors of those black abolitionists who were confronting the hazardous quagmire of Southern slavery while simultaneously negotiating the quicksand of Northern racism.

The predicament for black liberation that emerged in the encounter between the mutually antagonistic nationalist and integrationist perspectives continues to this day. The problem is evident in Louis Farrakhan's contentious, exclusive call to black men in the Million Man March. Black men were to be both the exclusive participants in the march and the primary agents in the drive for black equality. In the face of this dilemma, black nationalism confronts a haunting, historical, yet contemporary question. Did the nineteenth-century black liberation effort and does the twenty-first-century movement for equality require the establishment of common cause with and engagement of sympathetic whites? The question is important but remains unanswered. This chapter provides some possible answers.

In addition to the question of separatism or integration, the debate over the black liberation program reveals the vexing problem of black heterogeneity. The contemporary contest between black conservatism on the one hand and the civil rights establishment and radical black groups, including black nationalists, on the other is the most recent and perhaps the most sustained manifestation of this problem. It is a clash between black conservatives' individualism, which promotes black privatization, and black nationalism's collectivism, with its agenda of black collusion and activism. This confrontation drags black life to the brink of what Aaron Gresson calls a "black apocalypse" (15–16). It is a calamity that threatens to plunge African Americans into an abyss of infighting and self-destruction, thus precluding any hope of building on the successes of ancestors like the black abolitionists. The way out of this dilemma, Gresson argues, is for blacks to address black heterogeneity (15). The black activists who confronted conflicting visions of blackness in the 1840s sought their own way out. Whipper, Sidney, Ray, and other black abolitionists tried, through conflicting approaches, to develop an agenda for black liberation and black uplift. In the process, they revealed their efforts to define blackness.

What follows is an examination of the Whipper-Sidney debate as it related to an exclusively black effort to bring about liberation. This reveals the rhetorical growth and development of black nationalist ideology. First I explain the discord among abolitionists, including the "names" controversy, that culminated in the Whipper-Sidney debate. Then I analyze the arguments in both sets of letters to highlight the halting and uneven rhetorical development of black nationalist ideology. I show how the letters function ideologically to interpellate political subjects into the social world of nineteenth-century black struggle. Both Whipper and Sidney constituted subjects who were literary creations but who were introduced as real and free to choose their own path to freedom. Sidney's racialized subject was constructed on the basis of blackness, a common African ancestry, and the shared experience of oppression. In contrast, Whipper appealed to universal Christian principles and thus constituted in his rhetoric a universalist subject that transcended race to contest the perspective of the Albany Convention and Sidney.

This debate is important because the protagonists were clearly both speakers and actors in their discourse world who struggled to develop ideologies that contested for the souls of black folk. It also encapsulates most if not all of the arguments on both sides of the issue. Here we see the function of rhetoric in shaping African American identity at the intramural level within the African American discourse community. Blacks not only contended with the dominant Anglo-American narrative in carving out their own identity but also vigorously disputed among themselves the nature of such an identity. The intramural debate reveals the black abolitionist community as a heterogeneous black cultural space. Such heterogeneity, with its multiple perspectives on blackness, highlights the problem inherent in rhetorical efforts to fix black identity. Ernesto Laclau and Chantal Mouffe convincingly argue that such efforts to fix identity, marginal or not, are destined to fail. Mark McPhail, too, would later make this same argument with specific reference to black nationalists and black conservatives. Such efforts make visible their rhetorical nature and the ideological functions in the rhetoric employed. The equally vigorous names debate, the precursor of the Whipper-Sidney disputation, is where we must begin.

Early Debate over Black Identity: Precursors to Whipper and Sidney

Reverend Lewis Woodson, writing under the pseudonym Augustine, advocated the cause of black separatism in his "Ten Letters," published in the *Colored American* between 3 November 1837 and 13 March 1841.[4] In the first of these letters, he contended blacks "are a distinct class, and that our moral elevation is a work of our own" (Augustine, "Moral Work"). In his letter dated 13 July 1838, Woodson pointedly engaged Samuel E. Cornish, then editor of the *Colored American,* whose editorial of 23 June 1838 had rejected Woodson's thesis of black separatism as a prerequisite for equality (Augustine, "Farmer's Garden"). This dispute was primarily about black settlements in the United States; it provided, however, the forum for an exposé into the emerging perspective of some blacks about black-white integration (Ripley et al., *Black Abolitionist* 3: 256; Augustine, "Farmer's Garden"; *Colored American* 9 and 16 Feb. 1839). Woodson rejected the editor's thesis that contact, not separation, would eliminate prejudice. He contended, "[Y]ou tell us that *'contact'* is the most powerful engine in wearing out prejudices;—if so, why has it not worn out the prejudices of the whites in the cities?" Woodson used the biblical example of Abraham's separation from Lot (Gen. 13) and the founding fathers' Declaration of Independence from Britain as historical precedents that support separation and the establishment of autonomous societies "as a means of curing existing antipathies" and, for blacks, as a route to peace and progress (Augustine, "Farmer's Garden").

Woodson's nationalistic scheme of exclusive black settlements within the United States (a proposal influenced by his experience of successful black communities in Ohio) was lambasted by Cornish as *"colonization magnified"* (qtd. in Augustine, "Farmer's Garden"). This controversy points to the contortions and complexities faced by these black liberators. In this instance, Woodson, who actually opposed the program of the American Colonization Society, was accused of advocating a cause similar to that of his nemesis, a nemesis so acknowledged by a majority of Northern blacks. Furthermore, at the time, the American Colonization Society was lambasted by black nationalists. Woodson's scheme, however, was not emigration but migration; that is, he advocated not leaving the

United States but moving to a designated area within the country. The key distinction here, one that would be made repeatedly by subsequent black nationalists who advocated migration and emigration, was that this movement was to be effected by blacks at their own choosing.

Cornish's most telling point against black separatism, one that has continued to be a disconcerting if not haunting critique, was that if blacks were to gain equality, they would have to establish common cause with whites. He declared, "If we or our posterity ever possesses the inalienable rights of American citizens, it must be in identity of interests, and consequently in identity of communities and of intercourse with our white brethren" (qtd. in Augustine, "Farmer's Garden"). As Steele would argue one hundred fifty-two years later, moral power and not racial power should be the basis of black efforts for advancement (*Content* 19). Woodson rejected this argument on the basis of the experience of blacks in the United States. Continued racist practices have sustained the effectiveness of this response so much that it has been used by every advocate of black nationalism since Woodson. In the continuing fight for the rights of citizenship for blacks in contemporary America, Cornish's observation stalks separatist perspectives. However, shining the spotlight on the degrading experience of blacks in the United States, as Louis Farrakhan does so effectively, often closes off debate about the crucial issue of the means of achieving equality. Such a closure is counterproductive, as it often cuts off the necessary talk among the multiple perspectives within black communities, a talk encouraged by Gresson, perhaps as the basis through which such communities might begin to address the reality of their heterogeneity (Gresson 214). Where such silencing precludes the addressing of heterogeneity, it retards black communities by moving them closer to their own apocalypse. Woodson's approach was an unapologetic separation.

In presenting this perspective, Woodson, like Sidney, rejected the arguments of Cornish, Whipper, and other blacks who opposed black separatism (F. Miller 313). Woodson, who had served as corresponding secretary for the Pittsburgh auxiliary of the American Moral Reform Society, broke with the organization's leadership over their declared preference for integrated reform organizations. He advocated the development of black unity and black identity through separate black reform organizations, separate black settlements, black migration, and separate black schools and churches (Ripley et al., *Black Abolitionist* 3: 259–260; F. Miller). In so doing, he extended the nationalist ideas and separatism of Robert Alexander Young and David Walker and paved the way for Henry Highland Garnet and Martin Delany. This separatism was criticized by Frederick Douglass and other black Garrisonians, and of course, the Black Power movement with its push for independent black organizations is the target of strident criticisms from the new conservative voices. Woodson's letters and his exchange with the editor of the *Colored American* reflect the mood of black abolitionism out of which the call for the Albany Convention and an exclusive black effort emerged. This mood was marked by frustration with the inability to eliminate slavery. Equally frustrating were the continued insensitive and racist practices in Northern abolitionist and other reform movements.

The Albany Convention and the ensuing controversy were the culmination of another critical aspect of the development of nineteenth-century black identity: the simmering debate over names. The controversy grew out of the concern of black leaders such as Whipper that the promotion of separate black organizations and the use of distinctive black names would "encourage the colonizationist movement and increase racial prejudice." At the 1835 black national convention, Whipper successfully advocated a resolution that encouraged blacks to remove racial nomenclature from their schools, churches, and social institutions (Ripley et al., *Black Abolitionist* 3: 263). This passage led to increased pressure against complexional distinctions (Stuckey, *Slave Culture* 208). The American Moral Reform Society also held debates on the question of naming. One contested issue was the direction of the organization. Whipper and Robert Purvis agitated for an integrated organization, while Junius C. Morel, Frederick Hinton, and others sought to focus specifically on black concerns (Ripley et al., *Black Abolitionist* 3: 263).

Cornish underestimated the rhetorical significance and far-reaching implications of the decisions about naming when he scolded the contenders for "quarreling about trifles" in a 15 March 1838 editorial in the *Colored American*. He continued, "Nothing can be more ridiculous nor ludicrous, than their contentions about NAMES—if they quarrel it should be about THINGS" (*Colored American*). This position was curious considering that the *Colored American,* launched in the midst of the names controversy and open to the discussion, was deliberately so named to highlight the legitimacy of the claims that blacks made on America as their home. Cornish himself had outlined this position in his editorial in the maiden issue 4 March 1837. While he insisted on "colored" as the best appellation for blacks, he maintained that they should share America as home equally with whites (*Colored American* 4 Mar. 1837; Stuckey, *Slave Culture* 208–10). Moreover, the debate itself was carried out with insightful theoretical propositions, as the perspective expressed by William Watkins illustrates: "Permit us to say that words are used as the signs of our ideas, and whenever they perform this office, or are truly significant of the ideas for which they stand, they accomplish the object of their invention" (qtd. in Stuckey, *Slave Culture* 207). Watkins was writing in opposition to Whipper and supported use of the designator "colored" by blacks to identify themselves and their institutions. One can only surmise that Cornish thought the debate much too protracted, given the many THINGS that blacks needed to accomplish to gain equality. Sidney's reference to the focus and extent of the debate gives credence to this reading of Cornish. In the last of his four letters in response to Whipper, Sidney wrote, "[T]his endless clamoring about 'color,' is alike devoid of reason, as it is disreputable to us as a people. The people are perishing by oppression, and our leaders, one opposing the other upon a *word;* are metaphysicising upon *things*" (*Colored American* 13 Mar. 1841).

Naming is, of course, the first step in the rhetorical process of controlling and constraining the rhetorical subject. As Kenneth Burke suggests, persuasion begins with the act of naming (Burke, *Language* 44–80). Walt Whitman, too, contends that "[n]ames are the turning point of who shall be master" (Whitman 34; qtd. in Roediger 41). A crucial feature in the continuing contestation over black identity is the issue of names. As Stuckey argues, the names controversy among blacks in the nineteenth, twentieth, and twenty-first centuries is at its heart a contest over the individual and collective identity of blacks. Among ex-slaves, the assigning of African names was one way of furthering individual and collective consciousness, important to black progress (*Slave Culture* 194). This tension between individual and collective consciousness as the hallmark of black identity remains central to black intramural struggles. The notion of a collective consciousness as an indicator of a collective black identity has been for blacks an effective political tool to confront white supremacist practices in America. The rhetorical nature of this exercise is evident, however, in the disparate collection of people such a collective seeks to bring together as one, whether as "Africans," "blacks," or "African Americans." Still, the rhetorically constructed "people," "Africans," "blacks," or "African Americans" deployed in rhetoric had material consequences. After the American Colonization Society was launched in 1816, the use of the term "Africa" or names that connected blacks to Africa was a two-edged sword, as colonizers argued that Africa and not America was the home of blacks. Many blacks therefore avoided the appellation for fear of encouraging colonization (*Slave Culture* 194). Cornish bemoaned that, despite what these blacks called themselves, "their FRIENDS and their FOES, in the convention, in the Assembly and in the Senate; through the pulpit and the press, call them nothing else but NEGROES" (*Colored American* 15 Mar. 1838). Whipper and Sidney's contestation of these fundamental choices "marked a critical juncture in the development of black abolitionist thought" (Ripley et al., *Black Abolitionist* 3: 356; Stuckey, *Slave Culture* 211). My focus on Whipper and Sidney is not meant to suggest that they were the only significant protagonists continuing the debate in the 1840s. There were other voices.

Additional Voices

James McCune Smith, "one of the foremost black intellectuals of the antebellum period," outlined his strong opposition to the call for the Albany Convention in a letter to the editor of the *Colored American* dated 12 August 1840 and published August 15. Smith contended that he was "not at all opposed to all action on the part of the colored people, but [am] opposed to action based upon complexional distinction" (qtd. in Ripley et al., *Black Abolitionist* 3: 350).[5] In his 12 September 1840 editorial outlining his support of the Albany Convention and state conventions in general, Ray refers to the opposition of the *National Anti-Slavery Standard* and counters the objection to complexional distinction.[6] He charged, with sarcasm, "*a lily skin* is the *real simon pure* in this country. A skin colored like our own, has no right to say much, or do much, not even to hold a convention" (Ripley et al., *Black Abolitionist* 3: 347–48). This exchange is a representative sample of the divide created by this debate. Prominent black activists, equally committed to black liberation and black equality, disagreed sharply on the direction of abolitionism. Their eloquent and energetic defense reveals the strength of heterogeneity even as it provides a window into their developing ideologies.

Contesting the Role of the Black Subject

The "Four Letters" by Sidney defended exclusively black action to effect emancipation. Sidney argued, in the first letter, that blacks, as the oppressed, must work on their own behalf to extricate themselves from degradation. He stated, "[T]he *necessity* of effort to extricate ourselves from the deep pitfalls, and the loathsome cells of the dark prison-house of oppression, is a common conviction" (Sidney 13 Feb. 1841). He made this argument even more explicit in his second letter: "It is the irrevocable degree of nature, that our main hope of progress and elevation through life, shall depend upon our own energy and activity" (20 Feb. 1841). Not only did Sidney extend the argument of black self-liberation in his third letter, but he also refuted any claim that other agents or agencies could perform such functions on behalf of oppressed blacks. From Sidney's perspective, to qualify as an agent in the effort for freedom, those participating must have "a keen sense of actual suffering, and a fixed consciousness that it is no longer sufferable" (6 Mar. 1841). These qualifications account for the "essentially peculiar ability of the oppressed, and the necessary incapability of all others, even of the best of friends" to bring about such liberation (6 Mar. 1841). Sidney expressed sentiments declared earlier by William Hamilton, the "foremost black intellectual of the first quarter of the nineteenth century," when he argued, "the colored people of this country are oppressed; therefore the colored people are required to act"

(13 Mar. 1841; rpt. in Stuckey, *Slave Culture* 200–201, 214). As Marcus Garvey would later argue, "it takes a slave to interpret the feelings of the slave; it takes the unfortunate man to interpret the spirit of his unfortunate brother; and so it takes the suffering Negro to interpret the spirit of his comrade" (*Blackman* 21 May 1929; qtd. in T. Martin, *Race First* 90). As black women continue to remind us, notwithstanding this patriarchal rhetoric and the black and white patriarchy of the early nineteenth century, this suffering and this sensitive black subject was never exclusively male.

Sidney's perspective contrasts with that of Whipper. Responding to the minutes of the Albany Convention, Whipper, identified by Stuckey as the "prototype integrationist," wrote three polemics to editor Ray (*Ideological Origins* 27n. 17). In his first letter, Whipper addressed the first of several resolutions passed at the convention. The resolution stated,

> Resolved, that all laws established for human government, and all
> systems, of whatever kind, founded in the spirit complexional cast,
> are in *violation of the fundamental principles of Divine Law, evil in
> their tendencies,* and should therefore, be effectually destroyed. (*Colored American* 30 Jan. 1841)

On the basis of this resolution, Whipper challenged Ray and the convention movement to extend the eradication effort beyond the state and federal government to black "churches, schools, beneficial, and literary societies." Whipper contended, "Can we hope to be successful in reforming others before we procure a reformation among ourselves?" From his perspective, all people should depend on "principles and sentiments that are eternal and immutable. Principles that must and will dethrone slavery and obliterate prejudice" (*Colored American* 30 Jan. 1841). He therefore challenged what he called the "colorphobia" guiding the initiative. For him, this colorphobia embraced a distinctiveness in churches and other black institutions that was against "Christianity, republican freedom and our common happiness, and ought once now and forever to be abolished." Though only parenthetically, Whipper did acknowledge that the focus on color was a function of the experience of Sidney and other blacks. In speaking of colorphobia, he acknowledged, "and notwithstanding there may have been causes sufficient to implant it into our minds" (*Colored American* 6 Feb. 1841). He saw, then, that the nefarious conditions of nineteenth-century America encountered by individual blacks served to reinforce the consciousness of race. In short, black existence was a racialized one. America's dominant social phenomena, slavery and racism, were oppressive white supremacist practices that continued to define, defame, and destroy individuals on the basis of skin color.

Consistent with his minimal regard for immediate situational concerns, Whipper wrote all three letters without any knowledge of the firestorm they were causing or the content or tenor of the written responses. He was writing from Philadelphia, and the convention had been held in Albany, New York. As he noted in his third letter, "I have no means of ascertaining whether my letters of the 3d and 12th insts., have reached you" (Whipper 20 Feb. 1841). Notwithstanding Whipper's approach, the efforts of nineteenth-century black abolitionists were dominated by the complexity of their quotidian experience. For blacks, color was the significant marker of their lives. It circumscribed their existence and limited their ability to earn a livelihood, even to gain an education, not to mention their exclusion from participation in the public life of their country. Therefore, activists like Sidney sought to advance programs and practices grounded in the material experience of slavery, prejudice, oppression, and black struggle.

The complexity of the context within which black nationalist ideology emerged can be seen, for example, in the debate over emigration. Emigration was an integral, if problematic, aspect of the program of liberation and equality for blacks. In the Albany Convention, noted for its call for blacks to labor on their own behalf to achieve liberation and equality, there was also a strong resolution against emigration. Of course, emigration was to become one of the central elements of the black separatism championed by the likes of Alexander Crummell and Martin Delany (Crummell and Charles L. Reason objected to the resolution). The resolution read,

> Resolved, That this convention exceedingly deprecate any system of general emigration offered to our people, as calculated to throw us into a state of restlessness, to break up all those settled habits which would otherwise attach us to the soil, and to furnish our enemies with arguments to urge our removal from the land of our birth.[7]
> (*Colored American* 2 Jan. 1841)

In supporting this resolution, the convention continued to advance the earliest black objections to emigration schemes such as that of the American Colonization Society. It also utilized arguments similar to those employed in Walker's *Appeal to the Colored Citizens of the World*, claiming the United States was the country of blacks, "purchased by the exertions and blood of our fathers [and mothers], as much as by the exertions and blood of other men [and women]" (Walker 65; *Colored American* 2 Jan. 1841). These blacks sought an equality with Anglo-Americans but one achieved through the exclusive effort of blacks, who shared a unique history, culture, and color distinguishing them from whites.

With the need for acknowledgment alongside the desire for independent action, blacks confronted an awkward rhetorical challenge. The plight was even more precarious considering that, from the references in the discourse of the period, the rhetorical battle for acceptance by Anglo-America of the humanity that blacks shared with whites was not yet won. As Leon F. Litwack notes in reference to the Pennsylvania constitutional debates of 1837–38, Northern whites still employed the stock arguments of white supremacy. They referred to blacks as "a distinct, inferior caste," not qualified to exercise equal rights with whites (Litwack, *North* 76). How, then, could black advocates such as Sidney establish distinction without undermining the shared humanity that those before them had labored so long to establish? Deep frustration forced them to undertake the formidable task. The objection of other black activists, like Whipper, to the exclusive black focus was grounded in the argument that Christian principles and white partnership were necessary for successful black advancement.

Whipper's Rhetoric: Transcending Race Through Myth

Whipper interpreted the exigencies of nineteenth-century black suffering as a need for the application of eternal and immutable Christian principles, in short, the Christian myth so effective in explaining and defining American life. To address this need, Whipper promoted abolitionism by means of a collaboration between blacks and whites based on shared, universal, Christian principles. "With the advocates of such principles" Whipper opines, "I delight to labor" (Whipper 30 Jan. 1841). He advocated a deracinated, utopian subject. Whipper saw every distinction, especially those based on race, as odious, invidious, inconsistent, and against all principles of republican government, Christian virtues, and human rights. Thus he called for a collaborative effort between blacks and whites joined as one, representing the human family, and united not by color but by Christian principles. In so doing, Whipper effaced the differences between black and white and presented a futuristic utopian vision. This vision was particularly problematic in light of the dystopian realities blacks faced in their effort to persuade whites to acknowledge their most basic rights. By advocating emancipation through a collaboration between blacks and whites on the basis of universal Christian principles, Whipper proposed a maintenance of the status quo in abolitionism. In short, Whipper's perspective showed little accounting for the reality of black alienation. Here he faced a troublesome rhetorical challenge, as the Christian principles he advocated were the argued basis for various nineteenth-century reform movements, including abolitionism. In these societies, blacks heard idealistic proposals of principled partnerships from whites, but they also experienced arrogant paternalism. For example, Samuel Ringgold Ward charged white abolitionists with racism in a letter to Nathaniel P. Rogers, the editor of the *National Anti-Slavery Standard* (*National Anti-Slavery Standard* 2 July 1840). Ward especially responded to Rogers's objection to the call among black abolitionists for exclusive black liberation efforts within the convention. According to Ward, there "were too many who best love the colored man at a distance" (*National Antislavery Standard* 2 July 1840).

Whipper did not explicitly contest the existence of Sidney's unique black subject. He presented, however, a rhetorical revision of the character and identity of this subject. Whipper's focus on universal principles as the unifying features of his constituted human subject, which incorporated blacks and whites, transcended racial differences. This focus undermined the legitimacy of the exclusive role that Sidney claimed for blacks because Whipper's universal principles were proposed as replacements for the specific qualities of shared suffering, blackness, and common African ancestry proposed by Sidney as the basis for leadership in black liberation. Whipper's alternative, then, was a rhetorical contestation for the identity of the agent of black liberation and, as such, was a disputation against black separatism.

In making his point, Whipper relied on and emphasized the logic and consistency of his argument. His calls to both black activists and white supremacists were based on what he saw as universal Christian principles that would eventually result in the demise of oppression and the promotion of "brotherhood." He insightfully pointed to the contradiction of the convention's passing a resolution that challenged laws and systems based on color while it promoted an abolitionist program based on exclusive black agency. Whipper cited the convention's second resolution:

> 'Resolved, That the toleration of complexional difference in the State of New York is a stain upon its constitution, and attaches it to the great system of oppression in the land, so vital to our national character, since it is upheld not only in direct opposition to the common rights of humanity, but also runs counter to those political principles asserted by the framers of our republican government.'

He then argued,

> It is peculiarly appropriate for any people that have long been trodden under foot by the "iron heel" of any peculiar despotism that when they appeal to the rectitude of just principles on behalf of their deliverance that they should first exhibit to the world, that they were not only prepared to act upon those principles themselves, but that they had hurled the principle of despotism from their own borders. It speaks well for the purity of principle that must have existed in the convention to have passed such a resolution, yet it appears passing strange that such a body convened under a complexionally dis-

tinct call should so far transgress the principle of their own organization as virtually to declare it in direct opposition to the "rights of
humanity." (Whipper 6 Feb. 1841)

Whipper's contention is poignant in that the convention's appeal for the abolition of unjust laws and systems was proffered in the name of universal rectitude
and justice, and in "the light of reason, the principles of Christianity, and the
dictates of living and eternal right" (*Colored American* 2 Jan. 1841). Whipper's
challenge also highlights other problems spawned by the exclusive call, with race
as a primary basis of solidarity. These problems include the possible authentica-
tion of the white supremacist exclusive position, the encouragement of Anglo-
Americans to think of blacks as alien, the alienation of supportive others, and
the limiting of the program of liberation.

Within the context of nineteenth-century America dominated by Anglo-
American racist conceptions of what it meant to be an "American," any depiction of blacks as different from the white majority faced the danger of further
legitimizing black exclusion. Equally troubling was the danger of such a depiction serving as a foil against which white supremacist discourse could articulate
and authenticate white separatism and its attendant vice, black derogation. In
addition, within the context of such rhetorical contestation over identity and
legitimacy, whites who wished to support black causes could find themselves
alienated by both black and white exclusivism.

Though utopian and transcendental, Whipper's constituted subject reflects
a hopeful and futuristic, mythic vision. Through this vision, he sought to constitute partnership as the way forward for a nation constantly threatened by the
likelihood of a racially motivated civil war. From the perspective of the opening
years of the twenty-first century, Whipper's vision of collaboration based on a
shared commitment to human development is a desirable one. Such a vision is
even more poignant given America's ineffectual groping for a solution to its ar-
tificially created but debilitating racial division. The context within which he
advocated it undermined his effort, however, leaving him adrift in a seemingly
imaginary, paradisiacal world. Whipper's line of reasoning was therefore easily
countered and rejected by Sidney and others in whose lives race was the signal
marker. Whipper's rejection of black institutions as a part of his general excoriation of complexional classifications raises the question of the role of such institutions in the black struggle.

While Whipper questioned the legitimacy or at least the naming of these
institutions, including black newspapers, conventions, and churches, Sidney
embraced them. As Carla L. Peterson has noted, following Antonio Gramsci and
Benedict Anderson, such institutions are central to the struggle of subaltern

groups such as nineteenth-century blacks. These institutions provide a place for privately held sentiments to be made public, thus allowing for organized consent. These sites are used by blacks to create a sense of common purpose and of community. They therefore serve as sites for unity, collaboration, resistance, and struggle. It is reasonable, then, to argue that such institutions fostered Sidney's conception of blackness as part of "a deep horizontal comradeship" shared with blacks everywhere (Peterson 11). It is not surprising, then, that Sidney's emphasis on black pride and black self-determination, an extension of the earlier perspectives of Young and Walker, appealed to the convention and its delegates, many of whom were "free blacks." Sidney's distinctive augmentation of Young and Walker's perspective is a function of his advancement of an exclusive effort by blacks as an integral, if not central, aspect of abolitionism.

Sidney's Rhetoric: Embracing Race Through Ideology

In response to Whipper's appeal to universal principles, Sidney advanced self-exertion as the path to liberation. Sidney told of a people bound by their common ancestry and color who were further united by their shared suffering. Through such suffering, they developed a common commitment to liberation. Here we see the first ideological effect of Sidney's constitutive rhetoric, the constituting of a collective subject. Sidney constructed a collective black subject with specific and unique abilities. Sidney's discourse was ideological in that he sought to mask the rhetorical nature of this black subject. He assumed that the collective black subject existed in nature, outside his discourse. His narrative tendered a reference to this extrarhetorical entity. In the process, Sidney artfully constructed a united "people" qualified for the task of liberation by their common ancestry, their color, and their experience of oppression.

The Rhetoric of Descent

In Sidney's view, blacks were connected by their common African ancestry. The embrace and affirmation of his African ancestry is an integral part of Sidney's positive identification with blackness, which he made clear in his declaration, "We are descendants of Africans—colored people—negroes if you will. . . . 'Colored as we are, *black* though we may be, yet we demand our rights, the same rights as other citizens have'" (*Colored American* 13 Mar. 1841). Here Sidney employed one of the hallmarks of black nationalism, what Kwame Anthony Appiah calls "the rhetoric of descent" (*In My Father's* xi). In using the rhetoric of descent, black nationalists advance claims of black unity based on their common descent. Such a rhetoric also posits a transhistorical subject, the second ideological effect of constitutive rhetorics. In this scenario, ancestry is proffered as the connection linking Africans, blacks, and the collectivity presented in the discourse. This claim problematically assumes that shared African ancestry somehow links African Americans in unique ways, fostering, for example, common political aims. The problems with claims such as these are highlighted, for instance, in Charles T. Banner-Haley's contention that blacks could "at least in theory, trace their ancestry to Africa," but that "in point of fact most black Americans probably could not trace their heritage any further than a bill of sale from one slave-owner to another" (Banner-Haley xvii). In this observation, Banner-Haley points to the problematic of both the black heritage and black identity; issues confounded by the adaptation of blacks to their new, dominant American culture and the fading memory of Africa. There is no denying Stuckey's useful, if somewhat overstated, contention that "being of African ancestry and being treated accordingly [as inferior] formed a distinctive emotional bond for blacks everywhere in America" (*Slave Culture* 215). Still, this emotional bond does not preclude us from seeing that Sidney's effort to show a natural connection among this disparate group, scattered across the United States and throughout the world, was part of a rhetorical strategy to mobilize blacks to action. If blacks accepted their common link presented in this rhetorical transaction, they would complete the process of identification and be constituted as one. In Sidney's view, their color was another unifying principle for blacks.

The Rhetoric of Color

The exclusive focus Sidney advocated was not based primarily on "complexional cast," as Whipper argued, but, in Sidney's words, on the principle of "self-exertion the great law of our being" (*Colored American* 6 Mar. 1841). Even so, race was the primary unifying principle for Sidney and remains so for black nationalism. In responding to what he saw as Whipper's retreat from blackness, Sidney took an aggressive stance in the treatment of race, one that has come to mark twentieth-century black nationalism. He argued that blacks were pleased with their color, and white oppressors and others should adjust to that fact. "The color God has given us we are satisfied with; and it is a matter of but little moment to us, who may be displeased with it" (*Colored American* 13 Mar. 1841). For Sidney's collective subject, race was clearly a source of pride. It also united blacks as it distinguished them from whites and other subjects because race pride and unity based on race were inherent parts of Sidney's script. Therefore the protagonist in his story was positioned to embrace these important features. Race, then, was central to Sidney's conception of how America's slaves were to be emancipated and how her oppressed citizens should earn reprieve. While contending that the chosen course of exclusive action was not based on race, Sidney nevertheless clearly advocated race pride. Advocation of race pride was not unique to Sidney, as it was a general theme in black abolitionist discourse and one that continues in black nationalism. Sidney's expression of race pride, as well as the race pride of black nationalism, is an affirmation of blackness. It is part of a rhetorical strategy of refuting white supremacist derogation of blackness through confrontation with and, as it developed later, the demeaning of whiteness (C. Johnson 28–29). Yet Sidney argued that blacks were united not by their common ancestry and color but by the shared experience of the sufferings of slavery and oppression, all of which made them ready to bring about their own emancipation.

The Rhetoric of Shared Suffering

The averred readiness and commitment of this collective black subject to the task of liberation is another key textual feature presented in Sidney's discourse. This commitment is part of the motive and *telos* inherent in the subject of his narrative. Sidney's rhetorical magic, then, was in his masking of this commitment to liberation as the declared attitude of a collective group of individuals in the society. He presented this commitment as the free choice of nineteenth-century blacks. In so doing, Sidney engaged in the third ideological effect of constitutive rhetorics, the illusion of freedom. Sidney went further to contend that the "people" he spoke of developed their qualification on the basis of their historical experience. This history then became a part of the black nationalist narrative.

The material and historical-situatedness of action is a key issue in the ideology of black nationalism. Sidney pointed to this fact in his challenge of Whipper's "heaven-born truth." Sidney chastised such a focus as "despising all specific actions or means" (*Colored American* 6 Mar. 1841). Such specific means and actions, adapted as necessity demanded to meet the changing strategies and circumstances of white supremacist practices, was the breeding ground for black nationalists like Sidney and Lewis Woodson. For them, the cosmopolitan approach advocated by Whipper and others who opposed black autonomy was a theory that had no grounding either in reason or in the crucifix of their excruciating experience. In Sidney's view, "[d]uties arise from relations. Our responsibilities and obligations receive their hue and coloring from the situation." He was even more specific: "We sustain relations to our own people, so peculiar that white men cannot assume them" (*Colored American* 13 Mar. 1841). In contrast to Whipper's universalism, black nationalist ideology was based not on ubiquitous principles but on daily practical action. Its guiding principle was not grounded in philosophy, with its emphasis on ultimate questions of what ought to be done in a given situation, but was guided by phronesis: what could be done in a given situation, a more practical perspective. For advocates of the ideology, action taken should be grounded in history, common sense, and the experience of the oppressed.

To account for the commitment of his black subject to the task of liberation and to show how blacks were uniquely qualified for success in the venture, Sidney pointed to their experience of suffering. He contended that the shared experience of white oppression by American blacks uniquely qualified them for the program of their own deliverance. In making this claim, Sidney constituted oppression discursively as the basis for black unity while masking his rhetorical effort. This masking allowed him to chastise Whipper and others for overlooking this important qualification. For Sidney, Whipper's sentiments expressed in his letters were not new, but they were "singular and unfortunate" (*Colored American* 13 Feb. 1841). In his third letter, Sidney posed the question that best illustrates the principles undergirding black nationalist ideology's emphasis on exclusivity. He wrote,

> How is it possible, we ask, for men who know nothing of oppression, who have always enjoyed the blessedness of freedom, by any effort of imagination, by any strength of devotedness, by any depth of sympathy, so fully and adequately to express the sense of wrong and outrage, as the sorrowful presence and living desire of us who have drank the dregs of the embittered chalice? (*Colored American* 6 Mar. 1841)

Sidney's argument here represents a striking perspective of engaging alienated blacks in addressing their own alienation. As shown in the following chapter, this call was to be made more explicit in Garnet's "Address to the Slaves." In Sidney's view, an exclusive focus on the oppressed as the agents for their own liberation was based not so much on any perceived superiority of black over white but on what Sidney saw as an ability peculiar to the oppressed as a consequence of their experience of oppression. This peculiar ability came from a "keen sense of actual suffering and a fixed consciousness that it is no longer sufferable." Those not oppressed, then, did not possess this ability and thus could not function as agents of liberation, for "we occupy a position and sustain relations which they cannot possibly assume" and though "*they* are our allies—ours is the battle." This inability existed even in well-intentioned whites who were the best of friends to the black oppressed. Sidney noted that the Albany conventioneers "neither preclude[d] the necessity, nor . . . [forbade] the action of . . . [their] friends" in their call for blacks to act on their own behalf. For the conventioneers, this course of action was not born so much of race pride as of "reason and common sense, and the testimony of history" (*Colored American* 6 Mar. 1841). He observed, concerning Northern blacks, "though not chattels yet we are slaves. . . . through successive generations, each and every succeeding one receiv[ed] to itself the accumulated sufferings and indignities of all the preceding . . . down to our times" (*Colored American* 13 Feb. 1841).

Suffering, then, was the common experience and thus the common bond of all blacks and that which prepared them for effective action to bring about their own freedom. The problem with such a claim can be seen in Charles Johnson's observation that oppression is shared across racial lines (19). For example, even though there were particulars to American slavery, native Americans, like blacks, were its victims. As Martin Delany would later argue concerning blacks and Native Americans, "we are identical as subjects of American wrongs, outrages and oppression, and therefore one in interest" (Stuckey, *Ideological Origins* 214–15). Oppression, then, was common to both, if in different forms. The oppression to which Sidney referred was seen as uniting *only* the black subject constituted in his discourse. A hundred years after Sidney's claim, W. E. B. Du Bois would argue that he shared a bond with Africa based on a shared history of discrimination. The basis for Du Bois's claim points, however, to the role of rhetoric for both Sidney and himself, for as he contends, the "social heritage of slavery; the discrimination and insult; . . . [this heritage] binds together not simply the children of Africa, but extends through yellow Asia and into the South Seas" (*Dusk* 17). Appiah, who believes that this bond is "based on a hyperbolic reading of the facts" asks, of Du Bois (and of Sidney), "How can something he shares with the whole nonwhite world bind him to a part of it?" (*My Father's* 42). From the perspective of a constitutive rhetoric, Sidney and, later, Du Bois rhetorically constituted subjects who were constrained and constructed within such narratives. These were not subjects based on "the facts" but those whose roles were to fulfill the demands of the narratives in which they were constituted.

Constitutive Rhetoric and Social Action

The insertion of the subject into the social world is the ultimate persuasive function of constitutive rhetorics. While Whipper, Sidney, James McCune Smith, Charles B. Ray, and others contested the nature of the black subject, their efforts were geared at persuading blacks. From the perspective of constitutive rhetoric, this process of persuasion is ultimately an effort to insert a particular kind of subject into the social world for action. As Maurice Charland argues, this is not a process of persuasion in the sense in which rhetorical theory has traditionally considered it. It is not a rational or free choice but a rhetorical process. The subject is created with a history, motives, and a *telos*. Thus to be constituted as a subject in a narrative is to be positioned for the fulfilling of a predetermined course of action within the discourse ("Constitutive Rhetoric" 140).

Sidney created a self-conscious black subject aware of unique and exclusive qualifications based on history, ancestry, and race discursively constituted by the rhetor. Blacks who connected with this self-identity through the Althusserian process of interpellation would be inserted into the social world of action, already with a commitment to a particular type of political conduct based on their characteristics. The textual nature of Sidney's subject is seen in Appiah's observation that for African Americans, claims of common bond based on shared oppression, African ancestry, or race totters at close examination (*My Father's* 42). Whipper's opposing point of view serves to highlight even more that the presumed qualifications advanced by both advocates are discursive creations, a function of rhetoric. Viewing Whipper's and Sidney's letters from the standpoint of constitutive rhetoric illuminates the rhetorical nature of their claims. Yet it does not deny their power to use discourse, culture, and history to convince targeted, partisan individuals that they are part of a unified, unproblematic subjectivity. The result was that blacks who identified with Sidney engaged in exclusive actions for black abolitionism, while those hailed by Whipper's discursive efforts would be guided by universal Christian principles to act in concert with whites.

The establishment of the identity and role of the collective black subject is at the heart of the contestation between Sidney's black nationalism and Whipper's more integrationist approach. The internal debate of the black abolitionist movement saw a shift from the earlier efforts that concentrated on establishing the common humanity of blacks and whites. Sidney sought to construct a collective black subject interpellating slaves and "free blacks" as one yet distinct from others such as whites. Whipper, in contrast, called into being a black subject who was one with whites who espoused the common cause of liberty and equality. Sidney's was a racialized subject constructed on the basis of blackness, a common African ancestry, and the shared experience of oppression. Whipper questioned the expediency of Sidney's proposal, which called for the subject to be the primary, if not exclusive, agent in the struggle for black liberation. Whipper proposed an idealistic, deracinated subject unified by universal Christian principles. Sidney sought to interpellate his black subject as a social activist in preference to the previously-taken-for-granted white social activist. Whipper sought to assimilate the new black subject into a role of collaborator with the already active white subject.

The dilemma of black liberation that emerges in the encounter of these two perspectives and in the discourse of the black activists remains a central issue in the study of black nationalism. The call for an exclusive black effort in the struggle for equality was as troublesome when it was first articulated by Lewis Woodson and Sidney as it is today. The contemporary problem is evident from the voices raised in opposition to Louis Farrakhan's 1995 instantiation of Sidney's nineteenth-century call. Black separatist programs have united and empowered blacks since at least the days of Young and Walker, with significant success, Marcus Garvey and Malcolm X being the two successful embodiments of this separatist approach. Questions remain as to the long-term effects and the usefulness of such programs for contemporary, multicultural American life.

The embracing of race faces significant obstacles; so, too, do the efforts to transcend race. The perspective of black and white collaboration advanced by Whipper, Smith, and Cornish is no less problematic than Sidney's separatism. With race as the primary marker shaping the lives of Americans, pushing blacks to the bottom and whites to the pinnacle, blacks challenge race-transcendent programs as flights from reality. In addition, the political baggage of conservatism, such as the insensitivity toward racism that comes with contemporary instantiations of this perspective, creates new and additional challenges for its twentieth-first-century advocates. The continued evidence of American racism and its degrading impact on blacks further fuels the cause of black nationalist ideology and of separatist calls.

Michael Eric Dyson discusses the state of black leadership and points to Farrakhan and Colin Powell, the former joint chief of staff and present secretary of state, as contemporary representatives of the two distinct perspectives in question here (*Race Rules* 150–95). Dyson sees the two men as representing "the divided mind of black America" (154). This perspective is subject to the long-standing critique that it frames black life within the narrow binary opposites of separatist and integrationist. Dyson is accurate and insightful, however, in his depiction of Powell's program as a desire to *transcend* race and Farrakhan's as a desire to *translate* race, both of which are cut from the same cloth and which fall short of the more progressive desire to *transform* race advocated by Dyson (154). Race cannot be glossed, ignored, or transcended in the United States, where its national tentacles are tangled in a racialized history, racialized politics, and racialized economics. To translate race into every issue, however, is to foreclose viable options for the future. Race must be acknowledged as a central factor of life in the United States, and a clear commitment must be made to transform our long-standing and problematic treatment of race with its discredited biological trace. Let's treat race as an opprobrious fact of history and fashion from it new ways of relating to each other without denying our differences in appearance, culture, and ethnicity.

Sidney wrote that black nationalist ideology developed as a necessary response to the debilitating physical conditions of oppression of nineteenth-century blacks. There was also the significant supporting cast of both subtle and explicit supremacist discourse from Anglo-Americans, both "friends" and foes in the South as well as the North. Black nationalist ideology, then, was born in the face of slavery and the explicit and crude white supremacist efforts to trample blacks while exploiting their services. It is strange that its evolution was aided in part by those who claimed to be friends of blacks working on their behalf. For while blacks were struggling over the construction of a positive identity for themselves, as is evident in the names debate, notwithstanding what they called themselves to their friends and their foes, they were, as Cornish notes, "nothing else but NEGROES"

(Ripley et al., *Black Abolitionist* 3: 263). As Litwack's work indicates, north of slavery was not synonymous with north of racism.

Still, the need for shared existence on common territory and the joint use of limited resources continue to foil separatist tendencies and forces a rethinking of Whipper's concept of common humanity. Transcendence and the efforts to elide difference in the name of "color blindness" will continue to be rejected within the context of an America where race matters. Perhaps, then, the acknowledgment and embrace of racial difference can be a first step in transforming "race" and building more functional American communities. Integral to such a program would be a cooperative, long-range effort to make sure that while race matters, it should not rule. Rhetoric's role may be in the open construction (i.e., open to participatory efforts beyond just dominant groups or cultures) or reconstruction of categories that, while they acknowledge difference, may be more inclusive and thus more useful than race has been in the framing of our lives. Both the transcendence and the embracing of race as we know it have proved to be unfruitful paths: The transformation of race may prove to be more productive.

Though futuristic and optimistic, this more inclusive approach is not beyond our grasp and is worth our best efforts. It took years of struggle among themselves and between themselves and Anglo-Americans before antebellum blacks could gain the basic acknowledgment of being human, as well as the right to begin the process of public self-definition. Significant gains were made through the 1840s, but blacks were still a long way from their goal of freedom and equality. As the next chapter reveals, the decade preceding the Civil War was marked by an intense struggle for black citizenship.

5
Black Nationalism Matures: The Black Subject as Public Citizen

You can plead your own cause, and do the work of emancipation better than any others. . . . Think of the undying glory that hangs around the ancient name of Africa: and forget not that you are native-born American citizens, and as such, you are justly entitled to all the rights that are granted to the freest.
—H. H. Garnet, *The Black Abolitionist Papers*

A free [N]egro does not become a citizen merely because he is free. Such a person is no more a citizen than an alien is a citizen.
—Thomas Cooper, *Two Essays*

The effort of nineteenth-century blacks to create a collective identity with an effective public voice was a slow, uncertain, and difficult process. Early efforts focused on establishing the common humanity of blacks and whites. The 1840s and 1850s saw a shift in focus. Building on the appeals and limited successes of earlier abolitionists, advocates moved beyond claiming freedom and equality based on their common humanity. They began to argue that blacks were citizens. For example, the primary emphasis of the first black state conventions, convened in 1840 and 1841, was on suffrage. These New York gatherings were also the first to declare their independence from white abolitionists and the first to send an appeal to the state legislature (Bell, *Survey* 66; Schor 48). Important to these developments were many outstanding black and white abolitionists, who urged America to live up to its promises delineated in the Declaration of Independence.

The black public voice was expressed in a range of fora, including black conventions, black and white abolitionist meetings, the black church, and many newspapers. Between 1840 and 1860, there were several signal moments in black abolitionism. This chapter is a study of three such moments. Three speeches can be identified as significant emblems of the social and political consciousness of Northern blacks who agitated for black liberation during this period. The speeches are Henry Highland Garnet's "Address to the Slaves of the United States of America (delivered before the National Convention of Colored Citizens, Buffalo, NY, August 16, 1843)," Frederick Douglass's "What to the Slave Is the Fourth of July?: An Address Delivered in Rochester, New York [to the Rochester ladies antislavery society], on July 5, 1852," and Martin Robison Delany's "The Political Destiny of the Colored Race, (a report to the delegates at the first National Emigration Conference in Cleveland, August, 1854)."

Garnet's "Address," the first expression of militant black nationalism from the platform of the National Negro Convention, was given by the premier black abolitionist of the pre-Douglass years and perhaps the most influential figure in antebellum America in "advancing black nationalist ideas and projects" (Brewer 43; Stuckey, *Ideological Origins* 17). Douglass, the acknowledged chief spokesman of nineteenth-century black America, whom Waldo Martin called "the quintessential Afro-American leader of his day," delivered "What to the Slave Is the Fourth of July?" (Litwack and Meier 60). This speech, arguably the best antislavery oration ever, represented a significant expression of hope in America amid the growing black despair that marked the 1850s (Blackett, *Building* 212; McFeely 173; Lucaites, "Irony" 49). The despair is evident in "The Political Destiny," delivered by Delany, the chief spokesman for emigration among blacks in the 1850s. This comprehensive statement of black nationalism represents the growing sentiment among Northern blacks that emigration was their only dignified option in the face of a reinforced Fugitive Slave Law. These speeches by the leading spokesmen of black abolitionism represent significant milestones in black self-definition and self-determination.

Examined here is the rhetorical articulation of black nationalist ideology in its most mature state during the antebellum period, as blacks, contending for citizenship, grappled with the implications of self-representation from their position of alienation. To illuminate the rhetorical articulation of this ideology, it is important to situate these speakers and speeches within the historical contexts of the symbolic, national political environment of the 1840s and 1850s. During this period, the already savage oppression of blacks and their exclusion from considerations of citizenship were exacerbated. An understanding of this period reveals the rhetorical constraints and potentials these rhetors faced as they sought acceptance as Americans. They battled the dominant Anglo-American, constitutional, political, and popular notions of what it meant to be included among the Declaration of Independence's constituted persona, "all men," and that of the Constitution, "we the people" (Condit and Lucaites 69). After the symbolic context in which these speeches emerged is established, they are examined to highlight their functioning as part of nineteenth-century black ideology. Rhetorical functionality within Garnet's "Address" and Delany's "Political Destiny" are compared, with Douglass's "What to the Slave Is the Fourth of July?" used as a foil. By rhetorical functionality, I mean the way rhetoric functions as it persuades through the creation of audiences.

Garnet and Delany's speeches reflect increasing black disaffection with America, as well as growth and dynamism in the black public voice. As an offshoot of the differing perspectives, rigorous challenges, and critical exchanges among people like Garnet, Douglass, and Delany, black public discourse developed more complexity, sophistication, and radicalism. In addition, setting Douglass's view of the black struggle as a reinterpretation of the meaning of America against Garnet's militant proposal and Delany's emigrationist stance allows one to tease out the tensions between the pacifist and the militant, the American and the African, and the consequent rhetorical problems created as part of the separatist and integrationist dialectic within abolitionism. Critical to these issues is the role of memory and the American Revolutionary tradition in the framing of a collective African American public voice. These speeches are significant milestones both in the effort to construct a collective black identity with an effective public voice and in the lives of Garnet, Delany, and Douglass. Each of these men lived complex and sophisticated public lives that spanned decades and included a multiplicity of perspectives. (Schor; Ullman; Blight; Gilroy 19–71). We begin, then, by contextualizing these speeches within antebellum America's larger public effort to negotiate expansionism, slavery, and the related constitutional questions about the role of the federal government and the rights of states. Always, the issue that could not be detruded was the place of blacks in American society.

1850s America: Enacting the Anglo Perspective and Alienating African Americans

Henry Highland Garnet was a prominent leader of the effort to create a collective black public voice throughout the two decades preceding the Civil War and, to a lesser degree, the two decades beyond it (Schor xi–xii). He was born into slavery in Maryland, 23 December 1815, but escaped at age nine, when his parents took him and his sister Eliza to Pennsylvania by way of the underground railroad. The family finally settled in New York (Crummell 273–77; Schor 4, 8–9; Mann 12). Garnet eventually earned an education in the classical tradition and rose to become an ordained minister (Schor 3–24; G. Williams

579). William Brewer contends that Garnet was equal to Douglass in ability and intellect and that he "created the idea which Frederick Douglass tempered and presented to the world in a more palliative and acceptable form" (Brewer 52). Garnet became the first pastor of the Liberty Street Negro Presbyterian Church of Troy, New York (Brewer 43). By 1843, he had risen to prominence in the antislavery movements of the North on the basis of his broad area of service as a minister, a home missionary, and an organizer of black political activists (Schor 30).[1] Garnet's "Address" was the keynote speech at the National Negro Convention in Buffalo, New York, in 1843. This gathering marked the relaunching of the National Negro Convention after a seven-year hiatus since the fifth annual convention held in Philadelphia in 1835 (Bell, *Minutes* i–vi; Aptheker, *Documentary* 1: 159).

Garnet was one of the leaders in the call for this revival, part of a broader effort for aggressive political action to abolish slavery. The push for political action was encouraged by the Liberty Party with its plan to contest the 1844 national elections on a strong abolitionist platform and to break new ground as the "first American organization to nominate and run black men for office" (Ripley et al., *Black Abolitionist* 3: 413; Quarles, *Black Abolitionists* 184–86; and Pease and Pease, *They Would Be Free* 189, 197, 201–2). Blacks in New York had also recently won some concessions, such as the support of Governor William Seward, who refused to deliver fugitive slaves sought by the South and who endorsed an act establishing jury trials for runaway slaves (*National Antislavery Standard* 3 June 1841; Quarles, *Black Abolitionists* 83; Schor 48). Another component of the black abolitionist revival was a call for black separatism (Schor 49). This call precipitated acrimonious debates over abolitionism (the Whipper-Sidney debate being the most notable among black abolitionists), and it is within this context that Garnet developed his insurgency perspective.[2]

Garnet's militant, nationalist rhetoric reflected his own alienation from and frustration with American society. This frustration and alienation were, in part, a result of more than a decade of black conventioneering, pleading, petitioning, and general appeals to America's spirit of liberty and equality with only limited success. As Benjamin Quarles indicates in *Black Abolitionists*, "the early abolitionist movement was by no means barren of accomplishment, as it had rescued hundreds of Negroes illegally held in bondage" (12). These black abolitionists, however, had not achieved their major goal, the establishment of black equality, or even the first major step, the abolition of slavery. They continued to feel excluded from America's experiment in republican democracy. Garnet himself had experienced the horrors of knowing that his family had been attacked and scattered by slave hunters in New York, where they had escaped to freedom from slavery (Crummell 273–77; Schor 8–9).

Ironically, black abolitionists also felt excluded by white abolitionists from the effort toward emancipation. The result was Garnet's "Address," which brought to the convention movement and to black public discourse as a whole a militancy that reflected the frustration of blacks at their limited successes. Chagrin and alienation were also a response to the broader problems of slavery and racism.

Though Garnet's "Address" was not the first to suggest this kind of militancy, his call from the national platform of the most significant black abolitionist public forum was a declaration of independence from white abolitionists and marked a turning point toward a more militant, independent, black abolitionism (*Liberator* 16 Dec. 1833). Garnet scoffed at moral suasion and the commitment to nonviolent action inscribed in the Garrison-shaped "Declaration of Sentiments" issued by the American Antislavery Society in 1833. Instead, he advanced an appeal to violence as a viable option for emancipation. Garnet's controversial perspective spawned numerous debates, mostly about his appeal to violence (Schor 54–58). For example, Carelton Mabee identifies Garnet's call as "an encouragement to violence" and not a direct appeal to the slaves to revolt (60). Garnet's call for black separatism was followed by more such calls, however, as events in the national body politic further fueled the black separatist impulse (Schor 59–64). The call for black independence highlighted the plight of blacks in the North, including those in the abolitionist movement, and affirmed independent black institutions. Black abolitionism and white abolitionism, however, remained interdependent in significant ways. White abolitionism continued use the experience, credibility, and moral appeal of blacks, while black abolitionism used the funding and resources of white abolitionists.

Nineteenth-century racism was neither monolithic nor omnipotent. It varied in mode and degree with social class and geographic location. There were also pockets of antiracist sentiments among whites. For example, in *Abolitionism,* Herbert Aptheker argues that though many white abolitionists were racists, a few notable figures practiced racial equality. Also, in *Anti-Racism in U.S. History,* Aptheker contends that significant antiracist sentiment existed among whites of the lower classes. From the 1828 election of Andrew Jackson to that of James Buchanan in 1856, however, the proslavery political force, which officially adopted the name Democrats in 1844, won all but the 1840 and 1848 presidential elections (Beard, Beard, and Beard 239). From the John Tyler administration, beginning in 1841, through that of James Buchanan, ending in 1861, American expansionism often went hand in hand with the expansion of slavery, the promotion of popular sovereignty, and the continued exclusion of the black public voice. Proslavery expansionism was most obvious in the annexation of Texas; the war with Mexico, which resulted in the acquisition of the vast territory of New Mexico and California; and the acceptance of Kansas and Nebraska into the Union. The congressional rejection of the effort to prohibit slavery in the territories acquired during the Mexican War in 1846 and the political fallout of the Wilmot Proviso over the question of slavery in territories being considered as new states led to the Compromise of 1850. Important proslavery elements in this compromise were the strengthening of the 1793 Fugitive Slave Law and the promotion of popular sovereignty (Hopkins).

Even worse was the Stephen Douglas–led Kansas-Nebraska Act of 30 May 1854, which repealed the Missouri Compromise. This act pointed to popular sovereignty for settling the issue of slavery in new territories, with Congress committed to nonintervention. The repeal of the Missouri Compromise led to the formation of the Republican Party by some Northerners, including Whigs, Democrats, and Free-Soilers, all seeking to halt the spread of slavery in the territories (Beard, Beard, and Beard 251).

Two Supreme Court decisions were also important in this proslavery trend: *Prigg v. Pennsylvania,* which acknowledged the federal government's right to maintain slavery and thus upheld the Fugitive Slave Law, and later, *Dred Scott v. Sandford,* which declared the Missouri Compromise unconstitutional. Schor notes that *Prigg v. Pennsylvania* may have influenced Garnet toward the acceptance of violence (53). *Dred Scott v. Sandiford* undergirded popular sovereignty and government nonintervention in slavery in new territories and became a key factor in protests against the advance of Southern "slave power."[3] The effect on blacks was devastating. There was a pronounced increase in expeditions by slave hunters into Northern states to return or bring into slavery not only fugitive slaves in the North but free blacks as well. Northern blacks responded to the threat to their safety by holding "rallies, organiz[ing] vigilance committees and private militias, rais[ing] funds for the defense of alleged fugitives, and vow[ing] to resist slave catchers and federal efforts to enforce the law" (Quarles, *Black Abolitionists* 197–222, 229; Ripley et al., *Black Abolitionist* 4: 98–101). Prior to the *Dred Scott* decision, blacks considered the North, even with its debilitating racism, a refuge where fugitive slaves were relatively safe from such bounty hunters. Northern blacks now lived in greater fear as they realized, "'there is no North'; for there is none. The South goes clear up to the Canada line" (Carleton 20).

In addition, the Liberty Party, which contested the 1844 elections on the strong abolitionist platform of opposition to slavery in the states and territories, was rejected by the electorate when it received only sixty-two thousand votes (Beard, Beard, and Beard 250; Ripley et al., *Black Abolitionist* 3: 413–15). Because of its commitment to emancipation and racial equality, the Liberty Party had attracted blacks and won the support of black leaders such as Garnet, Charles B. Ray, and Samuel Ringgold Ward. It had also received the endorsement of the

Buffalo Convention and was viewed as an important vehicle for black political action toward abolition (Ripley et al., *Black Abolitionist* 3: 403, 413–15).

Through their participation in the Liberty Party, blacks like Garnet worked with white abolitionists who promoted the radical notion that the Constitution was an antislavery document.[4] To the distress of Garnet and other black advocates, however, the black cause was rebuffed at every level of American society. All branches of the federal government were dominated by white supremacist perspectives. In 1857, during Buchanan's presidency, for example, the Democrats had a majority in the Senate and the House of Representatives, and the Supreme Court had a majority of Democratic appointees (Beard, Beard, and Beard 249). During this period, then, black alienation was perhaps at its highest point in antebellum America. Northern blacks had their faith in America shaken to the core (Blight 1). Increasingly, it seemed there was no place in America for blacks beyond slavery. Responding to these developments, more and more black leaders promoted separatism and emigration as the only options for American blacks to live dignified lives.

The idea of emigration had an intermittent and uncertain history among nineteenth-century African Americans (Bell, "Negro Emigration" 132–42). Through the first three decades of the century, black leaders had largely rejected it as a viable option. With the developments of the 1840s and 1850s, however, and with blacks becoming more disconcerted about the possibility of a viable future in America, Northern blacks were increasingly considering their fortunes in places like Liberia, Haiti, the British West Indies, and California. Both the Liberian declaration of independence in 1847 and the 1850 Missouri Compromise undergirded this trend toward emigration (Bell, "Negro Emigration" 132–33). Up to this time, few outstanding black leaders had supported it, but in 1849, while still opposed to the American Colonization Society's notion that blacks could not rise to equality in America, Garnet publicly recognized emigration as a legitimate option for blacks (*North Star* 26 Jan. and 2 Mar. 1849; Bell, "Negro Emigration" 133–34; Bell, Introduction 7). In 1858, Garnet became president of the newly formed African Civilization Society, committed to the exploration of Africa as a place for black emigration. In black public discourse, the 1850s became "a feverish decade of proposals and counterproposals relating to emigration" (Delany and Campbell 7). By 1861, "'no Negro leader of first rank, with the possible exception of George Downing, was publicly championing the traditional stay-at-home-at-any-cost beliefs; most of them did not look unfavorably upon emigration—or championed it as the true road to progress'" (Bell, *Survey* 223; Schor 144–45). One leader in the emigrationist movement was Martin Robison Delany.

Delany is identified by Robert Levine as "an abolitionist, editor, doctor, novelist, political theorist, inventor, explorer, orator, and judge." Delany, like David

Walker, was born free, the son of a free woman and a plantation slave. He was taken by his mother from his birthplace, Charles Town, Virginia, to Pennsylvania under threat of arrest for her efforts to teach her children to read. In 1831, Delany began studying with Lewis Woodson, a strong early advocate for black self-determination. Delany went on to become editor of an early African American newspaper, the *Mystery*. Then for eighteen months, he co-edited the *North Star* with Frederick Douglass. He also attended Harvard's medical school but was kicked out of the program because of racism. In 1856, he moved to Canada, and in 1859, he visited the Niger valley as part of a program of African American settlement in West Africa. When this effort failed in 1862, he supported the war effort and recruited troops for the Union army. After the demise of Reconstruction, he returned to his efforts at African emigration, a program he pursued to the end of his life (Levine 2, 3). Earlier however, Delany, like Garnet, had been an outspoken opponent of emigration. As late as 1851, he still maintained that "the American Negro should not be lured away to lands beyond the bounds of the United States, not even Canada" (*Voice of the Fugitive;* Bell, "Negro Emigration" 134). In 1852, however, he established himself as the leading black voice for emigration with the publication of *The Condition, Elevation, Emigration and Destiny of the Colored People of the United States* (Ripley et al., *Black Abolitionist* 4: 126). This book outlined Delany's nationalist alternative to the integration efforts of blacks, led by Douglass, then the leading black spokesman. Douglass and Delany had worked together on Douglass's *North Star,* but during the 1850s, they shared sharp disagreements. Emigration and differing interpretations of Harriet Beecher Stowe's *Uncle Tom's Cabin* were two primary points of contention. Douglass viewed the text as pointing to potential black development in America, while Delany rejected it as the product of a racist colonizer (Levine 2–17). Emigration, which was popular among black abolitionists who viewed the Constitution as a proslavery document, continued to gain popularity, with even Douglass, the leading opponent, considering public endorsement, a move interrupted by the Civil War (Aptheker, *Documentary* 1: 363; Schor 144–45).

Against this backdrop, 102 delegates gathered on 24–26 August 1854 for the first National Emigration Conference in Cleveland, Ohio.[5] From the platform of this conference, Delany presented "The Political Destiny of the Colored Race," a condensed version of his 1852 book. This "most trenchant statement on black nationalism" is Delany's articulation of the collective black consciousness during this tense, aggressive march of Southern slave power (Stuckey, *Ideological Origins* 22). Delany's statement reflects the sense of alienation and lack of faith in America among many Northern blacks in the 1850s, who lived under the daily threat of abduction into slavery (Delany and Campbell 2). Delany's "Political Destiny" is an expansion of Garnet's perspective delivered twelve years later and, as such, bears comparison with it. Not every black abolitionist shared Garnet and Delany's militancy. In presenting his radical perspective at the Buffalo Convention, Garnet faced objections from black and white Garrisonians. Among them was Douglass, Garnet's chief black opponent. Douglass based his opposition on Garrisonian moral suasion and his proslavery characterization of the Constitution. As Douglass himself indicated, even as he planned to break with Garrison and launch the *North Star,* he was still "the known and distinguished advocate" promoting the principle of nonvoting based on the Garrisonian notion of the proslavery character of the Constitution (Douglass, *Life* 265–66).

Douglass escaped from slavery in Maryland in 1838. He settled first in New Bedford, Massachusetts, but after four years, moved to Lynn, Massachusetts. Between 1847 and 1872, Douglass lived in Rochester, New York. Working closely with Garrison, he soon became one of the leaders of the abolitionist movement in the North and was involved in almost every black convention of the period. After several disagreements between Douglass and the Garrisonians, a formal break in the relationship came in 1852 (P. Foner 59). Douglass's long and distinguished public career lasted from 1841 to his death in 1895. He made significant contributions as an orator, writer, and journalist. Douglass, Garnet, and Delany were among the top antislavery spokesmen of antebellum America. They, along with others such as William Wells Brown, Charles Remond, and J. C. W. Pennington, were part of the abolitionist vanguard that sought international support for the antislavery effort in America mainly through lecture tours in Britain.[6]

After his break with Garrison, Douglass reversed his perspective and argued that the Constitution did not support slavery. The break between Douglass and Garrison began in 1847 when Douglass moved from Lynn, Massachusetts, with its strong Garrisonian sentiment, to Rochester, New York, where there was strong support for a more strident political activism. The break was complete in 1851 when Douglass declared his opinion changed ("Change of Opinion"; Lucaites, "Irony" 55). As Douglass recalls, he concluded that the Constitution "was in its letter and spirit an antislavery instrument, demanding the abolition of slavery as a condition of its own existence, as the supreme law of the land" (*Life and Times* 266). The interpretation of the Constitution was the fulcrum on which national political issues turned. Debates of the issues that dominated American politics in nineteenth-century antebellum America, such as tariffs, banking, internal improvements, land distribution, and slavery, focused on constitutional interpretations and revealed sectional divisions between the North and the South. On the national scene, the two dominant perspectives were sharply framed in the 1830 Senate debate between Daniel Webster of Massachusetts, who advanced the predominance of the Union, and Robert Y. Hayne of South Carolina, who argued that the nation was a league of sovereign states. The latter view was championed by John Calhoun, also from South Carolina, who was then vice president to Jackson and, as such, presided in the Senate (Willis 127–28). A sharp divide between factions was especially evident in the political contests between Whigs and Democrats during the two decades prior to the Civil War. Democrats, who represented Southern interests, promoted a narrow interpretation of the Constitution, advocated states rights, and interpreted the Constitution as a proslavery document. By contrast, Whigs, who represented Northern interests, advanced a broad interpretation of the Constitution and argued for more power for Congress and for its right to control slavery in the territories (Beard, Beard, and Beard 236–48). Among abolitionists, the divide was equally acute. The Constitution was either "a sacred instrument" or "a covenant with death and an agreement with hell" (Ripley et al., *Black Abolitionist* 3: 442–45).

Douglass's conversion to the view that the Constitution was a "sacred instrument" meant that he could take a more effective political stance in opposition to proslavery sentiments. An antislavery interpretation of the Constitution meant that in their appeal for black equality, abolitionists could free themselves from the bind of having to circumvent the Constitution and appeal to the prior status of the Declaration of Independence and to a greater good (R. Cover 128, 133–35; McDorman 197). The appeal to the Declaration of Independence faced the effective rebuttal that it was not a legal document. In addition, the antislavery interpretation of the Constitution allowed for a jettisoning of the position that the nation was hopelessly committed to slavery from its very foundations, a potential dead end for blacks contending for a place in America (R. Cover 155; McDorman 197). This perspective that slavery was anomalous to American democracy allowed for a rhetorical challenge to the proslavery argument that presumed a symbiotic relationship between slavery and republican democracy.[7] This symbiotic relationship, first advanced by Charles Jared Ingersoll in his 1810 tract *Inchiquin, the Jesuit Letters* and institutionalized in Robert Walsh's *Appeal,* was central to the arguments of Southern elected officials such as Calhoun and Hayne (Tise, *Proslavery* 42–43; Lochemes 89). With this antislavery interpretation of the Constitution, abolitionists could claim that the perpetuation of slavery was a contemporary choice made by proslavery supporters in distortion of the legal foundation of the nation. Douglass best expressed his antislavery perspective of the Constitution and his hopeful approach to black inclusion in America in his "What to the Slave Is the Fourth of July?"

Within abolitionism, Douglass's change meant that he became a part of the active African American voice, including Garnet's, that pressured Northern white abolitionists to push the nation more aggressively to live up to its legal responsibility as outlined in the Constitution (Lucaites, "Irony" 55). Even so, Douglass's construction of the collective identity of blacks was different from the separatist sentiments expressed by both Garnet and Delany. Unlike separatism, which looked outside white America (and in some cases, outside the United States) for the development of dignified, black citizenship, Douglass confronted white America with its failure to acknowledge African American citizenship (55). Robert Cover's discussion of how marginalized groups such as abolitionists rearticulated legal decisions to fit their discourse communities, especially his distinction between marginalized efforts to build insular communities and efforts to engage in redemptive constitutionalism (95–172), serves as a point of entry into the distinctions between Garnet and Delany on the one hand and Douglass on the other.[8]

Cover argues that in the face of the perpetuation of slavery, especially the upholding of the Fugitive Slave Law, Garrisonians who strove for perfection gave up on any possibility of transformation. They gave up on the possibility that their participation in America under the government of the time could remove the scourge of slavery from the nation's life. They therefore chose "nomian insularity." In contrast, Douglass's "What to the Slave Is the Fourth of July?" demonstrated his commitment to redemptive constitutionalism. Nomian insularity identifies the notion of a minority community that frames itself within a narrative that sets it apart from the larger community, including its laws. Small communities choose nomian insularity when they believe the laws governing the majority neither reflect nor respect the history and stories of their community. Such laws are viewed as unjust, with inherent biases against the minority community. Their choice, then, is not to participate. Redemptive constitutionalism embraces the notion that the laws and the constitution are not inherently unjust but are applied unjustly. Minority communities facing such injustice practice redemptive constitutionalism when they seek to reform the system from within. Unlike Garrisonians who focused on the reality of American practices, Douglass stressed his experience as an escaped slave, transferring that experience into a vision of redemption for the nation and blacks in particular. Douglass's plan was to campaign for transformation and to help create the nation's public life.

Garnet's "Address" and Delany's "Political Destiny" represent a retreat from any effort to create "a general and public *nomos*" (R. Cover 133–36). Their disengagement from the state in their effort to redeem black life bore significant differences from that of abolitionists like Garrison and Wendell Phillips, but there are enough similarities for a viable comparison (R. Cover 134).[9] The concern of Garnet and Delany was the plight of blacks, and initially both were willing to strive for a place for the collective black voice in the general American *nomos*. Like the Garrisonians, though, continuously rebuffed by slavery's enduring character, they retreated to alternative measures. Garnet called for violent action, and Delany promoted emigration. Both promoted insularity by withdrawing from the effort to transform American public behavior in general and turning to the shaping of their particular communities.

Garnet's "Address" and Delany's "Political Destiny" as Constitutive Rhetorics of Black Ideology

This chapter extends the various treatments of Douglass's "What to the Slave Is the Fourth of July?," Garnet's "Address," and Delany's "Political Destiny" by focusing on nineteenth-century black identity.[10] These three speeches functioned as constitutive rhetorics and, as such, were significant responses to the then contemporary problem of establishing an effective, collective black identity. In addition to signifying the turning away from white abolitionism, Garnet's "Address" marks a milestone in the development of a black nationalist constitutive rhetoric begun in Robert Alexander Young's *Ethiopian Manifesto* and David Walker's *Appeal.* In a similar way, Delany's "Political Destiny" was part of the black ideological system of production. In short, these three documents were important parts of the emerging effort to create an effective, independent, collective, black public voice.

To counter the predominantly white narrative of dominance, which held that blacks had no history or culture before or beyond slavery, Garnet and Delany, like Young, Walker, and Sidney before them, presented their speeches as a new narrative with a reconstituted black history. Garnet also posited a new identity for blacks in his speech, although in so doing he went beyond Young and Walker's limited perspective of constituting blacks as different from their interpellation in proslavery narrative. Going further, Garnet incorporated the black collective subject as different from their constitution in the antislavery discourse of white, Northern abolitionists, which portrayed them as dependent on others for their development. In this new history, blacks were constituted as a people of African descent. They were one, without the distinction of "slave" and "free" and with a common ancestry and a common past.

In Garnet's narrative, heroism, cultural achievements, and laudable acts of resistance were part of the collective and continuous heritage of American blacks. Garnet posited this collective black subject to advance his political agenda of militant resistance to slavery and white domination. He interpellated blacks in his narrative notwithstanding barriers of time, place, and space. Garnet presented blacks as a free people. As a consequence, blacks held in slavery were called on to claim their freedom, and those in the North were encouraged to exercise their independence by rejecting the white abolitionist agenda of moral suasion advanced by the Garrisonians.

Delany continued Garnet's narrative by similarly fixing the identity of black people as a distinct collective with the right to determine their own fate. In "The

Political Destiny," Delany presented a comprehensive statement to the black community, outlining what for him was "the improbability of realizing our desires, and the sure, practicable, and infallible remedies for the evils we now endure" (Stuckey, *Ideological Origins* 195). In this statement, Delany delineated perhaps the most demanding call for black citizenship in this period. It went beyond the call for black suffrage and demanded full citizenship and equality within the context of black separatism. For Delany, "[a] people to be free must necessarily be *their own rulers,*" and therefore freedom for blacks required black autonomy (197). With this conviction, Delany extended Garnet's notion of blacks as a special people and advanced the concept that blacks in the United States were a nation within a nation who should therefore reject all efforts toward integration and work instead for autonomy and independence. Delany's "Political Destiny," then, was a continuation of Garnet's new rhetoric.

The three speeches by Garnet, Delany, and Douglass under consideration here make up a discourse that was constitutive in that it was concerned with the rhetorical transformation of persons into a collective entity or subject. This subject was then identified as being united in such a way as to elide divisions of interests, age, class, et cetera. Though this was not functionally true of blacks in either the North or the South, it was an important rhetorical strategy, for it authenticated the goal of presenting blacks as one people within the narrative. To ideologically advance the cause of black liberation, a part of which is the privileging of "black people" and their narratives, these advocates presented the collectives they constructed as natural.

The critical role of rhetoric in ideological programs such as those of Garnet, Delany, and Douglas is highlighted in their efforts to define "black people" rhetorically as part of a collectivization process. Neither the "Address," "The Political Destiny," nor "What to the Slave" used the terms "the people" or "the public." Yet Garnet, Delany, and Douglass did organize various beliefs from within the African American culture into political myths and presented them in an effort to call a black public or people into being as a means of legitimizing the goal of their new black narrative. Such a rhetoric was presented with the expectation that its black audience would complete the collectivization process. Public advocates like Garnet, Delany, and Douglass functioned, then, as the "flag-bearers" for the old longings of black America for political freedom and individual autonomy (McGee, "In Search" 240, 243).

In viewing these speeches as constitutive rhetorics, we see the crucial, continuing struggle over interpellation. Here Garnet, Delany, and Douglass sought to construct a narrative in which blacks were inscribed in a way different from their role in the traditional Anglo-American narrative. This rhetoric, in which black people were constituted as active, heroic, and united, ideologically highlighted black alienation and pointed blacks toward an activism that would help to bring about their own liberation. This is at once the rhetorical construction of black subjectivity and persuasion through identification. It is persuasion that relies on rhetoric to identify individual blacks with each other and, for Douglass, blacks with whites, making them consubstantial (Burke, *Rhetoric* 49–59, 62; Charland, "Constitutive Rhetoric" 133). Where such identification occurred, a desired by-product was the reconstruction of the social relations of reproduction in nineteenth-century America with dignified black citizens as its end product.

The New Narrative

Garnet's "Address": Confronting Alienation Through Separatism

Garnet's "Address" was an effort to engage black alienation as the primary focus for blacks. Garnet presented his "Address" as a direct statement to Southern blacks, with the convention audience framed as bystanders overhearing the monologue. He thus addressed an exclusively black audience, with all whites excluded. This speech, then, was a rejection of white domination, as Garnet broke free of the Garrisonian tradition of appealing to whites. The structure of the speech bears out this emphasis on black alienation as the basis for black action. Garnet began by establishing that he was speaking directly to Southern blacks, something that he contended had not been done before. This lack of even "a word of consolation and advice," he claimed, was part of the Northern self-centered focus that distanced Southern blacks from the liberation effort.

Second, he established the bonds shared by blacks in the North and those in the South. Third, he identified slavery as the cause for the division between Northern and Southern blacks, pointing to this white domination as having "fixed a deep gulf between you and us." He then established both the guilt and the hypocrisy of Anglo-Americans in their practice of slavery by characterizing them as "men calling themselves Christians . . . influenced by avarice and lust" who doomed "the first of our inured race" by forcing them into "unrequited toil and deep degradation."

Finally, Garnet pointed blacks to the acknowledgment of their alienation by contending that they should not submit to the degradation of slavery as their natural, Christian duty, as whites maintained. To do so, Garnet argued, was "sinful in the extreme." On the basis of their right to freedom, then, Garnet encouraged those held in slavery to "so torment the God-cursed slaveholders that they [would] be glad to let you go free" (Ripley et al., *Black Abolitionist* 3: 404, 407, 410).

Garnet's was a rhetorical effort to constitute and thereby unite blacks in America. He challenged the description of blacks in earlier, proslavery discourse as slaves or free blacks. These descriptions circumscribed blacks to a subservient role. The language of master versus slave and superior versus subordinate inherent in these designators was a concrete aspect of the black experience. The term "slave" carried with it the notion that blacks remain compliant, subservient, and acquiescent to the status quo. As slaves, blacks were property and therefore required to acknowledge that their owners always retained a position of superiority. Of course, these slave owners were primarily white.[11] This discourse, along with the related social conditions, ensured black alienation. Garnet's speech was an effort to manipulate this black experience toward emancipation. My redescription of "free blacks" simply as "Northern blacks" and "Southern slaves" as "Southern blacks" is an effort to show that the distinctions between "freedom" and "slavery" were called into question by Garnet's, Delany's, and Douglass's narratives.

The designators and distinctions created in the different narratives are important because blacks had to be constructed as both human *and* united to be able to act as subjects in their own liberation. Expressing an awareness of this necessity, Garnet's speech continued the earlier black struggles that sought to establish the humanity of blacks shared in common with whites. This continuation was part of the effort to challenge the naturalized social structure presented by whites and to portray blacks as able subjects in the effort toward freedom. Garnet's "Address" presented slavery and the general abjection and oppression of blacks as inconsistent with Americans for whom the call "liberty or death" motivated "thousands to fight in the holy cause of freedom." Slavery and the effort to make the sufferers content with it were, in Garnet's words, "the highest crime against God and man" (Ripley et al., *Black Abolitionist* 3: 406, 407).

Consistent with Young and Walker in their challenge to the narrative of oppression, Garnet identified all blacks as united by the bonds of oppression. To warrant social action against slavery and oppression, this new black narrative constructed blacks as united in their common humanity and called them into being as a collective on the basis of the common experience of suffering in America. Blacks in both North and South were identified as one because of their shared American experience of oppression and their common ancestry. This is different from what we shall see with Douglass where black alienation was employed to establish the commonality blacks shared with pre-Revolutionary American colonists alienated by Britain. The rhetorical nature of Garnet's strategy is highlighted by Sterling Stuckey's observation that in the early nineteenth century, some Northern blacks sought to distance themselves from Southern blacks identified as African and thus degraded (*Slave Culture* 204–11).

Garnet naturalized the notion of a shared experience of oppression by illustrating how blacks in the North experienced the sufferings of those in the South. He noted, "[W]hile you have been oppressed, we have also been partakers with you; nor can we be free while you are enslaved" (Ripley et al., *Black Abolitionist* 3: 405). This naturalization masked the rhetorical effect of the narrative. If blacks accepted their common link as presented in this rhetorical transaction, they would be likely to complete the process of identification and thus be constituted as a "people." Another consequence of this naturalization would be to acknowledge the proposed solution of self-liberation through united black engagement.

Garnet's "Address" not only sought to naturalize the connection of blacks through the common experience of oppression but also presented this experience as naturally qualifying blacks to act as subjects on their own behalf. Furthermore, he saw such action as the necessary and sufficient condition for the removal of bondage. In Garnet's view, oppression would be removed only when the oppressed rose up and took action. Garnet's view was thus consistent with Sidney's perspective expressed in his "Four Letters" in his invocation of Lord Byron's famous dictum, "'if hereditary bondmen would be free they must themselves strike the blow'" (Schor 55; Ripley et al., *Black Abolitionist* 3: 408).

What Garnet did not acknowledge was that the militant black subject ready to strike out for freedom on behalf of the duly constituted "black people" was purely fictive. This subject was a rhetorical construct, part of Garnet's ideological program of black nationalism accented, for example, by the difficulty faced by John Brown in his effort to recruit militant blacks and to gain the endorsement of black leaders, including Garnet and Douglass, as part of his 1859 violent offensive against slavery (Schor 60–1; Oates, *To Purge* 211–12). There was no ready, militant army of blacks available to fight for emancipation. The effective functioning of Garnet's rhetoric, however, turned on the fact that there were militant individuals looking to work for black liberation. These individuals were sporadic and in no way an organized, unified, or representative group. Yet, as a collective within Garnet's narrative, this militant force was potent.

It is understandable that Garnet's rhetorical choice stood in contrast to the subservient and impotent black subject of white supremacist discourse such as one finds in Walsh's *Appeal* and Thornton Stringfellow's "Bible Argument." Garnet's black subject also differed, however, from the black subject of the discourse of mainly white Northern abolitionists. They operated with the generally accepted view advanced by William Whipper in his "Letters" that blacks were unable to bring about their own emancipation and thus were dependent on Northern white advocacy for such liberation. The "Address" contested this view. Garnet called these abolitionists agents of black alienation. He argued that their efforts to achieve emancipation were ineffective, kept blacks from obtaining their own freedom, and furthered alienation.

Garnet characterized the efforts of Northern abolitionists this way:

> Your brethren of the North, East and West have been accustomed
> to meet to sympathize with each other, and to weep . . . we have
> addressed all classes of the free . . . we have never sent a word of
> consolation and advice to you. We have been contented in sitting
> still . . . earnestly hoping. But, we have hoped in vain. (Ripley et al.,
> *Black Abolitionist* 3: 403, 405)

This characterization accused Northern abolitionism of alienating Southern blacks
by engaging others as liberating subjects in the abolitionist cause while leaving these
blacks as helpless recipients of external aid. In Garnet's view, such a plan could not
result in the liberation of blacks, the supposed goal of this program. Rather, Northern whites were invoking the demon of the North, racial prejudice, and as Walker
had argued earlier, blacks needed to act on their own behalf because the efforts of
whites were not good enough. Garnet rejected the Northern abolitionists' approach
and argued that because of their experience of oppression, blacks were uniquely
qualified to act as subjects on their own behalf. He therefore called upon them
as a people to agitate for the freedom denied them in both the South and the
North by the twin demons of slavery and racial prejudice. "The Political Destiny" was also a call for blacks to take radical action on their own behalf. Frederick
Douglass, too, pointed to white hypocrisy, but as we shall see, he expressed hope
in his call to a white audience to acknowledge black citizenship.

Delany's "Political Destiny": The Biological and Social Bases of Separatism

"The Political Destiny" sought to convince blacks that they had no future in
America and that emigration was their best choice. Delany began his report by
establishing that blacks could never gain the privileges of *"citizenship"* or *"freemen"* because of their color, for "such privileges have never been enjoyed by any
colored man in the United States." Here, Delany rejected instances of black suffrage, available, for example, in New York, as evidence of citizenship, claiming
that such instances were never independent of whites, for "the suffrage of the black
man, independently of the white, would be in this country unavailable." He then
rejected proposals for integration as representing a loss of identity for blacks as a
distinct race, for "universal Anglo-Saxon predominance" was being propagated
as "universal brotherhood." The second and major portion of the report focused
on the "native characteristics peculiar to our [black] race" that establish black
superiority. Third, Delany argued that blacks in the United States would never
be able to exert the necessary political pressure to create legislation to change their
deplorable condition, "fixed by legal grades of distinction," because of their "nu-
merical feebleness" (Stuckey, *Ideological Origins* 195, 197, 202, 203, 223). The
final section of the report thus focused on emigration as the ultimate remedy.

In this report, Delany treated race in a caustic but coherent manner, showing race-based privilege among whites by contrasting it with black degradation. Delany posited that black separatism was based on biological essentialism and social survival. For Delany, blacks were inherently distinct from and superior to whites, but nineteenth-century blacks were degraded because of oppressive white customs and social practices. Thus he argued, "Among the whites, their color is made, by law and custom, the mark of distinction and superiority; while the color of the blacks is a badge of degradation, acknowledged by statute, organic law, and the common consent of the people." These manifestations, in Delany's view, were symptoms of a disease, a white pathology, and for him there was no cure that would allow for black and white coexistence. He therefore declared, "[T]he remedy is emigration." The purpose of this policy was, in the first place, to separate blacks from whites, for whom "[N]egro-hate [was] inseparable from their very being." More important, Delany believed this move allowed for the establishment of a nationality based on "the elementary principle of original identity"—black identity (Stuckey, *Ideological Origins* 199, 200, 201). For Delany, separation was necessary because black survival depended on such a move.

Delany presented black subordination in the United States as having a deleterious effect on black progeny, and as such, it ensured continued black dependence. The cycle had to be broken. Delany believed this would not be done through amalgamation with whites as "Americans." It could be achieved only through separation: "The truth is we are not identical with the Anglo-Saxon or any other race of the Caucasian or pure white type of the human family, and the sooner we know and acknowledge this truth the better for ourselves and posterity" (202). Delany's speech thus hailed a black subject who was distinctly different from and shared little in common with whites. This subject was in contrast to that of Douglass who used black and white difference ironically to establish commonalities.

Delany was unapologetic in his encomium to blackness and unsurpassed in his affirmation, which is worth repeating here:

> We have, then, inherent traits, attributes, so to speak, and native characteristics, peculiar to our race, whether pure or mixed blood; and all that is required of us is to cultivate these, and develop them in their purity, to make them desirable and emulated by the rest of the world.
>
> That the colored races have the highest traits of civilization, will not be disputed. They are civil, peaceable, and religious to a fault. In mathematics, sculpture and architecture, as arts and sciences, commerce and internal improvements as enterprises, the white race may probably excel; but in languages, oratory, poetry, music and paint-

ing, as arts and sciences, and in ethics, metaphysics, theology, and legal jurisprudence—in plain language, in the true principles of morals, correctness of thought, religion, and law or civil government, there is no doubt but the black race will yet instruct the world. (203)

This characterization of blackness reflected Delany's overall perspective about blacks and whites and his relationship to both. This perspective was illustrated in a 10 July 1852 letter to Douglass, which was excerpted by Victor Ullman as the opening statement for his biography of Delany. After excoriating Douglass for heaping upon his book (*The Condition,* sent to Douglass in May 1852 but passed over without comment by the *Frederick Douglass Paper*) "cold and deathly silence" unlike he supposedly would, had a white person sent it to him, Delany declared defiantly: "I care little but what white men think of what I say, write or do; my sole desire is to benefit the colored people; this being done, I am satisfied—the opinion of every white person in the country or the world, to the contrary notwithstanding" (Ripley et al., *Black Abolitionist* 4: 126–30; *Frederick Douglass' Paper;* Ullman ix).

Delany's challenge that white progress was usurpation of black rights and his general indictment of white aggression extended Walker's earlier characterization of whites as base and aggressive. It also set the tone for black separatist notions of whites as evil and devilish, a notion that has achieved its ultimate manifestation in Elijah Muhammad's brand of black nationalism (C. Johnson 28–29; Muhammad). Delany's nationalism was one of direct confrontation between blacks and whites. As Delany saw it, "for more than two thousand years, the determined aim of whites has been to crush the colored races wherever found." Blacks should, then, be ready to "meet them on vantage ground, or, at least with adequate means for the conflict" (Stuckey, *Ideological Origins* 204).

In addressing whether to share common cause with whites for black progress, Delany acknowledged the political potency of numbers: "Were the interest of the common people identified with ours, we, in this, might succeed, because we, as a class, would then be numerically superior." This struggle, as Delany saw it, however, was "not a question of the rich against the poor, nor the common people against the higher classes, but a question of white against black." For Delany, "the great issue, sooner or later, upon which must be disputed the world's destiny, will be a question of black and white" (223, 203). Delany's notion of the color line as a crucial political issue anticipated W. E. B. Du Bois, who receives most of credit for this perceptive, if not prophetic, observation.

Here are highlighted the insight, decisiveness, and probable pitfall of black separatist thinking. Black separatism identifies color as the central problem of American life with disastrous implications, especially for blacks. It acknowledges the potency of establishing common cause with whites and points to the strategic advantage of constructing the black cause as being in the self-interest of whites but chooses a path of separatism. The rejection of class for color has robbed black nationalism of an important facet of collaboration across color lines. The nefarious conditions that they faced cannot be denied, and from the perspective of black separatists, theirs was a noble choice between racial pride and degradation. Yet while this strategy fostered internal cohesion within the sympathetic elements of the black communities, it also distanced them from potential collaborators who were not black and from the larger American community, including blacks who questioned separatist sentiments. As our discussion of Douglass's "What to the Slave Is the Fourth of July?" will reveal, there were other options. Mark McPhail contends in his *Rhetoric of Racism* that the rhetoric of negative difference serves to reinscribe rather than negate racism even as it reveals the problematic move toward essentialist notions of black and white identity. Shelby Steele puts his critique differently. In *The Content of Our Character,* he asks, "Doesn't an insistence on black power call up white power"? (19, 20). The legitimacy of the black separatist approach continues to be debated. There are no easy answers, however, especially given that the black nationalism of Malcolm X, for example, declares the United States' experiment of integration a failed one. Still others argue that the effort toward integration was never undertaken with any commitment on the part of whites (Hochschild 46–145).

Undergirding the effort of nineteenth-century black abolitionists to mobilize fellow blacks to work toward liberation was the haunting awareness that "the rights of no oppressed people have ever been obtained by a voluntary act of justice on the part of the oppressors." Delany pointed insightfully to self-interest as the primary motivation for voluntary acts of justice by oppressors. While these acts may occur, "they are always actuated by the force of some outward circumstance of self-interest equal to a compulsion" (Stuckey, *Ideological Origins* 224). By arguing that the United States government was an enemy of blacks everywhere, Delany further reinforced his insular argument for blacks everywhere to unite as a nation for survival. His incorporation of international politics in the debate on black nationalism and black survival in general can be traced to Young and Walker even as it anticipated Pan-Africanism and the work of Marcus Garvey and Du Bois, whose black nationalism spanned significant international politics. This appeal to blacks to act as a united force on their own behalf has also been a constant and a recurring theme in more contemporary black nationalist discourse.

Garnet, Delany, and Black Nationalism's Ideological Effects

In his "Address," Garnet appealed to socially disenfranchised blacks as a collective, and by doing so he brought to the National Convention movement a new constitutive black abolitionist rhetoric. Delany's "Political Destiny" was an extension of this new rhetoric in which blacks were constituted as a unique and autonomous people. This new rhetoric set the ideological tone of black nationalism employed by subsequent black leaders. The new black identity presented by Garnet and extended by Delany became the cornerstone for subsequent programs for black development and advancement.

This calling into being of a black collective legitimized the goal of the new black narrative. This function was ideological in that blacks as a collective unit, "a public," did not exist in nature but were constructed by Garnet and Delany in the advocacy of their cause. In the rhetoric of contemporary black conservatives, who offer a vision of individual black identity, the collective identity of blacks is not without challenge. However, as activists Garnet and Delany sought to "organize dissociated ideological commitments into incipient political myths, visions of the collective life dangled before individuals in hope of creating a real 'people'" (McGee, "In Search" 243). Both advocates appealed to disparate elements in the past to present a black vision of dignity, freedom, and tenacious resistance against oppression. They revived dormant, emotional touchstones of collective black life and identified them as endemic to a common, black ancestry. The common history of oppression is one basis for the collectivization of blacks; the common heroic, black ancestry is the other.

Blacks as One: Interpellation and Identification

In the struggle over slavery, black abolitionists constructed narratives to recruit blacks or transform them into subjects constrained to serve the designated causes of each abolitionist. These causes varied from Walsh's proslavery perspective to the different antislavery positions of Garnet, Delany, and Douglass. Despite the variation among these causes, each was presented to individual blacks as a choice they could make. This presentation is especially true of activism for black liberation. The subjects of these narratives were fictional personae who were constructed and constrained in the framework of the discourse; nevertheless, such personae were important features in the rhetorical transactions. The way people are interpellated as subjects circumscribes what they can or cannot do. This interpellation not only limits their options but also points them in particular directions. As rhetors, Garnet and Delany were engaged in a critical battle for the way blacks would be constituted as a people.

Though both Garnet's "Address" and Delany's "Political Destiny" might be said to have failed to persuade the black community, both being minority opinions within the broader black community, they functioned as rhetorics of identification or consubstantiation. For example, Garnet's "Address" was rejected at the convention by a vote of nineteen to eighteen largely on the basis of opposition by Douglass, who "made some forcible remarks against its adoption" (Bell, "Negro Emigration" 142; Schor 56–57; and Bell, *Minutes* 18).[12] As part of the rhetorical process, the goals of a particular discourse may be achieved through identification and persons may be identified in terms of something that they share. Garnet and Delany sought black mobilization by establishing "signs of consubstantiality" as they tried to identify the common experiences of blacks everywhere that made them unique and distinguished them from whites (Burke, *Rhetoric of Motives* 55). This identification was achieved with significant help from the collective black subject constructed in their discourse. Examination of Garnet and Delany's speeches as constitutive rhetorics that sought to create identification allows exploration of the interesting rhetorical effects that they spawn. These effects include the construction of subjectivity and the ideological functions of rhetoric.

Through interpellation, this black nationalist narrative sought to fix what it meant to work for black liberation "through establishing, by selection and combination, a chain of equivalences" (62). In Garnet's "Address," for example, both Northern and Southern blacks were depicted as sharing oppression and alienation, along with the hope of freedom. This identification was ongoing, and its continuation can be seen in subsequent black discourse that similarly links all blacks to a common ancestry of militant black resistance efforts. Frederick Douglass was different in that he linked blacks seeking their freedom in America to Revolutionary white colonists who had claimed their freedom from British rule.

Affirming Africa and Negating America: Positing a Transhistorical Subject

The effort to connect blacks to a common ancestry posits a transhistorical subject. Constitutive rhetorics affirm this subject by establishing a continuum between past and present that links the living to the dead. Garnet and Delany, like Young and Walker, used the rhetorics of nostalgia and critical memory to provide blacks with a reconstituted history complete with laudable elements to counter the white narrative that posited a naturalized black degradation. This account was then presented to their black listeners as the natural and continuous heritage of blacks. In Garnet and Delany's new narrative, then, blacks were connected despite their separation by extended time spans and extensive distances.

In Garnet's "Address," heroic resistors to slavery such as Toussaint L'Overture, Denmark Vesey, Joseph Cinque, Madison Washington, and Nathaniel Turner were the authentic ancestors of black Americans. While these men were presented as villains by the supporters of slavery, Garnet presented them as "noble men! . . . who [had] fallen in freedom's conflict . . . [whose] names [were] surrounded by a halo of glory." They were "dead fathers [who spoke] to you from their graves" and connected through actions that reflected the black ancestral tradition on which blacks in America were being called to draw (Ripley et al., *Black Abolitionist* 4: 410).

Garnet's new black discourse presented a narrative history in which disparate actions were conceived to be part of the ongoing effort of the black community to resist oppression. Not only were disparate acts woven into a cumulative whole, but also individuals from different times and places were perceived to be part of a collective of the living and the dead. Through this linkage of the past with the present, Garnet's rhetoric identified blacks as part of a transhistorical subjectivity that spared no effort in the struggle for freedom, liberty, and human dignity.

Delany also posited a transhistorical subjectivity for his collective black subject. For him, blacks were part of the colored races with "the highest traits of civilization . . . a people who have freed themselves by the might of their own will, the force of their own power, the unfailing strength of their own right arms, and their unflinching determination to be free." Rather than focus on resistance efforts, however, he pointed to the continued black survival, even in the most adverse conditions, that was common to blacks across time. He claimed that in the difficult conditions of the South, whites had "*decreased* in numbers, [and] *degenerated* in character," while blacks had "*increased* in numbers, [and] *regenerated* in character." In Delany's view, these results were evidence that blacks were "a race capable of the endurance of more toil, fatigue, and hunger than any other branch of the human family" (Stuckey, *Ideological Origins* 203, 221, 216). In a marked departure from the approach taken by Garnet that further highlights the rhetorical functions of the two speeches, Delany distinguished between blacks in 1854 and those of fifty years earlier:

> Fifty years ago our fathers lived. . . . We are their sons but not the same individuals. . . . That which suited them does not suit us. . . . [T]hey were ignorant. . . . With education, we are conversant. . . . They once were held as slaves; to such a condition we never could be reduced. . . . They considered themselves favored to live by sufferance; we reject it as degradation. A subordinate position was all they asked for; we claim entire equality or nothing. The relation of master and slave was innocently acknowledged by them; we deny the right as such and pronounce the relation as the basest injustice that ever scourged the earth and cursed the human family. (219–20)

Delany used this sharp contrast to establish his claim that blacks were "no longer slaves, as were our fathers, but freemen; now fully qualified to meet our oppressors in every relation which belongs to the elevation of man, the establishment, sustenance, and perpetuity of a nation" (220). An embrace of this vision by the blacks making up Delany's convention audience and other blacks in the 1850s would highlight the disparity between their material condition in America and this constituted identity. Thus "The Political Destiny" was also an enactment of black alienation. On the face of it, this difference between Garnet and Delany might be considered as contradictory claims. More important, however, it points to the constitution of the black subject in these speeches as the ideological manifestation of a pliable fiction. It also points to intramural differences within black nationalism and its common goal of spotlighting black alienation as a basis for revolutionary black action. For Douglass, the focus was not so much on blacks as heroic or superior but as Americans. This focus was, then, the basis for his appeal to whites to acknowledge the rights of all Americans, including blacks.

Blacks Championing Their Liberation: The Illusion of Freedom

From his rhetorically constituted position of blacks as ideological subjects identified in such a way that freedom and liberty were a "natural" part of their lives, Garnet called upon blacks to choose to agitate for their essential freedom. He presented these subjects as free to agitate for the overthrow of slavery and the radical restructuring of the American society. Delany called upon his "new black people" to act so as to "transmit, as an inheritance to our children, the blessings of unrestricted civil liberty" (220). Such action was the necessary development that flowed from the new black narratives Garnet and Delany constructed. In making this appeal, they presented an illusion of freedom, for they positioned and constrained their constituted subject toward the fulfillment of a goal predestined by their narrative. As Maurice Charland observes, "subjects within narratives are not free, they are *positioned* and so constrained . . . [and] to be constituted as a subject in a narrative is to be constituted with a history, motives, and a *telos*" ("Constitutive Rhetoric" 140).

In the new narrative, blacks were interpellated as subjects with a clear history connected to heroic ancestors who battled for their freedom and who survived because of their superiority. In the "Address," this identification was motivated by the effort to overthrow slavery and radically reform the social structure of nineteenth-century America. "The Political Destiny" sought to mobilize blacks to organize for emigration as a way of uplifting one part of the race that would then function as a "reflex influence" on those held in bondage (Bell, Introduction 1).[13] In Delany's words "the redemption of the bondsmen depends entirely upon the elevation of the freemen; therefore, to elevate the free colored people of America, anywhere upon this continent, forbodes the speedy redemption of the slaves" (qtd. in Delany and Campbell 8). Therefore the idea that blacks, the collective subject constituted by this new narrative, were free to choose their course of action was nothing but an illusion. The effective function of rhetorics such as Delany and Garnet's is to replace the illusion of freedom proffered by other narratives with their own illusion of free choice.

Herein lies an important issue that evaluations of Garnet's and Delany's rhetoric must confront. Did the new narrative that they advanced interpellate blacks in such a way that their new illusion of freedom replaced the old? For example, in the penultimate paragraph of "The Political Destiny," published above the signatures of Delany and eleven other representatives to the Cleveland conference is Delany's outline of black nationalism's objectives to be achieved through emigration:

> [B]eing politically equal to the whites, physically united with each other by a concentration of strength; when worse comes to worse, we may be found, not as a scattered, weak, and impotent people as we now are separated from each other throughout the Union, but a united and powerful body of freemen, mighty in politics, and terrible in any conflict which might ensue. (Stuckey, *Ideological Origins* 225)

Though Delany points to blacks in their present conditions as "a scattered, weak, and impotent people," it is the vision of "a united and powerful body of freemen, mighty in politics, and terrible in any conflict" that becomes the future collective black subject. To the extent that blacks have continued to accept this vision and its inherent construction of black identity, linked to a rich tradition begun by ancient ancestors and incorporating artistic creativity and scientific advance, and that freedom and dignity were embraced at all cost, this new narrative was successful. Wilson Jeremiah Moses instructively contends that African Americans, "steeped in egalitarian mythology of the 'self-made man' [*sic*]," have always been ambivalent about claiming a noble lineage and so many prefer to trace their ancestry to "noble savages or virile barbarians" living in an "equatorial Eden" (*Afrotopia* 15). Delany's accounting claims for African Americans an historiography that incorporates decline and progress: from nobility to slavery and from Edenic naiveté to "complex free citizens."

With his ideological vision of black people as a collective, Garnet laid the groundwork for the black activism that Delany extended. Joel Schor notes that "by 1860, political action, violent methods, and emigrationist plans had become the means of choice for many black abolitionists" (59). These means have continually been championed by nationalists such as Edward Blyden, Marcus Garvey, Paul Robeson, Malcolm X, and more recently, Louis Farrakhan. Garnet's vision, extended by Delany and picked up in the narratives of black America from the nineteenth century to the present, suggests that this constitutive rhetoric was successful in its advancement of a black ideology. Nonetheless, prior to 1860,

Garnet and Delany's separatism faced significant challenges from, for example, the different perspective of Frederick Douglass. As shown in the next section, disparate outlooks emerged from the way these speakers engaged memory and the American Revolutionary tradition to tune a black public voice.

Separatism, Black Memory, and the American Revolutionary Tradition

In antebellum America, the call for black citizenship was a radical one with revolutionary undertones. As one might expect, then, black memory and the American Revolutionary tradition were constant sources of appeal. To varying degrees, this is true of all three of the speakers under consideration here.

The revolutionary tradition was invoked by Garnet as an ironic example of "the gross inconsistency of a people holding slaves, who had themselves 'ferried o'er the wave' for freedom sake." Garnet invoked the historical events both to highlight the Anglo-American hypocrisy of slavery and to hail blacks to revolutionary struggle. Garnet employed what Cover calls an insular strategy with redemptive elements as he sought to arouse an exclusive black community to verbal and even violent rejection of oppression but with the possibility of sharing common cause with whites under the banner of freedom and liberty. In so doing, Garnet castigated the church that "stood silently by," along with the law and public opinion that colluded to "curse," "oppress," and "destroy" blacks. Within black memory, "the Declaration was a glorious document" with "Godlike sentiments." However, when the colonists gained the power of government, even though "the sentiments of their revolutionary orators [had fallen] in burning eloquence upon their hearts," rather than emancipate the slaves "they added new links to our chains." To legitimize his call for a possible violent revolt, Garnet noted that in their endorsement of physical violence, the colonists had "with one voice . . . cried, LIBERTY OR DEATH" (Ripley et al., *Black Abolitionist* 3: 405, 406).

By consistently juxtaposing slavery and liberty throughout his speech, Garnet highlighted white hypocrisy as he pointed blacks to an acknowledgment of their own alienation. Garnet declared, "Slavery . . . is misery. . . . [U]nless the image of God is obliterated from the soul, all men cherish the love of liberty." For Garnet, Anglo-American oppressors seeking to make blacks "contented with a condition of slavery, [were committing] the highest crime against God and man," and of course, black submission was "sinful in the extreme." If blacks acknowledged that slavery and racism alienated them from their rights to liberty and, ultimately, their rights to citizenship, then it was likely that they would be ready to "choose liberty or death" (3: 406, 407, 409). This acknowledged alienation was Garnet's central tenet for black cohesion and mobilization to revolutionary action.

By opening his "Address" with a greeting to Southern blacks as "brethren and fellow citizens," Garnet claimed the rights of citizenship for those held in slavery even as he appealed to them as part of an insular community (3: 403). He attempted to demonstrate to these fellow citizens the material reality of the distance between them, in their present condition, and their rights as citizens—their alienation. The rejection of Anglo-America is even more thoroughgoing in Delany's "Political Destiny."

Delany argues for insularity, for even as he claims the African was the "first *available contributor* to the country, and consequently was by priority of right, and politically should be, entitled to the highest claims of an eligible citizen," he told his listeners that "we can never enjoy" such rights. Delany's speech was consistently antagonistic toward Anglo-American perspectives, which he saw as the promotion of white superiority. He left his most scathing attack, however, for the Fugitive Slave Law, "the crowning act of infamy on the part of the general government towards the colored inhabitants of the United States" (Stuckey, *Ideological Origins* 195, 227). The enforcement of this law cast the foreboding shadow of slavery beyond the Mason-Dixon line and to the Northern boundaries of the United States.

The enforcement of the Fugitive Slave Law gave credence to the slave power conspiracy with its encroachments on the hard-earned freedoms of Northern blacks. Set against the backdrop of the 1850 congressional compromise, which affirmed this white supremacist, racist legislation, Delany's 1854 statement reflected the somber mood of black-white relations that marked the period (22). Within this context of black degradation and threatened disintegration, Delany's nationalism with emigration as its centerpiece was an attractive alternative around which black life could coalesce, even as it distanced blacks from whatever paltry hope existed for citizenship in America. Of course, for separatists such as Delany, the uplift of some blacks and the "reflex influence" on those in bondage were their only hopes within the nation, dominated as it was by white supremacist perspectives. The appeal of another black nationalist, "Augustine," expressed in 1838, puts the black plight in perspective. In defending emigration to Canada and the West Indies, Augustine argued that he would "rather be a living freeman, even in one of these places, than a 'dead nigger' in the United States" (*Colored American* 3 May 1838). The argument used by blacks to reject the American Colonization Society's emigration scheme was that such emigration would leave enslaved blacks without hope. As a solution to this problem, Delany encouraged slave migration north to Canada, as well as south to Mexico, Central America, and the Caribbean (Stuckey, *Ideological Origins* 231). Always in the discourse there are strategies for resisting oppression.

As we shall see, Frederick Douglass's speech engages the American Revolutionary tradition to argue that whites needed to acknowledge the true American citizenship that was yet denied blacks. Douglass, whose speech is a study in irony, employed the tradition born of a violent revolution to offset a potentially violent black revolution. Douglass's hopeful view of America, when Northern blacks were expressing despair and embracing separatism and emigration, was based on his faith in what David W. Blight calls "American nationalism and mission" (Blight 27).

Integration, Black Memory, and the American Revolutionary Tradition

Douglass's "What to the Slave Is the Fourth of July?" expresses hope in the potential of America. Even though he spoke in the immediate shadow of the 1850 reaffirmation of the Fugitive Slave Law, Douglass embraced a hopeful and expansive view of America as the home of blacks as well as whites. Whereas Delany saw the Fugitive Slave Law as a manifestation of the essence of America, Douglass presented it as an aberration of the America conceived by the founders, the one for which blacks and whites should strive. Douglass addressed the more than five hundred people gathered at the Fourth of July celebration meeting of the Rochester Ladies' Antislavery Society as fellow-citizens. Yet he maintained a clear ironic distance between himself and whites throughout his speech by his continued identification of America as "your country." This speaks to both his awareness of existing disparities between Anglo-Americans and African Americans and his expansive conception of America as an idea with scope for blacks and whites.

Unlike Garnet and Delany, both of whom sought equality by establishing a collective black identity distinct and separate from whites, Douglass focused on America as an idea to be shared and fulfilled by all. His emphasis was on the tenets of freedom and equality through which this idea "America" was conceived by the founders of the republic. For Douglass, nineteenth-century white supremacist practices derogating black life were aberrations that both races needed to correct. Proceeding from his central thesis that the Declaration of Independence was "the RINGBOLT to the chain" of America's destiny, Douglass developed the concept of an inclusive America (Douglass, *Oration* 9). Even from his less than favorable vantage point of black alienation, Douglass affirmed the greatness of the Declaration of Independence and its signers.

Beginning with the title of his speech, Douglass sets up a tension between himself and his audience, the past and the present, the potential of America and the reality of nineteenth-century antebellum life, the glory of the celebration of independence with the Declaration as its crowning document and the desperate struggle of blacks for liberation from American bondage. These tensions found their first explosive release in Douglass's poignant questions, "What have I, or those I represent, to do with your national independence? Are the great principles of political freedom and of natural justice, embodied in that Declaration of Independence, extended to us?" (14). The way nineteenth-century black leaders answered these pivotal questions shaped their perspectives on black identity and black activism.

Douglass's answer to his own question was negative, a resounding "nothing!" He makes clear, however, his indictment of contemporary American practice. In affirming the extension of America's constitutional principles and the promise of the Declaration to blacks, Douglas had no equal. This affirmation informed and shaped his challenge to the black nationalists' separatist ideology and propelled him to advocate agitation by blacks for their place in their new home, not apart as a distinct group and not in another land.

Douglass was uncompromising in his repudiation of the perspective that the Constitution was a proslavery document. "In that instrument I hold there is neither warrant, license, nor sanction of the hateful thing; but, interpreted as it ought to be interpreted, the Constitution is a glorious liberty document." Douglass was prescient in his perspective of how citizens ought to approach the Constitution, anticipating the much heralded narrative turn in legal studies driven by the critical legal studies movement.[14] Rejecting the constructionist approach, Douglass argued, "[E]very American citizen has a right to form an opinion of the constitution, and to propagate that opinion, and to use all honorable means to make his opinion the prevailing one" (36).

While expressing hope in America by "drawing encouragement from the Declaration of Independence," Douglass nevertheless looked to the day when "Africa must rise and put on her yet unwoven garment." In Douglass's inclusive and hopeful perspective, we see a vision of an America built on the imagination. As David McCullough contends, this is the way it should be, for "the entire focus of the founding fathers was on the future; [for them,] America was built on the imagination." For Douglass, it was all about what America could become and should become on the basis of the promises of the Declaration of Independence. Though this progressive notion of America's history serves Douglass well here, as Nathan Huggins notes, in presenting this idealistic vision, which has become the "master narrative" of American history, the "founding fathers" sought to avoid the "deforming mirror of truth," the material reality of race and slavery (38–9, 25).

Garnet and Delany advocated black liberation through an active black separatist agenda with emigration as the primary solution, or at least with deep searching questions about the possibility of black existence. By contrast, Douglass contends for a place for blacks in America by challenging Anglo-America's exclusive and peculiar public dialogue framing America's past. The Anglo-American dominance had resulted in a conservative and naturalized view of America's revolutionary past. As James Jasinski notes, the late-eighteenth-century and early-nineteenth-century articulation of America's revolutionary experience fixed the meaning of the Revolution even as it significantly forgot features important to the nation's progress. Douglass destabilizes Anglo-America's sedimented notions of the American Revolution as an inevitable and natural phenomenon by pointing to the contingency of the event and to the choices made by the founding fathers as social actors (Jasinski 72).

Douglass's challenge was important because it represented an insertion of the black memory into the interpretation of America's past and the shaping of its future. As he contended, "we have to do with the past only as we can make it useful to the present and to the future," and Anglo-America's framing of the nation's revolutionary heritage served to justify the continued exclusion of African Americans (Blassingame 3: 366). This challenge was, then, part of Douglass's effort to engage in redemptive constitutionalism to champion black liberation and to contend for an America belonging to all, including blacks and whites.[15] In so doing, Douglass constructed a "concrete and inclusive conception of American equality" (Lucaites, "Irony" 56). He also constructed a black subject ready to participate equally with whites in the experiment of American democracy.

Through their call for violent resistance and emigration as the ultimate solution to black oppression, Garnet and Delany both demonstrated black frustration as they appealed to insularity. While the "Address" was ambivalent about the place of blacks in American society, "The Political Destiny" indicated Delany's unwillingness to continue battling for a place in America's public discourse.[16] Without granting the American Revolutionary tradition status as the source of the black radical tradition, Garnet and Delany both drew on it to legitimize their militant stance. Neither Garnet nor Delany, however, confronted what Jasinski calls Anglo-America's conservative "domestication" of the revolutionary tradition. Douglass sought to destabilize this conservative view in an effort to interpret the revolutionary tradition as having established the principles that provided a place for the black collective voice in the public dialogue that articulated the scope and structure of America (Jasinski 78).

Alienation and the Place of Rearticulation

Treatments of "What to the Slave Is the Fourth of July?" consistently point to the significance of Douglass's history as a former slave and to his continued experience as an oppressed American as elements that animate the rhetor's rearticulation of American history (Leroux; Lucaites, "Irony"; and Jasinski). Even so, there is more to be probed. John Louis Lucaites's treatment of these phenomena as providing an effective strategic platform for the performance of Douglass's critique of American practices will be extended here ("Irony"). Notwithstanding Steele, who contends that he resists the "seductive imagery of alienation," black alienation provides a potent place from which the collective black subject can present an effective, African American rearticulation of America (22). For this project, concerned with the construction of black identity, a development shaped in significant ways by race and alienation, the function of this perspective is a primary concern.

Amiri Baraka confronts black alienation in American literature and argues that black writers, isolated from mainstream America, are in a unique if not advantageous position from which to describe America. He contends that "this alienation should serve to make a very powerful American literature" (Baraka 164). As Baraka sees it, blacks have always occupied this place of alienation in American society, a place that should be put to use, since the vantage point is classically perfect—outside and inside at the same time. Patricia Hill Collins explores the position of black women as domestic workers and their perspective of the "outsider-within." She theorizes such a perspective as an effective standpoint for critical analysis (11). As J. Robert Cox observes, in our efforts to make use of the past, "memory is *always mediated* by the experience of a historical, material people." Though Anglo-Americans claimed the authority of the revolutionary tradition as the dominant group, "theirs [was] not the only story" ("Cultural Memory" 12). Black abolitionists such as Garnet, Delany, and Douglass inserted an alienated, historical, material, collective, black, public voice into America's public dialogue so as to mediate America's past, challenge the un-American story of exclusion, and tell a different story. This alienation provides Douglass with the perspective from which to celebrate the Revolution *because* it endangered the Anglo-American–dominated constitutional order and communal stability.[17]

This historical and material black experience of alienation is one of belonging and not belonging. It is an experience of Du Bois's "twoness." It is being African—from a different place, a place that, in the popular memory, had come to signify not only difference but backwardness and inferiority. This differentness is then confounded by the other aspect of twoness, being American. For Douglass, as it was for most blacks in America in 1852, America was the only home he knew and one that he and his ancestors had helped to build with their blood, sweat, and tears. It is this paradoxical situatedness that gives Douglass both his unique perspective and effective rhetorical *topoi*. This outside-inside perspective that represents the black experience in the nation is America's true irony. Irony is the trope of alienation. As Kenneth Burke indicates, "true irony, humble irony, is based upon a sense of fundamental kinship with the enemy, as one *needs* him [or her], is *indebted* to him [or her], is not merely outside him [or her] as an observer but contains him [or her] *within,* being consubstantial with him [or her]" (*Gram-*

mar 514). Ironically, then, in Douglass, the African American's alienated position, a position born of exclusion and domination, becomes rhetorically effective ground from which to restructure and diversify the landscape of American identity. Douglass's ironic perspective demonstrates the possibility of the African American challenge to racism embracing the shared responsibility with "others," including white America, for the creation of a more inclusive society. With the acknowledgment of consubstantiality, especially between blacks and whites, grounded in the material reality of the shared experience of slavery, racism, and genocide, there might yet be a way to confront white supremacy as a problem that crosses racial boundaries. Such an approach might facilitate expansive narratives encompassing African American, Asian American, Latin American, Anglo-American, and Native American recovery, among others. For such a narrative to be enacted, the alienated position of blacks, for example, is fruitful ground on which to start, but the goals have to include an acknowledgment of shared loss, however skewed, and ultimately shared recovery.

In Garnet and Delany's speeches, the rhetorical boon of alienation and oppression constructs a morally empowered collective black subject. This subject has as its motive and *telos,* however, the making of a dignified "black people." In the face of the ideological dominance and the hegemonic power of the Anglo-American white supremacist public voice, both Garnet and Delany present the possibility of a dignified, liberated black people only through violence or emigration. The alienated perspective rejected the ironic, with its paradoxical consubstantiation with the enemy. For Garnet and Delany, Burke's "fundamental kinship with the enemy" would have made them too much like the enemy, hypocritical. Instead they chose skepticism, sarcasm, and with a heavy dose of understandable bitterness, ultimately, separatism. This progression of thought is evident in the careers of both Garnet and Delany. As late as 1842, Garnet was still proposing conventional methods and rejecting violence as a means of emancipation. In that year he claimed, "[S]laveholders count upon numbers; we upon truth, and it is powerful and will prevail" (*Emancipator* 207). As noted before, Delany opposed emigration as late as 1851, insisting that America was the only home for himself and his fellow blacks. The ongoing oppression accompanying black alienation makes this progression an understandable if limited perspective. For Douglass it was different. This alienated position became the basis not only for a rupture in the dominant ideology but also for a deliberate reconfiguration of the ideology with an inclusive agenda. It is a rhetoric through which Douglass incredibly continues to express hope in America as a place for blacks. Douglass was the escaped slave, and as Cover observes, it was this escape that constituted for Douglass his redemption and the beginning of life, a redemption that he incorporated into his rhetoric as possible for all blacks (136–37).

For these three speakers, the "Revolution," with its juxtaposition of reform and renewal, would expose America's hypocrisy. Though Garnet used this tradition, with its emphasis on liberty, as the basis for black revolutionary action, it is in "What to the Slave Is the Fourth of July?" that we see an American future of possibilities for those previously alienated. Faced with similar conditions, Garnet and Delany opted for subversion or at least rejection of America and its supposedly noble Revolutionary tradition. Both adeptly exposed American hypocrisy, and while "The Political Destiny" rejected any possibility of blacks and whites sharing equality as American citizens, the "Address" did extend this hope. Only Douglass engaged in both the "subversion and reaffirmation" of this tradition (Jasinski 80).

Douglass's subversion was in his reinterpretation of the revolutionary tradition, and his reaffirmation was in his embrace of that tradition to shape his rearticulation of America as an idea of inclusion and equality rather than one of exclusion and oppression. Within Douglass's rearticulation, the voice of the eighteenth-century disenfranchised American colonist becomes synonymous with the voice of the nineteenth-century disenfranchised black American. Although Douglass's interpretation of sociopolitical change was more idealist than materialist, he was not oblivious to the reality that, in the face of oppression, separatism found sanction in the Revolution (W. Martin 110). He recounted the Revolutionary tradition and argued, "[W]ith brave men there is always a remedy for oppression. Just here the idea of a total separation of the colonies from the crown was born" (Douglass, *Oration* 7). The separatist impulse articulated by Garnet and Delany is within the American Revolutionary tradition, but the tradition was invoked to point to American hypocrisy, reject American institutions, and advance separatism. This rhetoric was insular, reinforcing beleaguered blacks as a unique community. The celebration of difference rather than the confrontation through difference would have been more idealistic than materially practical in the 1850s. Still, there is no avoiding that separatism faces the danger of what critics such as McPhail point out is its inherent invitation to the "other" to defend against it and, as such, its complicity in a never-ending cycle of negative difference. Douglass, however, chose to go beyond invoking the Revolutionary tradition to reject American institutions, contending instead for a place for blacks within them.

It is from this hopeful perspective that Douglass successfully exploited the irony of his assignment to present an epideictic oration in praise of the American Revolution and its offspring, independence. The irony was in Douglass's position as a former slave and a representative of blacks held in slavery in the South and held in contempt in the North: the alienated and degraded inhabitant of the nation became its prophetic voice of redemption.

This reading of Garnet, Delany, and Douglass indicates how ideas brought to the forefront of abolitionism by Garnet were extended by Delany and how both men sought to create a new society by focusing on blacks and casting them in the role of liberating subjects. Integral to this focus was the creation of a collectivized black subject. This creation was achieved through interpellation and identification in which blacks were presented as one on the basis of their common experience of oppression and suffering, along with their common ancestry. This collective black subject was one with an identity of black self-dependence and dignity, the foundations of black nationalism. This identity was distinct from the one created for blacks by white America. In contrast to previous descriptions of blacks as slaves and "free" blacks, this new black identity symbolized the mobilization of blacks to action and a critique of the white systems of domination.

To legitimize their advocacy of black liberation, Garnet's and Delany's narratives call a black public into existence by constructing blacks as a collective subject. A part of this effort to present blacks as one was the linking of the living and the dead. This new black subject was then called to exercise its freedom in the cause of black emancipation. Through these features, this new narrative functioned as a constitutive rhetoric with powerful ideological effects. The constituting of a collective subject, the positing of a transhistorical subject, and the advancing of the illusion of the freedom of the subject were the ideological effects identified in this rhetoric. These ideological functions were highlighted by the overt effort to naturalize their development within the narrative.

While Garnet, Delany, and Douglass performed these important functions in their narratives, their discourse employed a distinctly masculine, black subject to represent black subjectivity. The problem with this rhetorical process is that black women have always been part of the black struggle. Thus their exclusion from this discourse merits our attention, and as shown in the following chapter, scholars have been exploring the role of women in the discourse of racial uplift.

Like Garnet and Delany, Douglass spoke from the perspective of black alienation. Similar to Garnet's success, Douglass's was due partly to his experience as a former slave and as "one who continued to suffer in many respects," a suffering caused by racism. In short, his position of alienation became one of rhetorical empowerment (Leroux 46). Partly because of this, "What to the Slave Is the Fourth of July?" represents a different view of the collective black consciousness from that expressed in the "Address" and "The Political Destiny."

With his focus on the promise of America, Douglass provided a black perspective that served as a counterpoint to the largely separatist agendas of Garnet and Delany. Douglass's advocacy of a differently constituted subject in the same nineteenth-century context shared by Delany's and Garnet's subjects is evidence that contradictory subject positions simultaneously exist within cultures. Black subject positions continue to change as new discourses are introduced within the culture. Douglass projected a more hopeful, integrated future for America, a future in which blacks did not yield their rights to America or claim allegiance to Africa in contrast to America. Instead, Douglass's black subject contended for both its "Americanness" and its "Africanness" in one paradoxical, contorted, but distinctly human being.

While Douglass's speech was less militant than the other two, it was no less confrontational. For Douglass, blacks needed to point whites to the fact that they were not living up to the promise and potential of the young nation. America, then, was a nation that belonged not to whites but to both blacks and whites. It should be acknowledged that "What to the Slave Is the Fourth of July?" was an address to a predominantly white audience, while the "Address" and "The Political Destiny" were presented to predominantly black audiences. This difference does not, however, negate the fact that these speeches were geared to audiences beyond their immediate recipients, and Delany and Douglass "were often speaking to and about each other even when they were not engaged in direct debate" (Levine 12).

I have highlighted here the common themes shared by Garnet's "Address" and Delany's "Political Destiny," while pointing out the different perspective expressed in Douglass's "What to the Slave Is the Fourth of July?" Yet, neither do I wish to suggest that these two black nationalists consistently shared perspectives nor that they were always in disagreement with Douglass. They did not hold consistently the perspectives expressed in these speeches. Garnet, Delany, and Douglass, like their predecessors, peers, and progenitors, proceeded through trial and error, moving from one strategy to the next in an effort to break black bondage. As Stuckey has convincingly argued, Douglass and Delany (and, I would add, Garnet) were part of a continuing black liberation effort that predated them and in which each embraced at different times much of what is now seen as exclusive poles: integrationism on the one hand and nationalism on the other (Stuckey, *Ideological Origins* 26–27).

To highlight and to affirm various elements of the black past were part of their effort to create among blacks a "national culture." Such a culture is, in the words of Franz Fanon, "the whole body of efforts made by people in the sphere of thought to describe, justify, and praise the action through which that people has created itself and keeps itself in existence" (Fanon, *Wretched* 233). Though their perspectives were different, Garnet, Delany, and Douglass wanted to ensure that their people re-created and maintained themselves.

Ultimately, then, Garnet, Delany, and Douglass sought to develop among blacks a consciousness of a shared experience of suffering and commitment to self-development—nationalism. A consideration of these three advocates as nationalists allows for a rethinking of black nationalism. This system of thought that promotes black consciousness and self-development, instead of being linked to inevitable ends such as separatist practices and exclusionary politics, may be conceived as anchored in contingency, expediency, and pragmatic improvisation. This was the path of Garnet, Delany, and Douglass, one that remains open to contemporary blacks negotiating the quagmire of twenty-first-century American politics.[18]

The conception of black nationalism as a pragmatic strategy rhetorically framed, at least partly, in response to white supremacy invites a consideration of several related features. One such is the role of rhetoric in black survival strategies. In addition, we are reminded that black nationalism has always been a situated practice and its study will yield fruitful returns when considered alongside related white practices. Garnet and Delany viewed America through its dominant practices.

The nature and tone of the ideology that Garnet and Delany advanced turned on their interpretation of the treatment blacks received as a result of public practices and policies dominated by whites. Where such treatments suggested that racism was an anomaly that would eventually be rectified by the nation's liberal ideals of natural rights, liberty and equality for all, including blacks, Garnet and Delany promoted active black involvement in American public life. Even after his family was stalked by headhunters, Garnet campaigned on behalf of the Liberty Party only to see it dissipate after the indubitable rejection at the polls of its antislavery platform. In 1842, the year before his "Address," he still advocated the power of "truth" over violence in his program of emancipation (*Emancipator* 207). In 1859, he called for a "grand center of Negro Nationality" in West Africa (*Weekly Anglo-African;* Moses, *Afrotopia* 14). As head of the African Civilization society in 1861, he was forced to defend himself against claims that he was promoting the view that America was not home for blacks (*Frederick Douglass's Monthly;* Stuckey, *Slave Culture* 179). Delany, as Paul Gilroy contends and Levine endorses, cannot be fixed by any simplistic attempts to label him as "consistently either conservative or radical" (Gilroy 20; Levine 2). As late as 1851, Delany was urging blacks to remain in America. In the face of the ominous advance of the slave power and white supremacy in the 1840s and 1850s, both men began to interpret racism, white supremacy, and liberty as symbiotic in American life, not as Gunnar Myrdal would later see it, as a "glaring conflict in the American conscience" (Myrdal 21). Black separatism was their contingent, expedient, if not logical choice.

Douglass's argument that whites should live up to America's liberal ideals and acknowledge the rights of blacks as citizens should be seen not as a fixed and inevitable argument but as one based on Douglass's relatively new perspective in 1852 that slavery, racism, and black exclusion were antithetical to the America imagined by the "founding fathers." Of course, as noted before, in true contingent fashion, Douglass, too, would soon be on the verge of a public endorsement of emigration.

Garnet, Delany, Douglass, and numerous blacks since have advocated approaches to black life grounded in black memory and molded by the constraints of Anglo-American racist practices. In so doing, they advance a rhetoric that restructures their historical experience of alienation to advance their cause of black progress.

Collective black memory and white supremacy are themselves fluid features and, as such, continue to be reshaped. Consequently, improvisation and rhetorical dexterity have always been at the heart of black nationalism. The rhetorical product that emerges from these black efforts continues to shape and guide black lives alienated by racism. It is the construction of black lives that points us to the material function of black nationalist rhetoric. This is a rhetoric that creates and proscribes black life even as it describes it. Approaches that conceptualize black nationalism as an essential and inevitable practice of separatism will miss the rich store of black survival strategies it preserves. To frame Farrakhan, for example, as merely an extremist with a destructive separatist agenda panders to this view. Such approaches also fail to consider the changing face of America that both frames and features elements of black nationalism. Perhaps most important for our consideration, these approaches mask the significant role of rhetoric in the shaping of our social realities. Such a role includes the ability to produce and prohibit, develop and delimit reality.[19] They will miss the possibilities and complexities that emerge in the rhetoric of black nationalism as they function in its definition.[20]

6

The Ideology of Black Nationalism and American Culture

Conceivably there was and is a way out from the vicious cycle of degradation, an opening of better hope demanding an unprecedented and perhaps impossible measure of courage, honesty, and sheer nerve.

—Winthrop D. Jordan, *White over Black*

This study of the nineteenth-century development of black nationalist ideology provides some insight into ideological debate and identity formation. Such insight points to a rhetorical conception of alienation, especially that experienced and expressed by blacks in the face of white supremacist, Anglo-American discourse, the discourse of domination, and African American discourse, the discourse of freedom. By grasping the way rhetoric constructs alienation, we understand important aspects of African American discourse. Such an understanding demonstrates the pivotal role of rhetoric in the efforts of African Americans to constitute a viable black public voice in American political culture. Enactment of such a voice is central to the ideological struggle for the soul of America. Theorizing black nationalism as a rhetorical-material ideology thus allows for the demonstration of this world view functioning as a rhetoric to both discipline and describe black life for its own ends.

Focusing on exploring the rhetorical conception of alienation and examining the thesis that black nationalism is a rhetorical-material ideology, this chapter is simultaneously a summary, a synthesis, and a critical enactment of the collective conclusions of this study of nineteenth-century African American discourse.

This rhetorical-material reading of history points to a critical interpretation of the collective public memory in contemporary black life. Following the examination of the rhetorical-material functioning of black nationalist ideology and the exploration of the rhetorical conception of alienation are some critical rhetorical probes about the place of conservatism, radical black nationalism, and multiculturalism in contemporary America.

Important to this critical enactment and these collective conclusions are the implications for critical rhetorical theory and the understanding of black nationalism that emerge from this study. Part of the conclusion probes a number of peculiarities of the multifaceted ideology of black nationalism. A primary question focuses on black nationalism and black women. While the voice of black women in abolitionism is well established and acknowledged, its role in the development of black nationalism is not. The black female voice is muted in the development of this ideology. There is also the question of the function of black nationalism in the broader program of the black struggle for equality, including abolitionism, civil rights, and contemporary efforts toward multicultural life, with its commitment to egalitarian sharing of the nation and its resources. From a materialist conception of the rhetoric of black nationalism and from my notion of a rhetorical conception of alienation, important functions of this ideology that can be derived from observation of such a rhetoric at work in nineteenth-century black abolitionism. Also explored is the capacity of black nationalism to move beyond the leading role in the "strategy of opposition" to guidance in a "strategy of construction of a new order," to use the terms of Ernesto Laclau and Chantal Mouffe (189).

Black Nationalism as a Rhetorical-Material Ideology

Conceptualizing black nationalism as rhetorically material foregrounds ideology as the social tool necessary to mold people into mutable subjects able to respond to the demands of social existence. Important to this conceptualization is the spotlighting of the rhetorical. Black nationalism is a material ideology because it pragmatically directs its human charges to live as "'conscious subjects' within the totality of social relations" (Giddens 179). Black nationalism is also rhetorical because rhetoric plays a key role in the constitution of its narrative subjects who "do what they do because of who they are." In such constitution, rhetoric constructs individuals into a collective subject: a fictive being that transcends divisions such as interests, age, and class. Through its rhetoric, then, black nationalist ideology legitimizes its function as natural, normal, and taken for granted as it empowers its subjects to act "freely" (McGee, "In Search" 240). Through such rhetoric, the "god," the ideology, controls its subjects and determines their actions (Burke, *Language* 6).

Through the prism of a critical rhetoric, I examine black nationalism as a rhetorical-material ideology and thus show why it is easy to praise "black people" before blacks and, more important, how such individuals come to perceive themselves as part of a unique group: "black people." We can thus understand why nineteenth-century blacks, inhabited by this god, this ideology, "chose" to strive for the freedom their ancestors never knew. In other words, we see how black nationalism exercised its ontopolitical might even as it challenged the ontopolitical might of white nationalism (Kramer 3). Such a critical rhetorical enterprise advances the agenda of theorizing the relationship between power and discourse in that it looks beyond traditional conceptions of audience effects to the ways in which rhetoric literally creates its audience (Burke, *Rhetoric* 50; Charland, "Constitutive Rhetoric" 133, 134).

Important to the understanding of ideology is that black nationalism is a diminutive mode of resistance (at least in the number of people advancing it in nineteenth-century America). Black nationalism is at best one among many deuteragonists in America's story writ large, with the hegemonic ideology of white supremacy as the protagonist. Ideologies are not always dominant but are pervasive, ubiquitous, and always worthy of investigation. The components of diminutive or dominant ideologies, both the "dimensions of domination and freedom as they are exercised in a relativized world," should draw the attention of critical scholarship (McKerrow, "Critical Rhetoric: Theory" 91). The relative size of black nationalism makes it even more crucial that we investigate its power to unify and mobilize blacks, a power that we see, for example, in the Million Man March. The antecedents to the march are worth considering.

An Historical Summary of Black Nationalism

Michael West places the Million Man March in its historical context of the tradition of black nationalism and, in so doing, updates Wilson Jeremiah Moses's exploration of the flowering of black nationalism. West traces black nationalism beyond Moses's notion of the golden years of 1850–1925 through the Million Man March to 1999. West contends that black nationalism has had four moments in the African American experience: 1850–61, 1919–25, 1964–72, and 1984 to the present (81–100). Each moment has been preceded by precipitous developments in America that threatened the progress if not the very existence of a viable black community within the larger American community. Black nationalism then emerged or reemerged to counter America's antiblack agenda and to trump integrationist schemes with its own program of back separatism. In these moments of prominence, black nationalism provided blacks with the ideological equipment to confront white supremacist practices.

West's four moments exclude important black nationalists and black nationalist developments. They include Paul Cuffe and the post-Revolution generation, Robert Alexander Young, David Walker and the generation that faced colonization at its height, and as West acknowledges, the mid to late 1930s through World War II and McCarthyism, with the emergence of Elijah Muhammad's Nation of Islam, the mobilization of blacks in response to the Italian invasion of Ethiopia that led to the formation of the National Negro Congress and the Council on African Affairs—the era of George Padmore, W. E. B. Du Bois, Paul Robeson, and C. L. R James. West's four moments are instructive, however, and worthy of elaboration.

The first moment, 1850–61, discussed in chapter 5, was a response to events in America's political life highlighted by the Compromise of 1850, which rewarded Southern slaveholders by strengthening the notorious Fugitive Slave Act. The period included the infamous Dred Scott decision of 1857 and ended with the beginning of the Civil War, which promised the end of slavery and new possibilities for black America. As we have seen, this was a moment featured in the black public rhetorical arena by the debates of Henry Garnet, Martin Delaney, and Frederick Douglass. Separatism, self-determination, race pride, self-development, and emigration, primarily to Africa but also to the Caribbean, Mexico, Canada, and elsewhere, were the main themes. Black women, too, such as Sojourner Truth, came to the fore and tenaciously contended in public for the affirmation of black life.

The second moment, 1919–25, began with the violent white supremacist backlash against black enfranchisement and black political mobilization: a turning back from a promising experiment in democracy in the South after the Civil War. The experiment was formally abandoned with the Compromise of 1877 and the withdrawal and redeployment of federal troops in the South. From Reconstruction's still unfulfilled promise to each black family of "forty acres and a mule" and the turn of the century with Booker T. Washington's ascendancy, through the frightening reality of ongoing, barbaric lynchings, blacks looked to another war for possible redemption. After World War I, however, blacks were stunned by renewed racism, which included Northern mob violence. Hundreds of thousands of black men had joined the war with the hope of new opportunities at home to follow their victory over the Axis powers abroad. In the Great Migration, half a million blacks had fled segregation and racialized oppression in the South for the prospects of jobs and opportunities in the North, where they were joined by new black migrants from the Caribbean and Central America (Bontemps and Conroy; Lemann). These and other blacks were the targets and often the victims of the Red Summer of 1919 with its twenty-six "race riots," white mobs attacking black communities (Lewis 62).

The brand of black nationalism that surfaced in response was dominated by the Marcus Garvey–led Universal Negro Improvement Association whose slogan was "Africa for Africans, at home and abroad." Garvey tapped into palpable black alienation with its deep sense of frustration, displacement, and resentment even as he drew on his own rhetorical and organizing skill and prophetic vision to develop and lead what is still arguably "the largest black mass movement in Afro-American history" (T. Martin, *Race First* ix).[1] Though it drew its inspiration and its themes from nineteenth-century black nationalism, Garvey's success went beyond the scope, if not the imaginations, of Walker's, Garnet's, and Delany's nationalism. Black nationalism was now a mass movement. Its rhetoric of race pride, black uplift, self-determination, self-definition, black religion, and a return to Africa, all against the backdrop of the celebration of Africa as home, provided a mosaic that dominated black political culture in the United States and throughout the African diaspora. For example, Theodore Vincent argues that Garveyism "set in motion what was to become the most compelling force in Negro life—race and color consciousness" (14). The trumped-up charges and subsequent imprisonment and deportation of Garvey to Jamaica marked the end of the second moment of black nationalism.

The third moment, 1964–72, arrived with Malcolm X as its clear leader and his Organization of Afro-American Unity as its first significant institutional expression. This moment ticks within the long, painful hour of the civil rights struggle that ended de jure segregation in the United States but not the commitment of much of Anglo-America to white supremacy and a tenacious, vulgar fight for de facto segregation. Throughout the Civil Rights movement and beyond, even as Martin Luther King Jr. embodied the best in America, blacks continued to experience the worst of America, as harsh racism stalked their lives. The Watts uprising and the assassination of Malcolm X in 1965 at once demonstrated and deepened the alienation of the nation's black, urban poor youth. This was the era of Black Power as a worldwide phenomenon. In the United States, there was an ideological divide between two strands of black nationalism. On one side was the Black Panther party with its emphasis on political action for employment, jobs, education, and racial justice. This revolution was to be led primarily by working-class youth and to include alliances among blacks, Native Americans, and Chicanos and Hispanics, as well as white antiwar protestors. Cultural nationalism was on the other side of the spectrum, under the guidance of the US Organization, led by its founder and leading West coast cultural nationalist, Maulana Karenga. The cultural nationalists eschewed the political activism of the Panthers and their supporters in favor of a more racially exclusive, cultural rebirth among Africans in the diaspora.

This mid-twentieth-century rise of black nationalism symbolically ended with the demise of the National Black Political Assembly formed out of the Gary Convention of 1972. The convention had brought together black leadership of all stripes, including the cultural and the political nationalists. The demise of the

Panthers at the beginning of the 1970s, as a result of "state repression" and "self-destruction," including the abuse of drugs and the exploitation of women, marked the end of the era. The cultural nationalists continued their work, building for the next wave.

This wave began in 1984 and is described by West as a direct response to the widespread efforts to reverse progress made by blacks during the Civil Rights era. This backlash was symbolically and significantly embodied in the person and programs of Ronald Reagan. The rise of hip-hop culture, with its symbol rap music, signaled the coalescence of the black nationalist re-emergence in response to the Reagan phenomenon. Among the black middle class, there was an attraction to cultural nationalism expressed in the growth of the Black Arts Renaissance with Amiri Baraka in the forefront. This phenomenon, which included heritage tours, black studies, and the popularity of African prints in both sartorial styles and home decor, reflected Baraka's effort to bridge the radical political nationalism with cultural nationalism (Woodard). Amid this cultural renaissance, West argues, with no single organization emerging to give political leadership, Louis Farrakhan called on a million black men to join him in a march on Washington (84–92).

Farrakhan, himself a nonactivist, was well versed in the "rhetorically-strident tradition in black nationalism." This awareness explains the rhetorically astute themes of atonement and reconciliation that afforded black men the opportunity for a public collective expression of repentance and goodwill. West sees the Million Man March as running aground shortly after the event because of the lack of a program to bring about social change. He also contends that the support for the march must not be seen as an endorsement of Farrakhan's "anti-feminist, conservative black nationalism" (93). Farrakhan might have called the march, but in so doing, he facilitated the expression of sentiments well beyond his limited range. These were sentiments grounded in the long history of black struggle for dignity. One marcher declared,

> We marched against stereotypes. We marched against media that continue to portray Black men as criminals. We marched against conservative ideology that is anti-Black. We marched against angry white males who have concocted a myth that Black men are taking jobs away from them through affirmative action. We marched against the Contract with America. We marched against Rush Limbaugh, Newt Gingrich, and Jesse Helms. We marched against the Bell Curve. We marched to silence the skeptics. But we also marched for ourselves. (Cottman 25)

Other nationalist voices in the "national black community" were able to ex-

ploit the boon of goodwill from the event to advance the cause of black liberation. The Million Woman March of 25 October 1997 in Philadelphia had a more
progressive agenda. It was followed by an even more progressive and broad-based
event, the Black Radical Congress, a meeting in Chicago 19–21 June 1998. A
question central to this chapter is whether black nationalism can move beyond
facilitating the expression of an oppositional consciousness among blacks. First
to be examined, however, are the roots of black nationalism, which go deeper
than West's first moment, 1850.

Black nationalism is part of a black radical tradition that has its genesis in
Africa but has manifestations across the diaspora. Cedric Robinson demonstrates
this fact in *Black Marxism* and points to Du Bois, C. L. R. James, and Walter
Rodney who, like him, contested Eurocentric accounts of black radicalism as a
variant of European radicalism. Nineteenth-century black nationalist rhetoric
developed in the United States in response to material and symbolic black alienation wrought by American hegemonic, nineteenth-century white supremacy.
The white supremacist discourse framing black life became the immediate reason for the emergence of this strand of the black radical tradition. Consideration
of the rhetoric of nineteenth-century black nationalism, then, begins with the
key marker of its context, the rhetoric of nineteenth-century proslavery discourse
that advocated white supremacy: white nationalism.

The Ironic Soil of Black Nationalism: White Nationalism

From the mid-seventeenth century to the War of Independence, Americans advanced largely biblical, local, and unchallenged arguments in defense of slavery.
To meet the challenge of socioeconomic and political changes, the subsequent
proslavery defense simply modified and restated these early arguments (Jenkins
2). The Declaration of Independence, the Revolutionary War, and the rise of the
new nation transformed debate about slavery into a national one with international significance. To explain the rise of liberty, equality, and slavery in the
shadow of the Revolutionary War, the new nation had to craft arguments to unify
its proclamation of equality for "all men" while holding "black men" (and women)
in bondage. Between the Revolution and the rise of radical abolitionism in the
1830s, Revolutionary rhetoric based on natural rights became the main discursive challenge to slavery. Southern, white, proslavery advocates countered with
arguments that absolute freedom and equality were impractical, as an essential,
racial hierarchy was a necessity for social order. With the cotton gin and Southern agricultural boom still in the future, slavery was defended mostly as a necessary evil, thus keeping proslavery ideologies intact in the "new land of equality."
More ominous developments loomed, however. The abolition of slavery in the
North, the closing of the foreign slave trade, British criticisms of American sla-

very, and the rise of abolitionism, in addition to Revolutionary rhetoric, created a crisis for proslavery ideology.

These criticisms challenged the peculiar social formation and mode of social and relational reproduction of America's ideology. This challenge highlighted the contradiction between slavery and equality and questioned the unity of the proslavery ideology. It also represented a loss of the concept of a heroic white America. The nation needed a reconstitution of its ideological unity. Robert Walsh responded to the British contentions and provided just such a reconstitution in his *Appeal.* This treatise wove slavery and republicanism into a unified American vision based on conservative republican nationalism. Walsh's primer was so successful it became the representative proslavery text, one celebrated by no less than John Adams, James Madison, and Thomas Jefferson as a triumphal representation of American life. Walsh successfully demonstrated a rhetoric of white recovery.

An Appeal from the Judgements and other standard proslavery documents presented Southern whites as a superior race and blacks as imbecilic and inferior. These systematic and self-conscious defenses of slavery became part of a formal ideology, with advocates methodically advancing all possible arguments to support human bondage. This new American ideology re-produced equal whites and inferior blacks; slavery was now largely a positive good (Tise, *Proslavery* 16).[2] By rhetorically constituting individual whites into a collective, proslavery narrative unified whites and excluded blacks. The proslavery narrative effectively socialized the community by interpellating whites as naturally dominant and at the core of American civil society, while blacks were always the inferior alien outsiders. Elements of "white superiority" and "black inferiority" were ably woven into the systematic proslavery rhetoric, with its Judeo-Christian racist logic presuming white surveillance as a necessary restraint to black chaos (Cornel West, *Keeping Faith* 269).

Proslavery rhetoric bolstered slavery and, in tandem with whips and chains, buried blacks deeper in degradation by its presumption of both inherent, negative, black characteristics and self-evident, positive, white ones. It materially undergirded slavery by rhetorically constituting blacks and whites as social subjects always within a hierarchical structure that proved slavery was right and a part of the natural social order of society. The textual was made real. Blacks and whites experienced this rhetoric in ways that framed their lives as slaves and masters, property and owners, subordinate and superior, savages and saviors, and chaotic and civil. Through the stories they lived by, Anglo-Americans suppressed blacks. Anglo-American slave society, then, was based on this rhetorical-material ideology. Blacks responded. This response highlights the fact that the proslavery narrative constituted the ironic rhetorical culture that facilitated the emergence of black nationalism as its adversary.

Nineteenth-Century Black Nationalism

Early in the nineteenth century, blacks contested proslavery ideology by crafting an effective disarticulation of white supremacist discourse and by articulating a discourse that constituted an active, human, black subject. The contest for ideological dominance was a struggle to fix meaning and to control cultural practices. Even under threat to their own lives, blacks like Maria W. Stewart, David Walker, and Robert Alexander Young battled rhetorically for black liberation. Black nationalism worked with other abolitionist forces and with British criticisms of American life to challenge proslavery social formations and relations. Black nationalist discourse forced proslavery ideology into its own identity crisis. Some singular rhetorical productions animated the development of black nationalist perspectives.

Young's *Ethiopian Manifesto* and Walker's *Appeal* catalyzed early-nineteenth-century black activism. Young's *Manifesto* and Walker's *Address* were used by blacks to define themselves as part of a larger project of emancipation and self-determination. This effort to create a black identity was based on a common heritage and common expectations. The two documents claimed distinctive historical and cultural features and qualities of black life that revealed a pronounced nationalist-ideological bent. Functioning ideologically, then, these two foundation documents guided the organization of black public life.

The black cause was further aided by the constitutive rhetorics of black activists such as Stewart, William Whipper, Sidney, Henry Highland Garnet, Martin Robison Delany, Sojourner Truth, and Frederick Douglass. More specific to concerns addressed here, the Whipper-Sidney debate, Garnet's "Address to the Slaves of the United States of America," Douglass's "What to the Slave Is the Fourth of July?" and Delany's "Political Destiny of the Colored Race" were all part of a black nationalist discourse that presented a narrative account of "black people." In this black nationalist accounting, nineteenth-century blacks were an oppressed people within a country that they could call home because of their investment of blood, sweat, and tears. For black nationalists like Delany, blacks would be better served within their own nation. Such a nation could be established in the black motherland of Africa or the adopted country of America. In either case, according to the black nationalist narrative, the black nation was to be a self-governed entity independent of Anglo-America. According to Young, Walker, Sidney, Garnet, and Delany, to establish this independent black nation, American blacks needed to throw off the yoke of white oppression and claim their rights as a free people. Their rhetoric contributed significantly to the fight against slavery. Black nationalism developed as an important feature in nineteenth-century America because black life continued to be circumscribed by slavery and white supremacist rhetoric. This development was not without its own intramural challenges and changes wrought by events unfolding both within and outside organized black public life. Sidney put it tersely: "[T]here are differences among us" (*Colored American* 13 Feb. 1841).

Intramural struggles largely focused on separatist versus integrationist, pacifist versus militant, and American versus African dialectics. The following questions were asked: (1) Should abolitionist efforts involve sympathetic whites? (2) Should there be independent black social institutions? (3) Should blacks identify themselves as "colored," "black," "African," "American," or something else? (4) Should blacks be militant or pacifist? (5) Should blacks look to America as home or emigrate "back to Africa" or elsewhere? and (6) Should black people live among whites or as a geographically separate group? As these issues were contested, the rhetorical function of black nationalist ideology became clear: to constitute and reconstitute a mutable black subject.

The Whipper-Sidney debate of 1840–41 questioned the efficacy of separatism within abolitionism. In letters to the *Colored American,* both men crafted subjects to advance their disparate causes of separatism and integration. Though both supported the cause of nineteenth-century blacks, they constituted distinct subjects. Sidney constructed a racialized subject set apart by blackness, common African ancestry, and the shared experience of oppression. Whipper constituted a universalist subject that transcended race. The black subject was clearly not fixed in nature or culture but was pluralistic and amphibian, and rhetoric in the interest of different causes gave it different shapes. Still, the two perspectives articulated in this debate remain the polarized extremes of contemporary deliberation of black nationalism.

As the responses to Farrakhan's 1995 instantiation of Sidney's nineteenth-century call reveals, the appeal for an exclusively black effort for equality is as much a problem now as it was in 1840. Black separatist programs such as Garvey's Universal Negro Improvement Association have united and empowered blacks, both in North America and beyond. As a category, however, race has been used to marginalize African Americans and their concerns. It is therefore a two-edged sword, and questions remain as to its usefulness as an organizing principle for contemporary, multicultural, American life. Manning Marable persuasively argues, "Most contemporary socio-economic problems confronting black America cannot adequately be addressed by using the traditional racial strategies of 'integration' or 'separatism,' which have dominated black political discourse for more than a century" ("Plea" A15).[3]

The debates among nineteenth-century black leaders show the vigor and dynamism in the development and functioning of black nationalism. Such intramural contests also reveal that advocates in the 1840s and 1850s advanced black rhetorical strategies beyond claiming freedom and equality based on blacks' humanity and establishing the role and identity for blacks in the struggle for freedom. These advocates began to argue for freedom and equality based on the expressed claim that blacks were citizens. Garnet, Delany, and Douglass contended for a black public voice as citizens equal to other Americans. Theirs was a public rhetorical advocacy that contested Anglo-American notions of "the people." For these black advocates, blacks were "a people" who could claim their freedom and their place as part of the important American ideograph "the people." Where Garnet and Delany saw no prospect of a place for "their people" among "the [American] people" they proposed separation and independence. More important for considerations here, the radical contingency of this black nationalist ideology continuously adjusted to the vagaries of nineteenth-century black life even as it functioned as part of its creation. In addition, the rhetorical-material functioning of black nationalist ideology appropriately directed subjects to action or inaction. Such functioning emerged in the contested issues and in the actions taken by blacks in response to and as part of their rhetorical construction in the discourse. For example, in response to the call for emigration, some free blacks did leave America but most remained, another response to ideological prompting. Either way, none was unaffected.

Alongside physical slavery's chaining of black bodies, the rhetoric of white supremacy suppressed the black voice and, perhaps more insidious, alienated black lives. In the most cruel of ironies, blacks were often convinced of their impotence and dependence on white control (McColley 6). Such blacks were the subjects of the proslavery rhetoric of control (Bowers, Ochs, and Jensen 47–64). As Sidney argued in 1841, "one of the most malignant features of slavery . . . [is] that it leads the oppressor to stigmatize his victim with inferiority of nature, after he himself has brutalized him" (*Colored American* 6 Mar. 1841). To confront white supremacy, articulate their self-identity, and determine their own destiny, blacks had to confront their own alienation. They had to reject the image assigned them in the rhetoric of white supremacy: one of contentment in their degraded state. To awaken among their fellow black Americans "a bitterness and consciousness of degradation," they had to create an American story (*Colored American* 13 Feb. 1841). Their undertaking provides a rhetorical conception of alienation.

A Rhetorical Concept of Alienation

For this study, a rhetorical conception of alienation points to the role of rhetoric in the production of black identity. White supremacists constructed black identity to restrict blacks to social roles that fit a naturalized racial hierarchy of white superiority. These roles distinctly undermined the potential of blacks outside this socialization and were a significant part of the Anglo-American effort to complement and undergird physical slavery. With an interest in the way alienation functions rhetorically, we look beyond the physical and symbolic conditions themselves and see the discursive problems faced by blacks. Interpellated in a racist discourse that reified them as naturally subservient, blacks pointed to their awareness and feeling of alienation. To voice the distance between their constructed identity and their choices as social and biological beings, blacks expressed an "alternative consciousness" and engaged in an act of recreating and "repossessing the world" (Griffin 306; Burke, *Attitudes* 216). In Aaron Gresson's terms, they were in the process of racial recovery. In this process, they made visible their sense of the psychic distance between both their physical and discursive status on the one hand and their concept of their "true selves" on the other: they rhetorically made visible their discursive alienation.

Proslavery Rhetoric

In nineteenth-century America, such alienation was palpable, as whites not only dominated blacks with the physical accoutrements of slavery as part of their brutalization but also stigmatized them as inferior. In their discourse, they constructed social identities that reflected a debased and dominated life and consciously excluded the vast potential that black individuals always possessed. These Anglo-Americans rhetorically crafted black alienation. In the black responses to this two-pronged effort to distance them from their humanity are two problems: black compliance and black complicity.

Alienation took its full effect where blacks accepted these limited roles and reproduced them in their own discourse. White language marginalized blacks on the basis of race, and alienation occurred when blacks acquiesced to the descriptors imposed upon them within such language. In the black experience, then, alienation included more than just oppressive material conditions; it incorporated the language of blacks and whites. Black responses colluded with the white racist agenda. This is the phenomenon to which bell hooks refers in explaining her preference for the term "white supremacist capitalist patriarchy" rather than "racism." Blacks actively participated in white supremacy by acquiescing to notions of black inferiority.

The nineteenth-century Anglo-American proslavery narrative, here called the narrative of oppression, constituted a collective black subject that lacked the basic capacity necessary to claim humanity. Such a subject was imbecilic, without subjectivity, and always under the control and supervision of whites. Supervision was considered both necessary and in the interest of blacks, who by the 1840s numbered more than three million, about two million of whom were slaves. This narrative, of course, was an Anglo-American effort to facilitate social cohesion among whites, as well as to function as a rhetoric of control over blacks. It was an expression of white supremacy that served both the practical function of domination over blacks and the ideological function of rationalizing black-white relations of domination. It was an endeavor to distance blacks from their humanity, an act of alienation acknowledged among blacks and made visible by black nationalist rhetoric.

Such alienation maintained the racial hierarchy of nineteenth-century American life. More significant, it facilitated the willing participation of blacks in social relations that secured for themselves a fixed place at the bottom of the social order. Whites, of course, were always reinscribed at the top. This rhetorical functioning of alienation may be seen in the material and pragmatic effect the discourse had on both blacks and whites. The rhetoric of alienation could not be ignored by nineteenth-century Americans, whether black or white. It would be used to "form attitudes *and* induce actions in humans" (Burke, *Rhetoric* 41). Blacks and whites were induced by proslavery discourse to cooperate in the racist, hierarchical social relations of plantation slave societies.

From a twenty-first-century perspective, black and white interests were clearly not joined in nineteenth-century American slave societies. In fact, it is hard to believe that blacks could ever be persuaded that they were. Yet such is the power of rhetoric. Some blacks did accept the language that joined them to whites in social relations structured to condemn them to a position of inferiority based on race. Before our contemporary sensibilities prompt us to incredulity, we might consider the sobering reality of the effective functioning of modern capitalism, with its prolific rhetoric that identifies poor people as joined with the rich in a productive and mutually beneficial social relationship. Poor people have to be persuaded that "[t]he poor must be poor so the Rich may be Rich," to use the stark terms of W. E. B. Du Bois in *Dusk of Dawn* (162). The power of rhetoric is in its ability to effect identification. Sometimes that identification is as unlikely as the master-mistress and slave relationship that dominated antebellum American society. Constituted as subjects in discourse, individuals are recruited and "persuaded" to function in these roles. Inherent in such identification is the creation of factions. Thus constituted as slaves and masters-mistresses, blacks and whites belonged together even as they were separate. In such a scenario, the fabric of social power is woven by the hidden threads of discourse (McKerrow, "Critical Rhetoric: Theory" 92).

As an act of resistance, blacks wrestled for control over the construction of their own identity. In so doing, nineteenth-century blacks like Young and Walker began to develop a larger project of emancipation and self-determination that consisted of re-creating and repossessing the world. This undertaking included the articulation of a heroic and progressive collective black consciousness.

Black Nationalism and Alienation

Along with Young and Walker, Garnet, Delany, and Douglass used their unique perspectives as black men and, in the cases of Garnet and Douglass, as former slaves to highlight black alienation. They sought to restructure the relationship between blacks and whites by constructing and promoting an "African conscious-ness" among blacks (Stuckey, *Ideological Origins* 4).

The black nationalist struggle to awaken black Americans to a bitter conscious-ness of degradation provided a rhetorical account of alienation. Blacks needed to wrest rhetorical access to the dominant public fora from the clutches of white supremacy so they could constitute a human, vigilant, and heroic black public identity. Such an identity would contrast sharply with the imbecilic, subservi-ent, and animalistic one depicted in dominant white supremacist renderings of black life. The samples of black discourse examined here exemplify the develop-ment and materialization of black nationalist ideology and its inherent new black identity. This ideology unified and mobilized blacks while it challenged Anglo-American conceptions of black identity and authenticated its own.

The rhetorical articulation of black nationalism, then, was in part a struggle to confront the systems of meaning that produce black alienation. This struggle was true of black nationalism from its inception, with the birth of the collective black subject in Young's *Manifesto* and Walker's *Appeal,* through its most mature state during the antebellum period, with blacks contending for citizenship and grappling with the implications of self-representation from their position of alien-ation as seen in Garnet's "Address to the Slaves of the United States of America," Douglass's "What to the Slave Is the Fourth of July?," and Delany's "The Politi-cal Destiny of the Colored Race."

In establishing a black identity, black nationalists constructed a narrative of black life that functioned ideologically to constitute a collective black subject, to posit a transcendental subject, and to advance an illusion of freedom. This narra-tive served, first, to articulate black alienation. It did so by presenting the "true" identity of blacks, complete with their "true" history and culture. This identity was then set in contrast to nineteenth-century black conditions and the black sub-jectivity of Anglo-American white supremacist discourse. Having articulated this perspective, black nationalists employed alienation to mobilize apathetic and lethargic blacks to act in the interest of their own emancipation.

The second problem facing blacks in their response to the two-pronged assault of physical and rhetorical oppression, that of complicity, is highlighted by Mark McPhail in *The Rhetoric of Racism.* Unlike compliance, complicity results not from sharing the agenda of white supremacy but from efforts to oppose it. McPhail con-tends that in articulating a rhetoric of negative difference, black nationalism em-ploys the epistemic premises of racist rhetoric. This racist rhetoric presents a protagonist with an alleged essential quality of superiority: "whiteness." And as "whiteness" studies have made clear, this "essence" was often unmarked and as such was often signified by the marking of the Other as black, brown, or some *other race*. Where black nationalism presents an oppositional perspective based on the notion of essentialized blackness, "us," and an essentialized whiteness, "them," it shares with the perspective it opposes common foundationalist assumptions. In this way then, as we see in McPhail's notion of complicity, rhetorically, alienation premised on racism is perpetuated not just by whites on blacks or even by whites and blacks who support them. Racism is part of a linguistic dance often between black and white "victims" and "oppressors." This is not simply "blaming the victim"; rather it is an important insight into the problematic entailments of embracing essentialism.

McPhail's insight implies the possibility of black nationalism being shackled by what Gresson calls "the code word 'essentialist'" (55). These shackles can be broken, however. Because black nationalism seeks to deconstruct white racist notions of blacks as always Other, such a move always includes a process of essentializing, as Gayatri Spivak notes (Spivak 51). Black nationalism is a strategic rhetoric, however, and such a rhetoric can employ essentialism not as a fixed category but as a tentative one. This essentialism eschews claims of subjects who are "authentic" and "fixed" in any permanent sense. While remaining committed to its political agenda of emancipation, black nationalism can be fluid in its rhetorical and philosophical stance. Such a fluidity can be seen in black nationalism's approach to the problem of alienation.

Black nationalist ideology primarily provides a system of thought with modes of representation that affirm blackness and black life in general. In Molefi Kete Asante's view, black nationalism is an emancipatory politics that "liberates the mind from the duality of marginal existence" ("Systematic Nationalism" 124). To extend Asante's view, such liberation involves the rhetorically strategic use of the alienated position as an effective inside-outside perspective from which a collective African American public voice can reconstruct and rearticulate American identity both to create an acceptable place for black life and to guide the nation to concrete expressions of its highest ideals. As part of this effort, too, alienation was constructed as the basis for the motivation and mobilization of blacks for their own elevation. As we see here, the "motives, morality, and possible outcomes" of black nationalism are different from those of the racist discourse it opposes, black conservatives notwithstanding. Therefore, as Gresson notes, it ought to be considered differently and not simply discarded with the claim that it is essentialist (55).

The rhetoric of white supremacy functioned materially to conscript blacks to an underclass designated as their rightful status. This rhetorical function, in concert with the physical reality of slavery, ensured black alienation. Black nationalist discourses confront such rhetoric to create a different public consciousness and advance its own program of social and political activism. Important to this effort was black nationalism's constitution of a black collective identity.

It is in the confrontation between black nationalism and white nationalism that constitutive rhetorics create identities appropriate to the goals of such rhetorics. Here, ideologies create and recreate rhetorical realities at the expense of each other. In the challenge that black nationalism posed to the proslavery reified hierarchy and its racialized, transcendent subjectivity, the realm of subject formation and alienation is revealed as that of *doxa*. This is rhetoric's natural protean habitat. Rhetoric makes rescendent the transcendent subjects of opposing discursive practices, replacing them with textual beings of its own. Histories, epistemologies, and ontologies are created and contested as part of this process. In such a scenario, ossified black-white past meanings and identities are rendered fluid and contingent. Proslavery rhetoric was part of the system that created the hierarchy of white superiority and black alienation. It established what it meant to be black in relation to whites. By contrast, black nationalist rhetoric addressed the experience of alienation and sought to restructure what it meant to be black in relation to whites. The ideological effects that were appellative of black alienation are an important part of this discourse. These effects include the re-defining of blacks and the re-structuring of their social relations. With such an understanding of the epistemic and ontological functions of rhetoric in the historical struggle for black liberation, we can begin to understand African American political culture and the changes that take place within it. The past and its uses are crucial to our critical effort to understand contemporary life.

Sadly, the end of chattel slavery did not signal black acceptance and citizenship among Anglo-Americans (Williamson). For many nineteenth-century Anglo-Americans, "the existence of free blacks in any community, whether free or slave, [was] universally admitted to be an evil of no minor consideration" (Priest vii). What was an explicit sentiment in the nineteenth century continues to manifest itself, and even the United States government now acknowledges the troubling phenomenon of contemporary covert racism.[4] Whether overt or inferential, American racism continues to stalk its black citizens.

Slavery Ends, Racism Continues

The Jim Crow laws that continued through the first half of the twentieth century reveal the ugly face of this continued, overt American racism. Of equal concern is the less obvious, though no less notorious, manifestation of inferential racism. For a cursory look at these two egregious American practices, consider Frank Tannenbaum's 1946 assessment of blacks in the Americas. Within the context of the degrading ghost of slavery, Tannenbaum gushes that the survival

and adaptation of blacks to their circumstances in the New World are both cred-
itable and surprising. He observes, oddly, "he is active, self-assertive, and a living force. (He) [The black 'man'] has become culturally a European, or if you
will, an American, a white man with a black face" (41). Of course, just over forty
years later, Allan Bloom would bemoan the fact that blacks have not "melt [into
Anglo-America] as have all other groups"; "when everyone else has become a
'person,' blacks have become blacks" (19, 91–93). What Tannenbaum does not
identify is the pivotal role of rhetoric in the adaptation of black people to the
changing face of American oppression. While Tannenbaum acknowledges the
progress of blacks, he also reveals the superiority of his framework when he attributes black progress to the assimilation into whiteness. This tension spotlights
the ongoing problem of black identity and the dilemma blacks faced after Jim
Crow and continue to face in their efforts to negotiate contemporary American
political culture, even, and some might argue, especially, among sympathetic
whites. Tannenbaum's assessment, though courageous, is also curious in that it
provides insight into one of liberalism's blind spots.

Tannenbaum is reflexive enough to acknowledge that his work is a product
of its time. Grievously, though, blacks continue to experience racism even within
black-white coalitions that pursue black progress. Blacks have taken pains to make
visible to progressive whites both their execrable experience of inequality and the
racism implicit in the paternalistic practices and patronizing attitudes of white
"friends." These coalitions include the outstanding marathon of abolitionism,
the early years of the National Association for the Advancement of Colored People
(NAACP), and the Civil Rights movement. Black nationalists have led the effort to expose the racism of "friends." In response to the racist sentiments expressed by the early leadership of the NAACP, for example, Marcus Garvey excoriated the organization when he declared, "the greatest enemies of the Negro
are among those who hypocritically profess love and fellowship for him, when,
in truth, and deep down in their hearts, they despise and hate him" (T. Martin,
Race First 275; Garvey, *Philosophy* 2: 70). Similarly, Stokely Carmichael [Kwamè
Ture] charged, "[W]e've got to examine our white Liberal friends who come to
Mississippi and march with us, and can afford to march because our mothers,
who are their maids, are taking care of their house and their children" (6). This
is a form of racism that is predicated not on the white supremacist notions of
domination, oppression, and subjugation but on the basis of "friendly" exclusion of African Americans from significant circles of power. A black nationalist
ideology continues to find fruitful soil in such scenarios, as both the exclusion
to which the nationalists point and their leadership in confronting it resonate
with black people, many of whom share similar experiences. Still there is the
important question of whether black nationalism, functioning effectively as it

has in the role of what Laclau and Mouffe call a "strategy of opposition," can move us farther, taking the crucial step to becoming "the strategy of construction for the new order" (189; McPhail "Complicity of Essentializing" 166). It is that challenge to which I turn next.

Black Nationalism and Contemporary American Culture

Contemporary blacks continue to face perplexing problems in their effort to construct an effective black identity that will advance their causes in a majority white society. The modern diasporean problem of black alienation has been described in terms of visibility and namelessness. As a phenomenon of black life, it "can be understood as the condition of *relative lack of black power to represent themselves to themselves and others as complex human beings, and thereby to contest the bombardment of negative, degrading stereotypes put forward by white supremacist ideologies*" (Cornel West, *Keeping Faith* 16). In response to this claim of namelessness, Michael Eric Dyson contends that in hip-hop culture there is an overflow of naming (148–49). Yet this plethora of names within this aspect of African American performative culture is in some respects a response to the dominant frame of Anglo-American culture; when pushed, as in the case of the O. J. Simpson trial, it demonstrates that it still largely frames blacks in simplistic terms and in contrast to whites. The inability or lack of scope for effective naming is especially problematic, given the robust ensemble that makes up black life. The black world and the black image overflow with meaning "so rich and multisided that literally anything—and everything—can be found there, good and bad." Like the life-world of any group of complex humans it is a rich store of "contradictory material" (C. Johnson 11).

Despite years of struggle, most blacks still lack control of the means of production, and those with such control manufacture a monolithic, obnoxious product that is peddled as black identity. This product is then used as part of an effort to bracket black life, forcing it to the margins of American society and limiting its access to the myriad benefits of the "land of the free" (Wodak 199–226). These benefits are experienced as part of the common, taken-for-granted, everyday experience of Anglo-Americans, evident, for example, in *A Common Destiny* (Jaynes and Williams). Without the means of production, the ability to control identity is more apparent than real and we have not moved beyond the alienation problem. For all the progress in America, we have simply moved to a different stage of black alienation: away from the grotesque American nightmare of slavery and explicit oppression to the "American dream," with its facade of inclusion masking its disfiguring alienation. As hooks remarks, while blacks have gained some success in education and economics, the gains are minimal in "the field of representation[, which] remains a place of struggle" (*Black Looks* 1–3). As blacks know, those who constitute the identity of the subject set the agenda and are the likely beneficiaries of the resultant material action. Such action will come from individuals who act in the social world guided by their textual subjectivity. As blacks try to advance, their efforts toward self-representation continue. While black nationalism has played a significant role in this cause, there is much to be done.

The question is, does a black nationalist ideology provide the scope for the representation of contemporary blacks in such a way as to counter degrading stereotypes while it advances a common cause for equality? Can the concepts espoused by advocates like Farrakhan provide a reconfiguration of black alienation and black identification so as positively to restructure the relationship between African Americans on the fringes of American society and Anglo-Americans at its center? Put another way, for all its successes (and failures) in the past, can black nationalism's imagined black political community function effectively in the contemporary social, political, and rhetorical culture of the United States so as to have a firm chance at being successful in the battle of interpellation? It is this question that animates my excavation of black memory and my interrogation of the rhetorical problems that confront contemporary black nationalism as part of multicultural America.

Memory and Identity Formation

Critical memory, Houston Baker contends, is never free of "transgression and contamination of the past," and is "always uncanny . . . always in a crisis . . . the very faculty of revolution" (7). This is a faculty employed to good effect by black nationalists who advocate a revolution in response to years of black domination by Anglo-American white supremacist perspectives. Critical memory is an important site for African American identity formation. As Geneviève Fabre and Robert O'Meally avow, memory is where African Americans constantly renew their stock of "tragic consciousness," which makes them cautious and critical toward American life and history, embracing the notion that the past "has never really *passed*" (3). Following black nationalism, then, African Americans employ collective critical memory to contest history.[5] This use of memory is in contrast to the Anglo-American tendency to seek an escape from the burden of memory by focusing on the present and the future (Fabre and O'Meally 3). The difference, of course, is due partly to the fact that Anglo-American memory, with its own select remembering, dominates American life as America's true history. Still, blacks continue to contend for the place denied them by Anglo-American memory and historiography.

As in abolitionist rhetoric, critical memory is crucial in the social construction of contemporary reality, where different groups do the hard work exploring the possible readings of the "ensemble of experiences and documents" from the past, all of which provide sites with "a heap of signifying" (C. Johnson 20; Ellison 379). Anglo-American historiography has been used to suppress blacks and stymie black progressive efforts. Black nationalism provided history as the myth and ideology that blacks needed to contest dominant antiblack histories (Susman 5). Black nationalists then function, in Wilson Jeremiah Moses' terms, as "African vindicationists," not unlike "English vindicationists" before them (*Afrotopia* 15). In positing this shared memory for nineteenth-century black consumption, with its agenda of a common black identity, black nationalism inscribes a black subject with the unique perspective of independence and self-determination. Not only did black nationalist history challenge antiblack renderings of the past, it also posited a transhistorical subject and so fulfilled the ideological function of connecting contemporary blacks with an admirable past. This history also provided the material that served as the warrants for claims of a bright future for blacks as a people free of degradation and white oppression.

For black nationalists, critical memory is place, space, and identity. In short, to be black is to be able to think and feel on the basis of being the rhetorical "subject-who-remembers" (Dickinson 21). While not excluding black life in the New World, this "dialectic of remembering and forgetting" goes beyond the boundaries of the United States and certainly to a time before the experience of slavery (Nora 8). Important to this dialectic is critical memory's reclamation of Africa not only as a physical place, a home to which blacks could return, but as a psychological space from which blacks could trace their ancestry and reclaim a lost dignity. With some nostalgia, then, black writing continues to employ Africa to recall "racial ancestry and memory with considerable irony and surprise" (Dixon 23). In this rhetoric of nostalgia, black nationalism filled the past "with golden virtues, golden men and sterling events" (Baker, "Critical Memory" 7). This memorialization served to construct a black subject free of the taint of white subjugation. It is a black recovery process. In the mid-nineteenth century, this romanticized notion of blackness united blacks and energized them to overthrow slavery and oppression. As part of the effort toward continued black advancement, contemporary black nationalist conceptions have built upon the nineteenth-century notions of black identity, incorporating the struggle against slavery as a crucial component. Anglo-American perspectives, by contrast, have sought to restrict the use of black memory to "the gains we have made since the 1960s." In 1996, my seventeen-year-old daughter told me that in response to the already paltry efforts to celebrate black history month at Bloomington North High School in Indiana, white students who rejected the program often asked, "What else is there to learn? We already know about Dr. Martin Luther King." These Anglo-American perspectives often focus on blacks as a problem people, a people who have not embraced the opportunities offered by America. Whites therefore present a black subject who invokes a combatant, accusative memory that serves no productive purpose. The use of memory by whites in their own identity formation, however, reveals a different approach.

By their embrace of the double-barrel nomenclature "African American," blacks explicitly acknowledge the role of memory in their identity formation.[6] In contrast, whites often resist any form of hyphenation that would accentuate their immigrant status. Instead, whites often contend that they are simply "Americans," thus seeking to limit the scope of memory to be used in their identity formation to a naturalized notion of them as part of the espoused divine, pristine, seventeenth-century beginnings of America. They are supposedly God's emissaries, a part of the "Manifest Destiny" that is post-Columbian America (Horsman). This naturalization also underplays the significance of the Native American presence, as well as their vicious destruction at the hands of white settlers, and to mute the fact that, like most of the population, whites came to North America from elsewhere.

Memory then, this nearly forgotten rhetorical concept, is a crucial factor in coming to grips with our postmodern age. Our contemporary border crossings, fragmentation, and multiculturalization are not flights from a memory to which postmodernity returns seeking unity, as Greg Dickinson seems to suggest (21). Instead the nostalgic memory employed by those contesting multiculturalism often invokes a unity in America's past that is gossamer. This view, with its hand-wringing angst over contemporary fragmentation, uses its impaired nostalgic memory to scold present social practices. This is a flight from public memory. Invoking a shared public memory to look at America's past is likely to reveal that multiculturalism, at least from one perspective, is simply an effort to invoke a new past, giving voice to the previously suppressed. Here memory and the acknowledgment of its functions to construct fruitful and usable narratives from the past for the effective contemporary life of various national, ethnic, racial, or other groups can help us deal with our anxiety about our modern fragmentation. The present debate over the construction of the identity of blacks in the United States and, by extension, the construction of American identity or identities, often manifests itself as a debate over public memory. This raises significant questions about the role of public memory in contemporary political culture. Questions that critical scholarship might engage further include these facets: Where does collective memory begin? What should such memory entail? How should collective memory function in identity construction, deconstruction, and reconstruction?

This study of black nationalism reveals how rhetors created a collective black memory by drawing on black experiences prior to their American enslavement. These collective recollections provided the initial rhetorical ground from which later advocates could launch their efforts to contest the collective white memory and its account of black life, both prior to and since the beginning of their American experience. The use of memory, then, as a rhetorical strategy both facilitated the construction of a progressive, black, historical subject and provided a bridge that connected degraded blacks to an illustrious past. This transhistorical subject could then be depicted as free to choose the historical path of resistance, so cherished by the ancestors, or remain in the degraded unnatural state of white domination. This rhetorical subject was then used to challenge both the black and white subjects of proslavery rhetoric. Black nationalists used "black memory" to contest "white memory" and thus to create an American history with scope for blacks. Even so, black nationalism manifests striking limitations.

The Ideology of Black Nationalism and Its Problems

Cornel West indicts black nationalism for having decentered the freedom movement of the 1970s and 1980s. West charges what he calls "petit bourgeois nationalism" with having had four deleterious consequences for African America. First, the claim that black people within the United States constituted a nation served to isolate progressive black leftists, forcing them to embrace orthodox Marxism to advocate their concerns of class struggle and internationalism. Second, nationalism's macho image marginalized black women and caused the development of ineffective black feminine separatism. Here West echoes the multiple voices of black women such as Audre Lorde, bell hooks, Michele Wallace, and Toni Cade Bambara who see black men, not just nationalists, as breaking what Gresson calls the "collusive bonds" they share with black women through their masculinist notions of black life. Paradoxically, West's depiction of black feminine separatism as ineffective can be read as part of the antagonistic posture some black men adopt in response to black women's effort toward independent action. In addressing this problem in literature, Calvin Hernton notes that black men often relegate black women to the back burner and perceive it "as an offense for black women to struggle on their own let alone achieve something independently" (6). Third, its development of a parochial black rhetoric resulted in islands of internal dialogues that excluded progressive nonblack intellectuals and even some black ones. Fourth, black nationalism's move away from the church led to the freedom movement's loss of organic ties with the black community, especially the black church (Cornel West, *Keeping Faith* 268). These charges provide a template or set of *topoi* for discussing the problems of the ideology of black nationalism.

Insular Rhetoric and the Alienating of Potential Allies

The notion that blacks within the United States constitute a nation is one of the earliest facets of the ideology of black nationalism. It is a concept used to generate black pride, as it fostered a sense of unity among disenfranchised and down-trodden blacks searching for a sense of place and a secure identity. The nineteenth-century effort to identify blacks as one with Anglo-Americans in shared citizenship in the United States was an improbable if not futile one, given the structure of American society dominated by the white superiority perspectives. For both blacks and whites, this society had a fossilized racial hierarchy and the place of blacks was fixed at the bottom. This perspective resulted in widespread malaise and apathy among blacks facing a seemingly hopeless situation.

Black nationalists advocating black advancement sought to infuse hope into their black communities. In this undertaking, they faced the rhetorical challenge of publicly creating black pride in the face of overwhelming despair. They created in their discourse a collective black subject that fulfilled their goal of black activism. Beginning with Young's *Manifesto* and Walker's *Appeal,* these black nationalists constructed black people in the United States into a collective black subject with an illustrious past, replete with militant activism and credible achievements in the arts and sciences. Amidst intramural conflict, the notion of a distinct and separate black subject was extended to its most extreme perspective in Delany's "The Political Destiny" and the claim that blacks in the United States were a nation within a nation.

This separatist viewpoint has provided a world of existence for blacks distinct from the world created for them in Anglo-American discourse. In this separatist "nation within a nation," blacks found places and spaces where they could excel, find acceptance, and enjoy acknowledgment. Asante looks at the systematic nationalism of proponents such as Bishop Henry McNeal Turner, Edward Blyden, Marcus Garvey, and Elijah Muhammad and observes that they demonstrated that blacks were not alienated; they had simply never been a part of the American society. To find strength, then, Asante argues, "we affiliated with one another and grew to appreciate our strength" ("Systematic Nationalism" 123). Though true, this is only one aspect of black nationalism, the one that strengthened the call for the identification of Africa as home. Alongside this call, black nationalists were also making significant claims to the United States as a home for blacks. To do this, they crafted, in their rhetoric, black alienation.

The rhetoric of black nationalism highlighted the black condition in relation to that of whites. The relations of domination were presented and rationalized in white supremacist discourse as natural, God-ordained, and necessary for the smooth functioning of the society. By questioning and undermining this dominant American narrative, black nationalism rhetorically constructed black alienation. This construction involved the depiction of the black subject in prowhite discourse as functioning to distance black individuals from their natural humanity. In addition, black nationalism contended that Anglo-American accounts of black life were part of an effort to divide blacks in the North from those in the South, and to distance all blacks from their unique history and culture. Ultimately, black nationalism argued, Anglo-American efforts were conjured up to deny blacks their rightful place as equal citizens of America.

The effort to separate blacks from what was rightfully theirs was an act of alienation. If, as Asante argues, blacks never belonged, then their exclusion could continue to be rationalized as natural and necessary. For black activists such as Walker, Stewart, Garnet, Delany, and Douglass, however, the observation that blacks never belonged was true only in racist conceptions of America promoted and practiced as part of the framework of white supremacy. These blacks posited a rhetorical conception of alienation that focused on black interpellation in proslavery discourse as different from the potential of individual blacks. It is, as such activists argued, because blacks had a rightful claim on America that to accept their nineteenth-century roles, assigned by whites, was to be alienated. Because of Anglo-America's continued denial of such rights, black nationalism battled for black identity by seeking to establish a militant black subject with an admirable and unique history and culture.

The rhetoric of black nationalism has often been strident and exclusionary. It has strengthened internal cohesion while it fostered the creation of binary opposition between itself and other ways of thinking, even within the black community. Opponents of black nationalism, both blacks and whites, have often been excoriated as enemies and, in the case of blacks, as traitors. This has led to the isolation of black nationalism. Blacks who disagree with the radical ideology of people like Delany, Garvey, and Farrakhan have distanced themselves from black nationalism. The fortress mentality of walling off one group as distinct and special has been used by some radical black nationalists to further cement in-group loyalty by fomenting an "us versus them" discourse. Unfortunately, such a development leaves little space within black nationalism for alternative conceptions of black life. It has led, at best, to a tenuous relationship between black nationalists and others supporting black progress, especially where there is an advocacy of integration, collaboration, or other form of cooperation between blacks and whites. Sadly, others were alienated as well, including black women.

Black Nationalism and Masculinist Discourse: What of Black Women Activists?

For all the outstanding work of black nationalism toward black emancipation, it fell to black women to point out that it was to be an emancipation for all blacks, men and women. Such an observation exposes black nationalism as largely a masculinist enterprise that failed to acknowledge black men as an important part but not the whole of nineteenth-century black experience. With their own unique experiences, women made salient contributions to this struggle, though constrained by both racist and sexist practices such as the "cult of true womanhood." This cult was challenged by black women such as Maria Stewart and Sojourner Truth in their "indecorous" public speaking practices. The sexism these women faced is evident, for example, in Truth's 1867 insistence that she had "a right to just as much ('citizenship and suffrage') as a man," when black men argued that the right to suffrage proposed in the fourteenth amendment should focus exclusively on men (Yee 1). The significant role of nineteenth-century black women in elevating the race then should not be underestimated. An appreciation of the women's role is crucial, especially given that they, like black men, resisted oppression from the margins of a majority white society. In addition to racial hierarchy, however, the women also had to contend with patriarchal hierarchy, black and white. As a consequence of such patriarchal traditions, the black public sphere and its engines of reform were dominated by men's voices, with women largely involved in supporting roles. These women are aptly identified as the "brave," because of the tenacity that marked their enduring contribution despite the odds (Hall, Scott, and Smith; Peterson 6). For example, Stewart successfully challenged all these barriers to perform in public with pen and voice. Since the nineteenth century, black women have contested efforts to exclude their voices. In 1886, for example, distinguished black educator Anna Julia Cooper questioned the celebration of leading black men to the exclusion of black women in a speech titled "Womanhood a Vital Element in the Regeneration and Progress of a Race." Speaking of Martin Delany, she argued that no individual could "be regarded as identical with or representative of the whole [black race]" (30). Cooper's defense of the role of women in the struggle for black progress is significant, as it demonstrates the willingness of nineteenth-century black women to confront their own communities to correct masculinist myopia. One hundred years later, Deborah E. McDonald encounters the problem of a single man being used as the synecdoche of African Americans when she confronts Henry Louis Gates Jr's contention that Frederick Douglass was a representative man (*Figures in Black* 108). McDonald employs Cooper's critique and argues that such a perspective "reproduces the omission of women from view" (208). Since the early nineteenth century, beginning with Phyllis Wheatley and Stewart, black women activists not only confronted men but also spoke and wrote in public in collaboration with men.

From the early to mid nineteenth century, however, women participated in the black struggle primarily from within the confines of a "women's 'sphere,'" which was interpreted as limited to organizing all-female societies and raising funds to support the male leadership" (Yee 3; Blackett, "In Search" 307–8). Yet their work was no less significant than that of the men highlighted in this debate. In addition, as in the case of Charlotte Forten (Robert Purvis's niece), Mary

Ann Shadd Cary (Abraham Shadd's daughter), and Sarah Parker Remond (sister to Charles Remond), several women were related to prominent male leaders by blood or marriage and were actively involved in the black abolitionist effort (Peterson 10, 135).[7]

Appropriately, then, as part of the vibrant research program focusing on the role and efforts of black women, critics invite a rethinking of the scope and modes of evaluation of black women's role in the struggle for equality. Cheryl Gilkes, for example, cautions against overlooking the importance of "internal transformations" championed by women that functioned alongside the "persistent effort to combat racism" (Rogers-Rose 53). Patricia Hill Collins proposes a reclaiming of the black women's activist tradition as a way of reconceptualizing black women's activism and resistance and providing a more comprehensive analysis of power. Collins encourages the ongoing explorations of black women's significant, if often overlooked, role in organized struggle against slavery and white supremacy. In addition, she seeks a more careful assessment of black women's survival practices, including women's creation of "spheres of influence within existing structures of oppression" that do not necessarily confront oppressive structures but undermine them. These practices within the "women's sphere" also provide for black communities "the ties that bind," making possible public activism and the public resistance of oppression (140–61).

With a focus on the Nation of Islam, Cynthia S'thembile West examines the role of women to argue that the "'public' posture of the Nation emphasized a male agenda" (6). However, she contends that, like others before them, the women of the Nation make significant contributions that continue to be demeaned because of a long-standing gender-based prejudice that designates "women's work" as inferior (7). Consequently, she engages in a reevaluation of "women's work" in the Nation and joins the larger effort to reconceptualize women's contribution to the liberation of African people through a reevaluation of their spheres of influence. She highlights that notwithstanding the efforts to render them invisible, women continue to make substantial contributions to the premier black nationalist religious organization in the United States.

In the 1850s, when Sojourner Truth joined Francis Watkins Harper and others, the voices of black women abolitionists were much more prominent than before. These women, both by choice and as a function of social constraints, focused on issues of moral reform and worked as advocates of Christianity. Though they worked on a different front, however, Stewart, Harper, Forten, Truth, and others were partners to men such as Sidney and Whipper.

The "double jeopardy" of race and sex stalking black women persisted beyond slavery (Beale 90–100). In 1904, Mary Church Terrell contended that not only are "colored women" "handicapped on account of their sex, but they are almost everywhere because of their race" (King 42). Even today, the role of black women continues to be a contentious issue, and black women persist with their claim of being doubly oppressed by both racist and sexist practices. As Gerda Lerner has documented, black women have long lived in white America and continue to do so. The signal contemporary marker of this phenomenon was the experience of Anita Hill in the 1991 Senate Judiciary Committee hearings regarding the nomination of Clarence Thomas to the U.S. Supreme Court (Morrison). The problem is even more acute, however, within black nationalism's strident rhetoric and its exclusionary, militaristic overtones. Such a rhetoric serves to constitute black nationalism as a macho, male-dominated organization with little room for black women's public voices.[8] Incidentally, this militant stance continues to be one of the reasons why black nationalism is among the most scrutinized and policed aspects of black culture. As Tony Martin argues, black nationalism has "been a heavily persecuted ideology. The powers that be have sought to destroy nationalist movements with a fervor not usually experienced, even by less conservative integrationist movements" (*Pan-African Connection* ix). That it is perhaps the most organized sector of the black community is another.

Whereas nineteenth-century black women advocates worked primarily within the church, espousing moral reform as a means of racial uplift, the men, as the public voice of black nationalism, presented a more explicit challenge to America and its institutions. Most prominent among such challenges were those to the black church. Though the changing role of the black church admits to a more complex reading than West's blame of black separatism, his claim is worth investigating.[9]

The Black Church

The role of the church in black liberation is as central as it is enigmatic. That the black church was integral in the struggle for black liberation is beyond question. What is more problematic is the church's role in the construction of black identity. While an extensive treatment of the black church is beyond the scope of this project, the church's relationship with black separatism turns on issues of black identity and the means of the black struggle (Frazier, *Negro Church;* Lincoln). These contentious issues have put a continued strain on this relationship.

As Franklin Frazier argues, though the "Negro Church" offered a refuge from the hostile white world, it generally accepted white domination to which it offered no threat. The church dismissed black sufferings as temporary and transient. Also, the catharsis that the black church offered to those seeking status and a meaningful existence pointed them away from their daily sufferings to a future world of heavenly rewards. From the separatist perspective, the church was regressive in that it aided in the "accommodation to an inferior status" (*Negro Church* 51). C. Eric Lincoln also contends that while the black church has always "stood as the *symbol* of freedom," there was uncertainty as to whether it should also have been the "*instrument* of freedom" (108).

The black church has been indicted for incorporating white values and for presenting to black people a view of the world where "white" represents that which is pure and good and "black" represents that which is sinful and degraded. Frazier, for example, relates his experience of hearing a black preacher declare that "Pharaoh was a nigger and like all niggers who get power he oppressed the Jews who were God's chosen people" to argue that the image of God in the minds of some blacks "conformed to that of a kindly white planter" (*Negro Church* 96). In contrast, black nationalism focuses explicitly on race pride. In each of these issues, the rhetorical positions of the church and black separatism put them at ideological cross purposes. The partnership for freedom between the two has always been tenuous. To challenge white domination and promote black pride, then, black nationalism often worked outside and at times against the church. The result was a number of challenges to black nationalism, including a conservative reappraisal.

Contesting Blackness: Black Nationalism and the New Black Conservatism

A new conservative, black vision of race in America has emerged in recent years with an articulate public voice focusing on individual responsibility and minimizing past struggles as a basis for present agitation (Marable, *Speaking Truth* 62–68). This contending black vision highlights the rhetoricity of "black people," black nationalism's collective subject. More than that, on center stage of the struggle in the African American drama, it lays bare what Gresson calls "the myth of racial homogeneity" as it claims "authentic blackness" (ix).

For black nationalism to function effectively in American society, it must contend with the white supremacist discourse demeaning blackness, as well as multiple black voices contesting blackness, including the more recent crop of blacks, who, like Farrakhan, share common conservative values such as self-help, notions of family, and religious commitment. In striking contrast to black nationalism and to the black Civil Rights establishment, however, these newer black conservatives discredit both the historical role of white privilege and white oppression and that of black struggle and deprivation. This conservative black vision employs critical memory to mine an account of the black past different from that advanced by black nationalists such as Garnet, Delany, Garvey, and Farrakhan. Not surprising and more important, these conservatives map a different black future landscape. To them, the question of the present and the future is more important than that of the past. Within this context, the struggle over the future is more strident, since some of these new black conservatives were civil rights activists with a good grasp of African American history of struggle. For some of them, then, the problem is not so much the black past but the endangerment of the present and the future by the betrayal of the civil rights agenda for one of race and racial privileges. Central to this conservative vision is the aggressive advancement of an individual black subject who can fulfill the American dream on the basis of personal effort while eschewing collective black activism.

This alternative, black, American story is exemplified in the autobiographical narratives of George S. Schuyler, Clarence Thomas, and Ward Connerly.[10] It is the personal success story of blacks advancing to the top of American society amidst racism but with the help of "good white people"; a black endorsement of the Horatio Alger myth (this black endorsement was embodied earlier in Booker T. Washington's *Up from Slavery*), so much a part of the Anglo-American conception of the United States as a land of social mobility for all hardworking individuals. For example, Karl R. Wallace identifies Washington's life as "a brilliant example of the success-story formula" (2: 408). As part of this conservative affirmation, Connerly, a University of California Board of Regents member, contends large numbers of blacks are seeking independence from traditional (liberal) black dogma to advance their cause in contemporary America. In upbraiding liberal notions of African American struggles articulated by Rev. Jesse Jackson and the Civil Rights establishment, for example, Connerly protests that in America "we are preoccupied with race, it seeps out of every pore."[11] Joseph G. Conti and Brad Stetson, largely supportive of the conservative move, note that "this country is hearing a debate between two sets of ideas that are vying to direct the future of American blacks" (5). This conservative vision stands in direct contrast to the black nationalist vision of ongoing, collective black struggle for equality. The contending perspectives in the debate over the identity of blacks reveals that the character of the collective entity of "black people" and who it entails is problematic.

Beyond that, these conservative developments embody what Gresson identifies as the white recovery project rhetoric best exemplified in Reaganism. Curiously, an important aspect of this white recovery rhetoric is the "deconstruction of the oppressed." The black successes of the Civil Rights era were achieved against the backdrop of blacks being able to claim victimhood; pointing to the "nigger" status imposed on blacks by whites dramatized this national social predicament. The Black Power movement dramatized this predicament as international, with the connection of the black struggle in the United States to the struggle over colonialism worldwide. The civil rights successes for blacks then represented an indictment of whites and resulted in what Gresson calls the loss of white heroic status. Whites quickly moved into recovery mode, with white women and white students being the first to recover their "heroic" voices. Gresson contends that this white recovery was facilitated by the enlarged use of term "nigger" to allow first white women (in the women's liberation movement), then white students (in the student's rights and antiwar movements), and finally, white men (under Reaganism) to reenter the fray as victims, always with blacks as the new victim-izers, the new perpetrators of injustice. These developments allow for a recovery of white moral force and a weakening of black claims to victimhood; a disen-chantment with blacks and with the portrayal of them as victims (6–7). This reframing of blacks as perpetrators rather than as victims of oppression was ex-emplified in dramatic fashion with the 1990 publication of Steele's *Content of Our Character*. In this significant treatise with its central themes of black exploi-tation of white guilt and black oppression of whites, the author, a black man, signifies full-blown white recovery and the lack of "black racial unity" (8, 9). Steele provides insightful analysis of the problem of race in America and demonstrates the heterogeneity that must be acknowledged and embraced as part of a multi-cultural community. Still his insistence on articulating white pain and what he sees as black pathology compromises his project and reveals a regressive political agenda that reflects an awareness of the history of black suffering but a willing-ness, if not eagerness, to dismiss it. Steele was lauded primarily by white and black voices on the conservative side of the political spectrum, and he was lambasted by blacks and whites on the other side, some of whom even labeled him a trai-tor. Julius Lester faced similar reactions after his 1988 publication *Lovesong* (McPhail, "Complicity of Essentializing" 167–68).

Steele, along with Connerly and Thomas Sowell, occupy leading roles in this new black conservative army often accused of irresponsibly traipsing on the sa-cred black memory of struggle. Their alternative conception of blackness, how-ever, also brings into sharp relief the key role of rhetoric and collective memory in the use of the past as part of contemporary black identity formation and ideo-logical contestation. In addition, such contestations, past and present, make vis-ible the tenuous nature of claims to an essential black identity as they call into question projections of a unified black collective. From McPhail's perspective, these black conservatives who "do not speak the party line" ought to be welcomed as part of the conversation about black culture that Gresson invites, for it is their input that "illuminates the shifting and unstable boundaries that circumscribe African American culture and identity" (Gresson 214; McPhail, "Complicity of Essentializing" 167, 170). Stuart Hall too invites more debates about black iden-tity among blacks (*Race*). This intramural struggle for control of the identity of the black subject and the program for black advancement is not unlike earlier struggles, for as we see in the Whipper-Sidney debate and in the comparative exploration of Garnet's, Douglass's, and Delany's rhetoric, blacks in abolition-ism engaged in vigorous contentions for black advancement from a variety of perspectives. The advocates of black uplift sometimes changed their perspectives, depending on the challenges facing their black communities. With this in mind,

Gresson's and, later, McPhail's critical explorations of black conservative rhetoric are welcome developments.[12] Noteworthy too is the critical scholarship moving us beyond popular and often simplistic condemnations of Farrakhan's radical black nationalism by investigating his rhetoric with its complex mix of insular appeals (including the expressed hate mongering), religious dogmatism and conservatism, and patriarchal, militaristic agitation for black equality.[13] For example, John Arthos Jr. treats Farrakhan's Million Man speech as the performance of a shaman trickster and contends that Farrakhan and the March provided a space where blacks could find solace and strength, with both speaker and audience sharing a common understanding of the double voice and the double reading necessary to survive and thrive under the panoptic gaze of an unsympathetic mainstream culture. Steven Goldzwig sees Farrakhan's rhetoric as effecting symbolic realignment between Farrakhan and his audience to motivate action within his black audience.

McPhail extends Gresson's insightful analysis of the ideological and material complicity of black conservatives in the debate over identity and unity to show how these oppositional discourses limit both analytical and political action. McPhail grounds the debate between liberal and conservative voices in the historical black struggle (the rancorous Garvey–Du Bois verbal spats) to argue that essentialism and epistemic complicity are evident in the oppositional stance of both those advocating "Blackness" and those countering with notions of "the myth of Black unity" ("Complicity of Essentializing" 163). Both sides in these debates advance notions premised on "foundationalist or essentialist classifications" (163). Both contest for dominance with argumentative claims of difference premised on unreflexive claims of the essences of their chosen black (and white) subject. Of course, from the perspective of a critical rhetoric we see the functioning of the discursive formation. The subjects are not simply chosen; they are constructed. As McPhail, citing Laclau and Mouffe, acknowledges, they are always ambiguous, always incomplete, always polysemic, always amorphous, and thus always problematic (Laclau and Mouffe 121; McPhail 163). These discursive subjects resist closure even though they are "born" as a result of the "*desire* for . . . fullness." This is a desire shared in symmetry by oppositional perspectives, all with the goal of preeminence by displacement. The rhetoric of black nationalism, then, a rhetoric of freedom, articulated in direct opposition to the rhetoric of domination, such as white nationalism, shares with it a common desire for fullness and the limiting perspectives of "essentialized subjects and transcendent sensibilities" (164). Such a revelation calls for reflexivity and flexibility among black nationalists to foster self-critique and more effective emancipatory action, as there is still work to be done among all classes in black America.

Black Nationalism, the Black Underclass, and the Black Middle Class

The black underclass is fixed in Anglo-America's collective consciousness as scofflaws. This image is reinforced by Anglo-America's media representations. This is a group of black people constrained and contained within the steel bars of poverty and lack of opportunity, and interpellated within the dominant Anglo-American narrative as a pathological problem to be kept under the panoptical white gaze of America's judicial machinery. These blacks are patently alienated (W. Wilson, *Declining Significance* and *Truly Disadvantaged;* Glasgow). Notwithstanding the incredulous protestations of black and white conservatives about black pathologies and individual responsibility, this alienation is a major American problem and one that continues to have devastating effects on blacks with deleterious consequences for the nation. Black nationalism and rap music's strident lyrics readily articulate this alienation.

In more subtle terms, black nationalism, with its radical and often extreme manifestations and through its bold challenges of white supremacist practices, gives voice to an otherwise muted middle class caught in the straits of careers geared toward social mobility within an economy still controlled by whites.[14] Such white control often requires black quietism and compliance as part of the package of advancement. There is some truth in the observation that the crass racism of the pre–Civil Rights era, such as that expressed earlier by Mississippi governor and later senator James K. Vardaman, has simply become invisible. Vardaman claimed,

> I am just as opposed to Booker T. Washington as a voter, with all his Anglo-Saxon reinforcements, as I am to the coconut-headed, chocolate-colored typical little coon, Andy Dotson, who blacks my shoes every morning. Neither is fit to perform the supreme function of citizenship. (qtd. in Stone 26)

As evidenced by *The Bell Curve,* with its deceptive veneer of intellectual respectability and its array of public defenders, many Anglo-Americans still presume blacks prima facie to be inferior, incredible though it may seem. This is much like the Supreme Court of Mississippi, which earlier "presume[d] a Negro *prima facie* to be a slave" (qtd. in Frazier, *Negro Church* 31).

This dilemma makes for uncertainty and sometimes confusion for middle-class blacks, which leads, for example, to Charles T. Banner-Haley's contention that it is often unclear what the black middle class wants to be. He argues, however, that black middle-class ideology throughout the twentieth century has been informed by the desire to be included in American society while maintaining a distinct racial identity. This is Du Bois's classic statement of the problem of the African American who "ever feels his [or her] twoness—an American, a Negro; two souls, two thoughts, two unreconciled strivings; two warring ideals in one dark body, whose dogged strength alone keeps it from being torn asunder" (*Souls* 5). In their effort, then, to merge their "double selves into truer and better selves" and to fulfill their desire to advance against the odds of American racism, middle-class blacks have effectively manipulated black nationalist ideology by rejecting the separatism of radical black nationalism and embracing racial solidarity (5; Banner-Haley 9, 10). It is as it is expressed, that this middle-class black alienation takes on material existence. Not only does the historical black nationalist political practice of race pride as a basis for solidarity continue to serve black causes, but its rhetorical conception of alienation provides an avenue to identify a long-denied form of black alienation.

Blacks continue to demonstrate an age-old black survival strategy of adapting to, configuring, and reconfiguring exigencies, a tradition clearly part of nineteenth-century black abolitionist practices. Charles P. Henry refers to this practice as "the hallmark of black politics: an ability to combine individualism and community as well as sacred and secular" (Henry 94). This ability is sorely needed in the confrontation between the individualized and the collective visions of black identity that now stalks black culture. However, with respect to the alienation of the black middle class and without the black narrative exemplified in James Baldwin's *Notes of a Native Son,* Sam Fulwood III's "Rage of the Black Middle Class," Ellis Cose's *Rage of the Privileged Class,* and Feagin and Sikes's *Living with Racism: The Black Middle Class Experience,* there would be no material phenomenon, as such, to demand redress. Though the feelings may have been present among blacks, other voices would have continued unabated, their construction of a black middle class used as white supremacist, Anglo-America's poster child for its story of black mobility. This is a subject used as the star witness for the prosecution of the black underclass for its "crime" of being lazy and un-American. Black nationalism's articulation of black alienation, however, continues to keep black folks alive as it confronts this effort at black debasement and fosters the alienation of other progressive forces interested in the struggle for justice. The centrality of race in this encounter remains a vexing problem.

Black Nationalism's Biggest Challenge: The Problem of Race

Espousing race is problematic, but the effort to transcend it is no less vexatious. Radical or immediatist abolitionism, which saw blacks and whites working together, in contrast to earlier gradualist efforts that excluded blacks, had its apogee in the mid-1830s. As part of the flurry of public efforts against slavery, black women such as Susan Paul, Grace and Sarah M. Douglass, Harriet Purvis, and Sarah and Margaretta Forten organized antislavery activities for women. By 1836 more than five hundred antislavery societies had been established in the North. This growth in interracial efforts was also marked by a linking of moral reform and racial uplift with the attendant expectation that the human condition would improve and that slavery and racial prejudice would be eliminated. In the face of a thriving slave society and increased racism, however, by the 1840s blacks had judged this venture a failure and began to call for independent black action (Ripley et al., *Black Abolitionist* 3: 12–18). Even so, black abolitionists such as Whipper, James McCune Smith, and Samuel Cornish challenged black separatism and advocated ongoing black-white collaboration. With race as the primary marker shaping the lives of nineteenth-century Americans, such calls entailed their own impediments. Furthermore, they remain subject to the ready criticism of being disingenuous utopian desire. Even into the twenty-first century, such criticisms maintain their veracity as long as whiteness continues to accrue wages while functioning as social capital and blackness accrues surveillance while functioning as a social stigma. As Sidney argued, the black nationalist ideology was a response to the physical and rhetorical manifestation of white supremacy. This is an Anglo-American ideology continuously supported and undergirded by the racist rhetoric of whites, including both friends and foes of blacks. For even while blacks were struggling over the construction of a positive identity for themselves, as is evident in the names debate, whatever blacks called themselves, they were, as Samuel Cornish noted, "nothing else but NEGROES" (3: 263). Likewise today, students continue to indicate that "nigger" remains a popular sobriquet among white college students to describe blacks.[15] The increase in bigotry and brutality of white supremacist practices followed by a resurgence of black nationalist sentiments has since become a pattern, as Michael West's historical survey at the beginning of this chapter reveals.

Black nationalism has constantly been attuned to the collective needs of blacks in America, and thus its collectivist vision readily emerges when it is needed rather than in reaction to white nationalism per se. By making race its central organizing principle, nineteenth-century black nationalism has passed what Kwame Anthony Appiah calls "a burdensome legacy" on to twenty-first-century Pan-Africanism and more contemporary nationalisms (Appiah 5). According to Appiah, this legacy predisposes contemporary black nationalists to assume racial solidarity among blacks (5). Important as it is for internal group cohesion—especially for disenfranchised blacks in America—this assumed solidarity is textual, a construct of the rhetoric seeking to advance black causes. Such solidarity is often espoused in exclusive terms, precluding any possibility of collaboration with whites or other groups. Where race continues to serve as a fixed entity loaded with the historical baggage of Anglo-American racism and where black nationalism is inflexible, it provides little rhetorical scope for creative and innovative solutions to our shared social problems, often predicated on "race." From this perspective, black nationalism is in desuetude, but it can be flexible.

The positions of black abolitionists, especially black nationalists, have been long debated and increasingly accepted for their flexible and changing positions on issues such as integration versus separatism and Africa versus America as home for blacks. That black nationalist leaders such as Garnet and Delany were flexible in their ideology is now generally accepted. Accounts that point out the adaptability of these leaders to difficult and changing situations, though insightful, leave untouched the rhetorical nature of such changes. How does the collective black subject facilitate the changes in the persuasive appeals of the narrative of black nationalism? Perhaps more significant, how is this protean collective subject created? From the perspective of a constitutive rhetoric, a perspective that reveals people are constituted in discourse, we can tell that the identity and character of "the people" are open to constant rhetorical revision. As part of this rhetorical flexibility, the terms "blacks," "Africans," "black Americans," or "African Americans" function materially to identify and position black people in America with respect to their history and future. This positioning is, to extend Goldzwig, a "symbolic realignment" of blacks to their history and thus their "true" selves. It addresses their alienation and places them symbolically on equal footing with the dominant group (Goldzwig 211). It is an effort to disconnect from the enemy at the level of an inferior and to reengage at the new level of equals. As long as black nationalism's rhetoric persists in its inward focus, however, it will continue to build in-group solidarity while it increases the distinction between an essentialized "us" and "them," thus reducing the chances for fruitful collaboration.

Central to the issue of race is its progeny, racism. Gresson's insight that racism has become a problematic *topos* is worth exploring. Racism seems to be a place on the American discourse landscape that, in the mind of many white and some black Americans, especially conservatives, has been mined of all its rhetorical resources. Speakers and audiences, it seems, are weary of racism as a rhetorical situation. It has deteriorated and needs to be reconfigured and reconceptualized if it is to usefully serve the discourse of liberation. In McPhail's terms, oppositional claims of racism invite counterclaims and precipitate a downward spiral of negative differences. Still the problem of color, hair, and bone haunts us. Liberation efforts concerned with race have to artfully negotiate the rhetoric of racism as it reflexively contends with its own implication in the process. The philosophical challenge presented by essentialism might be addressed with the use of "strategic essentialism," which calls for a contingent and mutable approach to the identification of subjects and their essences. Such a move facilitates a political solution that includes the building of coalitions across "racial" lines and thus rendering as problems notions of essential racial categories. Paradoxically, the shattering events of 11 September 2001 that destroyed approximately three thousand lives might serve at least one useful purpose. It might refocus our collective eyes across racial divides and onto our shared target of inviting the nation to live up to its creed. While I am reluctant to join the black intellectual elite, especially the conservatives, who, in their positions of privilege, urge us to transcend race by thinking beyond our blackness (because most blacks in America have no choice but to live racialized lives), I must confront a hard question: Can black nationalism's "truth," which Louis Farrakhan calls "an answer to your [white] racism," suffice in our efforts to combat racism and advance common causes for justice (Goldzwig 214)? If black nationalism maintains its separatist agenda, guided as it is by its problematic notion of essentialized identities, the answer is an easy no. Yet separatism and essentialism are not fixed features of this discursive system.

The need for multicultural, American existence continues to foil separatist tendencies. By embracing contingency rather than inevitability, difference rather than homogeneity, and social and intellectual fragmentation rather than seamless systematic approaches, we may yet create ways to celebrate our differences. We may yet transform "race." With its own radical contingency, black nationalist ideology, often in mutated form, addresses some of the salient issues of our social relations in contemporary life and, as such, frames our lives in significant ways.

Contemporary Challenges, Contingent Responses

In employing a material conception of rhetoric in this study, I have described the historic role of discourse in the black struggle for freedom and justice and the critical rhetorical reconstruction of memory as an ideological tool. A little scrap of *his*tory about the antebellum period can serve here as a gentle reminder of this functioning. In defending his notorious work *Cotton Is King* against the claim that it was an apology for American slavery, David Christy argued that he was "writing history and not recording his own opinions" (Elliott 28). In the face of such histories, American stories that selectively forget blacks or remember them only "as a people who have been docile, passive, parasitic, imitative," African American resisters have since the seventeenth century consistently recrafted a more inclusive story of America (Aptheker, *Documentary* introd., vol. 1; R. Cover 172).

With their lives dominated and demarcated by white supremacist perspectives, nineteenth-century blacks crafted an identity through which they could articulate their collective concerns and advance their cause of freedom. Interpellated in this discourse are progressive, militant subjects; blacks who were previously inscribed in proslavery discourse as passive and subservient could now assert their humanity as active subjects with the freedom to choose their social roles. Perhaps most important, black nationalist rhetoric questioned the reified black-white social relationship of the period. In proslavery discourse, this relationship was fixed in the naturalized racial hierarchy of white supremacist societies. Black nationalist rhetoric pointed it out as part of the functioning of white supremacist perspectives.

The relationship was a rhetorical crafting of alienation. Unmasked, such alienation became the basis for a variety of contingent, black nationalist appeals that ranged from Walker's call to violent uprising and Delany's desire for emigration to Douglass's claims of full citizenship.

In discussing these stories of resistance, I have highlighted different rhetorical strategies for conceptualizing alienation and struggle and for engaging race ideologically. My primary goal has been to advance the cause of justice in a more inclusive America. As Tony Martin states in defense of Garvey's project on race pride, "he set out with self-conscious candor to oppose the propaganda of race pride and nationhood to the contrary ideas of white supremacy, African inferiority, white man's burden and Caucasian manifest destiny" (*Race First* 90). The focus on racial distinctions was, of course, a rhetorical strategy for the debate over power. As Walter Rodney contends, "Black Power is not racially intolerant," for within black nationalist ideology, "the moment that power is equitably distributed among several ethnic groups then the very relevance of making the distinction between groups will be lost" (*Groundings* 29). Yet race continues to be a contradiction for black nationalism.

In contemporary American society, race is still used ideologically as a tool for alienation and fragmentation among people. Critical rhetoricians can expose such functioning and facilitate our wholesome, shared existence by problematizing and theorizing sedimented notions such as race, identity, difference, and alienation.

D. W. Griffith's *Birth of a Nation* (based on John Dixon's *Klansman* and President Woodrow Wilson's favorite film) is one crass and notorious example of where race has been used in popular culture for ideological effect. Even so, between the release of the film in 1915 and his death in 1948, Griffith "defended himself as a film maker with no political or ideological view in mind" (Bogle 16). The use of race for such purposes in contemporary American culture is not as vulgar as it was in *The Birth of a Nation*. Indeed, in contemporary America, race prejudice has become more sophisticated and subtle in its manifestation. With credible evidence, an impressive assembly of both professional and lay witnesses endorse the call for the biology of race to be buried without a trace (Hall, *Race*). The ghost of color, hair, and bone still stalks the landscape of our contemporary discussions about crime, welfare, education, housing, bank loan policies, and American identity (Hartman). Race, racism, and white supremacy are recalcitrant. In 1940, for example, Du Bois bemoaned the fact that, in America, not the philosophy of Thomas Jefferson, the crusade of William Lloyd Garrison, or the reason of Charles Sumner could prevail against the white superiority, imperialism, and race hate of John Calhoun, Jefferson Davis, and Ben Tillman, respectively (*Dusk* 139). We are forced therefore, to continue to attend to the unstable, malleable social entity called race.

Treating race as part of a process might be our best approach (Jordan, *White Man's* xi). In this undertaking, the rhetoric of black abolitionism can serve as a primer to guide us through the hazardous but necessary negotiation of race on the scabrous terrain of contemporary, multicultural America. The journey is hazardous because of the ideological mines that lurk just out of view but necessary because the terrain is that of our shared existence. As Asante contends, "symbolic imperialism rather than institutional racism, is the major social problem facing multicultural societies" (*Afrocentric Idea* 56).

There are still good reasons to "bore in" and traipse across the cherished and privileged domains of knowledge production (Wander 1). Therefore the challenge to provide emancipatory critique is presented to rhetorical scholarship in the face of the traditional practice of rhetorical criticism and theorizing, which has been to approach the study of discursive practices in ways that undermine the usefulness of the exercise for programs geared toward liberation and equality. Included here are the programs of blacks in the United States. Traditional approaches, with their idealistic conceptions of issues to be addressed by rhetoric, have reinscribed modes of domination in their conceptions, for example, of "rhetorical situations" as prerhetorical developments that call forth particular rhetorics.[16] Such approaches highlight the blind spots of rhetoric while undermining the potential of rhetorical theory as a major force in the crucible of public life, where power is constructed, deconstructed, used, and abused for human service and servility (Charland, "Rehabilitating Rhetoric").

Critical rhetorical theory can serve a useful function for marginal and oppressed groups such as blacks by facilitating the investigation of ways in which rhetors give salience to issues or situations. This use allows for fruitful investigations of the ways in which dominant discourse communities or dominant sections of discourse communities repress alternative voices through their "noisy command" and imposition of silence on other voices. Critical rhetorical scholarship will then be in a position to examine the ways in which these repressed and even fragmented voices construct imagined communities, shatter imposed silences, and resist domination through their counterdiscourse (C. Peterson 14).[17] This examination will allow for an understanding of the ways in which "denied knowledges" are constructed and legitimized (Bhabha 156). It allows rhetoric to consider, for example, the *kynicism* as represented by rap music's cynical impertinence that evokes only deadly laughter, if any (Sloterdijk 101–12; Charland, "Norms" 342).[18] As Dyson constantly reminds us with sermonic eloquence, even with rap's negative baggage of misogyny and valorization of crime, its angry rhythm and rhyme are an obstreperous instantiation of a voice from the *pagus* that forces a reconsideration of the *polis* and its exclusive consensus (Powell; Lyotard, 135–41; Charland, "Norms" 342). In nineteenth-century America, black abolitionism had such a voice, both irreverent and bawdy.[19] It was the voice of those who had "seen their own children or their own parents sold like hogs," often seen as hogs themselves, challenging those who controlled the press and pulpit, who represented "stability and respectability and who dominated the political apparatus" (Aptheker, *"One Continual Cry"* 21). Like the black voice excluded from the respectable nineteenth-century Anglo-American *polis,* rap— black nationalism's crass contemporary instantiation—often stands outside the norms of rhetorical culture today, even though its problematic is acknowledged as significant ground for rhetorical action.

Within black communities, "signifying," or the double voice that is an integral part of discourse, provides for critical rhetoricians a rich store of rhetorical artifacts and *topoi* worth studying (Gates, *Signifying*). Such studies would reveal sites of cultural resistance, vibrant cultural knowledge production, and various phases and stages of hybridity, as these vibrant groups navigate and negotiate their search for a fair share of the rights of life in the United States. Such negotiations focus on a self-determined structuring and restructuring and an autonomous articulation and rearticulation of indigenous and co-opted signs to create active black social beings capable of fighting for justice as they responsibly fulfill the role of American citizens (Burke, *Language* 137). Indeed, in certain cultural contexts, black people are always talking about talk, to rephrase Gates (xi). If Gresson, Hall, McPhail, and others are right, we have to keep on talking if we are to keep on living. The ground certainly is fertile for rhetorical seeding. Claude McKay's sonnet "America" expresses well the love-hate relationship that many blacks share with their homeland:

> Although she feeds me bread of bitterness,
> And sinks into my throat her tiger's tooth,
> Stealing my breath of life, I will confess
> I love this cultured hell that tests my youth!

> (McKay 59)

The rhetorical approach portends an intriguing conversation that questions saliencies and silences, absences and presences, production and consumption, the denied and the legitimized. It is out of the conundrum of shouts and silences, repression and rebirth that the ideology of black nationalism emerges with its own symphonic and cacophonous sounds, seeking resonance amidst the ongoing noisy effort to construct salience. Always, the contingent cultivates creativity.

Rhetoric and Emancipation

A rhetorical conception of black nationalism allows for useful explorations of the adaptability and resilience of this ideology and the malleable subject it constitutes. With an understanding of rhetoric as material, we can account for the fluidity with which the collective subject of black nationalism is constituted and reconstituted to meet the daily challenges that blacks face in the United States. We are also able to see the distinct challenges presented to Anglo-America by this black fiction. Black nationalism, then, should be considered neither a fixed nor an idealistic phenomenon. It is a way of thinking, a way of being in the world, predicated on rhetoric. Note, for example, the approach of the Moorish Science Temple of America, led by Noble Drew Ali (Timothy Dew), which termed blacks "Moorish-Americans." This organization sought for blacks a national identity that constituted what they argued to be their origins in Egypt but rejected the terms "Negro" and "black," which they saw as synonymous with death (Frazier, *Negro Church* 69–71). There are many others, such as C. Eric Lincoln's "Black-americans" and the latest construction, "people of color" (107; Foster).[20] In other words, "black people" can change or, more accurate, "black people" can be changed. Indeed, all "people" are made.

Because black nationalism's constituted black subject is a rhetorical construct, it is a pliable product of the narrative that seeks black equality. Within a rhetoric grounded in their realities, "black people" can be changed to meet and create rhetorical exigencies appropriate to the contemporary scenario. The effectiveness of this discourse will depend primarily on its ability to interpellate individual African Americans by placing before them images with which they can identify. As Farrakhan did with the Million Man March, black nationalist rhetors continue to seek a collective black subject they can insert into contemporary America for effective social action.

Since black nationalism can be fluid and flexible, the versions of this ideology espoused by other rhetors can be distinct from that advanced, for example, by Farrakhan. Indeed, they need to be, for Farrakhan's brand of black nationalism remains subject to telling critiques like that offered by Cornel West. With its militant, macho image, Farrakhan's conservative, patriarchal separatism, predicated on "racial fundamentalism, pushes oppressed minorities into an intellectual and political ghetto" as it excludes constituents crucial to the black cause, such as black women and progressive whites (Marable, "Plea" A15). While maintaining the critical tenets of black pride, contemporary black nationalism can expand its base by incorporating other activists and appealing to a broader constituency.[21] As Marable suggests, new approaches to black alienation must account for "new social, economic, cultural, and global forces at work that are rapidly restructuring African-American communities, as well as Africa and the black diaspora" (Marable, "Plea" A15).[22] Collins, hooks, and Dyson, among others, advance similar conceptions. Garveyism, for example, demonstrated that black nationalism could mobilize the black diaspora. Contemporary approaches need to build on but go beyond the black nationalism of Garvey or Farrakhan to incorporate the multiple perspectives of women, Latinos and Latinas, and other diasporic voices such as those in Africa, Brazil, the Caribbean, and the rest of the Americas, all of whom are also "exploring the complex relationships between racial identities, inequality, and power" (Marable, "Plea" A15). Indeed, for effective functioning, progressive, contemporary efforts may need to be rhetorically recrafted as an undertaking under a different rubric. For, as Marable argues,

> A new paradigm is required, one that would involve scholars who seek to substantially transform the society that perpetuates black inequality. This new approach must reach out, in particular, to the young generation of black Americans born after the civil rights and black power movements, who are increasingly under assault by the forces of unemployment, imprisonment and social alienation. ("Plea" A15)

In this study, not only do we see the scope and flexibility of black nationalism, but with the notion of constitutive rhetoric we can begin to understand the power of discourse to form social identities and to move audiences to action. This understanding takes us beyond traditional notions of persuasion to the much more instructive concept of Burkean identification in which rhetoric constitutes audiences by making persons consubstantial. Through this process of identification, rhetoric functions ideologically as it "persuades" through the construction of subjectivity. Such an understanding is critical to explorations of the effective rhetorical functioning of discourse and its power to move people to action.

Despite the limitations of black nationalism, such rhetoric will continue to be powerful. As demonstrated in the Million Man March, even with its inherent problems, the rhetoric of black nationalism presents to blacks a picture of themselves that contains praiseworthy features and bears enough resonance with their experience so as to hail them and insert them into the social world as a collective entity. Within this context, Farrakhan, for example, with his rhetoric of agitation, invokes a public persona that embodies the tensions of black alienation. As such he becomes the heroic figure unafraid to confront the enemy and lead the chant of NO (Goldzwig 212). Black nationalist rhetoric allows blacks to experience themselves as African Americans or "black people" and in turn to be "persuaded" as such. To be African American within such black nationalist rhetoric is thus to be hailed, to be one with those who have contended with slavery and past oppression. This transhistorical subject is established and authenticated when contemporary blacks continue the black tradition of struggle.

To achieve effective social activism, a collective entity is presented as naturally existing prior to the discourse. This key rhetorical function seeks to mask the ideological program of such a discourse. It is particularly potent in a discourse presented as that which naturally represents the given reality of "a people." Discourses like these, functioning effectively as part of the social relations of reproduction, create social beings who fulfill defined, if hidden, textual agendas. Unfortunately, this process sometimes redounds in skewed power relations among groups of individuals. Such was the case with Anglo-America's proslavery narrative. In contemporary America, black nationalism tenders a separatist vision for popular consumption. Where this product is consumed and embraced by black Americans it functions as a powerful force mobilizing them to action. To advance the black cause significantly in twenty-first-century, multicultural America with an especially large majority Anglo-American culture, however, the black nationalist vision has to extend its appeal beyond an exclusively black audience. This extension of appeal must include the acknowledgment that the notion of race as a fixed category is inherently regressive.

The black struggle for freedom and equality has continued unabated since the nineteenth century, with the 1960s marking its apogee of success in the United States.[23] The place of blacks in American society continues to be a contentious issue, since race continues to contort American culture, determining consciousness, "facts and fantasies" (Hacker ix). Still, few dispute the major hurdles faced by the black underclass trying to survive in the land of liberty. More complex and convoluted, however, are questions about the black middle class and their struggle to thrive and gain an equal footing with Anglo-Americans. Recent studies suggest that the alienation of the black middle class is perhaps worse than that of the black underclass, and the rage of the black middle class is attracting the attention of scholars in such areas as psychology and literature. For both classes, black nationalism articulates the experience of black alienation in an effort to improve the plight of blacks and to advance the cause of equality even as it inscribes its own problems of separatism.

In 1965, Herbert Aptheker, in an assessment of the impact of David Walker's *Appeal*, argued that the genius of the work was in its projection of tasks for succeeding generations, beginning with the eradication of slavery in its own generation, to fulfil America's promise of full equality. Aptheker's observation is instructive. He continued, "[T]he nation could not survive with slavery in the nineteenth century; it will not survive with Jim Crow in the twentieth century" (*"One Continual Cry"* 59–60). Furthermore, the nation will not survive with its insidious institutional and symbolic racism in the twenty-first century. With blood and pain, we have eliminated slavery and Jim Crow. With the same assiduity (and, it is hoped, reduced human cost), we can attenuate the last major scourge blocking the nation's path to at least a striving toward its promise of unalienable rights.

As part of the "great and unprecedented conversation about race" aimed at "lift[ing] the burden of race and redeem[ing] the promise of America," critical rhetoricians can play a crucial role (Clinton "Race Relations").[24] We can unmask race in rhetoric that hides its usage, as in the phenomenon that Toni Morrison calls "race talk," with which popular culture, in its everyday practice, and many white Americans in their daily talk are bold enough "hide" race right out in the open (qtd in hooks, *Killing Rage* 3–4). This racial cryptography, this hiding of a message in plain sight, is facilitated by a renewed sense among many whites that the indictment of white racism is dated. Such a program is aided by black conservative voices. Shelby Steele, for example, contends blacks are the new racists.

Nineteenth-century black nationalists rhetorically constructed an alternative vision of America to contend for a place for dignified black life. In so doing, they crafted a rhetorical conception of alienation to redeem the world and save black life from domination and destruction in the clutches of white supremacy. The contemporary task is equally daunting and no less urgent. We can point the way beyond the notion of black people as a problem for America. Instead, we can advance the idea that dealing with this challenge demands not only collaboration and creativity across the treacherous divide we now call race but also an investigation of the very concepts of race and how they function in our ongoing public conversation that shapes American identities.[25] In short, we can begin the hard work of transforming our conception of race, unfortunately still woman's and "man's most dangerous myth." Ashley Montagu is still right. Always important to this undertaking should be the lesson from jazz, the truly American art form, that "difference need not be antagonistic" (Kramer 4). Multiple significations and new contingent realities must be created as we move beyond anticipated meanings, roving alongside Proteus to re-create the known future while we re-create an unknown past (Griffin 308). Maybe the United States is not a narrow tribe or even a group of narrow tribes after all, but like Tiger Woods, Alice Walker, Paula Gunn, and so many others of acknowledged, mixed heritage, we are all "multicultural events" not only through biological connections but also through rhetorical rapprochement (Takaki, *Different Mirror* 427). *E pluribus unum?* Why not? Frederick Douglass's imagined community and Robert Walsh's ultimate nightmare are "one flesh and blood, and of one political family!" (Walsh 390). Linnaeus then, Proteus now.[26]

Notes

■

Works Cited

■

Index

Notes

1. The Making of a Constitutive Rhetoric of Black Ideology

1. The march was called by black Muslim leader Louis Farrakhan in collaboration with a coalition of African American leaders. On the day of the march, President William Clinton addressed the issue of black and white race relations in a speech at the University of Texas in Austin. See Clinton, Address. The Rodney King affair and the 1992 Los Angeles riot, along with the publication of Herrnstein and Murray's *The Bell Curve,* the trial and acquittal of O. J. Simpson, and Republican congressional efforts to dismantle affirmative action programs established in the mid-1960s all served to generate public discussions about race. Noteworthy too is that in response to the masculinist stance of the Million Man March, Philadelphia community activists Asia Coney and Phile Chionesu called for a Million Woman March, which was held in Philadelphia 25 October 1997 with the theme "repentance, resurrection, restoration."

2. Harding made this comment as part of his argument that this ideology was not very different from King's post-1963 perspective. He posited that this perspective of self-determination motivated King's 1968 promise of assembling an army of the poor for a march on Washington. For a discussion of a 1985 mass meeting in Madison Square Garden and Farrakhan's involvement, see Banner-Haley 5–7. For further discussion of Farrakhan, his work, and his ideology, see Lester, "Time Has Come"; Crouch, "Nationalism of Fools," in his *Notes of a Hanging Judge* 165–75; Reed, "False Prophet"; Reed, "False Prophet II"; and Curry, "Remaking."

3. See Bagdikian; Berry; Jackson; and Mauer and Huling 14. On 11 September 2001, terrorists crashed hijacked jetliners in New York, Washington, and southwestern Pennsylvania, killing approximately three thousand people. The suspected hijackers in question, all of whom died in the crashes, have been identified as men from Saudi Arabia, Syria, and the United Arab Emirates. Since then, the most feared individuals have become Arab men. Some contend, however, that this response is still grounded in a specific fear of black men.

4. See Blumstein; Kennedy; Klein; Lynch and Sabol; Mauer and Huling; Mauer and Sentencing Project; Petersilia.

5. For a sample of the growing number of works created to assess the march, see Curry, "After"; Henry, "Africological Analysis"; M. West. In footnote 37, West lists several publications that account for the influence of the Million Man March (100).

6. These efforts are chronicled in works ranging from Woodson's *Negro Orators* to *The Black Abolitionist Papers* with its companion volume, *Witness,* both edited by Ripley et al. For excellent surveys of this literature, including primary documents, biographies, and other secondary documents, see the bibliographic essay in *Witness* 279–89 and Blackett, *Beating.* The groundswell of research and scholarship in this area has been promoted by the Civil Rights movement, which fueled the launching of black studies departments in universities across the nation. For example, on 4 and 5 June 1973, the National Archives and Record Service sponsored a conference entitled "Federal Archives as Sources for Research on Afro-Americans" (R. Clarke ix).

7. For a discussion of these developments in rhetorical criticism, see Lucaites, Condit, and Caudhill 1–18.

8. The deleterious effects of slavery and racism on blacks, their social institutions, and the black family in particular has been recorded in such works as Du Bois, *Souls;* Myrdal, *American Dilemma;* K. Clarke, *Dark Ghetto;* Frazier, *Negro Family;* Franklin, *From Slavery;* Herskovits, *Myth;* Gutman, *Black Family;* Hill, *Strength of Black Families;* Scanzoni, *Black Family;* and Patterson, *Slavery and Social Death.* Though there are debates about the actual condition of the black family, there is no denying the negative effects of racism on it.

9. De Vos notes,

> Anomy, or anomie in French, was introduced by [Émile] Durkheim as an etic concept to indicate a failure in social cohesion due to problems occurring in either or both the external and internalized regulatory systems keeping a society together. Alienation is the subjective experience of anomy in Durkheimian theory. (xiv)

10. For an extensive survey of this literature, see Schacht.

11. See Marcuse; Adorno and Horkheimer; and Lukács. See also McKerrow, "Marxism."

12. The original source for this quotation is Vera Kutzinski, "American Literary History as Spatial Practice." *American Literary History* 4 (1992): 555. See Hochschild 1–12.

13. In his essay "Minority Cultures in Western Political Theory," Kymlicka points to this limitation in the Marxist political theory and tradition: "Indeed, Marxists have, if anything been more indifferent or hostile to the claims of minority cultures" (4–5). Kymlicka also provides a bibliographical listing of texts

that address the issue of minority cultures in the Marxist tradition (376). Still there has been significant rapprochement between blacks and communism. See, for example, Padmore; Robinson; Naison; and W. James. For an extensive discussion of efforts to establish a rapprochement between Marxist theory and black nationalism, see McKelvey 168–74.

14. See McGee, "'Ideograph'"; Wander; Condit and Lucaites; McKerrow, "Critical Rhetoric: Theory and Praxis" and "Critical Rhetoric and the Possibility of the Subject"; and Foss 291–302.

15. The argument of "the people" as a myth is further developed in McGee and Martin, "Public Knowledge"; and in McGee, "Power to the <People>."

16. See also Fiske.

2. The Narrative of Oppression: Preserving Slavery

1. Genealogical inquiry is one of three methodological moments identified by Cornel West as part of his genealogical materialist analysis. For West, a genealogical materialist analysis is one that "replaces Marxist conceptions of history with Nietzschean notions of genealogy, yet preserves the materiality of multifaceted structured social practices" (*Keeping Faith* 265–69).

2. Walsh's "work appeared late in September 1819, went through two editions in America and was reprinted in London" (Lochemes 91n. 6). I use the second edition, hereafter referred to as the *Appeal*.

3. Judge Samuel Sewell's widely distributed and influential antislavery pamphlet *The Selling of Joseph: A Memorial*, elicited a response from Judge John Saffin. In his pamphlet *A Brief and Candid Answer to a Lately Printed Sheet Entitled the Selling of Joseph (1701)*, Saffin sought to answer each of Sewell's arguments and in so doing produced "probably the first written defense of slavery in American history." See Jenkins 4, 39, 51. For what exists of Saffin's pamphlet, see George H. Moore 251–56 and Godell 103–12.

3. Early Roots of Black Nationalism: The Birth of the Black Subject

1. The *Manifesto* was published in New York and is dated 13 February 1829. The *Appeal* was first published in Boston 28 September 1829, with a third edition published in 1830 (the edition used in this study; Wiltse xii; Stuckey, *Ideological Origins* 38–39). The *Appeal* went through three editions before Walker's mysterious death in 1830. Also to appear in 1829 was a third, less influential book of poems, *The Hope of Liberty*, written by a slave, George Moses Horton, and published by Joseph Gales, editor of the *Raleigh Register* (Eaton 324; Aptheker, *"One Continual Cry"* 52, 27–28).

2. See also Styron, whose work elicited a strong response from blacks, as chronicled in J. H. Clarke, *William Styron's Nat Turner*. The ensuing contest over

the interpretation and use of the words "rebellion," "insurrection," and "massacre" points to the importance of rhetoric in efforts to make sense and use of the past. As Clarke, quoting Aptheker, notes, "[H]istory's potency is mighty. The oppressed need it for identity and inspiration; oppressors for justification, rationalization and legitimacy" (vii).

3. See Jones; Dow; Condit and Lucaites 70n. 3; and Aptheker, *To Be Free* 11–30.

4. See James H. Johnson.

5. See Condit and Lucaites 131.

6. See Norton 152–53.

7. For a detailed examination of naming, see Mulin, chapters 1–3.

8. For a discussion of the invention of Africa, see Appiah. For black nationalist conceptions of Africa and Western civilizations, see Moses, *Alexander Crummell.*

9. See Forman; and Williams and McDonald.

10. Later, blacks explicitly rejected the property argument in favor of equality based on rights. This change is evident, for example, in the debate over voting rights. In the petition emanating from the 18–20 August 1840 Albany Convention of Colored Citizens, blacks claimed "an equality, not of property or favor, but of rights is the firmest foundation of liberty, and that on which democracy is founded" (Stuckey, *Ideological Origins* 242–43).

11. See, for example, B. Edwards, *History;* Gardner, *History of Jamaica.* Though it covers a different period, 1860–80, Du Bois, *Black Reconstruction,* provides ample evidence of racist historiography. See especially "The Propaganda of History," 711–37. Among those indicted for their racist historiography are Charles and Mary Beard's highly acclaimed *Rise of American Civilization* and the prestigious *Encyclopedia Britannica,* 713–15. See also Walsh, *An Appeal,* in which he accuses Britain and other European nations of covering up their practice of sending criminals and other undesirables to their colonies, including America.

12. Included in this contest are important facets of black history such as black life before the European arrival in Africa and later the Americas. This "chang[ing of] the perspectives of conventional historiography," is important in the context of African diasporan experience, not just in the United States (Nettleford 60). As Nettleford argues, this issue is important for the advancement of Afro-Caribbean people as well. In his discussion, Nettleford points to such historians as Elsa Goveia, C. L. R. James, Eric Williams, and Walter Rodney who, in the cause of Afro-Caribbean development, challenge conventional historiography of the Caribbean and tell another story (57–61). As the title indicates, Rodney's "African History in the Service of Black Revolution" is an exposé of the black use of African history to resist and counter white domination (Nettleford 60).

13. For one such contestation, see Lefkowitz.

4. Contesting Blackness: The Rhetorical
Empowerment of the Black Subject

1. Ripley et al., *Black Abolitionist* 3: 356, identifies Garnet as the most likely to have written under the pseudonym Sidney. Sterling Stuckey argues that Sidney is probably a pseudonym of either Alexander Crummell or Garnet (*Ideological Origins* 15–17). Stuckey later concurs with Ripley and argues that Sidney was "almost certainly Garnet" (*Slave Culture* 211).

2. See Bell, *Survey.*

3. Wesley indicates that the Liberty Party was founded 1 April 1840. Quarles identifies the date as 1839 (*Frederick Douglass* 183). The party was formed in time to contest the 1840 elections. In contesting the elections of 1844, however, the party's platform against slavery in the states and territories was rejected by the electorate (Beard, Beard, and Beard 250–51).

4. In "The Father of Black Nationalism," Miller contends that Woodson, Delany's teacher, is the "father of Black Nationalism" and that in these letters, "Woodson outlined the basic positions Delany later enunciated in the 1850s" (311–13). The "Ten Letters by Augustine," are reprinted in Stuckey, *Ideological Origins* 118–48. These ten were not the only letters that Woodson wrote to the *Colored American* during this period. See Ripley et al., *Black Abolitionist* 3: 256–60.

5. Smith's letter was first published in the *Colored American* (New York) 15 August 1840 and reprinted in Ripley et al., *Black Abolitionist* 3: 345–46. On two previous occasions, 27 July and 4 August 1840, Smith had expressed his opposition to racially separate conventions and had moved resolutions against the call for the Albany Convention. The *Colored American* noted his opposition but failed to print Smith's resolutions against the convention (3: 349).

6. The choice between state and national conventions was also being hotly debated at the time. See Ripley et al., *Black Abolitionist* 3: 345–47.

7. See Delany and Campbell; and Blackett, "In Search" and "Martin R. Delany."

5. Black Nationalism Matures: The Black Subject as Public Citizen

1. For detailed treatments of Garnet's background, see Schor; Ofari; and Stuckey, *Slave Culture* 138–92.

2. Herbert Aptheker wrote that "the kernel of this militancy" within America may be found in the 1688 Germantown Quaker protest against slavery. As one might expect, this militancy is also reflected in literature distributed during the Revolutionary War that urged black freedom through rebellion. For a discussion of evidence of this early militancy, see Aptheker, *"One Continual Cry"* 22–28; and Ripley et al., *Black Abolitionist* 3: 403. Cedric Robinson, however, observed

that black radicalism is a specifically African response to the experience of oppression (97).

3. See Hofstadter 309–13; Beard, Beard, and Beard 250–51; and David Brion Davis, *The Slave Power Conspiracy.*

4. Advancing this notion were the radical constitutionalists, typically viewed as eccentrics. Their views were best expounded in Alvan Stewart's "New Jersey Argument" used in *State v. Van Buren* and *State v. Post* (1845) to argue that the new state constitution of 1844, because of its "all men are by nature free and independent" clause, had effectively abolished slavery (See Godell; Spooner; and Stewart). As Lucaites notes, Spooner's *Unconstitutionality* became the handbook for the Liberty Party and those who followed, seeking to invoke the Constitution on behalf of abolitionism ("Irony of 'Equality'" 53–54; Wiecek, 254–58). Black abolitionists committed to political action often disagreed over which party, Whig, Liberty, or Free-Soil, could best advance their cause (Ripley et al., *Black Abolitionist* 4: 93–97).

5. The delegates were led "by two distinguished churchmen, William C. Munroe (president of the Convention), and William Paul Quinn of Indiana (its first vice-president)" and by Delany (Bell, "Negro Emigration" 140; Delany and Campbell 27). For a discussion of the strident disagreement between Douglass and Delany during this period, see Levine.

6. The details of these lecture tours in Britain are well documented by Blackett, *Building.*

7. Hochschild investigates the anomaly and symbiosis theses to discuss racism in post–civil rights America.

8. McDorman uses Cover's framework to discuss African Americans' responses to the 1857 Supreme Court's decision in *Scott v. Sandiford.* I use it here, in a broader context, to account for select African American responses to the dominant Anglo-American public voice that frames the nation's identity.

9. As Cover notes, Garrisonians believed that their withdrawal would ultimately lead to the dissolution of the government. The Garrisonian withdrawal "did not entail physical or social insularity, but a radical insularity of the normative world alone."

10. See Leroux; Lucaites, "Irony"; Jasinski; Andrews; Stuckey, *Slave Culture* 138–92; Litwack and Meier; Ernest 109–79; Stuckey, *Ideological Origins* 1–29; Gilroy; and Levine. While there have been several treatments of "What to the Slave Is the Fourth of July?," Garnet's "Address" and Delany's "Political Destiny" have received relatively less attention. Robert S. Levine, for example, studies the writings of Delany and Douglass and argues that because of his separatist position, Delany "has been marginalized and for the most part ignored." Levine writes that the representative status granted to Douglass in recent American literature

anthologies obscures other nineteenth-century male writers, including Garnet (3, 4). John Ernest, in a similar vein, notes that Delany has received scant attention from literary scholars but that there is a "growing interest in his life as an early example of black nationalism" (109).

11. For a discussion of black slaveholders in the United States during the nineteenth century, see Kroger. Of course, D'Souza employs these slaveholders to support his thesis that the United States has come to the end of racism.

12. For a discussion of the issues involved in Garnet's and Douglass's disagreements in the period of this convention, including the rift in the Northern abolitionist movement, disagreements over moral suasion versus political action, and support for the Liberty Party, see Brewer 36–52; Wesley 32–74; Schor 47–87; and Ofari.

13. As Bell explains, black nationalists of the period, Delany among them, reasoned that the uplift of the black race anywhere, including Canada, the Caribbean, and Africa, would help liberate those held in slavery. This effect they identified as the "reflex influence," in which "Ethiopia might stretch forth her hand." They used as an example the Puritans who were able to throw off the oppression of England only after some of them had established their own viable government in another land.

14. See Hasian, Condit, and Lucaites; and McDorman. The work of such scholars as Robert Cover and Roberto Unger are the primary texts of critical legal studies. For a discussion of the development of and the debate surrounding critical legal studies, see Cornel West, *Keeping Faith* 195–247.

15. Douglass has been widely acknowledged as one of nineteenth-century America's leading orators and a champion of liberation and equality. See, for example, Rogers 203–4; W. Allen; Gregory; Higginson, *American Orators* 87–91; Blight 4; W. Martin, "Frederick Douglass," in Higginson, *American Orators* 139–45; and Lucaites, "Irony" 47–69.

16. Schor contends that though Garnet experienced anguish in the face of a march for "slave-power," he never gave up on America. He notes, "[W]hile Garnet was becoming increasingly anguished, there is no evidence that he was yielding to [David] Walker's abject despair. Although Garnet ultimately sanctioned resistance, nowhere did he specifically repudiate the possibility of eventual triumph in America" (Schor 54; Stuckey, *Slave Culture* 180–83).

17. Jasinski notes that Anglo-American postratification articulation rationalized the Revolution as a deliberate act of reform, with the Constitution as its natural end product. "The Revolution could then be celebrated without endangering the Constitutional order or communal stability." In short, the Revolution became a conservative naturalized event rather than a radically contingent revolt (74).

18. Robert S. Levine, in his treatment of Douglass and Delany, seeks to "replace inevitability with contingency, univocal politics with pragmatic (and principled) improvisation" (5).

19. Cornel West, *Prophesy Deliverance* 47–65, highlights such functioning in a discussion of the logic of modern discourse in the service of white supremacy and modern racism.

20. Molefi Kete Asante writes that African American protest speaking and writing is "in the employ of a determinism defined by the possibilities and complexities of social protest within a larger society, and is further constricted by the peculiarity of the black experience" (*Afrocentric Idea* 111).

6. The Ideology of Black Nationalism and American Culture

1. For arguments to the contrary, in which the author demeans Garvey and his supporters, see Pickens 3: 380.

2. Duncan J. MacLeod argues that the Revolution altered the ideological climate in America by helping to create a "new ethic of benevolent slaveholding." He notes that the "attempt to reconcile slavery and freedom in a single coherent view of society led to an attribution to the Negro of characteristics by virtue of which his slavery could be explained and maybe even justified" (11).

3. Marable argues that the "integrationist" approach has successfully created an expanded black middle class that may have diverted attention from class inequality and poverty. The black lower class has therefore been left untouched. This integrationist approach was largely the agenda of the Martin Luther King Jr.–led Civil Rights movement. "The opposite approach of group separatism, characterized by Gayatri Spivak as 'identitarianism,' encloses African-Americans within the narrow boundaries of their own experiences" ("Plea").

4. In a September 2000 report, the "United States government admitted that racism remains a stubborn problem" and that contemporary racism continues in "subtle" and "elusive" forms (S. Ross).

5. Here I use Pierre Nora's notion of memory as an employer of "spaces, gestures, images and objects" and that which is alive in the collective mind to challenge history, "the reconstruction of that which no longer exists" (7–9). In so doing, however, I affirm Melvin Dixon's critique of Nora's Eurocentric bias toward recorded European history as revealed in the disparaging comments on non-European memory (18).

6. Keith B. Richburg and Whoopi Goldberg, to the contrary, rhetorically craft a different conception of themselves as "black American."

7. See Hall, Scott, and Smith; Yellin and Van Horne; Yellin; Yee; Lerner; Giddings.

8. See Lasch 117–68; M. Wallace.

9. For a discussion of the changing role of the black church in the black struggle, see Frazier, *Negro Church;* Lincoln; and Litwack, *Trouble* 378–403.

10. See, for example, Schuyler.

11. Connerly, a leading activist in the effort to dismantle affirmative action programs, points to Steele's *The Content of Our Character* and to Richburg's *Out of America* to support his claim that blacks are seeking independence from traditional black dogma. In addition to the above works, the standard texts articulating the ideology of these conservatives are Faryna, Stetson, and Conti; D'Souza; Collier and Horowitz; Lester, *Lovesong;* and earlier, Sowell.

12. See, for example, McPhail, "Complicity of Essentializing Difference." For an investigation of the rhetoric of some of the leading public advocates of this conservative position, see Smith, "Transcending Politics."

13. See, for example, McPhail, "Passionate Intensity"; Goldzwig; Pauley; and Arthos.

14. See Frazier, *Black Bourgeoisie* and *Negro Church* 80–5; Cose, *Rage;* Landry; and Brooks. Brooks (34–105, 106–28) treats both the African American middle class and the African American "poverty class."

15. Shared by students in Gordon.

16. As Trevor Parry-Giles has shown, such approaches can be traced back to Aristotle and forward to Lloyd Bitzer. See Bitzer; Vatz; and C. Miller.

17. Here I make use of Peterson's summary of the discussion of colonial discourse from Bhabha's "Signs Taken for Wonders" and her paraphrasing of the function of silences in postcolonial texts from Ashcroft, Griffiths, and Tiffin.

18. Charland employs Peter Sloterdijk's discussion of the kynicism-cynicism dialectic to point to the absence of "the Sophistic love of paradox and linguistic play" from Thomas B. Farrell's *Norms of Rhetorical Culture* (Charland, "Norms" 339).

19. To the argument that Frederick Douglass, for example, argued in such a way as to fit the norms of nineteenth-century rhetorical culture, I reply that the abolitionist movement as a whole was considered outside the *polis.* In addition, the Douglass we have recorded is the polished speaker—the best of nineteenth-century (black) American society—only after years of public speaking. Sojourner Truth might be more representative.

20. Foster, identified as a "former high school teacher in southern California," generally excoriated the NAACP, the Urban League, and the Civil Rights movement. She blamed the movement for the fragmentation of America in the 1990s and argued that Jesse Jackson instructed the media to refer to blacks as "African Americans" and they have complied. She bemoans that there is now a movement in California to identify blacks and Latin Americans as "people of color." This movement was begun, she notes, because of the numbers and for political purposes.

21. Spike Lee's *Get on the Bus* is an exposé of the ideological commitments of twenty African American men on a bus journeying to the Million Man March. It provides insight into a range of interpretations of black nationalism employed by African Americans with some adherence.

22. For a caution against political activity replacing legitimate black scholarship, see Gates, "A Call to Protect."

23. In *Keeping Faith* (271–91), West surveys African American struggles for liberation from 1960 to 1995. In his discussion of this period under the title "The Paradox of the African American Rebellion," he uses the sixties not as a chronological category encompassing ten years but as a "heuristic rubric" that renders key elements and events of black struggle intelligible (271).

24. In this speech, broadcast live on CNN, the president called for a conversation on race. He also announced the appointment of a seven-member advisory board to "define, develop, and recommend concrete solutions" to the problems of race relations in the United States. The National Communication Association's 1997 Summer Conference on Racial and Ethnic Diversity in the 21st Century: A Communication Perspective, held 24–27 July 1997 at the Capital Hilton in Washington, DC, and its published proceedings under the same name are a productive start.

25. Orlando Patterson suggests "ethnicity" rather than "race" as a useful marker to guide our discussions of the various social groupings of Americans (*Ordeal*).

26. See Linnaeus; Jordan, *White over Black* 220–21; Cornel West, *Prophesy Deliverance* 55–56; and Omi and Winant.

Works Cited

Adams, John Quincy. *Writings of John Quincy Adams.* Ed. Worthington Chauncy Ford. 7 vols. New York: Macmillan, 1913–17.

Adorno, Theodore, and Max Horkheimer. *Dialectic of Enlightenment.* New York: Herder, 1972.

Allen, Theodore W. *The Invention of the White Race. I. Racial Oppression and Social Control.* London: Verso, 1994.

Allen, William G. "Orators and Orations, An Address Before the Dialexian Society of New York Central College, June 22, 1852." *The Liberator* [Boston] 29 Oct. 1852.

Althusser, Louis. *Lenin and Philosophy: And Other Essays.* Trans. Ben Brewster. New York: Monthly Review, 1971.

Anderson, Benedict. *Imagined Communities: Reflections on the Origin and Spread of Nationalism.* Rev. ed. London: Verso, 1993.

Anderson, Margaret L., and Patricia Hill Collins, eds. *Race, Class and Gender: An Anthology.* Belmont, CA: Wadsworth, 1992.

Andrews, William L., ed. *Critical Essays on Frederick Douglass.* Boston: Hall, 1991.

Angus, Ian, and Lenore Langsdorf, eds. *The Critical Turn: Rhetoric and Philosophy in Postmodern Discourse.* Carbondale: Southern Illinois UP, 1993.

Appiah, Kwame Anthony. *In My Father's House: Africa in the Philosophy of Culture.* New York: Oxford UP, 1992.

Aptheker, Herbert. *Abolitionism: A Revolutionary Movement.* Boston: Twayne, 1989.

———. *Anti-Racism in U.S. History: The First Two Hundred Years.* Westport, CT: Praeger, 1993.

———, ed. *A Documentary History of the Negro People of the United States.* 6 vols. New York: Citadel, 1951–73.

———. *"One Continual Cry": David Walker's Appeal to the Colored Citizens of the World (1829–1830), Its Setting and Its Meaning.* New York: Humanities P, 1965.

———. *To Be Free: Studies in American Negro History.* 2nd ed. New York: International, 1968.

Armstrong, George D. *The Christian Doctrine of Slavery.* 1857. New York: Negro UP, 1967.

Arthos, John, Jr. "The Shaman-Trickster's Art of Misdirection: The Rhetoric of Farrakhan and the Million Man March." *Quarterly Journal of Speech* 87 (2001): 41–60.

Asante, Molefi Kete. *The Afrocentric Idea.* Rev. ed. Philadelphia: Temple UP, 1998.

———. *Afrocentricity.* Trenton, NJ: Africa World, 1989.

———. "Systematic Nationalism." *Journal of Black Studies* 9 (1978): 115–28.

Ashcroft, Bill, Gareth Griffiths, and Helen Tiffin. *The Empire Writes Back: Theory and Practice in Post-colonial Literatures.* London: Routledge, 1989.

Augustine [Lewis Woodson]. "The Farmer's Garden." *Colored American* 28 July 1838. Rpt. in Stuckey, *Ideological Origins* 136.

———. "Moral Work for Colored Men." *Colored American* 2 Dec. 1837 (rpt. in Stuckey, *Ideological Origins* 119); 27 Jan. 1838.

Aune, James Art. "Cultures of Discourse: Marxism and Rhetorical Theory." Williams and Hazen 157–72.

Awkward, Michael. *Negotiating Difference: Race, Gender, and the Politics of Positionality.* Chicago: U of Chicago P, 1995.

Bagdikian, Ben H. *The Media Monopoly.* 2nd ed. Boston: Beacon, 1987.

Baker, Houston A., Jr. "Critical Memory and the Black Public Sphere." *The Black Public Sphere: A Public Culture Book.* Ed. The Black Public Sphere Collective. Chicago: U of Chicago P, 1995. 7–37.

Baker, Kenneth, ed. The New International Version Study Bible. Grand Rapids: Zondervan, 1985.

Bakhtin, Mikhail. *Speech Genres and Other Late Essays.* Trans. Vern W. McGee. Austin: U of Texas P, 1986.

Baldwin, James. *Notes of a Native Son.* Boston: Beacon, 1990.

Banner-Haley, Charles T. *The Fruits of Integration: Black Middle-Class Ideology and Culture, 1960–1990.* Jackson: UP of Mississippi, 1994.

Baraka, Amiri [LeRoi Jones]. *Home: Social Essays.* New York: Morrow, 1966.

Barnes, Gilbert H. *The Antislavery Impulse, 1830–1844.* New York: Appleton-Century, 1933.

Beale, Frances. "Double Jeopardy: To Be Black and Female." *The Black Woman: An Anthology.* Ed. Toni Cade. New York: New American Library, 1979. 90–100.

———. *Race, Racism and American Law.* 3rd ed. Boston: Little, 1973.

Beard, Charles A., and Mary R. Beard. *The Rise of American Civilization.* New ed. Two vols. in one. New York: Macmillan, 1934.

Beard, Charles A., Mary R. Beard, and William Beard. *The Beards' New Basic History of the United States.* 1944. Garden City, NY: Doubleday, 1968.

Bell, Howard Holman. Introduction. Delany and Campbell 1–22.

————, ed. *Minutes of the Proceedings of the National Negro Conventions 1830–1864.* New York: Arno, 1969.

————. "The Negro Emigration Movement, 1849–1854: A Phase of Negro Nationalism." *Phylon* 9 (1959): 132–42.

————. *A Survey of the Negro Convention Movement, 1830–1861.* New York: Arno, 1969.

Benson, Thomas W., ed. *Rhetoric and Political Culture in Nineteenth-Century America.* East Lansing: Michigan State UP, 1997.

Berry, Mary Frances. *Black Resistance, White Law: A History of Constitutional Racism in America.* 1971. New York: Penguin, 1994.

Bhabha, Homi K. "Signs Taken for Wonders: Questions of Ambivalence and Authority under a Tree Outside Delhi, May 1817." *Critical Inquiry* 12 (1985): 144–65.

Bitzer, Lloyd F. "The Rhetorical Situation." *Philosophy and Rhetoric* 1 (1968): 1–14.

Bizzell, Patricia, and Bruce Herzberg, eds. *The Rhetorical Tradition: Readings from Classical Times to the Present.* 2nd ed. Boston: Bedford–St. Martin's, 2001.

Black, Edwin. *Rhetorical Criticism: A Study in Method.* Madison: U of Wisconsin P, 1978.

————. "The Second Persona." *Quarterly Journal of Speech* 56 (1970): 109–19.

Blackett, Richard J. M. *Beating Against the Barriers: Bibliographical Essays in Nineteenth Century Afro-American History.* Baton Rouge: Louisiana State UP, 1986.

————. *Building an Antislavery Wall: Black Americans in the Atlantic Abolitionist Movement, 1830–1860.* Baton Rouge: Louisiana State UP, 1983.

————. "In Search of International Support for African Colonization: Martin R. Delany's Visit to England, 1860." *Canadian Journal of History* 10 (1975): 307–24.

————. "Martin R. Delany and Robert Campbell: Black Americans in Search of an African Colony." *Journal of Negro History* 52 (1977): 1–25.

Blackman 21 May 1929.

Blassingame, John W., ed. *Frederick Douglass Papers.* 5 vols. New Haven: Yale UP, 1979–82.

Blight, David W. *Frederick Douglass' Civil War: Keeping Faith in Jubilee.* Baton Rouge: Louisiana State UP, 1989.

Bloom, Allan. *The Closing of the American Mind: How Higher Education Has Failed Democracy and Impoverished the Souls of Today's Students.* New York: Simon, 1987.

Blumstein, Alfred. "On the Racial Disproportionality of United States Prison Populations." *Journal of Criminal Law and Criminology* 73 (1982): 1259–81.

Bogle, Donald. *Toms, Coons, Mulattoes, Mammies, and Bucks: An Interpretive History of Blacks in American Films.* Expanded ed. New York: Continuum, 1989.

Bontemps, W. Arna, and Jack Conroy. *They Seek a City.* New York: Doubleday, 1945.

Bormann, Ernest. *Forerunners of Black Power: The Rhetoric of Abolition.* Englewood Cliffs, NJ: Prentice-Hall, 1971.

Bosmajian, Haig. *The Language of Oppression.* Lanham, MD: UP of America, 1983.

Bowers, John Waite, Donovan J. Ochs, and Richard J. Jensen. *The Rhetoric of Agitation and Control.* 2nd ed. Prospect Heights, IL: Waveland, 1993.

Brewer, William M. "Henry Highland Garnet." *Journal of Negro History* 13.1 (1928): 36–52.

Bridges, George, and Rosalind Brunt, eds. *Silver Linings: Some Strategies for the Eighties.* London: Lawrence, 1981.

Brooks, Roy L. *Rethinking the American Race Problem.* Berkeley: U of California P, 1990.

Burke, Kenneth. *Attitudes Toward History.* 3rd ed. Berkeley: U of California P, 1984.

———. *A Grammar of Motives.* 1945. Berkeley: U of California P, 1969.

———. *Language as Symbolic Action: Essays on Life, Literature, and Method.* Berkeley: U of California P, 1966.

———. *A Rhetoric of Motives.* 1950. Berkeley: U of California P, 1969.

Campbell, Karlyn Khors. "In Silence We Offend." Wood and Gregg 137–49.

———. *Man Cannot Speak for Her.* 2 vols. New York: Praeger, 1989.

———. "The Rhetoric of Radical Black Nationalism: A Case Study in Self-Conscious Criticism." *Central States Speech Journal* 22 (1971): 151–60.

Campbell, M. "Aristotle and Black Slavery: A Study in Race Prejudice." *Race, a Journal of Race and Group Relations* 15 (1974): 283–98.

Carleton, George Washington. *The Suppressed Book about Slavery.* 1864. The American Negro: His Hist. and Lit. Ed. William Loren Katz. New York: Arno and *New York Times,* 1968.

Carmichael, Stokely [Kwamè Ture]. "Black Power." Ts. of speech delivered at Cobo Auditorium, Detroit, 30 July 1966.

Cartwright, Samuel. "The Prognathous Species of Mankind." *Cotton Is King, and Pro-Slavery Arguments.* Elliott 707–12, 714–16.

Catterall, Helen H., ed. *Judicial Cases Concerning American Slavery and the Negro.* Washington, DC: Carnegie Institution, 1926.

Centers for Disease Control and Prevention. 1998. *Epidemiological Notes and Reports: Acquired Immune Deficiency Syndrome.* 10 Sept. 2001 <http://www.cdc.gov>.

Centre for Contemporary Cultural Studies. *The Empire Strikes Back: Race and Racism in 70s Britain.* London: Hutchinson, 1982.

"Change of Opinion Announced." *North Star* 23 May 1851.

Charland, Maurice. "Constitutive Rhetoric: The Case of the *Peuple Québécois.*" *Quarterly Journal of Speech* 73 (1987): 133–50.

———. "Norms and Laughter in Rhetorical Culture." *Quarterly Journal of Speech* 80 (1994): 339–42.

———. "Rehabilitating Rhetoric: Confronting Blind Spots in Discourse and Social Theory." *Communication* 11 (1990): 253–64.

Christy, David. "Cotton Is King: Or, Slavery in the Light of Political Economy." Elliott 18–267.

Clarke, James F. *Anti-Slavery Days: A Sketch of the Struggle Which Ended in the Abolition of Slavery in the United States.* New York: AMS P, 1972.

Clarke, John Henrik, ed. *William Styron's Nat Turner: Ten Black Writers Respond.* Boston: Beacon, 1968.

Clarke, Kenneth. *Dark Ghetto.* New York: Harper, 1965.

Clarke, Robert L., ed. *Afro-American History: Sources for Research.* Washington, DC: Howard UP, 1981.

Clinton, William Jefferson. Address. University of Texas, Austin. 16 Oct. 1995.

———. "Race Relations Speech." University of California, San Diego. 14 June 1997.

Cobbs, Price M., and William H. Grier. *Black Rage.* New York: Basic, 1968.

Coffin, Joshua. *An Account of Some of the Principal Slave Insurrections.* New York: 1860.

Collier, Peter, and David Horowitz, eds. *Second Thoughts about Race in America.* Lanham, MD: Madison, 1991.

Collins, Patricia Hill. *Black Feminist Thought: Knowledge, Consciousness, and the Politics of Empowerment.* Perspectives on Gender. 2. New York: Routledge, 1991.

Colored American [New York] 4 Mar. 1837; 13 May 1837; 15 Mar. 1838 (rpt. in Ripley et al., *Black Abolitionist* 3: 263); 3 May 1838 (rpt. in Bell, Introduction 5); 28 July 1838; 9 and 16 Feb. 1839 (rpt. in Stuckey, *Ideological Origins* 136–46); 15 Aug. 1840 (rpt. in Ripley et al., *Black Abolitionist* 3: 345–46); 12 Sept. 1840; 2 Jan. 1841 (rpt. in Stuckey, *Ideological Origins* 250); 30 Jan. 1841; 6 Feb. 1841; 13 Feb. 1841 (rpt. in Stuckey, *Ideological Origins* 150); 20 Feb. 1841; 6 Mar. 1841 (rpt. in Stuckey, *Ideological Origins* 156); 13 Mar. 1841 (rpt. in Stuckey, *Ideological Origins* 160).

Condit, Celeste Michelle, and John Louis Lucaites. *Crafting Equality: America's Anglo-African Word.* Chicago: U of Chicago P, 1993.

———. "Reconstructing <Equality>: Cultural and Counter-cultural Rhetorics in the Black Martyred Vision." *Communication Monographs* 57 (1990): 5–24.

Connerly, Ward. "Affirmative Action and Civil Rights." Claremont McKenna College, Claremont, CA: C-Span. 31 May 1997.

Conti, Joseph G., and Brad Stetson. *Challenging the Civil Rights Establishment: Profiles of a New Black Vanguard.* Westport, CT: Praeger, 1993.

Cooper, Anna Julia. "Womanhood a Vital Element in the Regeneration and Progress of a Race." *A Voice from the South.* Introd. Mary Helen Washington. 1892. New York: Oxford UP, 1988.

Cooper, Thomas. "Two Essays: 1 on the Foundation of Civil Government: 2 on the Constitution of the United States [and the Questions That Have Arisen under It]." Columbia, SC: J. M. Faust, 1826.

Cooper, Wayne. *Claude McKay: Rebel Sojourner in the Harlem Renaissance.* New York: Schocken, 1987.

Cornish, Samuel, and John B. Russwurm. "To Our Patrons." *Freedom's Journal* 16 Mar. 1827: 1.

Cose, Ellis. "The Key to Farrakhan's Middle Class Appeal." *Newsweek* 30 Oct. 1995: 42.

———. *The Rage of a Privileged Class.* New York: Harper, 1993.

Cottman, Michael H. *Million Man March.* New York: Crown, 1995.

Cover. *Time* 27 June 1994.

Cover, Robert. "Nomos and Narrative." *Narrative Violence and the Law: The Essays of Robert Cover.* Ed. Martha Minow, Michael Ryan, and Austin Sarat. Ann Arbor: U of Michigan P, 1992.

Cox, J. Robert. "Cultural Memory and Public Moral Argument." Van Zelst Lecture in Communication, May 1987. Evanston: Northwestern U, 1988.

———. "Memory, Critical Theory, and the Argument from History." *Argument and Advocacy* 27 (1990): 1–13.

Cronon, Edmund D. *Black Moses: The Story of Marcus Garvey and the Universal Negro Improvement Association.* Madison: U of Wisconsin P, 1955.

Crouch, Stanley. *Notes of a Hanging Judge: Essays and Reviews, 1979–1989.* New York: Oxford UP, 1990.

Crummell, Alexander. *Africa and America.* Springfield, MA: Willey, 1891.

Cruse, Harold. *The Crisis of the Negro Intellectual: An Historical Analysis of the Failure of Black Leadership.* New York: Morrow, 1967.

Curry, George E. "After the Million Man March." *Emerge* Feb. 1996: 38, 41.

———. "The Remaking of Louis Farrakhan: Some Straight Talk and a Few Tears for Malcolm from the Minister." *Emerge* Aug. 1990: 28+.

Curry, Leonard P. *The Free Black in Urban America, 1800–1850: The Shadow of the Dream.* Chicago: U of Chicago P, 1981.

Davidson, Basil. *Africa in History: Themes and Outlines.* Rev. ed. 1966. Collier: New York, 1991.

Davis, David Brion. "A Comparative Approach to American History: Slavery." Foner and Genovese 60–68.

————. "Free at Last: The Enduring Legacy of the South's Civil Victory." *New York Times* 26 Aug. 2001.

————. *The Problem of Slavery in the Age of Revolution, 1770–1823.* Ithaca, NY: Cornell UP, 1975.

————. *The Problem of Slavery in Western Culture.* Ithaca, NY: Cornell UP, 1966.

Delany, Martin Robison. *The Condition, Elevation, Emigration, and Destiny of the Colored People of the United States.* 1852. New York: Arno, 1969.

————. "The Political Destiny of the Colored Race" (a report to the delegates at the first National Emigration Conference in Cleveland, August 1854). Stuckey, *Ideological Origins* 195–236.

Delany, Martin Robison, and Robert Campbell. *Search for a Place: Black Separatism and Africa.* 1860. Ann Arbor: U of Michigan P, 1969.

Denton, Robert. Series foreword. *The Cold War as Rhetoric: The Beginnings, 1945–1950.* Lynn Boyd Hinds and Theodore Otto Windt Jr. New York: Praeger, 1991. xiii–xv.

De Vos, George A. *Social Cohesion and Alienation: Minorities in The United States and Japan.* Boulder, CO: Westview, 1992.

Dew, Thomas R. "The Abolition of Negro Slavery." *American Quarterly Review* 12 (1832): 189–265.

————. *Review of the Debate in the Virginia Legislature of 1831 and 1832.* Richmond: T. W. White, 1832.

Dick, Robert C. *Black Protest: Issues and Tactics.* Westport, CT: Greenwood, 1974.

Dickinson, Greg. "Memories for Sale: Nostalgia and the Construction of Identity in Old Pasadena." *Quarterly Journal of Speech* 83 (1997): 1–27.

Dixon, Melvin. "The Black Writer's Use of Memory." Fabre and O'Meally 18–28.

Dodd, William E. *The Cotton Kingdom: A Chronicle of the Old South.* New Haven: Yale UP, 1919.

Donald, James, and Stuart Hall, eds. *Politics and Ideology.* Milton Keynes, England: Open UP, 1986.

Do the Right Thing. Dir. Spike Lee. Forty Acres and a Mule Filmworks, Universal Pictures, 1989.

Douglass, Frederick. *Autobiographies: Narrative of the Life. My Bondage and My Freedom. Life and Times of Frederick Douglass.* Ed. Henry Louis Gates Jr. New York: Library of America, 1994.

————. *Life and Times of Frederick Douglass.* Introd. George L. Ruffin. 1881. New York: Citadel, 1991.

————. *My Bondage and My Freedom.* New York: Miller, 1885.

————. *Narrative of the Life of Frederick Douglass: An American Slave.* 1845. New York: Penguin, 1968.

————. *Oration, Delivered in Corinthian Hall, Rochester* ["What to the Slave Is the Fourth of July?"]. Rochester, NY: Lee, Mann, 1852.

————. "What to the Slave Is the Fourth of July?: An Address Delivered in Rochester, New York, on July 5, 1852." Blassingame, 359–88.

Dow, George Francis. *Slave Ships and Slaving.* 1927. Cambridge, MD: Cornell Maritime P, 1968.

Dred Scott v. Sandiford 60 U.S. 393 (1857).

Drewry, William Sidney. *The Southampton Insurrection.* Washington, DC: Neal, 1900.

D'Souza, Dinesh. *The End of Racism : Principles for a Multiracial Society.* New York: Free, 1995.

Du Bois, W. E. Burghardt, ed. *Black Reconstruction: An Essay Toward a History of the Part Which Black Folk Played in the Attempt to Reconstruct Democracy in America, 1860–1880.* 1935. Studies in American Negro Life. Ed. August Meier. New York: Atheneum, 1983.

————. *Dusk of Dawn: An Essay Toward an Autobiography of a Race Concept.* New York: Harcourt, 1940. Rpt. with a tribute by Martin Luther King Jr. New York: Schocken, 1971.

————. *The Negro Church: Report of a Social Study Made under the Direction of Atlanta University; Together with the Proceedings of the Eighth Conference for the Study of the Negro Problems, Held at Atlanta University, May 26th, 1903. Atlanta University Publications (Numbers 7–11—1903–1906)* Atlanta: Atlanta UP, 1903. Vol 2. New York: Octagon, 1968. 2 vols.

————. *The Souls of Black Folk.* 1903. New York: Signet, 1969.

————. *The Suppression of the African Slave Trade to the United States of America.* Baton Rouge: Louisiana State UP, 1969.

Dwight, Timothy. *Remarks on the Review of Inchiquin's Letters.* Boston: Samuel T. Armstrong, 1815.

Dyson, Michael Eric. *Race Rules: Navigating the Color Line.* New York: Vintage, 1997.

Eaton, Clement. "A Dangerous Pamphlet in the Old South." *The Journal of Southern History* 2 (1936): 323–34.

"Editorial Comment: On Thinking the Black Public Sphere." *Public Culture* 7 (1994): xi–xiv.

Edwards, Bryan. *The History, Civil and Commercial, of the British Colonies in the West Indies.* 3rd. Ed. London: Printed for John Stockdale, 1801.

Edwards, Jonathan. *The Injustice and Impolicy of the Slave-Trade and of the Slavery of the Africans: Illustrated in a Sermon Preached Before the Connecticut Society for the Promotion of Freedom, and for the Relief of Persons Unlawfully Holden in Bondage, at Their Annual Meeting in New-Haven, September 15,*

1791. By Jonathan Edwards, D. D. Pastor of a Church in New-Haven.; to Which Is Added, a Short Sketch of the Evidence of the Abolition of the Slave-Trade, Delivered Before a Committee of the British House of Commons. Providence: John Carter, 1792.

Elkins, Stanley M. "Slavery in Capitalist and Non-Capitalist Cultures." Foner and Genovese 8–26.

Elliott, E[benezer] N[ewton], ed. *Cotton Is King, and Pro-Slavery Arguments: Comprising the Writings of Hammond, Harper, Christy, Stringfellow, Hodge, Bledsoe, and Cartwright, on This Important Subject.* 1860. The Basic Afro-American Reprint Library: Books on the History, Culture, and Social Environment of Afro-Americans. New York: Johnson Reprint, 1968.

Ellison, Ralph. *Invisible Man.* New York: Random, 1952.

Emancipator and Free American 3 Mar. 1842.

Entman, Robert. "Modern Racism and Images of Blacks in Local Television News." *Critical Studies in Mass Communication* 7 (1990): 332–45.

Ernest, John. *Resistance and Reformation in Nineteenth-Century African-American Literature: Brown, Wilson, Jacobs, Delany, Douglass, and Harper.* Jackson: U of Mississippi P, 1995.

Essien-Udom, E. U. *Black Nationalism.* Chicago: U of Chicago P, 1962.

Fabre, Geneviève, and Robert O'Meally, eds. *History and Memory in African-American Culture.* New York: Oxford UP, 1994.

Fanon, Franz. *Black Skin, White Masks.* New York: Grove, 1967.

———. *The Wretched of the Earth.* New York: Grove, 1963.

Farrakhan, Louis. "Day of Atonement." Madhubuti and Karenga 9–28.

Farrell, Thomas B. *Norms of Rhetorical Culture.* New York: Yale UP, 1993.

Faryna, Stan, Brad Stetson, and Joseph G. Conti, eds. *Black and Right: The Bold New Voice of Black Conservatives in America.* Westport, CT: Praeger, 1997.

Faust, Drew Gilpin, ed. *The Ideology of Slavery: Proslavery Thought in the Antebellum South, 1830–1860.* Baton Rouge: Louisiana State UP, 1981.

Feagin, Joe R., and Melvin P. Sikes. *Living with Racism: The Black Middle Class Experience.* Boston: Beacon, 1994.

Fineman, Howard. "The O. J. Verdict, Farrakhan's March: America Is Obsessed with Black and White. Can Clinton, Powell, or the GOP Unify Us—or Will Politics Divide the Country Even More?" *Newsweek* 23 Oct. 1995: 31–33.

Fiske, John. "Television: Polysemy and Popularity." *Critical Studies in Mass Communication* 4 (1986): 391–408.

Fitzhugh, George. *Cannibals All, or Slaves Without Masters.* 1857. Cambridge: Harvard UP, 1973.

———. *Sociology of the South, or The Failure of Free Society.* 1845. New York: B. Franklin, n.d.

Fogel, W. Robert. *Without Consent or Contract: The Rise and Fall of American Slavery.* New York: Norton, 1989.

Foner, Laura, and Eugene D. Genovese, eds. *Slavery in the New World: A Reader in Comparative History.* Englewood Cliffs, NJ: Prentice-Hall, 1969.

Foner, Philip S. *Frederick Douglass.* New York: Citadel, 1964.

Forman, James. *The Making of Black Revolutionaries.* 1972. Washington, DC: Open Hand, 1985.

Foss, Sonja K. *Rhetorical Criticism: Exploration and Practice.* 2nd ed. Prospect Heights, IL: Waveland, 1996.

Foster, Ezola. *Problems in American Schools.* C-Span 2. 30 Nov. 1997.

Foucault, Michel. *Power/Knowledge.* Trans. C. Gordon, L. Marshall, J. Mephau, and K. Soper. Ed. C. Gordon. New York: Pantheon, 1980.

Franklin, John Hope. *The Free Negro in North Carolina.* Chapel Hill: U of North Carolina P, 1943.

———. *From Slavery to Freedom: A History of Negro America.* 5th ed. New York: Knopf, 1988.

Frazier, E. Franklin. *Black Bourgeoisie.* Glencoe, IL: Free, 1957.

———. *The Negro Church in America.* 1963. Pub. with C. Eric Lincoln, *The Black Church Since Frazier.* Memoir by Everett C. Hughes. New York: Schocken, 1974.

———. *The Negro Family in the United States.* Chicago: U of Chicago P, 1939.

Frederick Douglass' Paper [Rochester, NY] 23 July 1853.

Frederick Douglass's Monthly [Rochester, NY] Feb. 1859.

Fulwood, Sam, III. "The Rage of the Black Middle Class." *Signs of Life in the U.S.A.* Eds. Maasik and Solomon. 462–70.

Gardner, William James. *A History of Jamaica from Its Discovery by Christopher Columbus to the year 1872, Including an Account of Its Trade and Agriculture; Sketches of the Manners, Habits, and Customs of All Classes of Its Inhabitants; and a Narrative of the Progress of Religion and Education in the Island.* London: F. Cass, 1971.

Garnet, Henry Highland. "Address to the Slaves of the United States of America." Ripley et al. 3: 403–12.

Garvey, Marcus M. *The Philosophy and Opinions of Marcus Garvey, or, Africa for Africans.* Centennial ed. Comp. Amy Jaques Garvey. Pref. Tony Martin. Dover, MA: Majority, 1986.

Gates, Henry Louis, Jr. "A Call to Protect Academic Integrity from Politics." *New York Times* 4 Apr. 1998: A13+.

———. *Figures in Black: Words, Signs, and the "Racial" Self.* New York: Oxford UP, 1987.

————. *The Signifying Monkey: A Theory of Afro-American Literary Criticism.* New York: Oxford UP, 1988.

Genovese, Eugene D. *Roll, Jordan, Roll: The World the Slaves Made.* New York: Vintage, 1976.

————. *"Slavery Ordained of God": The Southern Slaveholders' View of Biblical History and Modern Politics.* Gettysburg, VA: Gettysburg College, 1985.

————. *The World the Slaveholders Made: Two Essays in Interpretation.* Middletown, CT: Wesleyan UP, 1988.

Get on the Bus. Dir. Spike Lee. 15 Black Men Forty Acres and a Mule Filmworks, Columbia Pictures, 1997.

Giddens, Anthony. *The Nation-State and Violence.* Berkeley: U of California P, 1985. Vol. 2 of *A Contemporary Critique of Historical Materialism.* 2 vols.

Giddings, Paula. *When and Where I Enter: The Impact of Black Women on Race and Sex in America.* New York: Bantam, 1984.

Gilkes, Cheryl Townsend. "'Holding Back the Ocean with a Broom': Black Women and Community Work." Rogers-Rose 217–32.

Gilroy, Paul. *The Black Atlantic: Modernity and Double Consciousness.* Cambridge: Harvard UP, 1993.

Glasgow, Douglas G. *The Black Underclass: Poverty, Unemployment, and Entrapment of Ghetto Youth.* San Francisco: Josey-Bass, 1980.

Godell, Abner. "John Saffin and His Slave Adam." *Colonial Society of Massachusetts Publications* 1 (1895): 85–112.

Goldberg, David Theo. *Racist Culture: Philosophy and the Politics of Meaning.* Cambridge, MA: Blackwell, 1993.

Goldberg, Whoopi. *Book.* New York: Morrow, 1997.

Goldzwig, Steven. "A Social Movement Perspective on Demaguery: Achieving Symbolic Realignment." *Communication Studies* 40 (1989): 202–28.

Goodell, William. *Views of American Constitutional Law, in Its Bearing upon American Slavery.* Utica, NY: Jackson and Chaplin, 1844.

Goodman, Paul. *Of One Blood: Abolitionism and the Origins of Racial Equality.* Berkeley: U of California P, 1998.

Gordon, Dexter B., instr. Class discussion. Diversity and communication course. Tuscaloosa: U of Alabama, spring 1998.

Gregg, Richard B. "The Ego-Function of the Rhetoric of Protest." *Philosophy of Rhetoric* 4 (1971): 71–91.

Gregory, James. *Frederick Douglass: The Orator.* Springfield, MA: Willey, 1893.

Gresson, Aaron David, III. *The Recovery of Race in America.* Minneapolis: U of Minnesota P, 1995.

Griffin, Cindy L. "Rhetoricizing Alienation: Mary Wollenstonecraft and the

Rhetorical Construction of Women's Oppression." *Quarterly Journal of Speech* 80 (1994): 293–312.

Grossberg, Lawrence, and Jennifer Daryl Slack. "An Introduction to Stuart Hall's Essay." *Critical Studies in Mass Communication* 2 (1985): 87–90.

Gutman, Herbert G. *The Black Family in Slavery and Freedom, 1750–1925.* New York: Vintage, 1976.

Guy-Sheftall, Beverly. *Books, Brooms, Bibles, and Ballots: Black Women and the Public Sphere, Daughters of Sorrow: Attitudes Toward Black Women, 1880–1920.* New York: Carlson, 1990.

Hacker, Andrew. *Two Nations: Black and White, Separate, Hostile, Unequal.* New York: Scribner's, 1992.

Haiman, Franklin. "The Rhetoric of the Streets: Legal and Ethical Considerations." *Quarterly Journal of Speech* 53 (1967): 99–114.

Hall, Gloria T., Patricia Bell Scott, and Barbara Smith, eds. *All the Women Are White, All the Blacks Are Men, But Some of Us Are Brave: Black Women's Studies.* Old Westbury, NY: Feminist, 1992.

Hall, Stuart. *Race: The Floating Signifier.* Dir. Sut Jhally. Videocassette. Media Education Foundation, 1996.

———. "Signification, Representation, Ideology: Althusser and the Post-Structuralist Debates." *Critical Studies in Mass Communication* 2 (1985): 90–114.

Hammond, James Henry. *Gov. Hammond's Letters on Southern Slavery: Addressed to Thomas Clarkson, the English Abolitionist.* Charleston, SC: Walker and Burke, 1845.

———. "Letter to an English Abolitionist." Faust 170–205.

———. *Two Letters on Slavery in the United States, Addressed to Thomas Clarkson, Esq.* Columbia, SC: Allen, McCarter, 1845.

Harding, Vincent. Address. Symposium on Martin Luther King and the Million Man March. Atlanta. 15 Jan. 1996.

———. *There Is a River: The Black Struggle for Freedom in America.* New York: Harcourt, 1981.

Hariman, Robert I. "Status, Marginality, and Rhetorical Theory." *Quarterly Journal of Speech* 72 (1986): 38–55.

Harper, William. "Memoir on Slavery." *The Pro-Slavery Argument* 1–98.

Hartman, Roy. "Blinded by the White: We Caucasians Would Prefer to Ignore Our Preferences." *Riverfront Times* 29 Apr. 1998: 2.

Hasian, Marouf, Jr., Celeste Michelle Condit, and John Louis Lucaites. "The Rhetorical Boundaries of the Law: A Consideration of the Rhetorical Culture of Legal Practice and the Case of the 'Separate but Equal' Doctrine." *Quarterly Journal of Speech* 82 (1996): 323–42.

Henry, Charles P. *Culture and African American Politics.* Bloomington: Indiana UP, 1990.

Hernton, Calvin. "The Sexual Mountain and Black Women Writers." *Black Scholar* 16 (1985): 2–11.

Herrnstein, Richard J., and Charles Murray. *The Bell Curve: Intelligence and Class Structure in American Life.* New York: Free, 1994.

Herskovits, Melville J. *The Myth of the Negro Past.* Boston: Beacon, 1941.

Higginson, T[homas] W[entworth]. *American Orators and Oratory.* Cleveland: Imperial, 1901.

———. *Black Rebellion: A Selection from Travellers and Outlaws.* New York: Arno and *New York Times,* 1969.

———. "Gabriel's Defeat." *Atlantic Monthly* 10 (1862): 337–45. Rpt. in Higginson, *Black Rebellion* 185–214.

Hill, Robert B. *The Strength of Black Families.* New York: National Urban League, 1971.

Hinds, Lynn Boyd, and Theodore Otto Windt Jr. *The Cold War as Rhetoric: The Beginnings, 1945–1950.* New York: Praeger, 1991.

Hochschild, Jennifer L. *The New American Dilemma: Liberal Democracy and School Desegregation.* New Haven: Yale UP, 1984.

Hofstadter, Richard, ed. *Great Issues in American History: From the Revolution to the Civil War, 1765–1865.* New York: Vintage, 1958.

Holland, Edwin Clifford. *A Refutation of the Calumnies Circulated Against the Southern & Western States, Respecting the Institution and Existence of Slavery among Them. To Which Is Added, a Minute and Particular Account of the Actual State and Condition of Their Negro Population. Together With Historical Notices of All the Insurrections That Have Taken Place since the Settlement of the Country, by a South-Carolinian.* 1822. New York: Negro UP, 1969.

hooks, bell. *Black Looks: Race and Representation.* Boston: South End, 1992.

———. *Killing Rage: Ending Racism.* New York: Holt, 1995.

Hope, Dianne S. "Communication and Human Rights: The Symbolic Structures of Racism and Sexism." *Speech Communication in the 20th Century.* Ed. Thomas W. Benson. Carbondale: Southern Illinois UP, 1985. 63–89.

Hopkins, James F., ed. *Henry Clay Papers.* Vol 10. Lexington: U of Kentucky P, 1992.

Horsman, Reginald. *Race and Manifest Destiny.* Cambridge: Harvard UP, 1981.

Horton, George Moses. *The Hope of Liberty.* Raleigh, NC: Joseph Gales, 1829.

Hubbart, Henry Clyde. "Pro-Southern Influence in the Free West, 1840–1865." *Mississippi Valley Historical Review* 20 (1933): 45–62.

Huggins, Nathan I. "The Deforming Mirror of Truth: Slavery and the Master Narrative of American History." *Radical History Review* 9 (1991): 25–48.

Hughes, Henry. *Treatise on Sociology, Theoretical and Practical.* 1854. New York: Negro UP, 1968.

Ingersoll, Charles Jared. *Inchiquin, the Jesuit Letters, During a Late Residence in the United States of America: Being a Fragment of a Private Correspondence Accidentally Discovered in Europe: Containing a Favorable View of the Manners, Literature, and State of Society of the United States, and a Refutation of Many of the Aspersions Cast upon This Country by Former Residents and Tourists.* New York: I. Riley, 1810.

Jackson, Jesse. *Legal Lynching: Racism, Injustice, and the Death Penalty.* New York: National, 1995.

Jacobson, Matthew Frye. *Whiteness of a Different Color: European Immigrants and the Alchemy of Race.* Cambridge: Harvard UP, 1998.

James, C. L. R. *The Black Jacobins: Toussaint L'Ouverture and the San Domingo Revolution.* 2nd ed. New York: Vintage, 1963.

James, Winston. *Holding Aloft the Banner of Ethiopia: Caribbean Radicalism in the Early Twentieth Century.* London: Verso, 1998.

Jasinski, James. "Rearticulating History in Epideictic Discourse: Frederick Douglass's 'The Fourth of July to the Negro.'" Benson 71–89.

Jaynes, Gerald David, and Robin M. Williams Jr., eds. *A Common Destiny: Blacks and American Society.* Committee on the Status of Black Americans, Commission on Behavioral and Social Sciences and Education, National Research Council. Washington, DC: National Academy P, 1989.

Jefferson, Thomas. *Notes on the State of Virginia.* Ed. William Peder. Introd. and notes by the ed. Chapel Hill, NC: N.p., 1955.

Jenkins, William Sumner. *Pro-Slavery Thought in the Old South.* 1935. Gloucester, MA: Smith, 1960.

Jhally, Sut, and Justin Lewis. *Enlightened Racism: The Cosby Show, Audiences, and the Myth of the American Dream.* Boulder, CO: Westview, 1992.

Johnson, Charles. *Being and Race: Black Writing since 1970.* Bloomington: Indiana UP, 1988.

Johnson, James H. "The Participation of White Men in Virginia Negro Insurrections." *Journal of Negro History* 16 (1931): 158–67.

Johnson, James Weldon. *Negro Americans, What Next?* New York: Viking, 1935.

Jones, Howard. *Mutiny on the Amistad: The Saga of a Slave Revolt and Its Impact on American Abolition, Law, and Diplomacy.* New York : Oxford UP, 1987.

Jordan, Winthrop D. *The White Man's Burden: Historical Origins of Racism in the United States.* New York: Oxford UP, 1974.

———. *White over Black: American Attitudes Toward the Negro, 1550–1812.* Chapel Hill: U of North Carolina P, 1968.

Katz, William Loren. *Black Indians.* New York: Macmillan, 1986.

Kaufmann, Walter. "The Inevitability of Alienation." Introductory essay. *Alienation.* By Richard Schacht. Garden City, NY: Anchor, 1970. xv–lviii.

Kennedy, Randall. *Race, Crime, and the Law.* New York: Pantheon, 1997.

Kermode, Frank, ed. *The Tempest.* By William Shakespeare. London: Arden Shakespeare, 1954.

Kinney, James. *Amalgamation! Race, Sex, and Rhetoric in the Nineteenth-Century American Novel.* Contributions in Afro-American Studies. John W. Blassingame Sr. and Henry Louis Gates Jr., ser. advisors. Westport CT: Greenwood, 1985.

King, Deborah K. "Multiple Jeopardy, Multiple Consciousness: The Context of a Black Feminist Ideology." *Signs* 14 (1988): 42–72.

Klein, Stephen P. *Racial Disparities in Sentencing Decisions.* Santa Monica, CA: Rand, 1991.

Kolchin, Peter. *American Slavery, 1619–1877.* New York: Hill, 1993.

———. "In Defense of Servitude: American Proslavery and Russian Proserfdom Arguments, 1760–1860." *American Historical Review* 85 (1980): 809–27.

Kramer, Eric Mark, ed. *Postmodernism and Race.* Westport, CT: Praeger, 1997.

Kroger, Larry. *Black Slaveowners: Free Black Slave Masters in South Carolina, 1790–1860.* Jefferson, NC: McFarland, 1985.

Kuhn, Thomas. *The Structure of Scientific Revolutions.* Chicago: U of Chicago P, 1962.

Kymlicka, Will, ed. *The Rights of Minority Cultures.* New York: Oxford UP, 1995.

Laclau, Ernesto, and Chantal Mouffe. *Hegemony and Socialist Strategy: Towards a Radical Democratic Politics.* London: Verso, 1985.

Landry, Bart. *The New Black Middle Class.* Berkeley: U of California P, 1987.

Lasch, Christopher. *The Agony of the American Left.* New York: Knopf, 1969.

Lefkowitz, Mary R. *Not Out of Africa: How Afrocentrism Became an Excuse to Teach Myth as History.* New York: Basic, 1996.

Lemann, Nicolas. *The Promised Land: The Great Black Migration and How It Changed America.* New York: Vintage, 1991.

Lerner, Gerda, ed. *Black Women in White America: A Documentary History.* New York: Vintage, 1973.

Leroux, Neil. "Frederick Douglass and the Attention Shift." *Rhetoric Society Quarterly* 21 (1991): 36–46.

Lester, Julius. *Lovesong: Becoming a Jew.* New York: Holt, 1988.

———. "The Time Has Come." *New Republic* 28 Oct. 1985: 11–12.

Letters to the editor. *Time* 18 July 1994: 5.

Levine, Robert S. *Martin Delany, Frederick Douglass, and the Politics of Representative Identity.* Chapel Hill: U of North Carolina P, 1997.

Lewis, Rupert. *Marcus Garvey.* Trenton, NJ: Africa World, 1988.

Liberator, The [Boston] 27 Feb. 1833; 16 Dec. 1833: 198 (rpt. in Reid 342–47).

Lincoln, C. Eric. *The Black Church Since Frazier.* Pub. with *The Negro Church in America.* Memoir by Everett C. Hughes. New York: Schocken, 1974.

Linnaeus, Carolus. *Natural System.* 1735.

Liston, Robert. *Slavery in America: The History of Slavery of Black America Series.* New York: McGraw, 1970.

Litwack, Leon F. *North of Slavery: The Negro in the Free States, 1790–1860.* Chicago: U of Chicago P, 1961.

———. *Trouble in Mind: Black Southerners in the Age of Jim Crow.* New York: Knopf, 1998.

Litwack, Leon F., and August Meier, eds. *Black Leaders of the Nineteenth Century.* Urbana: U of Illinois P, 1988.

Lochemes, M. Frederick. *Robert Walsh: His Story.* Washington, DC: Catholic U of America P, 1941.

Loewen, James W. *Lies My Teacher Told Me: Everything Your American History Textbook Got Wrong.* New York: New, 1995.

Logan, Shirley Wilson. *"We Are Coming": The Persuasive Discourse of Nineteenth-Century Black Women.* Carbondale: Southern Illinois UP, 1999.

———. *With Pen and Voice: A Critical Anthology of Nineteenth-Century African-American Women.* Carbondale: Southern Illinois UP, 1995.

Lucaites, John Louis. *Flexibility and Consistency in Eighteenth-Century Anglo-Whiggism: A Case Study of the Rhetorical Dimensions of Legitimacy.* Diss. U of Iowa, 1984. Ann Arbor: UMI, 1990.

———. "The Irony of 'Equality' in Black Abolitionist Discourse: The Case of Frederick Douglass's 'What to the Slave Is the Fourth of July?'" Benson 47–69.

———. "Visualizing 'The People': Individualism vs. Collectivism in *Let Us Now Praise Famous Men.*" *Quarterly Journal of Speech* 83 (1997): 269–88.

Lucaites, John Louis, Celeste Michelle Condit, and Sally Caudhill, eds. *Contemporary Rhetorical Theory: A Reader.* New York: Guilford, 1999.

Lukács, Georg. *History and Class Consciousness: Studies in Marxist Dialectics.* Trans. Rodney Livingstone. 1922. Cambridge: MIT, 1988.

Lynch, James P., and William J. Sabol. "The Use of Coercive Social Control and Changes in the Race and Class Composition of U.S. Prison Populations." American Society of Criminology Conf. Hyatt Regency Hotel, Miami. 9 Nov. 1994.

Lyons, Adelaide Avery. "The Religious Defense of Slavery in the North." *Trinity College Historical Society Papers* 13 (1919): 5–34.

Lyotard, Jean-François. *The Lyotard Reader.* Cambridge, MA: Basil Blackwell, 1989.

Maasik, Sonia, and Jack Solomon, eds. *Signs of Life in the U.S.A.: Readings on Popular Culture for Writers.* Boston: Bedford, 1994.

Mabee, Carelton. *Black Freedom: The Non-Violent Abolitionists from 1830 Through the Civil War.* New York: Macmillan, 1970.

MacLeod, Duncan J. *Slavery, Race and the American Revolution.* London: Cambridge UP, 1974.

Madhubuti, Haki R. "Took Back Our Tears, Laughter, Love and Left a Big Dent in the Earth." Madhubuti and Karenga 3–4.

Madhubuti, Haki R., and Maulana Karenga, eds. *Million Man March/Day of Absence: A Commemorative Anthology.* Chicago, Los Angeles: Third World and U of Sankore P, 1996.

Mann, Kenneth Eugene. "Nineteenth Century Black Militant: Henry Highland Garnet's Address to the Slaves." *Southern Speech Communication Journal* 36 (1970): 11–21.

Marable, Manning. "A Plea That Scholars Act upon, Not Just Interpret, Events." *New York Times* 4 Apr. 1998: A13+.

———. *Speaking Truth to Power: Essays on Race, Resistance, and Radicalism.* Boulder, CO: Westview, 1996.

Marcuse, Herbert. *One-Dimensional Man: Studies in the Ideology of Advanced Industrial Society.* 1964. Boston: Beacon, 1966.

Marsh, Luther R., ed. *Writings and Speeches of Alvan Stewart, on Slavery.* New York: A. B. Burdick, 1860.

Martin, Tony. *Marcus Garvey, Hero.* Dover, MA: Majority, 1983.

———. *The Pan-African Connection: From Slavery to Garvey and Beyond.* Cambridge, MA: Schenkman, 1983.

———. *Race First: The Ideological and Organizational Struggles of Marcus Garvey and the Universal Negro Improvement Association.* Dover, MA: Majority, 1976.

Martin, Waldo E., Jr. *The Mind of Frederick Douglass.* Chapel Hill: U of North Carolina P, 1984.

Marx, Karl, and Friedrich Engels. *The German Ideology.* Parts 1 and 3. Ed. R. Pascal. New York: International, 1947.

Mauer, Marc. *Young Black Men and the Criminal Justice System: A Growing National Problem.* Washington, DC: Sentencing Project, 1990.

Mauer, Marc, and Malcolm C. Young. *Truths, Half-Truths, and Lies: Myths and Realities about Crime and Punishment.* Washington, DC: Sentencing Project, 1996.

Mauer, Marc, and the Sentencing Project. *Race to Incarcerate.* New York: New, 1999.

Mauer, Marc, and Tracy Huling. *Young Black Americans and the Criminal Justice System: Five Years Later.* Washington, DC: Sentencing Project, 1995.

McColley, Robert. *Slavery and Jeffersonian Virginia.* Champaign: U of Illinois P, 1964.

McCullough, David. *Great American Perspectives.* C-Span. 25 Jan. 1996.

McDonald, Deborah E. "In the First Place: Making Frederick Douglass and the Afro-American Narrative Tradition." Andrews 192–214.

McDorman, Todd F. "Challenging Constitutional Authority: African American Responses to *Scott v. Sandiford.*" *Quarterly Journal of Speech* 83 (1997): 192–209.

McFeely, William S. *Frederick Douglass.* New York: Norton, 1991.

McGee, Michael Calvin. "The 'Ideograph': A Link Between Rhetoric and Ideology." *Quarterly Journal of Speech* 66 (1980): 1–17.

———. "In Search of 'the People': A Rhetorical Alternative." *Quarterly Journal of Speech* 61 (1975): 235–49.

———. "A Materialist's Conception of Rhetoric." McKerrow, *Explorations* 23–48.

———. "Power to the <People>." *Critical Studies in Mass Communication* 4 (1987): 432–37.

———. "Technical Terms and Meaning." Online posting. 16 July 1997. CRTNET news group. 16 July 1997. <http://lists1.cac.psu.edu/cgi-bin/wa?ao=crtnet> (e-mail: crtnet@natcom.org).

McIntyre, Carshee C. L. *Criminalizing A Race: Free Blacks During Slavery.* New York: Kayode, 1984.

McKay, Claude. *Selected Poems of Claude McKay.* Biog. note by Max Eastman. 1953. New York: Twayne, 1981.

McKelvey, Charles. *The African-American Movement: From Pan-Africanism to the Rainbow Coalition.* New York: General Hall, 1994.

McKerrow, Raymie E., ed. *Argument and the Postmodern Challenge.* Annandale, VA: SCA, 1993.

———. "Critical Rhetoric and the Possibility of the Subject." *The Critical Turn: Rhetoric and Philosophy in Postmodern Discourse.* Ed. I. Angus and L. Langsdorf. Carbondale: Southern Illinois UP, 1993. 51–67.

———. "Critical Rhetoric in a Postmodern World." *Quarterly Journal of Speech* 77 (1991): 75–78.

———. "Critical Rhetoric: Theory and Practice." *Communication Monographs* 56 (1989): 91–111.

———, ed. *Explorations of Rhetoric.* Glenview, IL: Scott, 1982.

———. "Marxism and a Rhetorical Conception of Ideology." *Quarterly Journal of Speech* 64 (1980): 1–16.

McMillan, Terry, et al. *Five for Five: The Films of Spike Lee.* New York: Stewart, Tabori, and Chang, 1991.

McPhail, Mark Lawrence. "The Complicity of Essentializing Difference: (De)-constructing the Color Line: Complicity and Black Conservatism." *Communication Theory* 7 (1997): 162–78.

————. "From Complicity to Coherence: Rereading the Rhetoric of Afrocentricity." *Western Journal of Communication* 62 (1998): 114–40.

————. "Passionate Intensity: Louis Farrakhan and the Fallacies of Racial Reasoning." *Quarterly Journal of Speech* 84 (1998): 416–29.

————. "The Politics of Complicity: Second Thoughts about the Social Construction of Racial Equality." *Quarterly Journal of Speech* 8 (1994): 343–57.

————. *The Rhetoric of Racism.* Lanham, MD: University P of America, 1994.

Mehlinger, Louis. "The Attitude of the Free Negro Toward African Colonization." Uya 24–40.

Mfume, Kweisi. Press conference. Washington, DC. 11 Dec. 1995. C-Span.

Miller, Carolyn R. "Genre as Social Action." *Quarterly Journal of Speech* 70 (1984): 151–67.

Miller, Floyd J. "The Father of Black Nationalism: Another Contender." *Civil War History* 17 (1971): 310–19.

Minow, Martha, Michael Ryan, and Austin Sarat, eds. *Narrative Violence and the Law: The Essays of Robert Cover.* Ann Arbor: U of Michigan P, 1992.

Montagu, Ashley. *Man's Most Dangerous Myth: The Fallacy of Race.* 6th ed. Walnut Creek, CA: AltaMira, 1997.

Moore, Carlos. *Were Marx and Engels White Racists?* Chicago: Institute of Positive Education, 1972.

Moore, George H. *Notes on the History of Slavery in Massachusetts.* 1866. New York: Negro UP, 1968.

Morgan, Edmund S. *American Slavery, American Freedom: The Order of Colonial Virginia.* New York: Norton, 1975.

Morrison, Toni, ed. *Race-ing Justice, En-gendering Power: Essays on Anita Hill, Clarence Thomas, and the Construction of Social Reality.* New York: Pantheon, 1992.

Moses, Wilson Jeremiah. *Afrotopia: The Roots of African American Popular History.* Cambridge: Cambridge UP, 1998.

————. *Alexander Crummell: A Study of Civilization and Discontent.* New York: Oxford UP, 1989.

————. *The Golden Age of Black Nationalism, 1850–1925.* Hamden, CT: Archon, 1978.

Mouvement Souveraineté-Association. Founding political manifesto, 1968. *Le manuel de la parole: Manifestes Québécois.* Vol. 3. Ed. Daniel Latouche and Diane Poliquin-Bourassa. Sillery, PQ: Editions du boreal express, 1977. 97.

Muhammad, Elijah. *Message to the Blackman in America.* Chicago: Muhammad Mosque of Islam No. 2, 1965.

Mulin, Michael. *Africa in America: Slave Acculturation and Resistance in the American South and the British Caribbean, 1736–1831.* Urbana: U of Illinois P, 1992.

Myrdal, Gunnar. *An American Dilemma: The Negro Problem and Modern Democracy.* New York: Harper, 1944.

Naison, Mark. *Communists in Harlem During the Great Depression.* New York: Grove, 1983.

Nash, Gary B. *Race and Revolution.* Madison, WI: Madison House, 1990.

National Anti-Slavery Standard 2 July 1840 (rpt. in Ripley et al. *Black Abolitionist* 3: 340–41); 12 Sept. 1840; 3 June 1841, 207.

National Communication Association's 1997 Summer Conference on Racial and Ethnic Diversity in the 21st Century: A Communication Perspective, July 24–27, 1997, Capital Hilton, Washington, DC. Annandale, VA: National Communication Association, 1997.

Nettleford, Rex M. *Caribbean Cultural Identity, The Case of Jamaica: An Essay in Cultural Dynamics.* Kingston: Institute of Jamaica, 1978.

Nora, Pierre. "Between Memory and History: *Les Lieux de Mémoire.*" *Representations* 26 (1989): 7–24.

North Star [Rochester, NY] 26 Jan. 1849; 2 Mar. 1849.

Norton, Anne. *Alternative Americas: A Reading of Antebellum Political Culture.* Chicago: U of Chicago P, 1986.

Oates, Stephen B. *The Fires of Jubilee: Nat Turner's Fierce Rebellion.* New York: Harper, 1975.

———. *To Purge This Land with Blood: A Biography of John Brown.* New York: Harper, 1970.

Ofari, Earl. *"Let Your Motto Be Resistance:" The Life and Thought of Henry Highland Garnet.* Boston: Beacon, 1972.

Oliver, William. *The Violent Social World of Black Men.* New York: Lexington, 1994.

Ollman, Bertell. *Alienation: Marx's Concept of Man in Capitalist Society.* 2nd ed. Cambridge: Cambridge UP, 1976.

Olmstead, Frederick Law. *A Journey Through Texas: Or a Saddle-Trip Through the Southwestern Frontier.* 1857. Austin: U of Texas P, 1978.

Omi, Michael, and Howard Winant. *Racial Formations in the United States: From the 1960s to the 1980s.* London: Routledge, 1986.

Ono, Kent A., and John Sloop. "Commitment to Telos—A Sustained Critical Rhetoric." *Communication Monographs* 59 (1992): 48–60.

Padmore, George. *Pan-Africanism or Communism.* 1956. Garden City NY: Doubleday, 1971.

Palmer, Edwin H., ed. Exodus. The New International Version Study Bible. Grand Rapids: Zondervan, 1985.

Parry-Giles, Trevor. "Public Issue Construction and Rhetorical Access: The 1985 Banning of *Real Lives—At the Edge of the Union* in Great Britain." Diss. Indiana U, 1992.

Patterson, Orlando. *Freedom in the Making of Western Culture*. Vol. 1. New York: Basic, 1991.

———. *The Ordeal of Integration: Progress and Resentment in America's "Racial" Crisis*. Washington, DC: Civitas/Counterpoint, 1997.

———. *Slavery and Social Death: A Comparative Study*. Cambridge: Harvard UP, 1982.

Paulding, James Kirke. *The United States and England: Being a Reply to the Criticism on Inchiquin's Letters, Contained in the Quarterly Review for January, 1814*. New York: A. H. Inskeep, 1815.

Pauley, John L., II. "Reshaping Public Persona and the Prophetic *Ethos:* Louis Farrakhan at the Million Man March." *Western Journal of Communication* 62 (1998): 512–536.

Pease, Jane H., and William H. Pease. *Black Utopia: Negro Communal Experiments in America*. Madison: State Historical Society of Wisconsin, 1963.

———. *They Who Would Be Free: Blacks' Search for Freedom, 1830–1861*. New York: Atheneum, 1974.

Perkins, Howard C. "The Defense of Slavery in the Northern Press on the Eve of the Civil War." *Journal of Southern History* 9 (1943): 501–31.

Petersilia, Joan. *Racial Disparities in the Criminal Justice System*. Santa Monica, CA: Rand, 1983.

Peterson, Carla L. *Doers of the Word: African American Women Speakers and Writers in the North (1830–1880)*. New York: Oxford, 1995.

Phillips, Ulric Bonnell. *American Negro Slavery: A Survey of the Supply, Employment and Control of Negro Labor as Determined by the Plantation Regime*. 1918. Baton Rouge: Louisiana State UP, 1966.

Pickens, William. "The Emperor of Africa: The Psychology of Garveyism." Aptheker, *Documentary History* 3: 379–86.

Porter, Dorothy. *Early Negro Writing*. Boston, MA: Beacon 1971.

Powell, Kevin. "Hip-Hop Nation 2000." *Essence* Aug. 1997: 76+.

Priest, Josiah. *Bible Defense of Slavery; or, The Origin, History, and Fortunes of the Negro Race, as Deduced from History, Both Sacred and Profane, Their Natural Relations—Moral, Mental, and Physical—to the Other Races of Mankind, Compared and Illustrated—Their Future Destiny Predicted, etc*. Glasgow, KY: Rev. W. S. Brown, M.D. Rpt. Detroit: Negro History P, n.d.

Prigg v. Pennsylvania 41 U.S. 539. 1842.

Pro-Slavery Argument, The; As Maintained by the Most Distinguished Writers of the Southern States, Containing the Several Essays, on the Subject, of Chancellor Harper, Governor Hammond, Dr. Simms, and Professor Dew. Charleston: Walker, 1852. Rpt. ed. New York: Negro UP, 1968.

Quarles, Benjamin. *Black Abolitionists*. 1969. New York: Da Capo, 1991.

———. *Frederick Douglass.* 1948. New York: Atheneum, 1969.

Record, Wilson. *The Negro and the Communist Party.* 1956. New York: Atheneum, 1971.

Reed, Adolph, Jr. "All for One. None for All." *Nation* 28 Jan. 1991: 86–92.

———. "The Rise of Louis Farrakhan." *Nation* 21 Jan. 1991: 37+.

Reid, Ronald F., ed. *Three Centuries of American Rhetorical Discourse: An Anthology and a Review.* Prospect Heights, IL: Waveland, 1988.

Richardson, Marilyn, ed. *Maria W. Stewart, America's First Black Woman Political Writer: Essays and Speeches.* Bloomington: Indiana UP, 1987.

Richburg, Keith B. *Out of America: A Black Man Confronts Africa.* New York: Basic, 1997.

Ripley, C. Peter, et al., eds. *The Black Abolitionist Papers.* 5 vols. Chapel Hill: U of North Carolina P, 1985–92.

———, eds. *Witness for Freedom: African American Voices on Race, Slavery, and Emancipation.* Chapel Hill: U of North Carolina P, 1993.

Robinson, Cedric J. *Black Marxism: The Making of the Black Radical Tradition.* London: Zed, 1983.

Rodney, Walter. *Groundings with My Brothers.* 1969. Introd. Omawale. London: Bogle-L'Overture, 1975.

———. *How Europe Underdeveloped Africa.* London: Bogle-L'Overture, 1972.

Roediger, David R. *The Wages of Whiteness: Race and the Making of the American Working Class.* London: Verso, 1991.

Rogers, Nathaniel P. "Herald of Freedom." *Newspaper Writings.* Concord, NH: John R. French, 1847.

Rogers-Rose, La Frances, ed. *Black Woman.* Beverly Hills, CA: Sage, 1980.

Ross, Frederick A. *Slavery Ordained of God.* 1857. New York: Negro UP, 1969.

Ross, Sonya. "Gov't Report: Racism Still in U.S." 21 Sept. 2000. <blacknews@blacknews.net> BlackNews. 21 Sept. 2000.

Sapir, Edward. *Selected Writings of Edward Sapir in Language, Culture, and Personality.* Ed. David Mandelbaum. Berkeley: U of California P, 1949.

Scanzoni, John H. *The Black Family in Modern Society.* Chicago: U of Chicago P, 1971.

Schacht, Richard. *Alienation.* Garden City, NY: Anchor, 1970.

Schmitt, Richard. *Alienation and Class.* Cambridge, MA: Schenkman, 1983.

Schor, Joel. *Henry Highland Garnet: A Voice of Black Radicalism in the Nineteenth Century.* Westport, CT: Greenwood, 1977.

Schuyler, George S. *Black and Conservative.* 1966. New Rochelle, NY: Arlington, 1971.

Scott, Robert L. "On Viewing Rhetoric as Epistemic." *Central States Speech Journal* 18 (1967): 9–17.

Scott, Robert L., and Donald K. Smith. "The Rhetoric of Confrontation." *Quarterly Journal of Speech* 55 (1969): 1–8.

Sentencing Project, The, with Human Rights Watch. *Losing The Vote: The Impact of Felony Disenfranchisement Laws in the United States.* Washington, DC: Sentencing Project, 1998.

Shapiro, Walter. "Unfinished Business: A Sweeping Survey of Race Relations Finds That Black Progress Has Stalled Because of a Stagnant Economy and White Resistance to Equality." *Time* 7 Aug. 1989: 13–16.

Shome, Raka. "Postcolonial Interventions in the Rhetorical Cannon: An 'Other' View." *Communication Theory* 6 (1996): 40–59.

Sidney, Thomas [Henry Highland Garnet]. "Four Letters, in response to William Whipper." *Colored American* 13, 20 Feb.; 6, 13 March 1841. Rpt. in Stuckey, *Ideological Origins* 149–64.

Silbey, Joel H. "Pro-Slavery Sentiment in Iowa, 1836–1861." *Iowa Journal of History* 55 (1957): 289–318.

Sloterdijk, Peter. *The Critique of Cynical Reason.* Trans. Michael Eldred. Minneapolis: U of Minneapolis P, 1987.

Smith, Arthur L. [Molefi K. Asante]. *The Rhetoric of Black Revolution.* Boston: Allyn, 1969.

Smith, Goldwin. *Does the Bible Sanction American Slavery?* Cambridge: Sever, 1863.

Smith, Sherri B. "Transcending Politics: Conservative Black Rhetoric in the African American Community." Diss. Penn State U, 1996.

Souljah, Sistah. *No Disrespect.* New York: Vintage, 1996.

Sowell, Thomas. *Race and Economics.* New York: McKay, 1975.

Spivak, Gayatri. *The Postcolonial Critic: Interviews, Strategies, Dialogues.* Ed. S. Harasym. New York: Routledge, 1990.

Spooner, Lysander. *Address of the Free Constitutionalists to the People of the United States.* 2nd ed. Boston: Thayer and Eldridge, 1860.

Stanback, Marsha Houston, and Barnet Pearce. "Talking to 'the Man': Some Communication Strategies Used by 'Subordinate' Social Groups. *Quarterly Journal of Speech* 67 (1981): 21–30.

Steele, Shelby. *The Content of Our Character: A New Vision of Race in America.* New York: Harper, 1990.

Stewart, Alvan. "Argument, On the Question Whether the New Constitution of 1844 Abolished Slavery in New Jersey." *Writings and Speeches of Alvan Stewart, on Slavery.* Ed. Luther R. Marsh. New York: A. B. Burdick, 1860. 272–367.

Stone, Chuck. *Black Political Power in America.* Rev. ed. New York: Delta, 1970.

Strine, Mary S. "Cultural Diversity and the Politics of Inquiry: Response to Mattison and McPhail." *Communication Theory* 7 (1997): 178–85.

Stringfellow, Thornton. "The Bible Argument: Or, Slavery in the Light of Divine Revelation." Elliott 459–521.

———. "A Brief Examination of Scripture Testimony on the Institution of Slavery." *Richmond Religious Herald* 25 Feb. 1841.

———. *A Brief Examination of Scripture Testimony on the Institution of Slavery. In an Essay First Published in the Religious Herald and Republished by Request, With Remarks on a Letter of Elder Galusha of New York to Dr. Richard Fuller of South Carolina.* Washington, DC: Congressional Globe Office, 1850.

———. *Scriptural and Statistical Views in Favor of Slavery.* Richmond: J. W. Randolph, 1856.

Stuckey, Sterling, ed. *The Ideological Origins of Black Nationalism.* Boston: Beacon, 1972.

———. *Slave Culture: Nationalist Theory and the Foundations of Black America.* New York: Oxford UP, 1987.

Styron, William. *The Confessions of Nat Turner.* New York: Random, 1967.

Susman, Warren I. *Culture as History: The Transformation of American Society in the Twentieth Century.* New York: Pantheon, 1984.

Takaki, Ronald. *A Different Mirror: A History of Multicultural America.* Boston: Little, 1993.

———. *A Pro-Slavery Crusade.* New York: Free, 1971.

Tannenbaum, Frank. *Slave and Citizen: The Negro in the Americas.* 1946. New York: Vintage, 1963.

Terrill, Robert E. "Colonizing the Borderlands: Shifting Circumference in the Rhetoric of Malcolm X." *Quarterly Journal of Speech* 86 (2000): 67–85.

Thiong'o, Ngugia wa. *Decolonizing the Mind.* London: Curry, 1981.

Thomas, Ewart. Editor's preface. *Groundings with My Brothers.* By Walter Rodney. 1969. London: Bogle-L'Overture, 1975. 5–6.

Tise, Larry E. "The Interregional Appeal of Proslavery Thought: An Ideological Profile of the Antebellum American Clergy." *Plantation Society* 1 (1979): 58–72.

———. *Proslavery: A History of the Defense of Slavery in America, 1701–1840.* Athens: U of Georgia P, 1987.

"To Our Readers." *Time* 4 July 1994: 4.

Towner, Lawrence W. "The Sewell-Saffin Dialogue on Slavery." *William and Mary Quarterly* 21 (Jan. 1964): 40–52.

Ullman, Victor. *Martin R. Delany: The Beginnings of Black Nationalism.* Boston: Beacon, 1971.

United States. Cong. Senate. *Cong. Globe* 10 Jan. 1838. 25th Cong., 2nd sess., app. 61–62.

Uya, Okon E., ed. *Black Brotherhood: Afro-Americans and Africa.* Lexington, MA: Heath, 1971.

Van Dijk, Teun A. *Communicating Racism: Ethnic Prejudice in Thought and Talk.* Beverly Hills, CA: Sage, 1987.

Vatz, Richard. "The Myth of the Rhetorical Situation." *Philosophy and Rhetoric* 6 (1973): 154–61.

Vaughn, Alden T. *Roots of American Racism: Essays on the Colonial Experience.* New York: Oxford UP, 1995.

Vincent, T[heodore] G. *Black Power and the Garvey Movement.* Berkeley, CA: Ramparts, n.d.

Voice of the Fugitive 24 Sept. 1851.

Walker, David. *David Walker's Appeal, in Four Articles; Together With a Preamble, to the Colored Citizens of the World, But in Particular, and Very Expressly, to Those of the United States of America.* Ed. Charles M. Wiltse. 1830. New York: Hill and Wang, 1965.

Wallace, Karl R. "Booker T. Washington." *History and Criticism of American Public Address.* Ed. William Norwood Brigance. Vol 2. New York: McGraw Hill, 1943. 407–34. 2 vols.

Wallace, Michele. *Black Macho and the Myth of the Superwoman.* New York: Dial, 1979.

Walrond, Eric D. "Imperator Africanus Marcus Garvey: Menace or Promise?" *A Documentary History of the Negro People in the United States.* Ed. Herbert Aptheker. Vol 3. Secaucus, NJ: Citadel, 1977. 386–403. 6 vols. 1951–73.

Walsh, Robert. *An Appeal from the Judgements of Great Britain Respecting the United States of America. Part First, Containing an Historical Outline of Their Merits and Wrongs as Colonies; and Strictures upon the Calumnies of the British Writers.* 2nd ed. Philadelphia: Michell, Ames, and White, 1819.

Wander, Philip C. "The Ideological Turn in Modern Criticism." *Central States Speech Journal* 34 (1983): 1–18.

Washington, Booker T. *Up from Slavery.* New York: 1901.

Weekly Anglo-African 10 Sept. 1859.

Wesley, Charles H. "Negroes in Anti-Slavery Political Parties." *Journal of Negro History* 29.1 (1944): 32–74.

West, Cornel. Forum on Race and Criminal Justice. Harvard U. Nov. 1996. C-Span.

———. *Keeping Faith: Philosophy and Race in America.* New York: Routledge, 1993.

———. *Prophesy Deliverance: An Afro-American Revolutionary Christianity.* Philadelphia: Westminister P, 1982.

———. *Race Matters*. Boston: Beacon, 1993.

West, Cynthia S'thembile. *Nation Builders: Female Activism in the Nation of Islam, 1960–1970*. Diss. Temple U, 1994. Ann Arbor: UMI, 1997.

West, Michael O. "Like a River: The Million Man March and the Black Nationalist Tradition in the United States." *Journal of Historical Sociology* 12 (1999): 81–100.

Whipper, William. "Three Letters." *Colored American* 30 Jan., 6 and 20 Feb. 1841.

Whitman, Walt. *An American Primer*. Ed. Horace Traubel. 1904. San Francisco: City Light, 1970.

Wiecek, William. *Sources of Antislavery Constitutionalism in America: 1760–1848*. Ithaca, NY: Cornell UP, 1977.

Williams, David Cratis, and Michael David Hazen, eds. *Argumentation Theory and the Rhetoric of Assent*. Tuscaloosa: U of Alabama P, 1990.

Williams, Eric. *Capitalism and Slavery*. 1944. New York: Russell, 1961.

Williams, George. *A History of the Negro Race in America, 1619–1880*. 2 vols. 1883. New York: Arno, 1968.

Williams, James. *Letters on Slavery*. Miami: Mnemosyne, 1969.

Williams, Jayme Coleman, and William McDonald, eds. *The Negro Speaks: The Rhetoric of Contemporary Black Leaders*. New York: Noble and Noble, 1970.

Williams, Raymond. *Culture and Society: 1780–1950*. 1958. New introd. New York: Columbia UP, 1983.

Williamson, Joel. *A Rage for Order: Black-White Relations in the American South Since Emancipation*. New York: Oxford UP, 1986.

Willis, Gary. *Lincoln at Gettysburg: The Words that Remade America*. New York: Simon, 1992.

Wilson, August O. Opening lecture. "Writing Race Across the Atlantic World, 1492–1763," 25th Alabama Symposium on English and American Literature. University of Alabama, Tuscaloosa. 27–29 Sept. 2001.

Wilson, William Julius. *The Declining Significance of Race*. Chicago: U of Chicago P, 1978.

———. *The Truly Disadvantaged: The Inner City, the Underclass and Public Policy*. Chicago: U of Chicago P, 1987.

Wiltse, Charles M. Introduction. *David Walker's Appeal, in Four Articles; Together with a Preamble, to the Colored Citizens of the World, but in Particular, and Very Expressly, to Those of the United States of America*. By David Walker. Ed. Charles M. Wiltse. 1830. New York: Hill and Wang, 1965. vii–xii.

Wish, Harvey. "American Slave Insurrections Before 1861." *Journal of Negro History* 23 (1937): 299–320.

———. "Slave Disloyalty under the Confederacy." *Journal of Negro History* 23 (1938): 435–50.

———. "The Slave Insurrection Panic of 1856." *Journal of Southern History* 5 (1939): 206–22.

Wodak, Ruth, ed. *Language, Power and Ideology: Studies in Political Discourse.* Amsterdam: John Benjamin, 1989.

Wood, Julia T., and Richard B. Gregg, eds. *Toward the 21st Century: The Future of Speech Communication.* Cresskill, NJ: Hampton, 1995.

Woodard, Komozi. *A Nation Within a Nation: Amiri Barake (LeRoi Jones) & Black Power Politics.* Chapel Hill: U of North Carolina P, 1999.

Woodson, Carter G. *The History of the Negro Church.* Washington, DC: N.p., 1921.

———. *Negro Orators and Their Orations.* 1925. New York: Russell, 1969.

Woodward, C. Vann. *The Strange Career of Jim Crow.* 2nd rev. ed. New York: Oxford UP, 1966.

Wrage, Ernest J. "Public Address: A Study in Social and Intellectual History." *Quarterly Journal of Speech* 33 (1947): 451–57.

Wright, Donald. *African Americans in the Colonial Era: From African Origins Through the American Revolution.* Arlington, IL: Harlan Davidson, 1990.

X, Malcolm, with Alex Haley. *The Autobiography of Malcolm X.* 1964. New York: Ballantine, 1973.

Yee, Shirley J. *Black Women Abolitionists: A Study in Activism, 1828–1860.* Knoxville: U of Tennessee P, 1992.

Yellin, Jean Fagan. *Women and Sisters: Antislavery Feminists in American Culture.* New Haven: Yale UP, 1990.

Yellin, Jean Fagan, and John C. Van Horne, eds. *The Abolitionist Sisterhood: Women's Political Culture in Antebellum America.* Ithaca, NY: Cornell UP, 1990.

Young, Robert Alexander. *The Ethiopian Manifesto, Issued in Defense of the Black Man's Rights, in the Scale of Universal Freedom.* 1829. Stuckey, *Ideological Origins* 30–38.

Zinn, Howard. *A People's History of the United States.* New York: Harper, 1980.

Index

abolitionists: women's contributions to, 8–9. *See also* black abolitionists; white abolitionists

Adams, John, 168

Adams, John Quincy, 50

Adorno, Theodore, 25

African Civilization Society, 130

Africanity, 9

African Methodist Episcopal Church, 73

Afrocentricity, 11–15; coherence theory and, 17–18; complicity theory and, 18

Albany Convention of Colored People, 101–2, 110; on names, naming, 108

Alger, Horatio, 189

Ali, Noble Drew (Timothy Dew), 199

alienation: black (*see* black alienation); ideological (*see* ideological alienation); Marx, Engels on, 24–28; rhetorical concept of, 29–39; separatism and, 137–43

Allen, Richard, 73, 94

Allen, Theodore W., 41–42

Allen, Woody, 37

Althusser, Louis: on ideology, 25, 33, 38; on interpellation, 36; on practice and ideology, 1

American and Foreign Antislavery Society, 103

American Antislavery Society, 103

American Colonization Society: background of, 73–74; on inevitable black failure in America, 65; on names, naming, 109; opposition to, 106, 112; plan of, for emancipation, 49; proslavery sentiment of, 94; and scheme to remove free blacks, 85; support of white abolitionists by, 75

American Moral Reform Society, 107

American Revolutionary ideologies, 46–47

Amistad (slave ship), 76

Anansi (trickster figure), 14

Appeal from the Judgements of Great Britain Respecting the United States of America, An (Walsh), 42–61

Anderson, Benedict, 115

Anderson, Margaret, 16

antecedent rhetoric, 5

antislavery societies: antislavery schism and, 103; gradualist, 73

Appeal, in Four Articles (Walker), 72–100

Appiah, Kwame Anthony, 194; on black-on-black bond, 121; on bond with Africa, 120; on fathers of Pan-Africanism, 78; on rhetoric of descent, 116

Aptheker, Herbert, xiii, 202; on black challenge of white respectability, 71; on history, 96; on racial equality practiced by whites, 128; on seventeenth-century blacks, xiii; on Walker, and American institutions, 94; on Young, 79

Aristotle, 47

Armstrong, George D., 62

Arthos, John, Jr., 191

Asante, Molefi Kete, 183–84, 197; and Afrocentricity, 11–13; and Afrocentrism, 6; on black nationalism, 175; on critical scholarship, 10; on Marx, 28

Augustine. *See* Woodson, Reverend Lewis

Aune, James, 26

back-to-Africa call, black nationalism and, 79–80

Bacon's Rebellion, 57

Baker, Houston, 178
Bakhtin, Mikhail, 20, 25
Baldwin, James, 89, 193
Bambara, Toni Cade, 182
Banner-Haley, Charles T., 28–29, 117, 192
Baraka, Amiri, 154, 166
Barness, Gilbert H., 8
Beard, Charles, 84
Beard, Mary, 84
Beard, William, 84
Benezet, Anthony, 48
Benjamin, Walter, 25
Benton, Thomas Hart, 77
Bethel Church, 73
Bible, use by blacks, 72
"Bible Argument: or, Slavery in the Light
    of Divine Redemption" (Stringfellow),
    43, 54–57
Birney, James, 8
Birth of a Nation (Griffith), 197
Bizzell, Patricia, 14
Black, Edwin, 5, 34, 37
black abolitionists: on blacks as citizens,
    124; black women as, 8; goals of, 127;
    heterogeneity of, 105–6; public voice
    of, 125–60; rhetorical scholarship and,
    10; rhetorical undertakings of, 6; role
    of, in abolition, 7; as transformative of
    antebellum black Americans, 6; white
    abolitionists and, 128; women's contri-
    butions to, 8–9
black alienation: black nationalism and,
    171–76; language of white supremacy
    and, 27, 29; rearticulation of American
    history and, 153–60; separatism and,
    137–43
Black Arts Renaissance, 166
black conservatism, 188–93
black convention movement, 101–4
black history, acknowledgment of, 4
black identity: as basis for slavery, 52–53;
    black convention movement and, 102;
    contemporary American culture and,
    179–82; as contingent, socially con-
    structed reality, 6; early debate over,
    106–10; public rhetorical construction
    of, 103–20; separatism and, 107

black middle class: contemporary Ameri-
    can culture and, 192; Million Man
    March and, 28
black nationalism: alienation and, 171–76;
    back-to-Africa call and, 79–80; begin-
    nings of, 69–100; black church and,
    187–88; black conservatism and, 188–
    93; black women and, 162, 182, 184–
    87; contemporary American culture
    and, 178–203; genealogical tracing of,
    5; historical summary of, 163–67; and
    identification as one, 144–45; ideologi-
    cal alienation and, 21–29; ideology of,
    4, 6–20, 161–63, 182; integration and,
    151–53; of Malcolm X, 143; mascu-
    linist problems of, 182, 184–87; nine-
    teenth-century, 169–71; Pan-African-
    ism and, 99; philosophy as, 5; public
    rhetorical efforts of, 5–6; public voice
    of, 125–60; race and, 113–20, 193–96;
    rearticulation of American history and,
    153–60; reconception of, 6; rhetorical
    articulation of, 125; rhetorical concep-
    tion of, 199–203; rhetoric as, 5; sepa-
    ratism and, 149–51; white national-
    ism and, 167–68; white past and, 95;
    women activists and, 184–87
black Northerners: and black nationalism
    ideology, 78; free blacks as redescription
    of, 138; indictment of, 55–56; opposi-
    tion to colonization by, 74
Black Panther party, 165–66
Black Power movement, 107, 189
Black Radical Congress, 167
black rhetorical strategies, 11
blacks: alienation of (*see* alienation; black
    alienation); and black church, 187–88;
    and black conservatism, 188–93; and
    black convention movement, 102; as
    citizens, 124; claiming America, 93–94;
    as collective subject, 33–35; and "color-
    phobia," 111; and complexional dis-
    tinction, 110–12; and constitutive rhet-
    oric and social action, 120–23; and
    contemporary American culture, 178–
    203; degradation of, reasons for, 80;
    exclusivity and, 102; free (*see* black

Northerners); heterogeneity of, 105; identification of, as one, 144–45; ideological alienation and, 21–29; liberation and freedom of, 147–49; a Messiah and, 90–91; names for, 87–88, 122; as natural slaves, 64–67; as Other, 55; as a people, 100; as a problem people, 2, 180; public voice of, 125–60; race and, 116–20; racial essentialism and, 18; racist effect on, due to color, 22–23; rearticulation of American history, and, 153–60; reconstituted history of, 145–47; reconstitution of, 100; religion of, and black liberation, 90–94; rhetorical construction of, as human beings, 70; rhetorical myth and, 83; rhetorical revision of, 97; rhetorical undertakings of, 6; self-naming by, 87–88, 108–10; as slaves (*see* black Southerners; slavery); as society within a society, 22–23; as transhistorical subject, 35–36; transhistorical subjectivity of, 146; as united force, 143; voices of, reclamation of, 70–71; white naming of, 87, 122; women activists and, 184–87

black Southerners: as property, 56–57; redescription of slaves as, 138. *See also* slavery

black women: activist tradition of, 184–87; antislavery activities of, 193; as black abolitionists, 8; and black feminine separatism, 182; and black nationalism, 162, 182, 184–87; contributions of, to abolitionism, 8–9; early work of, 71–72; elevation of blacks by, 72; establishment of educational institutions, benevolent societies by, 74; exclusion of, in rhetorical process, 157; Million Woman March and, 167; as part of the struggle, 157; public affirmation of black life by, 164; as reminder to men, 111; women's rhetoric and, 11. *See also* women

Blassingame, John, Sr., 7

Bloom, Allen: and black nationalism, 177

Blyden, Edward W., 78, 148, 183

Bormann, Ernest, 5

Bosmajian, Haig, 15–16

Brewer, William, 127

British West Indies, 130

Brooks, Roy L., 28

Brown, John, 65, 76, 81, 139

Brown, William Wells, 132

Bryan, Andrew, 73

Buchanan, James, 128, 130

Buffalo Convention, 130

Burke, Kenneth: on black alienation, 154–55; on identification, 29; on names, naming, 109; on the negative in language, 17; on persuasion, 32; on representative anecdote, 43; on the symbolic, 34–35

Bustill, Cyrus, 73

Byron, Lord, 139

Calhoun, John, 70, 133, 197

Caliban, 56

California, 128, 130

Campbell, Joseph, 19

Campbell, Karlyn Khors, 8, 10

Carmichael, Stokely (Kwamè Ture), 177

Cary, Mary Ann Shadd, 185–86

Charland, Maurice, 30–31, 120, 147; on audiences, 34; on calling people into being, 32–33; on constitution of people, 37; constitutive rhetoric concept of, 6

Cherokee, 94

Childs, Maria, 9

Christy, David, 65, 196

Cinque, Joseph, 145

Civil Rights era, 165, 189

Clarke, James F., 76

Clay, Henry, 74, 94

Cobbs, Price M., 89

coherence: and race, 31; theory and rhetoric of, 17–18

collective subject, 33–35

Collins, Patricia Hill, 9, 13, 16, 154, 186, 200

colonization of Africa: Anglo-American desire for, 73; black opposition to, 71–75; effect of self-naming by blacks on, 108; forced removal of free blacks for, 85; Walsh on, 48; white abolitionist support of, 75. *See also* emigration

"colorphobia," 111
communication scholarship, 16
complexional distinction, 110–12, 117
complicity, theory and rhetoric of, 17–18
Compromise of 1850 (Missouri Compromise), 129, 164
Compromise of 1877, 164
Condit, Celeste Michelle, xv; on black abolitionists, 7; on ideology, 46; on justice within shared communities, xv; on "the people," 30; on the word "equality," 15
confrontation, rhetoric of, 10
Connerly, Ward, 189–90
conservatism, black, 188–93
Constitution: as antislavery document, 132–33; as proslavery document, 132; and redemptive constitutionalism, 134; "We the people" in, 30, 84, 126
constitutive rhetoric, 31–39; and identity, 30
Conti, Joseph G., 189
Cooper, Anna Julia, 185
Cooper, Thomas, 124
Cornish, Samuel E., 74, 106–8, 122, 193–94
Cose, Ellis, 3, 193
Council on African Affairs, 164
Cover, Roger, 134, 149, 155
Cox, J. Robert, xv, 154; on history viewed ideologically, xv
Creole (slave ship), 76
crime, as black problem, 3
critical rhetorical scholarship, 10, 15; of Condit and Lucaites, 15
Crummell, Alexander, 78, 99, 112; on America, 94; as Sidney (*see* Sidney)
Cruse, Harold, 5, 79
Cuffe, Paul, xiii, 164

Davidson, Basil, 97
Davis, David Brion, 63, 76
Davis, Jefferson, 197
Declaration of Independence, 92, 106, 124, 126; use by blacks, 72
Delany, Martin Robison, xiv, 160, 183–85, 188, 190, 194, 196; on American Revolution, 156; background of, 131; and black alienation, 137–38, 154–55, 173–74; and black collective subject, 144–45; and black liberation, 125, 158; and black nationalism, 79, 99, 159, 164–65, 169, 171; black nationalist constitutive rhetoric of, 135–36; black public discourse and, 126; on black race pride, 90; on blacks and Native Americans, 120; and black-white color line, 142–43; and collective black subject, 157; on emigration, 112, 130; as first black nationalist, 78; militancy of, 132, 147–48; and narrative history of blacks, 146; nationalist, separatist ideas of, 107; separatism and, 134, 140–41, 149–50, 152–53
Democrats, prior to Civil War, 133
Denton, Robert, 27
Dew, Thomas Roderick, xiii; as apologist, 46; on best interests of white Southerners, 57; proslavery discourse of, 50; proslavery documents of, 43
Dick, Robert C., 11
Dickson, Greg, 181
Dixon, John, 197
Dodd, William E., 57
Dotson, Andy, 192
Douglas, Grace, 193
Douglas, Sarah M., 193
Douglas, Stephen, 129
Douglass, Frederick, xiv, 154, 160, 184, 190, 196, 203; on American Revolution, 156; antislavery position of, 144; background of, 132; and black alienation, 138, 155, 173–74; on black liberation, 125; and black nationalism, 159, 164–65, 169, 171; black nationalist constitutive rhetoric of, 136; and black public discourse, 126; on blacks and whites together, 141–42; and blacks as citizens, 150; on blacks linked to Revolutionary white colonists, 145; and collective black subject, 157; on the Constitution, 132–33; on hypocrisy, 86; and Delany, 131; militancy of, 139; on potential of America, 151–53, 158; and separatism, 107, 149; and white abolitionists, 133–34

Downing, George, 130
Drake, St. Clair, 96
Dred Scott v. Sandiford, 129, 164
Drew, Timothy (Noble Drew Ali), 199
Du Bois, W. E. B., 167, 191–92, 197; and black alienation, 154, 173; and black nationalism, 164; on blacks as a problem, 2; and the black-white color line, 142; on bond with Africa, 120; on international slave trade, 78; on life of Southern slaveholder, 85–86; Pan-Africanism of, 143; on philosophy of black nationalism, 5; on Southern slaveholders, 85–86
Dwight, Timothy, 45
Dyson, Michael Eric, 2, 178, 198, 200

Eaton, Clement, 81
Egyptians, 83
Elkins, Stanley, 65
Elliot, Ebenezer Newton, 41
emigration, 112, 130–31. *See also* colonization of Africa
Engels, Friedrich, 24–27
Entman, Robert, 16
equality, as contested ideograph, 15
Essien-Udom, Essien Udosen, 13
Esu Elegbara (trickster god), 14
Ethiopian Manifesto, The (Young), 72–100
Eurocentrism, 12
European rhetoric: effect of, on Afrocentricity, 12

Fabre, Geneviève, 179
Fanon, Franz, 5, 89, 158
Farrakhan, Louis, 160, 184, 188, 191, 195, 200–201; and black nationalism, 99, 148, 166, 170, 178; on degrading experience of blacks, 107; discursive acts of, 21; on divine purpose of slavery, suffering, 87; on equality, call for exclusive black effort, 121; on God and blacks, 87; on liberation through self-exertion, 122; militant stand of, 91; and Million Man March, 1, 4, 104; on Elijah Muhammed, 87; nationalist ideology of, 1

Feagin, Joe R., 193
Fineman, Howard, xv
Fitzhugh, George, 62–63
Floyd, John, 76
Fogel, Robert, 22
Forten, Charlotte, 185–86
Forten, Margaretta, 193
Forten, Sarah, 193
Foster, Abigail Kelly, 103
Frankfurt School, 25
Frazier, Franklin, 187–88
Free African Society, 73
free blacks. *See* black Northerners
freedom, and illusion of, 36–38
French Revolution, 49
Fugitive Slave Law, 125, 129, 134, 150
Fulwood, Sam, III, 193

Gabriel. *See* Prosser, Gabriel
Garnet, Eliza, 126
Garnet, Henry Highland, xi, xiv, 81, 160, 184, 188, 190, 194; on alienation, 119; on America, 94; on American Revolution, 156; on *Appeal,* 82; background of, 126–27; and black alienation, 137–38, 154–55, 173–74; and black collective subject, 143–45; and black liberation, 125, 158; and black nationalism, 159, 164, 169, 171; black nationalist constitutive rhetoric of, 135–36; and black public discourse, 126; on blacks as citizens, 124; and collective black subject, 157; and Liberty Party, 103, 129, 130; militancy of, 128, 131–32, 139, 140, 147–48; and narrative history of blacks, 146; nationalist, separatist ideas of, 107; separatism and, 134, 149–50, 152–53; as Sidney (*see* Sidney); solicitation of letters of, by Ray, 104; and white abolitionists, 133
Garrison, William Lloyd, 197; and accusation of collaboration with Walker, 76; and antislavery schism, 103; on depreciation of women's influence, 9; response of, to *Appeal,* 81; role of, in abolition, 8; support of American Colonization Society by, 75

Garvey, Marcus Mosiah, 183, 188, 191, 196; and black nationalism, 99, 148, 164–65, 170, 177; on black-on-black empathy, 111; on black race pride, 90; and blacks as a people, xi; and creation of a people, 100; on equality, call for exclusive black effort, 121; Pan-Africanism of, 143; Pan-Africanist influence on, 80; standoff between, and communism, 28; on white history, 95–96

Garveyism, xi, 165, 200

Gary Convention of 1972, 165

Gates, Henry Louis, Jr., 7, 14, 185, 199

Genovese, Eugene D., 56–57, 67, 70, 88

George, Nelson, 37

Gilkes, Cheryl, 186

Gilroy, Paul, 159

Goldberg, David, 67

Goldzwig, Stephen, 21, 191, 195

Goodman, Paul, on black abolitionists, 8

gradualist antislavery societies, 73

Gramsci, Antonio, 115

Grassi, Ernesto, 17

Great Migration, 164

Greece, 95

Green, Beriah, 8

Gregg, Richard B., 11, 19–20

Gresson, Aaron David, III, 182, 188–91, 199; and black alienation, 172, 175; on black heterogeneity, 105; on heterogeneity, 107; on racial essentialism, 18; recovery concept of, 6, 31; on rhetoric, 19–20; on The Signifying Monkey, 14

Grice, Hezekiah, 74

Grier, William H., 89

Griffith, D. W., 197

Grimké, Sarah, 8

Grossberg, Lawrence, 38

Gunn, Paula, 203

Guy-Sheftall, Beverly, 8

Haiman, Franklin, 10

Haiti: black emigration to, 130; white on black history of, 95

Haitian Revolution: as byproduct of French Revolution, 49; effect of, on white

Southerners, 76; liberation achieved by, 98; proslavery discourse on, 55

Hall, Prince, xiii, 73, 199

Hall, Stuart, 38, 190

Hamilton, William, xiii, 110

Hammond, James Henry, 34; proslavery discourse of, 50; proslavery documents of, 43; on slave revolt, 65; on slaves, free blacks, 84; on whites as superior race, 66

Harding, Vincent: on black abolitionists, 7; on Million Man March, 1

Hare, Nathan, 5

Hariman, Robert, 53

Harper, Frances Watkins, 186

Harper, William, xiii, 43; proslavery discourse of, 50

Harper's Ferry, 65

Hayne, Robert Y., 132

Hegel, Georg Wilhelm Friedrich, 24

Henry, Charles P., 193

Hernton, Calvin, 182

Herzberg, Bruce, 14

Hill, Anita, 187

Hinton, Frederick, 108

hip-hop culture, 166

history: black, acknowledgment of, 4; as useful tool, 5

Holland, Edwin Clifford, 56

hooks, bell, 182, 200, 202; and black alienation, 172; and black nationalism, 178; on black rage, 89–90; on masculinist discourse, 9

Hope, Dianne, 16

Horton, Africanus, 78

Huggins, Nathan, 152

Hughes, Henry, 62–63

ideological alienation, 21–29; language and, 23–24; Marx and Engels on, 24–27; race and, 6; rhetorical conception of, 6

ideology: American Revolutionary ideologies, 46–47; black, constitutive rhetoric of, 31–33, 135–37; black, emergence of, 72–78; and constitutive rhetoric, 31–33; embracing race through, 116–20;

Marx, Engels on, 24–28; and particular perspectives, 25; of proslavery discourse, narrative, 40–68; of slavery, 43–46
Ingersoll, Charles Jared, 44–45; on relationship of slavery, republican democracy, 133
insurrections, 75–77
integration, 143, 151–53
international slave trade, abolishment of, 73
interpellation: and black abolitionists, 36–39; of blacks as one, 144–45; of blacks into collective entity, 98; inscription of people by narrative, 36

Jackson, Andrew, 75, 128
Jackson, Reverend Jesse, 189
Jamaica, 165
James, C. L. R., 164, 167
Jasinski, James, 153
jazz, lesson of, 202–3
Jefferson, Thomas, 47, 83, 168, 197; thesis of black inferiority, 83
Jesus, 93
Jhally, Sut, 28–29
Jim Crow laws, 176, 202
Johnson, Charles, 120
Jones, Absalom, 73
Jordan, Winthrop D., 42, 161

Kansas, 128–29
Kansas-Nebraska Act, 129
Karenga, Maulana, 165
Katz, William Loren, 40
King, Martin Luther, Jr., 165, 180
Knapp, Isaac, 76, 81
Koch, Ed, 3
Kolchin, Peter, 42
Kuhn, Thomas, 13

Laclau, Ernesto, 191; on black identity, 106; on black nationalism, 162, 177; on ideological discourse, 45–46; on marginality, 18
language: and alienation, 23–24; power of, 15–17; of white supremacy, 29
Lee, Spike, 37

Lerner, Gerda, 187
Lester, Julius, 19, 190
Levine, Robert, 130, 159
Lewis, Justin, 28–29
Liberia, 130
Liberty Party, 103, 127, 129–30
Liele, George, 73
Lincoln, C. Eric, 187–88, 200
Litwack, Leon F., 113, 123
Locke, John, 93
Loewen, James W., 96
Logan, Shirley Wilson, 8
Lorde, Audre, 182
Lucaites, John Louis, xv; on black abolitionists, 7; on black alienation, 153; on blacks as a people, 82; on ideology, 46; on justice within shared communities, xv; on "the people," 30; on the word "equality," 15
Lukács, Georg, 25
Lundy, Benjamin, 81
lynchings, 164

Mabee, Carelton, 128
Madhubuti, Haki R., 4
Madison, James, 73, 168
Malcolm X. See X, Malcolm
Marable, Manning, 170, 200
Marcuse, Herbert, 25
Martin, Tony, 80, 96, 187, 196
Martin, Waldo, 125
Marx, Karl, 24–27
Massachusetts Antislavery Society, 103
Massachusetts General Colored Association, 74
McCullough, David, 152
McDonald, Deborah E., 185
McGee, Michael Calvin, xv; on abolition, rhetoric of, xv; on argument as presentist reasoning, xv; on blacks as a people, 82; on collective subject, 33; on ideology, 30; on rhetoric, 25, 29
McIntyre, Carshee C. L., 85
McKay, Claude, 199
McKelvey, Charles, 5
McPhail, Mark Lawrence, 190–91, 195, 199; on American Revolution, 156;

McPhail, Mark Lawrence *(continued)*
    and black alienation, 175; on black iden-
    tity, 106; and black-white color line,
    143; coherence concept of, 6, 31; cri-
    tique of Afrocentrism by, 14; on persua-
    sion, 32; on race, rhetoric studies, 10,
    16–19; on racism and rhetoric, 15–17
Messiah, 90–91
Mexican War, 128–29
Mfume, Kweisi, on race relations, 1
militancy, 89–90, 127
Miller, Maria. *See* Stewart, Maria W.
Million Man March, 166, 191, 200–201;
    and black middle class, 28–29; and
    black nationalism, 163; as different pic-
    ture of black men, 3–4; effect of, on
    race debate, 1; exclusivity of participa-
    tion in, 104; ideology of, 5
Million Woman March, 167
Missouri Compromise (Compromise of
    1850), 129, 164
Monroe, James, 74
Montagu, Ashley, 202
Moorish Science Temple of America, 199
Morel, Julius C., 108
Morgan, Edmund S., 48, 57
Morrison, Toni, 202
Moses, Wilson Jeremiah, 11, 14; on black
    ambiguity toward lineage, 148; and
    black nationalism, 163, 180; on blacks
    as a fallen race, 96–97
Mouffe, Chantal, 191; on black identity,
    106; on black nationalism, 162, 177;
    on ideological discourse, 45–46; on
    marginality, 18
Moynihan, Daniel Patrick, 3
Muhammed, Elijah, 183; and black na-
    tionalism, 99, 164; and black-white
    color line, 142; on divine purpose of
    slavery, suffering, 87
Murrant, John, 73
Myrdal, Gunnar, 159

naming: self-, by blacks, 87–88, 108–10,
    122; white, of blacks, 87, 122
National Association for the Advancement
    of Colored People (NAACP), 177

National Black Political Assembly, 165
National Emigration Conference, 131
nationalism. *See* black nationalism
National Negro Convention, 74; and black
    nationalism, 164; relaunch of, 103, 127
Nation of Islam, 164, 186
Native Americans, 120
Nebraska, 128–29
New Mexico, 128
Ngugia wa Thiong'o, 12
Nkrumah, Kwame, 5
Norton, Anne, 69–70, 93

Oliver, William, 3
Ollman, Bertell, 26
O'Meally, Robert, 179
oppression, tenets of, 50–68
Organization of Afro-American Unity, 165
Otis, Harrison G., 81
Owen, John, 77

Padmore, George, 164
Pan-Africanism: black nationalism and, 99;
    fathers of, 78; influence of, on Garvey, 80
Patterson, Orlando, 97
Paul, Susan, 193
Pearce, Barnet, 15
Pease, Jane H., 7
Pease, William H., 7
Pennington, J. C. W., 132
Peterson, Carla L., 8, 115
Phillips, Wendell, 134
popular sovereignty, 128–29, 132
Porter, Dorothy, 80
Powell, Colin, 122
Prigg v. Pennsylvania, 129
proslavery discourse, narrative, 40–68
Prospero, 56
Prosser, Gabriel, 49, 75
Purvis, Harriet, 193
Purvis, Robert, 108

Quakers, 48
Quarles, Benjamin, 7, 127

race: in America, 2; as basis for slavery, 52–
    53; black nationalism and, 193–96;

blackness as Other, 29; coherence and, 31; embracing, through ideology, 116–20; ideological alienation and, 6; proslavery discourse, narrative, and, 40–68; recovery and, 31; as social category, 2; transcendence of, through myth, 113–16; transcendence, translation, transformation of, 122; as unifying principle, 117

racism: complexional distinction and, 110–12; contemporary covert, 176; continuance of, 176–78; language of, negative consequences of, 15–17; rhetoric of, 15–17

Randolph, John, 87

rap music, 166, 192

Ray, Charles B., 104, 110–11, 120, 129; on conflicting visions of blackness, 105

Reagan, Ronald, 166

Reaganism, 189–90

Reason, Charles L., 112

rebellions, 75–77

Record, Wilson, 28

recovery: and race, 31; rhetorics of, 20–21; *Signifying Monkey* as message of, 14; theme of, 21

Red Summer of 1919, 164

religion: and black liberation, 90–94

Remond, Charles, 132

Remond, Sarah Parker, 186

rhetoric: antecedent, 5; constitutive, 31–39; new approaches to, 10–11; of persuasion and argumentation, 17; rhetorical criticism and, 10; role of, in black struggle, 11; of the streets, 10

Richardson, Marilyn, 8

Robeson, Paul, 99, 148, 164

Robinson, Cedric, 97–98, 167

Rochester Ladies' Antislavery Society, 151

Rodney, Walter, 27, 91, 167, 197

Rogers, Nathaniel P., 113

Ross, Frederick A., 56

Russwurm, John B., 74

Saffin, John, 48

Sapir, Edward, 40

Schmitt, Richard, 27

Schor, Joel, 148

Schuyler, George S., 189

Scott, Robert, 10

Sentencing Project, 2–3, 23

separatism, 107, 137–43, 149–51, 182–84

September 11, 2001, racialized stock responses to, xv

Seward, Governor William, 127

Shapiro, Walter, 23

Shome, Raka, 19

Sidney, xiv, 102, 186, 194; on black conventions, 101; and black nationalism, 98, 169–70; black nationalist constitutive rhetoric of, 135; on black nationalist ideology, 122; on conflicting visions of blackness, 105; on liberation through self-exertion, 116–17; militancy of, 139; on names, naming, 109; and persuasion of blacks, 120; on programs based on black experience, 112; rhetorical nature of claims by, 121; on separatism, 110, 113–14; on shared suffering, 119; on specific means, actions, 118

signifying, 14

Sikes, Melvin P., 193

Simpson, O. J., 3

Sistah Souljah, 89, 91, 99

Slack, Jennifer Daryl, 38

slavery: American expansionism and, 128–29; American Revolutionary ideologies and, 46–47; and *An Appeal from the Judgements of Great Britain Respecting the United States of America*, 42–61; and "Bible Argument: or, Slavery in the Light of Divine Redemption," 43, 54–57; biblical defense of, 54–55, 61, 64, 67; as black progress, 61–64; as consistent with American values, 57–61; defense of, 47–50; ideology of, 43–46; insurrections and rebellions, 75–77; blacks as natural for, 64–67; as perpetual institution, 64–67; proslavery discourse, narrative, 40–68; and slaves (*see* black Southerners)

slaves. *See* black Southerners

Smith, Donald, 10

Smith, James McCune, 110, 120, 122, 193
Smitherman, Geneva, 14
Sowell, Thomas, 190
Spivak, Gayatri, 19, 175
Stanback, Marsha Houston, 15
Steele, Shelby, 190, 202; on black advancement, 107; on black alienation, 154; on black heterogeneity, 102; and black-white color line, 143; on race as issue, 28
Stetson, Brad, 189
Stewart, Maria W., xii, 71–72, 169, 184–86
Stowe, Harriet Beecher, 131
streets, rhetoric of, 10
Strine, Mary S., 18
Stringfellow, Thornton, xiii; as apologist, 46; and "Bible Argument: or, Slavery in the Light of Divine Redemption," 43, 54–57; and biblical defense of slavery, 54–55, 67; on blacks, 139; on Hebrew laws, 62; on hereditary bondage, 64; proslavery discourse of, 50; proslavery documents of, 43; on slavery as civilizing for blacks, 97; on slavery as salvation, 61; on whites as agents of God, 57; on whites as superior race, 66
Stuckey, Sterling, xiii, xiv; on black liberation, 158; on black nationalist ideology, 9, 79; on black-on-black emotional bond, 117; on black resistance efforts, 9; on Delany as first black nationalist, 78; on distancing of Northern, Southern blacks, 138; on names, naming, 88, 109; on seventeenth-century blacks, xiii; on Walker, morality, violence, 90; on white domination and life in Africa, 61
Sumner, Charles, 197
Susman, Warren I., 95

Tannenbaum, Frank, 62–63, 176–77
Tappan, Arthur, 103
Tappan, Lewis, 103
Terrel, Mary Church, 186–87
Texas, 128
Thomas, Clarence, 187, 189
Thomas Aquinas, 47

Tillman, Bill, 197
Toussaint L'Overture, 49, 76, 145
transhistorical subject, 36–38
Truth, Sojourner, 185–86; and black nationalism, 164, 169; on masculinist discourse, 9; as role model, 72
Turner, Bishop Henry McNeal, 183
Turner, Nat, 49, 75–76, 145
Tyler, John, 128

Ullman, Victor, 78, 142
Uncle Tom's Cabin (Stowe), 131
Universal Negro Improvement Association, 164, 170
US Organization, 165

van Dijk, Teun A., 16
Van Horne, John C., 8
Vardaman, James K., 192
Vesey, Denmark, 49, 75–76, 145
Vincent, Theodore, 165

Walker, Alice, 203
Walker, David, xiii, 69, 183–84, 196, 202; accusation of collaboration of, with Garrison, 76; on America for blacks, 93, 112; and American founding documents, 92; antislavery response to *Appeal* of, 81; and *Appeal, in Four Articles*, 72–100; background of, 78–79; and black alienation, 138, 173–74; and black nationalism, 164–65, 169; black nationalist constitutive rhetoric of, 135; on black race pride, 90; on blacks as a people, 82, 84; and the black-white color line, 142; as catalyst for black activism, 72; challenge of white history by, 95; construction of collective black subject by, 98–99; denunciation of racism, proslavery activities by, 94; on equality, call for exclusive black effort by, 121; first publication of, 74; on God and blacks, 86; on Haitian Revolution, 98; life of, 78–79; on names, naming, 87–88; nationalist, separatist ideas of, 107; in opposition to back-to-Africa call, 80; on racist depictions of blacks,

83; radical abolitionism of, 8; on religion and a Messiah, 90–91; on response
to oppression, 89; rhetorical significance of, 100; on whites, 85–86
Wallace, Karl R., 189
Wallace, Michele, 9, 182
Walsh, Robert, xii, 68, 203; on African
colonization, 48; on American civil society, 47; and *An Appeal from the Judgements of Great Britain Respecting the
United States of America*, 42–61; background of, 45, 50; on blacks, 139; defense of slavery by, 42–43, 46, 63, 64,
144, 168; as model for Stringfellow,
67; on necessity of white governance, 94;
reconstitution of American ideology by,
49; on relationship of slavery, republican democracy, 133; significance of
work of, 44; on slaveholders, 85; on
slaves, free blacks, 84; on whites as superior race, 66
Wander, Philip, 30
Ward, Samuel Ringgold, 113–14, 129
Washington, Booker T., 164, 189, 192
Washington, George, 47
Washington, Madison, 145
Watkins, Gloria Jean. *See* hooks, bell
Watkins, William J., 75, 101, 108–9
Watts uprising, 165
Webster, Daniel, 74, 132
Weld, Angelina Grimké, 8
West, Cornel, 2, 182; on assimilationist ap-
proach, 83; on black constitution of
public voice, 70; on black nationalism,
178; on Judeo-Christian racist logic, 66
West, Cynthia S'thembile, 186
West, Michael O., 194, 200; on Million
Man March, 5, 163, 166
Wheatley, Phyllis, 185
Whigs, prior to Civil War, 133
Whipper, William, xiv, 186, 193; and black
conventions, 101–2; and black na-
tionalism, 169; on blackness, 105; on
blacks, 139; on black, white collaboration, 122; on complexional distinction,
117; and concept of common humanity, 123; on focus on color, "colorpho-

bia," 111–12; heaven-born truth of,
118; as integrationist, 111; on integration of Albany Convention of Colored
People, 108; on names, naming, 109;
and persuasion of blacks, 120; rhetorical nature of claims by, 121; sentiments
of, attacked by Sidney, 119; on separatism, integration, 104; utopian vision of,
113–16
Whipper-Sidney debate, 102–5, 169–70,
190
white abolitionists: black abolitionists' influence on, 7–8; and blacks as citizens,
124; conversion from gradualists of,
74–75; use of black abolitionists by,
128; women's contributions to, 8–9
white identity, reconstruction of, 85
white Northerners, Southern claims
against, 76–77
white Southerners, and survival of the
South, 77
white supremacy: bolstering of, by black
servility, 22; language of, 27, 29; proslavery discourse, narrative of, 40–68;
white nationalism, black nationalism,
and, 167–68
white women: contributions to abolitionism, 8–9, 103. *See also* women
Whitman, Walt, 109
Williams, Eric, 41
Williams, Peter, 73
Wilmot Proviso, 129
Wilson, August O., 92
Wilson, Woodrow, 197
Wiltse, Charles M., 68, 78, 81
Wish, Harvey, 77
women: contributions of, to abolitionism,
8–9; rhetoric of, 11; role of, in American
and Foreign Antislavery Society, 103. *See
also* black women; white women
Wood, Julia T., 11
Woodfolk (Woolfolk), Ben, 75
Woods, Tiger, 203
Woodson, Reverend Lewis: as Augustine,
106; on black advancement, 107; and
black nationalism, 99; and Delany, 131;
on equality, 121; on inability to abolish

Woodson, Reverend Lewis *(continued)*
slavery, 108; and separatism, 150; on
specific means, actions, 118
Woolman, John, 48
World War I, 164
Wrage, Ernest J., 30
Wright, Elizur, Jr., 8

X, Malcolm: and black nationalism, 99,
148, 165; on black rage, 89; and black-
white color line, 143; efforts of, 91; on
equality, call for exclusive black effort,
121; on progress, 67

Yee, Shirley J., 8
Yellin, Jean Fagan, 8
Young, Robert Alexander, xiii, 183; on
America for blacks, 93; and American
founding documents, 92; background
of, 79; and black alienation, 138, 173–
74; and black nationalism, 169; black
nationalist constitutive rhetoric of, 135;
on blacks as a people, 69, 82, 84; as
catalyst for black activism, 72; and construction of collective black subject,
98–99; on equality, call for exclusive
black effort, 121; and *Ethiopian Manifesto,* 72–100; first publication of, 74;
on God and blacks, 86–87; life of, 79;
nationalist, separatist ideas of, 107; in
opposition to back-to-Africa call, 80;
on racist depictions of blacks, 83; on
religion and a Messiah, 90–91; on response to oppression, 89; rhetorical significance of, 100; on slaveholders, 86;
and unity ideology, 78

Dexter B. Gordon is a professor in the Department of Communication and Theatre Arts and the director of the African American Studies program at the University of Puget Sound, where he teaches rhetoric and cultural studies with a focus on African American and Caribbean discourse communities. His "Struggle and Identity in Jamaican Talk," published in *Our Voices,* third edition (2000), won the 2000–2001 Best Book Chapter Award from the African American Communication and Culture Division and the Black Caucus of the National Communication Association.